Empathy and its development

Cambridge Studies in Social and Emotional Development

General Editor: Martin L. Hoffman
Advisory Board: Nicolas Blurton Jones, Robert N. Emde, Willard W. Hartup, Robert A. Hinde, Lois W. Hoffman, Carroll E. Izard, Jerome Kagan, Franz J. Mönks, Paul Mussen, Ross D. Parke, and Michael Rutter

Empathy and its development

Edited by

NANCY EISENBERG

Arizona State University

and

JANET STRAYER

Simon Fraser Univesity

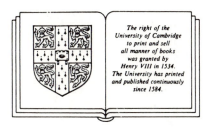

The right of the
University of Cambridge
to print and sell
all manner of books
was granted by
Henry VIII in 1534.
The University has printed
and published continuously
since 1584.

CAMBRIDGE UNIVERSITY PRESS

Cambridge
New York   New Rochelle   Melbourne   Sydney

Published by the Press Syndicate of the University of Cambridge
The Pitt Building, Trumpington Street, Cambridge CB2 1RP
32 East 57th Street, New York, NY 10022, USA
10 Stamford Road, Oakleigh, Melbourne 3166, Australia

First published 1987

Printed in the United States of America

Library of Congress Cataloging-in-Publication Data
Empathy and its development.
(Cambridge studies in social and emotional
development)
Includes index.
1. Empathy.   2. Developmental psychology.
I. Eisenberg, Nancy.   II. Strayer, Janet.   III. Series.
[DNLM: 1. Empathy. WB 575.E55 E55]
BF575.E55E453   1987   155.2′32   87–11622

British Library Cataloguing-in-Publication Data
Empathy and its development. – (Cambridge
studies in social and emotional
development).
1. Empathy
I. Eisenberg, Nancy   II. Strayer, Janet
152.4   BF575.E55

ISBN 0 521 32609 5

Contents

Contributors

Mark A. Barnett
Department of Psychology
Kansas State University
Manhattan, KS 66506

C. Daniel Batson
Department of Psychology
University of Kansas
Lawrence, KS 66045

Janet Beavin Bavelas
Department of Psychology
University of Victoria
Victoria, BC V8W 2Y2
Canada

Alex Black
Department of Psychology
University of Victoria
Victoria, BC V8W 2Y2
Canada

Brenda K. Bryant
Department of Applied Behavioral
  Sciences
University of California, Davis
Davis, CA 95616

Denise Bustamante
c/o Nancy Eisenberg
Department of Psychology
Arizona State University
Tempe, AZ 85287

Nancy Eisenberg
Department of Psychology
Arizona State University
Tempe, AZ 85287

Richard A. Fabes
Department of Home Economics
Arizona State University
Tempe, AZ 85287

Norma Deitch Feshbach
Graduate School of Education
UCLA
405 Hilgrad Avenue
Los Angeles, CA 90024

Jim Fultz
Department of Psychology
Northern Illinois University
DeKalb, IL 60115-2892

Martin L. Hoffman
Department of Psychology
New York University
6 Washington Place
New York, NY 10003

Charles R. Lemery
Department of Psychology
University of Victoria
Victoria, BC V8W 2Y2
Canada

Randy Lennon
Department of Educational
  Psychology
University of Northern Colorado
Greeley, CO 80639

James Marcia
Department of Psychology
Simon Fraser University
Burnaby, BC V5A 1S6
Canada

Robert F. Marcus
Institute of Child Study
University of Maryland
College Park, MD 20742

Robin M. Mathy
Department of Sociology
Indiana University
Bloomington, IN 47405

Paul Miller
Department of Psychology
Arizona State University
Tempe, AZ 85287

Bert S. Moore
Department of Psychology
University of Texas, Dallas
Richmond, TX 75083-0688

Jennifer Mullett
Department of Psychology
University of Victoria
Victoria, BC V8W 2Y2
Canada

Paul Mussen
Institute of Human Development
University of California, Berkeley
Berkeley, CA 94720

Robert Plutchik
Department of Psychiatry
Albert Einstein College of Medicine
1300 Morris Park Avenue
Bronx, NY 10461

Patricia A. Schoenrade
Department of Psychology
University of Kansas
Lawrence, KS 66045

Ervin Staub
Department of Psychology
University of Massachusetts
Amherst, MA 01003

Janet Strayer
Department of Psychology
Simon Fraser University
Burnaby, BC V5A 1S6
Canada

Ross A. Thompson
Department of Psychology
  Burnett Hall
University of Nebraska
Lincoln, NE 68588-0308

Lauren Wispé
Building 158 SC, Room 134
University of Oklahoma
Norman, OK 73069

Preface

Among the many self-evident problems in modern society are the lack of communication and understanding between individuals and groups and the frequent occurrence of inhumane and uncaring behavior. Many factors, both societal and psychological in nature, may contribute to these problems. There is a great need, particularly at this time in human history, for information about these factors and their precise role in the development and maintenance of affective bonds, understanding, and caring actions among people.

One factor long considered to be a mediator or contributor to positive human interaction and altruistic behavior is empathy or its potential derivative, sympathy. There is now some empirical evidence to support such a view. Therefore, it is important that we fully understand the nature of empathy, its development, and its role in behavior. With such an understanding, we may be able to improve the quality of human interrelationships.

To understand empathy, scientific investigation is needed. Although psychologists have been studying empathy (defined in this book as having an affective component) for several decades, most of the work reported in the literature has been done in the past 15 years. Indeed, research on this topic has increased dramatically in recent years. However, there are few books in which the research and theory concerning empathy have been integrated, and most of these have been written primarily from the perspective of clinical psychologists (who tend to define empathy somewhat differently from many developmental and social psychologists). Thus, a considerable body of information is available, but it is in need of evaluation and organization.

For the aforementioned reasons, we felt that it was time for investigators interested in the development of empathy and its relation to social behavior to organize and present the major findings and conceptualizations in the field, and to evaluate current methods for assessing empathy. This volume is an effort to accomplish these goals. We hope that this book will not only inform its readers, but also lead to further and better research as well as stimulate interest in this very important topic. Perhaps by doing so, it will, in a small way, help to meet the urgent need for a better understanding of factors affecting the quality of human relationships.

This volume is the product of a group effort. We are indebted to the contributors for their thoughtful presentations and their help in completing the project. In addition, we are grateful to Sally Carney for her assistance in the preparation of the manuscript. Work on this volume was funded by grants from the National Institutes of Health (a biomedical grant administered through Arizona State University and a Career Development Award [1KO4HD00717]) and from the National Science Foundation (BNS-8509223) to Nancy Eisenberg, and by grants from the Child Development Foundation and the Social Sciences and Humanities Research Council of Canada (Strategic Area Grant 498-82-0027) to Janet Strayer. We are truly grateful for this support. The first editor also wishes to thank Jerry Harris for his continuing support and input throughout the duration of this project. The second editor wishes to express her appreciation to her interested colleagues and research assistants, and to express special thanks to J. M., who retained resilience and good humor at both the high and low altitudes along the flight of ideas.

Introduction

1   Critical issues in the study of empathy

Nancy Eisenberg and Janet Strayer

The role of empathy and related processes such as sympathy in social and moral development has been debated for centuries by philosophers as well as psychologists (e.g., Allport, 1937; Blum, 1980; Hume, 1777/1966; Titchener, 1924). Moreover, empathy has been an important concept in contemporary developmental, social, personality, and clinical psychology (e.g., Batson & Coke, 1981; Dymond, 1949; Goldstein & Michaels, 1985; Hoffman, 1984). However, in part because of its wide-ranging application, the notion of empathy is, and always has been, a broad, somewhat slippery concept – one that has provoked considerable speculation, excitement, and confusion.

Indeed, identifying the topic of this edited volume as empathy does not clarify for many readers exactly what will be discussed. Some people take the term *empathy* to refer to a cognitive process analogous to cognitive role taking or perspective taking (e.g., Deutsch & Madle, 1975); others take it to mean a primarily affective process (having some cognitive components) (e.g., Feshbach, 1978; Hoffman, 1984); still others, primarily clinicians, view empathy as a process that serves a communicatory and/or information-gathering function in therapy (e.g., Goldstein & Michaels, 1985).

The history of the term is an interesting topic in itself, which is discussed in chapter 2. The perspectives of the contributors to this volume, although diverse, are not nearly so varied as has been the use of the term both historically and in present-day psychology. For most of the contributors, empathizing involves the vicarious sharing of affect – this is the critical similarity that underlies our different perceptions of both the role of cognition in this affective process and the exact nature of the process itself. Consider the similarities in the following definitions of empathy:

> an affective response more appropriate to someone else's situation than to one's own (Hoffman, chapter 4)
>
> other-oriented feelings of concern, compassion, and tenderness experienced as a result of witnessing another person's suffering (Batson, Fultz, & Schoenrode, chapter 8)

3

empathy denotes the vicarious experiencing of an emotion that is congruent with, but not necessarily identical to the emotion of another individual (Barnett, chapter 7)

a definition of empathy that requires that an observer share the general emotional tone of another – whether or not there is direct emotional match – seems appropriate for most purposes. . . . It seems appropriate to regard *both* kinds of empathic responding reactions requiring minimal inference from an observer and those requiring much greater inferential role taking as anchor-points on a continuum of empathy (Thompson, chapter 6)

empathy viewed multidimensionally may be initiated by one's attention to a person in a salient stimulus event (real or symbolic). . . . Subsequent phases of the empathic process may entail motor mimicry, classical conditioning, association, imaginal transposition of self and other, and similar processes as part of the reverberation that links the other person's experience to our own and permits affect sharing (Strayer, chapter 10)

Social perspective taking entails cognitive understanding of the feelings and motives of others and, as such, is an instrumental skill. Empathy, on the other hand, entails emotional responsiveness to the feelings experienced by others and, as such, is an expressive experience (Bryant, chapter 11)

Empathy has been defined as "the capacity for participating in, or a vicarious experiencing of another's feelings, volitions, or ideas and sometimes another's movements to the point of executing bodily movements resembling his" (*Webster's Third New International Dictionary*, 1971). This definition has several implications. First, it suggests that empathy is an internal state or experience similar to an emotion. Second, it implies that this emotional state can sometimes be recognized through imitative bodily movements (Plutchik, chapter 3)

an affective state stemming from apprehension of another's emotional state or condition and which is congruent with it (Eisenberg & Miller, chapter 13)

In all of the definitions just mentioned, the sharing of affect is a primary component. However, several contributors depart from the general view represented by these quotations. For example, Wispé, in chapter 2, does not really emphasize his own definition of empathy; he views empathy in more cognitive terms than do the other contributors:

"Empathy" refers to the attempt by one self-aware self to comprehend unjudgmentally the positive and negative experiences of another self. These emotions and reactions are often unclearly understood by the other person . . . so one important aspect of the process is empathic accuracy inasmuch as the purpose of empathy is often (but not necessarily) to provide understanding for one or both parties. Empathy depends upon the use of imaginal and mimitic capabilities and it is most often an effortful process.

Marcia (chapter 5) defines empathy from the perspective of a clinician or, more precisely, from the perspective of various groups of clinicians. He adopts Reik's (1949) definition of the empathic process in psychotherapy, a model that provides a focus for discussion of its development in Strayer's chapter as well. In Reik's view, empathy has an affective component, particularly in what Reik refers to as the "reverberation phase." However, the last phase in Reik's model is said to be particularly important for the clinician. It is defined as the "moving back from the merged inner relationship to a position of separate identity that permits a response to be made that reflects both understanding of the other as well as separateness from them" (Marcia, chapter 5). Thus, in addition to emphasizing affect, Reik's definition includes "detachment," which refers to a highly cognitive process and seems to involve some neutralization of emotion.

A brief reading of the contributors' definitions of empathy, however, may be misleading. The similarities in their conceptualizations of empathy may well be greater than these brief quotations suggest. Even Wispé, who defines empathy in more cognitive terms than do many of the contributors, defines sympathy in somewhat the same way as they define empathy:

> Sympathy refers to the heightened awareness of the suffering of another person as something to be alleviated . . . sympathy intensifies both the representation and the internal reaction to the other's predicament. (Wispé, 1986, p. 318)

The lack of consistency in the usage of the terms *empathy* and *sympathy* has given rise to considerable confusion. In reality, there is no correct definition of empathy, just different definitions. Because this volume is about empathy, it seems appropriate to open the discussion with our own definition of empathy and to compare it with definitions of related concepts. We should also look at some of the general issues relevant to many of the chapters in this volume.

Definitional issues

Empathy

In our view, empathy involves sharing the perceived emotion of another – "feeling with" another. This vicarious affective reaction may occur as a response to overt perceptible cues indicative of another's affective state (e.g., a person's facial expressions), or as the consequence of inferring another's state on the basis of indirect cues (e.g., the nature of the other's situation). Thus, we define empathy as an emotional response that stems from another's emotional state or condition and that is congruent with the other's emotional state or situation. This definition is quite similar to Hoffman's (1982) and implies that one can empathize with a broad range of affects.

Several important issues concerning the conceptualization of empathy also need to be clarified here. One is the degree of self–other differentiation when empathizing. Some theorists assume that empathy involves an "as if" distinction – that there is at least a minimal differentiation between self and other when empathizing (e.g., Feshbach, 1978; Kohut, 1978; Rogers & Truax, 1967). Others (e.g., Hoffman, 1982) assume that such a differentiation does not necessarily take place in the early phases of empathy. Thus, there is some question whether it is empathy or merely a precursor to empathy when one experiences vicarious emotion and is not aware of where the affect originated. For example, an infant may experience contagious affect without recognizing the source of the affect. If infants truly do not differentiate between their own and others' affect, their vicarious experiencing should then be considered a potential precursor of empathy, not empathy itself. However, even young children may have some primitive understanding of the difference between their own and others' affective responding.

Sympathy

Another critical issue is how to distinguish between empathy, sympathy, and personal distress. Sympathy, like empathy, has been defined in a multitude of ways. Wispé's (1986) definition is perhaps representative of the ones most widely accepted today. For him, sympathy refers to

> the heightened awareness of the suffering of another person as something to be alleviated. There are two aspects to this definition of sympathy. The first makes reference to the increased sensitivity to the emotions of the other person. Sympathy intensifies both the representation and the internal reaction to the other person's predicament. The second aspect involves the urge to take whatever mitigating actions are necessary; that is, in sympathy the suffering of the other person is experienced immediately as something to be alleviated. (p. 318)

Our definition of sympathy is, in general, consistent with that of Wispé. Sympathy is "feeling for" someone, and refers to feelings of sorrow, or feeling sorry, for another. That is to say, sympathy often involves feelings of concern, although the conscious cognitive realization that one is concerned about another's welfare is an outcome, rather than a part, of sympathizing. Often sympathy is the consequence of empathizing, although it may be possible for sympathy (as well as empathy) to result from processes such as cognitive perspective taking. Whether or not empathy always mediates sympathizing is an open question.

Our and Wispe's definition of sympathy is in marked contrast to that of some clinicians. For example, in Katz's (1963) view, sympathy involves heightened attention to one's own feelings and the assumed similarity between one's own and another's feelings. Similarly, Goldstein and Michaels (1985) have stated that "the sympathizer, in contrast [to the empathizer], is more preoccupied with his or her own feelings in response to the other and thus is less able to respond to, for, or with the other in a manner sensitive to the other person's actual ongoing emotional world and context" (p. 8). In attempting to differentiate between sympathy and empathy, Goldstein and Michaels suggest that the latter involves role taking, adeptness at reading nonverbal cues, sensitivity to the full range and depth of the other's affective state or situation, and communication of a feeling of caring, or at least sincere attempts to understand in a nonjudgmental or helping manner (see also Keefe, 1979; Macarov, 1978). Goldstein and Michaels's definitions of empathy and sympathy reflect a current perspective among clinicians, which differs somewhat from that of nonclinicians.

Personal distress

When perceiving cues related to another's distress, some people may experience an aversive state such as anxiety or worry that is not congruent with the other's state and, what is more important, that leads to a self-oriented, egoistic reaction or concern. Batson (e.g., Batson & Coke, 1981) has labeled such a response "personal distress" and has suggested that the experiencing of personal distress leads one to attempt to alleviate one's own aversive state. Personal distress, therefore, is conceptually quite different from both empathy (which is, in essence, neither an egoistic nor other-oriented response) and sympathy (which involves a clear other-orientation). Nonetheless, owing to the conceptual and methodological limitations of existing research, personal distress undoubtedly is confused with sympathy and empathy in much of the literature (see Batson, Fultz, & Schoenrode, chapter 8, for an exception to this confusion).

Many researchers disagree about the relation of personal distress to empathy. For Batson (Batson & Coke, 1981), the two types of affective reactions are conceptually unrelated, although owing to the relation of both to other relevant factors (e.g., general affective arousability), they are positively correlated. For Hoffman, however, feelings of "global distress" (Hoffman, 1982) or "empathic distress" (Hoffman, 1976), whereby young children confuse their own and others' feelings and act as if they themselves are experiencing another's distress, is an early stage in the development of empathy. Thus, Hoffman does not consider such personal distress to be distinct from empathy (Hoffman, 1982).

Our view is somewhat more akin to that of Batson, although we do agree with Hoffman that "contagious" personal distress is an early precursor of the development of empathy. We believe that personal distress can occur either independently of empathy or as an outcome of an initial empathic experience. In the latter case, the individual's initial empathizing is experienced as an aversive reaction and, consequently, the individual focuses on his or her own affective state. However, it also is likely that empathizing leads one to focus on the other person rather than solely on the self. Indeed, in most cases involving persons older than infants, one would expect empathy to engender feelings, which, if sufficiently strong, would prompt the empathizer to attempt to locate whether their source is self- or other-derived. This process would not be expected to occur if the feelings aroused are weak or if the individual is distracted by competing events.

Projection

Although we are concentrating on definitional issues here, it is useful to differentiate between empathy and projection. Projection is defined as "the act of ascribing to someone or something else one's own attitudes, thoughts, etc." (*Random House College Dictionary*, 1980, p. 1058). Thus, projection differs from our definition of empathy in two ways: (1) it is a cognitive process that does not necessarily involve affect, and (2) the direction of the process is from self to other, rather than vice versa (see Feshbach, 1978). There is, therefore, a clear conceptual distinction between empathy and projection. Nonetheless, as Strayer points out in chapter 10, differentiating projection and empathy becomes an issue when researchers try to measure empathy.

The role of cognition in empathy

Although the role of cognition in empathy is discussed in many chapters of this book, especially those by Hoffman (chapter 4) and by Strayer (chapter 10), we should at least touch on this topic here because it has direct bearing on the definition of empathy. A number of cognitive processes of varying sophistication can be viewed as contributing to empathy. The complexity of these cognitive processes probably varies, depending upon the age of the individual and other personality and situational factors. At the most basic level, the ability to differentiate between self and other and between one's own and another's affective responding is necessary for empathizing, at least according to our definition of the concept (see Hoffman, 1982, 1984 for a more detailed discussion of these processes). Recall, however, that Hoffman (e.g., 1982) does not think differentiation processes are necessary for primitive empathic responding and has suggested, for example, that emotional reactivity based upon the classical conditioning of cues of another's distress to one's own distress is a form of empathy. As mentioned earlier, whether or not one considers these primitive emotional reactions to be empathy or a possible precursor of empathy depends upon how the individual chooses to define empathy.

Hoffman (1982) also has described the role of several other cognitive processes in empathy. One of his early developing modes of empathic response involves the direct association between cues of another's emotional state and the potential empathizer's memories of past experiences of a similar emotion. The example he cites is that of a girl who sees a boy cut himself and who then cries herself. The sight of blood or some other cue in the situation reminds the girl of her own past experiences of pain and evokes an empathic distress response. The fact that such a process depends on a general associative mechanism and at least a minimal degree of cognitive processing implies some self–other differentiation. Thus, we agree with Hoffman that this mode of response is empathic.

Another mode of empathic response discussed by Hoffman is that based on symbolic association, that is, the association between cues that symbolically indicate another's feelings and the observer's own past distresses. For example, hearing a description of another in distress may evoke empathy by means of association. This mode of empathy requires the ability to interpret symbols, which is, of course, a cognitive skill. Moreover, inasmuch as this mode of empathy is based upon a relatively advanced level of cognitive functioning, it is likely to entail at least the minimum degree of self–other differentiation specified in our definition of empathy.

Another cognitive skill cited as playing a role in empathy (e.g., Feshbach, 1978; Hoffman, 1982) is the ability to role take. According to Feshbach, two types of cognitive processes are essential for empathizing: (1) the ability to discriminate and label affective states in others, and (2) the ability to assume the perspective and role of another person. The former capability is more basic and is necessary for role taking.

We agree with Hoffman and Feshbach that role taking based upon the identification and labeling of others' affective states often is involved in the process of empathizing. However, it also is likely that individuals frequently discern the other's state and empathize without actually labeling the emotion or taking the other's role. As has been suggested by Karniol (1982), people may discern another's situation by retrieving from memory information related to cues concerning another's affective state. According to Karniol,

> We are suggesting, then, that need awareness is reached through the accessing of stored situational information which provides an interpretational context for the sequence of action and goals in the situation. Thus, need awarenesss is not dependent on imaginative attempts to understand what the other is thinking, feeling, or experiencing. (p. 260)

Karniol (1982), in her presentation of an information-processing model, was attempting to demonstrate that role taking is not always necessary for prosocial behavior. However, her point also applies to the role of cognition in empathy. It is likely that people often empathize not because they have put themselves cognitively in another's place, but because they have retrieved relevant information from their memories that has enabled them to understand another's situation or feelings. This notion is similar to Hoffman's view of the role of direct association in empathy, although the process Karniol describes may be more conscious and effortful.

In summary, many cognitive processes appear to play a role in empathy. Some are quite simple, such as those involved in the direct association between another's visual cues of distress and memories of one's own distress, whereas other modes of cognition entail more sophisticated information-processing or inferential capabilities. The development of the more sophisticated of these capabilities is no doubt age-related (see Karniol, 1982; Shantz, 1983). There is clear evidence that role-taking capabilities increase with age, and one would also expect children's store of information relevant to interpreting situational cues to increase as a function of experience and cognitive development. Thus, it is reasonable to assume (as has Hoffman) that developmental changes in cognitive processing capabilities are directly related to the development of both empathy and sympathy (which he considers to be a sophisticated mode of empathy).

The role of empathy in prosocial development

One reason for the considerable interest in empathy and related constructs is the assumption of many psychologists and philosophers that empathy (or sympathy) mediates prosocial behavior (e.g., Batson & Coke, 1981; Blum, 1980; Eisenberg, 1986; Feshbach, 1982; Hoffman, 1981; Hume, 1777/1966; Staub, 1979). Indeed, whether such a relation exists is discussed in many of the chapters in this volume (e.g., chapters 4, 8, and 13) and in much of the literature on altruism (e.g., Eisenberg, 1982, 1986; Radke-Yarrow, Zahn-Waxler, & Chapman, 1983; Rushton & Sorrentino, 1981; Wispé, 1978). In fact, in some of the early work on sympathy (Murphy, 1937), prosocial behavior and sympathy were not clearly differentiated.

The general finding in the relevant research (see Eisenberg & Miller, chapter 13) is that empathy and/or sympathy is positively related to prosocial behavior (i.e., voluntary behavior intended to benefit another; see Eisenberg & Miller, chapter 13). However, this does not necessarily imply that empathy always results in prosocial behavior, or even the desire to engage in prosocial actions. According to our definition of empathy, the arousal of empathic feelings may or may not lead to attempts to assist another. Indeed, in some cases, empathic arousal in reaction to another's need or distress may lead to feelings of personal distress and self-focus. In other situations, empathizing may be associated with sympathizing, which often, but not always, leads to prosocial responding. (Sympathy can be expected to be most closely associated with altruistically motivated prosocial behaviors, but various factors may inhibit the sympathizing individual from behaving altruistically.) In yet other instances, empathic arousal may simply dissipate or be less salient than some other feeling or consideration (e.g., cost to the self for assisting). Moreover, individuals can empathize with a variety of affects – including happiness, sadness, and anger – and in some of these instances should not be expected to act in a prosocial manner (see Cialdini,

Kenrick, & Baumann, 1982; Feshbach, 1982; Rosenhan, Salovey, Karylowski, & Hargis, 1981; Sterling & Gaertner, 1983).

To summarize, the relation between empathy and prosocial behavior is neither direct nor inevitable. Many factors must be considered when one is attempting to predict the relation between the two (see Eisenberg, 1986).

Overview of the book

The book is divided into four main parts. Part I is mainly about conceptual and theoretical issues. Historical perspectives of the construct of empathy are reviewed (Wispé), and perceptions of empathy and its role in human functioning from developmental (Hoffman), clinical (Marcia), and evolutionary (Plutchik) perspectives are presented. The authors of these chapters present their own perspectives rather than a catalogue of all possible perspectives; nonetheless, they provide an overview of several major approaches to the study of empathy, along with some interesting new ideas.

In Part II, research concerning empathy during the early years (Thompson), childhood (Barnett), and adulthood (Batson et al.) is reviewed. The authors of these chapters discuss many of the major conceptual issues concerning empathy within a given age span and integrate the results of the available empirical work.

Special topics and research projects are examined in Part III. Strayer considers affective versus cognitive inputs to empathy and tells how to assess both types of inputs. Eisenberg and Miller review the literature on the relation of empathy to altruism, and Lennon and Eisenberg look at age and gender differences in empathic responding. In these three chapters, the primary emphasis is on review, theoretical and empirical integration, and the interpretation of research findings, with some of the authors' own research also presented.

In the remaining chapters in Part III, the authors present recent findings and their implications for the study of empathy: Bryant examines differences in the roles of empathy and perspective taking in children's adjustment and social functioning and the correlates of each; Feshbach examines issues related to empathy and to adjustment and empathy in the familial context; and Bavelas et al. look at the concept of mimicry and its possible role in empathy and conclude that mimicry serves a different function than has generally been assumed in the past.

In Part IV, the strengths and weaknesses of various methods for operationalizing empathy are reviewed. Those indices include the picture-story procedures typically used with children (Strayer), self-report of affective state in experimental studies (Batson), facial/gestural measures (Marcus), questionnaires (Bryant), and physiological measures (Eisenberg, Fabes, Bustamante, & Mathy). The authors of these sections present relevant research and discuss issues of interest to anyone who desires to assess empathy. We hope that this section will be useful to those who wish to evaluate extant research as well as those planning future investigations.

A final component of this book is the commentaries provided by Bert Moore, Paul Mussen, and Ervin Staub. Their insights are a valuable contribution to the volume and to our understanding of empathy.

We hope that the following chapters will convey some of the excitement associated with the study of empathy, which is now an emerging area of research, and that they will demonstrate the importance of this aspect of human functioning.

References

Allport, G. W. (1937). *Personality: A psychological interpretation.* New York: Holt.

Batson, D., & Coke, J. S. (1981). Empathy: A source of altruistic motivation for helping. In J. P. Rushton & R. M. Sorrentino (Eds.), *Altruism and helping behavior: Social, personality, and developmental perspectives* (pp. 167–211). Hillsdale, NJ: Erlbaum.

Blum, L. A. (1980). *Friendship, altruism, and morality.* London: Routledge & Kegan Paul.

Cialdini, R. B., Kenrick, D. T., & Baumann, D. J. (1982). Effects of mood on prosocial behavior in children and adults. In N. Eisenberg (Ed.), *The development of prosocial behavior* (pp. 339–359). New York: Academic Press.

Deutsch, F., & Madle, R. A. (1975). Empathy: Historic and current conceptualizations, and a cognitive theoretical perspective. *Human Development, 18,* 267–287.

Dymond, R. F. (1949). A scale for the measurement of empathic ability. *Journal of Consulting Psychology, 13,* 27–33.

Eisenberg, N. (Ed.) (1982). *The development of prosocial behavior.* New York: Academic Press.

Eisenberg, N. (1986). *Altruistic emotion, cognition, and behavior.* Hillsdale, NJ: Erlbaum.

Feshbach, N. D. (1978). Studies of empathic behavior in children. In B. A. Maher (Ed.), *Progress in experimental personality research* (Vol. 8, pp. 1–47). New York: Academic Press.

Feshbach, N. D. (1982). Sex differences in empathy and social behavior in children. In N. Eisenberg (Ed.), *The development of prosocial behavior* (pp. 315–338). New York: Academic Press.

Goldstein, A. P., & Michaels, G. Y. (1985). *Empathy: Development, training, and consequences.* Hillsdale, N.J.: Erlbaum.

Hoffman, M. L. (1976). Empathy, role-taking, guilt, and development of altruistic motives. In T. Lickona (Ed.) *Moral development and behavior: Theory, research and social issues* (pp. 124–143). New York: Holt, Rinehart, & Winston.

Hoffman, M. L. (1981). Is altruism part of human nature? *Journal of Personality and Social Psychology, 40,* 121–137.

Hoffman, M. L. (1982). Development of prosocial motivation: Empathy and guilt. In N. Eisenberg (Ed.), *The development of prosocial behavior* (pp. 218–231). New York: Academic Press.

Hoffman, M. L. (1984). Interaction of affect and cognition in empathy. In C. E. Izard, J. Kagan, & R. B. Zajonc (Eds.), *Emotions, cognition, and behavior* (pp. 103–131). Cambridge: Cambridge University Press.

Hume, D. (1966). *Enquiries concerning the human understanding and concerning the principles of morals* (2d ed.). Oxford: Clarenden Press. (Original work published 1777)

Karniol, R. (1982). Settings, scripts, and self-schemata: A cognitive analysis of the development of prosocial behavior. In N. Eisenberg (Ed.), *The development of prosocial behavior* (pp. 251–278). New York: Academic Press.

Katz, R. L. (1963). *Empathy: Its nature and uses.* New York: Free Press.

Keefe, T. (1979). The development of empathic skill. *Journal of Education for Social Work, 15,* 30–37.

Kohut, H. (1978). *The search for self* (Vol. 2). New York: International Universities Press.

Macarov, D. (1978). Empathy: The charismatic chimera. *Journal of Education for Social Work, 14,* 86–92.

Murphy, L. B. (1937). *Social behavior and child personality.* New York: Columbia University Press.

Radke-Yarrow, M., Zahn-Waxler, C., & Chapman, M. (1983). Prosocial dispositions and behavior. In P. Mussen (Ed.), *Manual of child psychology: Vol. 4. Socialization, personality, and social development* (E. M. Hetherington, Ed.) (pp. 469–545). New York: John Wiley & Sons.

Reik, T. (1949). *Listening with the third ear.* New York: Farrar, Straus.

Rogers, C. R., & Truax, C. B. (1967). The therapeutic conditions antecedent to change: A therapeutic view. In C. R. Rogers (Ed.), *The therapeutic relationship and its impact: A study of psychotherapy with schizophrenics.* Madison, WI: University of Wisconsin Press.

Rosenhan, D. L., Salovey, P., Karylowski, J., & Hargis, K. (1981). Emotion and altruism. In J. P. Rushton & R. M. Sorrentino (Eds.), *Altruism and helping behavior: Social, personality, and developmental perspectives.* Hillsdale, NJ: Erlbaum.

Rushton, J. P., & Sorrentino, R. M. (Eds.) (1981). *Altruism and helping behavior: Social, personality, and developmental perspectives.* Hillsdale, NJ: Erlbaum.

Shantz, C. V. (1983). Social cognition. In P. H. Mussen (Ed.), *Handbook of child psychology: Cognitive development* (Vol. 3, pp. 495–555). New York: Wiley & Sons.

Staub, E. (1979). *Positive social behavior and morality. Vol. 2: Socialization and development.* New York: Academic Press.

Sterling, B. S., & Gaertner, S. L. (1983). The effects of anger on helping behavior. *Academic Psychology Bulletin, 5,* 221–227.

Titchener, E. (1924). *A textbook of psychology.* New York: Macmillan.

Wispé, L. (1978). *Altruism, sympathy, and helping: psychological and sociological principles.* New York: Academic Press.

Wispé, L. (1986). The distinction between sympathy and empathy: To call forth a concept, a word is needed. *Journal of Personality and Social Psychology, 50,* 314–321.

Part I

Historical and theoretical perspectives

2   History of the concept of empathy

Lauren Wispé

Tracing the history of the concept of empathy in modern psychology was a difficult, but rewarding, assignment. It was difficult because every decade or so a new growth of psychological concepts, or new uses for old ones, makes the old field impassable. The trails back have become overgrown with redefinitions, reinterpretations, and benign neglect. We no longer remember the important debates in which these concepts took shape. We don't even remember where they originated, or with whom. They have disappeared like the smoke from a long burned-out campfire. Then upon the same site, with materials we think are fresh and theories we think are new, we kindle another fire. At the same time, it has been a rewarding assignment, because a chapter on the history of empathy may help to refurbish our knowledge about the history of modern psychology. As we try to understand the present status of the concept of empathy, knowing where we have been may help us to decide where we want to go.

The concept we know today as empathy began as *Einfühlung* in late-nineteenth-century German aesthetics and was translated as empathy in early twentieth-century American experimental psychology. The concept was utilized by many personality theorists of the 1930s; was borrowed, cherished, and revitalized, especially by Rogerian psychotherapists, during the 1950s; had a brief encounter with conditioning theorists during the 1960s; and most recently has been called into service by social and developmental psychologists as an explanation for altruistic behavior. There have been some – relatively slight – differences of emphasis and connotation in the term *empathy* from one field to another, but there has also been a remarkable consistency of usage and meaning. To complicate matters, however, a number of other terms – *sympathy, role taking, perspective taking,* and so on – may, or may not, refer to similar, or identical, psychological processes. For reasons to be discussed later, these will not be considered in detail here.

In this chapter we consider the concept of empathy as it has been used in psychology specifically. We follow a roughly chronological order, and we quote

17

exactly the definitions of empathy so that readers can see for themselves the changes that have occurred in the concept as it has become more widely used.

Einfühlung in aesthetics

The term *empathy* is of comparatively recent origin, having been coined by Titchener (1909) as a translation of the German word *Einfühlung*, which had its origins in German aesthetics. The art critic Edgar Wind (1963) reported that the term *Einfühlung* was first used by Robert Vischer in 1873 in his discussion of the psychology of aesthetics and form perception. Vischer, according to Wind (1963), gave the theory of *Einfühlung* its "earliest and most eloquent statement," and his views "had a wide currency among art historians of his generation, perhaps because he was an art historian in his own right" (p. 150). Vischer's psychology of aesthetic appreciation involved a projection of the self into the object of beauty.

This idea was quickly picked up by others. Karl Groos (1892), better known to behavior scientists for his work on play, used a similar idea involving aesthetic satisfaction as the activity of "inner imitation" (Kovach, 1974). The process implied by *Einfühlung* was described for the first time in English by the English critic and novelist Vernon Lee (Violet Paget) in a lecture given in London in 1895 (Wellek, 1970, p. 169). She translated *Einfühlung* as sympathy, explaining that "the word *sympathy*, with-feeling – (*einfühlen*, 'feeling into,' the Germans happily put it) – as the word *sympathy* is intended to suggest, this enlivening . . . is exercised only when our feelings enter, and are absorbed into, the form we perceive" (Wellek, 1970, p. 170). She wrote in another connection about "those tautnesses of muscles . . . which, translated into similar strains in our own persons, make us fully realize movement" (Wellek, 1970, p. 171). Thus, apparently independently, she has discovered the basic idea of muscular mimicry and *Einfühlung*. There is no doubt that the idea of *Einfühlung* was in the wind in aesthetics by the late nineteenth century, where it meant that aesthetic enjoyment is an objectification of self-enjoyment. Although psychologists usually credit Theodor Lipps (1903, 1905) with having discovered empathy, it would be more accurate to say that he organized and developed the formula for psychology.

Einfühlung in Germany

Clearly, the concept of *Einfühlung* had its roots in German aesthetics, but our concern is the way it was used in psychology. Among psychologists at that time there were men like Brentano (1874/1924), Lipps (1903, 1905), and Prandtl (1910) for whom psychology was the study of immediate experience. Of these, Lipps and Prandtl wrote specifically about *Einfühlung*. Lipps was one of the few important figures in German psychology who managed to remain independent of Wundt's influence (Boring, 1950, p. 427). In his early work, on optical illusion, Lipps concluded that subjects projected themselves into the stimulus configurations. He explained illusions (some of them) in terms of the characteristics of those who viewed them. These ideas influenced his work on the psychology of aesthetics, for which he is probably best known, although he wrote widely on psychology in general. He first developed his ideas about *Einfühlung* in a monograph entitled *Einfühlung, innere Nachahmung, und Organempfindungen* (1903), in which he wrote that the appearance in the senses of the object of beauty may provide the object of aesthetic satisfaction, but is not itself the aesthhetic satisfaction. Rather, it is the striving self that is aesthetically pleased. It is the self that feels itself striving, yielding, overcoming obstacles – in short, feels various internal activities. Thus aesthetic satisfaction consists of the object, but does not reside in the object. It is in the self. This distinction between self and object is at first hard to grasp, but it is the crux of the concept of *Einfühlung*. *Einfühlung* implies that the apprehension of the sensible object involves an immediate tendency in the beholder to a particular kind of activity.

Later Lipps (1905) extended his analysis to how we know others. He wrote that one should not speak of a proud gesture, but rather a gesture of pride. The beholder ''sees'' shame *in* the blushing, anger *in* the clenched fist, joy *in* the radiant smile (Stein, 1964, p. 70). It is in the nature of language to designate these as a unity of experience, but it is rather the inner activities of the person, which resonate with the stimulus of the object to which it is inextricably bound, that provide the meaning. In this way, *Einfühlung* provides one aspect of what we know about other selves. However, Lipps noted that there are two other spheres of knowledge beside knowledge of others: There is knowledge of self and knowledge of things. One knows about oneself through apperception and about things through sensory information.

The debate became rather abstruse, as Allport (1937) pointed out. Knowledge about others, Allport argued, must be something more than, or above, empathy or motor mimicry. A ''proud'' gesture, a ''joyous'' laugh, describe those qualities in another sentient being. So first there must be a realization of the consciousness of the other. There can be no proud or joyous *stones*. Yet we use the same words to describe both inanimate and animate objects, as in ''The water in the brook danced joyously downstream.'' For Lipps, *Einfühlung* meant that the beholder of the gesture of pride simultaneously experiences an individual who is experiencing pride. But it also meant, more generally, that the observers project themselves into the objects of perception. This is the only way to grasp certain kinds of aesthetic appreciation, the only way to grasp the leafless tree that stands *naked* against the wind, the person *weighed down* with sorrow. Although many of his critics considered this wild animism, Lipps argued that qualities of certain kinds are experienced by the perceiver as ''in'' rather than ''about'' the object. Objects are felt as well as seen.

Prandtl (1910), although less well known than Lipps, wrote an important book on the nature of empathy. He introduced an associative explanation for empathy. Although he agreed that persons can know only their own inner lives – even when they think they are understanding others – he believed that it is only their own imagining or thinking that they know. This act of ''animation'' can come about in two ways, either by ''empirical empathy'' (association) or by empathy through feeling. The former is easier to understand than the latter. Empirical empathy depends upon prior reproduction of feeling and assumes that such feelings have been previously felt as the person's own feelings. It can be explained in the following manner. Sometime in the past a person may have stamped his/her foot at the same time that the full fury of feelings was consciously presented. Later the person sees someone else stamp his/her foot, and thinks how furious that person must be. The other person's fury is not given directly, but rather is inferred. ''Empathy through feeling'' is closer to Lipps's version of empathy. In both kinds of empathy, however, there is the characteristic experience that something is going on in the perceiver that also exists in the object.

Thus Lipps, Prandtl, and the others used *Einfühlung* to explain how a person grasped the meaning of aesthetic objects and the consciousness of other persons. Most of these writers found the core of empathy in the experience of inner imitation – or motor mimicry, as it later came to be called. This can be done, of course, only by a generous interpretation of *Einfühlung*, and this particular kind of experience may occur only for a limited sample of viewers. Nevertheless, *Einfühlung*, understood in this very general sense, became the way of understanding all forms of psychic participation. Furthermore, *inner Nachahmung*, inner imitation, and motor mimicry, were precursors – and psychologically richer versions – of what today we refer to as vicariousness. This does not mean that these terms are synonymous. It merely means that the problem of explaining that objects are felt as well as seen is still with us.

Titchener on empathy

Titchener borrowed Lipps's notion of *Einfühlung*, but eventually shifted the emphasis from internal acts to content. What he meant by *Einfühlung* was complicated, changeable, and hard to render into current psychological language. When he coined the term *empathy*, Titchener (1909) thought one could not know about the consciousness of another person by reasoning analogically from one's own mental processes to those of another. One could do this only by inner imitation, as he said, ''in the mind's muscle.'' In his *Experimental Psychology of the Thought Processes* (1909), he wrote, ''Not only do I see gravity and modesty and pride and courtesy and stateliness, but I feel or act them in the mind's muscle. That is, I suppose, a simple case of empathy, if we may coin that term as a rendering of *Einfühlung"* (p. 21). One can scarcely imagine a more auspicious introduction into the psychological jargon than by Titchener, himself. His influence was great. His erudition was massive. His competence in modern languages, as well as Greek and Latin, was considerable. And his interest in etymology led him to translate *Einfühlung* as "empathy" via the Greek *empatheia,* which means literally "in" (*en*) "suffering or passion" (*pathos*). *Einfühlung* means "to feel one's way into," and the etymological similarity between empathy and sympathy did not escape Titchener. He wrote that empathy was "a word formed on the analogy of sympathy" (1924, p. 417, fn.). Given the recent uses of the term, it is important to note that Titchener did not mean "identification," or he would have referred to *Einsfühlung,* nor did he mean "vicarious feelings," which in German would be *Nachgefühl.* "Inner imitation" (*inner Nachahmung*) might have been an acceptable rendition of *Einfühlung.* This was what Groos (1892) meant by it. But Titchener did not mean any of these.

Although it is well known that Titchener invented the term *empathy,* what he meant by it is not clear. When he delivered his *Lectures on the Experimental Psychology of the Thought Processes* (1909), Titchener was into a defense of the "doctrine of sensation and image" as the basis of the psychology of the higher mental processes. Today we have forgotten that then there were psychologists who were "sensationalists" and that there were those who believed in "imageless thought." Sensationalism as "the theory that all knowledge originates in sensation," Titchener (1909, pp. 23–24) quoted with approval "is . . . primarily a theory of the origin of knowledge, not a theory of the genesis of thought." Along with sensations went imagery. Titchener was an imaginer. He found imageless thought unacceptable for himself. He wrote, "My mind, then, is of the imaginal sort" (1909, p. 7), and, indeed, his writing testifies to this. He began his *Lectures,* for example, this way:

> If I chance to be reflecting on the progress of science, there is likely to arise before my mind's eye a scene familiar to my childhood – the flow of the incoming tide over a broad extent of sandy shore. The whole body of water is pressing forward, irresistibly, as natural law decrees. . . . My mind . . . is prone to imagery; and this image, of check and overflow in the van of a great movement, has come to represent for me the progress of science. (1909, p. 3)

It strikes us today as utterly quaint that a great experimental psychologist would ever write that "the progress of science" *meant* "the incoming tide over a . . . sandy shore."

As in the quotation above, Titchener spent more time on visualization of meanings, but there was also auditory and kinesthetic imagery. He was having trouble distinguishing kinesthetic sensation from kinesthetic images when he noticed that

> if you compare an actual nod of the head with the mental nod that signifies assent to an argument, or the actual frown and wrinkling of the forehead with the mental frown that signifies perplexity. . . . The sensed nod and the frown are coarse and rough in outline; the imaged nod and frown are cleanly and delicately traced. . . . I represent the meaning of affirmation, for instance, by the image of a little nick felt at the back of the neck, – an experience which, in sensation, is complicated by pressures and pulls from the scalp and throat. (1909, p. 21–22)

This was what he meant by kinesthetic imagery. But in all ways kinesthetic and visual sensations and images were similar. Therefore it was possible that visual and kinesthetic images could combine to share the task of logical meanings. That was what he meant when he wrote that one could not only "see gravity and modesty and pride and courtesy and stateliness" but could also "feel" or "act" them in one's kinesthetic imagery. This was the "simple case of empathy." It was a kind of metaphor to describe an often fleeting coalescence of visual and kinesthetic imagination. There was no doubt in Titchener's mind about "the subjective reality" of such images, or of "these attitudinal feels," which seemed to be closely related (1909, p. 181). They were experiences "acted out" in imagination as a form of motor empathy (1909, p. 185). One cannot *see* stateliness. One can *see* only an object moving. One can add the stateliness only by what Titchener called "kinesthetic imagery" that had come for that person to mean stately.

By the time Titchener's *Beginner's Psychology* was published (1915), the concept of empathy had grown in importance. He wrote that

> We have a natural tendency to feel ourselves into what we perceive or imagine. As we read about the forest, we may, as it were, *become* the explorer; we feel for ourselves the gloom, the silence, the humidity, the oppression, the sense of lurking danger; everything is strange, but it is to us that strange experience has come. We are told of a shocking accident, and we gasp and shrink and feel nauseated as we imagine it; we are told of some new delightful fruit, and our mouth waters as if we were about to taste it. This tendency to feel oneself *into* a situation is called EMPATHY; – on the analogy of sympathy, which is feeling *together with* another; and empathic ideas are psychologically interesting because they are the converse of perceptions; their core is imaginal, and their context is made up of sensations, the kinaesthetic and organic sensations that carry the empathic meaning. Like the feeling of strangeness, they are characteristic of imagination. In memory, their place is taken by the *imitative* experiences, which repeat over again certain phases of the original situation. (1915, p. 198)

Thus empathy was important in imagination, which Titchener frequently contrasted with memory.

In addition, empathy helped to explain other things, for example, some optical illusions, emotions, and moral sentiments. With regard to moral sentiments, empathy enables one to "realize the attitudes and responses of those who . . . have reached the same level," so that there can be a "freemasonry among all men and women who have at any time really judged" (1915, p. 293). In other words, those of intellectual and moral similarity can reach one another by empathy. At this point in Titchener's thinking, then, empathy had become an important instinctive tendency (p. 205).

In Titchener's later writings (1924), the concept of empathy became less important. He now defined empathy rather succinctly as a "process of humanizing objects, of reading or feeling ourselves into them" (1924, p. 417), and used it to explain optical illusions, where "we read ourselves, or feel ourselves, into the lines of the figure" (1924, p. 333). "Motor empathy" (1924, p. 514) is mentioned again in connection with imagining mental comparisons.

Although Titchener moved from an act to a content psychology, he was not able to maintain that difficult distinction consistently. Moreover, the concept of empathy itself changed, so it is hard to summarize exactly what Titchener meant by the term. In the beginning (1909), it represented an amalgamation of visual and muscular/kinesthetic imagery (after Lipps) by which certain kinds of experiences were possible. Later (1915) it became a feeling, or projecting, of one's self into an object, and its implications were more social. It was a way to "humanize our surroundings." But Titchener also used empathy to explain certain kinds of optical illusions, and this came closer to motor mimicry (Woodworth, 1938, p. 645). Titchener thus harbingered the dual role of empathy, in perception and in society. In assessing his contribution to empathy theory, one is constrained to observe that experimenters who have cultivated a field long and intensively deserve a hearing even when their conclusions go idiosyncratically beyond their data.

Where did empathy theory go from there? It seemed to lose ground in experimental psychology. In an imposing presentation of pre-Hullian experimental psychology, Woodworth (1938) referred to "The empathy theory of Theodor Lipps" as one of the principal explanations for optical illusions. Interpreting Lipps, he wrote, "A vertical line, resisting gravity, suggests effort and thus appears longer than an equal horizontal. One part of the Müller–Lyer figure suggests expansion and the other limitation and thus the first line appears the longer" (p. 645). This is because the observer's "emotional and reactive nature is stimulated" (p. 645). Similarly, he noted that when identifying emotions from facial photographs, the observer can "imitate the pose and notice 'how it feels' – the method of empathy; or imagine a situation in which the pose would be appropriate" (p. 249). Although Woodworth recommended neither approach, both are derivatives of Lipps's and Titchener's empathy theory. But experimental psychology was by then becoming more behavioral, and a late-nineteenth-century concept like empathy, straight out of aesthetics, had no place in it.

Empathy in personality theory

At this point we must make a policy decision. By about the first part of the twentieth century the idea of *Einfühlung*/empathy was – intellectually speaking – everywhere. Although it was called by different names and utilized in different contexts and in different fields of the social sciences, the question of empathy – how one knows the consciousness of another – was current. Space does not allow us to explore all of these variations. Nor would that be a good idea, because there were subtle differences of emphasis among them. A few examples may suffice to make the point, however. The term *ejective consciousness* was used by Baldwin (1897) to mean that "other people's bodies, says the child to himself, have experiences *in them* such as mine has" (p. 8). For Washburn (1932), ejective consciousness was "One's idea of what is going on in other minds" (p. 395). Clearly ejective consciousness is similar to the idea of empathy. Piaget and Inhelder (1963) wrote about the development of *perspective taking* among children, and some psychologists (e.g., Underwood & Moore, 1982) have utilized this term, including affect in empathy. Sociologists (Cooley, 1902; Mead, 1934) were concerned with role taking and wrote about the development of the self, the internalization of social norms, and the assumption that in human interaction the person not only develops those responses appropriate to his part in the relationship but also incorporates in his reaction system the responses of the significant others in the situation. This explanation was put in a communication or interaction framework, but the idea of *Einfühlung*/empathy was clear. Mead (1934) wrote that "the exercise of what is often called 'social intelligence' depends upon the given individual's ability to take the roles of, or 'put himself in the place of,' the other individuals implicated with him in a given social situation" (p. 218). Given the general connotation of terms like *perspective taking* and *role taking,* it is hard to be specific, but it is clear that they are in a sense similar to empathy. However, because they are probably not quite the same, we limit ourselves in the rest of this chapter to those psychologists, and others, who have referred specifically to empathy.

The term *empathy* found its new life in the emerging field of personality. This is as it should have been, because empathy was always about personality. It had to wait for the psychology of personality to be born! And within the area of personality, it was used by personality theorists and psychotherapists of widely different persuasions. It is not a historical accident that the concept of empathy was more important for psychotherapists, especially for those who were not behaviorally inclined, like Rogers and Kohut. In personality theory there were rival constructs, especially imitation and sympathy, but the concept of empathy was important.

We consider briefly four quite different personality theorists (Allport, 1937; Dollard & Miller, 1950; Downey, 1929; Murphy, 1947) and show how the concept of empathy was used in each of their systems. Among psychotherapists, the selection is made for us, because the concept of empathy is closely associated with Rogers (1942, 1951, 1957, 1975) in the field of academic psychology and with Kohut (1959, 1971, 1977, 1980, 1984) in the field of psychoanalysis (see also Kahn, 1985). It is not generally recognized, however, that Freud, too, was aware of *Einfühlung* and used it in his discussions of humor (1905–1906) and social psychology (1921/1949). Let us briefly discuss Freud's use first, since it came first chronologically.

In his discussion of humor, Freud (1905/1960, p. 186) used *Einfühlung* to mean that "we take the producing person's psychical state into consideration, put ourselves into it and try to understand it by comparing it with our own." Since Freud had Lipps's books in his library, his idea of *Einfühlung* may have been influenced by Lipps. In his *Group Psychology* (1921/1949), however, Freud introduced a new idea, "that we are faced by the process which psychology calls 'empathy' (*Einfühlung*) and which plays the largest part in our understanding of what is inherently foreign to our ego in other people" (p. 66). Although Freud was more interested in the concept of identification, and the way in which it led to empathy by way of imitation, he wrote that empathy enabled us "to take up any attitude at all toward another's mental life" (1921/1949, p. 70). His idea that empathy provided a way of understanding "what is inherently foreign to our ego" seems not to have been developed further.

We turn now to Downey's (1929) work, which is interesting because it exemplifies the transition of the concept of empathy from aesthetics to personality. She had an interest in both fields and wrote knowledgeably about them:

> Famous analysts among psychologists and art-critics have given us many subtle modulations of the doctrine of inner imitation and of psychic participation. Their technical term for this process of psychic participation is *empathy*, or a process of "feeling-in" in which motor and emotional attitudes, however originating, are projected outside of the shelf. . . . From one point of view we subjectify an object; from another point of view, we objectify the self. . . . Our understanding of persons is moulded by something akin to empathic processes. Through subtle imitation we assume an alien personality, we become aware of how it feels to behave thus and so, then we read back into the other person our consciousness of what his patterns of behavior feels like. (pp. 176–177)

Downey noted that empathy had become a "much-inclusive term covering not only mimetic reactions . . . but also . . . the problem of the projection of all self-experiences into the object'' (p. 177). It is interesting that she not only put empathy back into aesthetic appreciation, from which it came, but also anticipated its use in understanding personality – a point made later by clinicians.

G. W. Allport's (1937) important personality book presented one of the better English versions of Lipps's empathy theory, although Allport criticized Lipps's theorizing – as did most of the phenomenologists by whom Allport was most influenced (especially Scheler, 1912/1954; Stein, 1964). On the other hand, Allport noted that ''the imitative assumption of the postures and facial expressions of other people plays a greater part in ordinary life than is commonly realized'' (p. 530). Thus, he used motor imitation in part, along with inference and intuition, to explain personality. In a later revision of his book, he defined empathy as the ''imaginative transposing of oneself into the thinking, feeling, and acting of another'' (1961, p. 536). He believed that empathy ''stands midway between'' inference, on the one hand, and intuition, on the other. But many personality theorists would disagree. Kohut (1971), for example, thought that empathy and intuition were quite different processes, and Titchener, at least in his early work, did not accept the inference theory. Much later, Allport concluded that the ''process of *empathy* remains a riddle in social psychology. . . . The nature of the mechanism is not yet understood'' (1968, p. 30).

Allport was certainly correct in pointing out that empathy remained ''a riddle.'' At that time empathy was considered a blend of associationism and intuition. Some would argue that it was associationist and that intuition was nonscientific. At any rate, in the conclusion to his personality book, Allport argued for a blend of intuition and inference in terms that allowed a place for what today would be called empathy: ''Our understanding of personality comes, then, partly, from without, but partly also from within. The first cues come from the structuration of the outer field; where these prove insufficient (as they usually do) then memory, imagination, and abstract conceptualization come to aid the process'' (1937, p. 548). Titchener (1924) made clear that empathy was a crucial aspect of imagination and abstract comparisons, so it is arguable that the process of empathy was not far removed from Allport's personality theory, even if the word ''empathy'' was less used. At any rate, Allport's book helped legitimate and organize the personality area and helped to establish the concept of empathy in current personality theory.

A decade later, G. Murphy (1947) wrote his highly regarded personality book. In it he defined the aesthetic and the personality aspects of empathy as, respectively,

> [(1) an] attribution to a natural object or a work of art of the feelings or attitudes aroused in one by the surroundings (actual or depicted) of that object, as when a column seems to plant itself doggedly under a too heavy pressure as a man

might do. (2) Direct apprehension of the state of mind of another person without
. . . feeling as that other person does.'' (p. 985)

He expanded on these definitions of empathy, writing that empathy applied

> to *putting oneself in the place of* either a living or a non-living thing. Exactly
> as an individual puts himself in another's place, assumes his spatial position
> and its appurtenances, glows with pride, suffers in his embarrassment, so he
> puts himself in the place of a pillar that is too slender to support the shaft, and
> he judges it inappropriate. (p. 414)

Murphy made more explicit the overt physical participation of empathy. Murphy
(1947) wrote that ''his muscles tighten as he watches the tug of war; his larynx
tires and his heels rise as the soprano strains upward.'' (p. 414). The ''inner
activities'' of Lipps, Prandtl, and Titchener had become, as it were, overt
expressions.

Although one might not expect to find the concept of empathy in a liberalized
Hullian version of personality theory, Dollard and Miller (1950) provided a standard definition of empathy as ''copying the other person's feelings or responding
with appropriate signs of emotion'' (p. 93). They also provided a more behavioral analysis of empathy in therapy. They wrote: ''As the patient's verbal responses unroll, the therapist rehearses them. In other words he listens to the
patient. If the therapist has emotional responses attached to the sentences he
rehearses, these emotions occur – constituting the basis of sympathy or empathy'' (p. 282). Despite the different orientation, this is obviously a description
of empathy.

The theoretical diversity of the last three personality theories – all of which
concern empathy – shows how the concept of empathy had spread by 1945.
Nonetheless, there was general agreement about the concept of empathy, although up to that time it had only been applied, rather than analyzed. Thus, it
still remained very much ''a riddle.''

Empathy in therapy

Perhaps the most important recent work on empathy has been that of
Carl Rogers (1942, 1951, 1957, 1975). He has had enormous influence in the
area of individual counseling, but most people have forgotten, or never knew
about, the times during which he was most influential, beginning with the 1950s,
when hopes for psychology ran high. At that time the debates about psychotherapeutic methods were heated, and excitement was great. Rogers (1975), himself, wrote, ''I cannot exaggerate the excitement of our learnings as we clustered
about the machine which enabled us to listen to ourselves, playing over and over
some puzzling point at which the interview clearly went wrong, or those mo-

ments in which the client moved significantly forward'' (p. 3). This was just after World War II. Many psychologists had participated in the war, and they were now ready to improve the world. It was in this climate that the Rogerian idea of empathy was reborn.

The concept of empathy was important to Rogers's theory of personality and crucial to the kind of psychotherapy in which he became involved (1957, 1975). One of the main points Rogers makes is that people have self-actualizing tendencies that will promote their growth and well-being unless these potentials are frustrated or perverted. To put it more directly, Rogers argued that human nature was Good rather than Evil. The positive forces in personality development could be thwarted, however, especially during childhood, by the disparagements of those significant others. Exposure to this kind of interpersonal environment then precluded the development of information and behaviors that could serve as a guide to fulfillment and productivity in adulthood. Rogerian therapy tried to provide an atmosphere of acceptance and openness to new ideas and behaviors, which, according to Rogers, could only be created by conditions of congruence, positive regard, and empathy. These were the essential attitudes for the psychotherapist. Under these conditions, Rogers maintained, the person would find his/her own best life. Therefore Rogerian therapy was not nondirective; it was inner directed. Moreover, in the therapeutic situation, empathy was ''one of the most potent factors'' (1975, p. 3).

Rogers offered two definitions of empathy. Earlier, he had written that empathy meant ''to perceive the internal frame of reference of another with accuracy and with the emotional components and meanings which pertain thereto as if one were the person, but without ever losing the 'as if' condition'' (1959, p. 210–211). Later (1975), he wrote that empathy was a ''process,'' and that it involved

> entering the private perceptual world of the other and becoming thoroughly at home in it. It involves being sensitive . . . to the changing felt meanings which flow in this other person. . . . It means temporarily living in his/her life, moving about in it delicately without making judgments, sensing meanings of which he/she is scarcely aware. . . . It includes communicating your sensings of his/her world as you look with fresh and unfrightened eyes at elements of which the individual is fearful. It means frequently checking with him/her as to the accuracy of your sensings, and being guided by the responses you receive. . . . To be with another in this way means that for the time being you lay aside the views and values you hold for yourself in order to enter another world without prejudice. (p. 4)

This is perhaps the most complete and insightful description of empathy to date. Although the description is long, perhaps empathy is too complex a phenomenon for a short definition. To adopt this kind of attitude – whether in a therapeutic or experimental situation – is, as Rogers said, complex and demanding (1975, p. 4).

It is not our purpose to discuss the clinical impact of empathy in client-centered therapy, or any other kind of therapy. Note, however, that the most persistent investigations of the process of empathy, especially in psychotherapy, were carried out by Rogers and his students. Although most – but not all – of their findings are related to therapy, their conclusions about empathy have much more general significance. Without doubt, the present popularity of empathy as a construct comes from Rogers's emphasis on it, and his definition put it squarely into an objective, researchable, personality framework. Some of these studies are referred to in the remainder of this chapter. However, the clinicians were less concerned with a theory of empathy than with finding a term to convey that particular attitude of nonjudgmentally entering "another's perceptual world" they regarded as important in psychotherapy. Their choice of terms was well made, because Rogers's descriptions of empathy are quite compatible with those of Titchener.

Almost from the beginning, Rogers's insistence upon an empirical approach led to research, not only on the process of clinical empathy, but also on a series of empathy scales. Interestingly, the first empathy scale (Dymond, 1949) was devised under the direction of a sociologist (Cottrell, 1950) rather than a Rogerian psychotherapist. The early scales represented attempts to measure empathic ability, and they involved a kind of imaginative role taking. This focus on empathic accuracy led researchers to explore some of the problems in judging accurately another person's characteristics (Bender & Hastorf, 1953; Gage & Cronbach, 1955; Hastorf & Bender, 1952; Hobart & Fahlberg, 1965; Marwell, 1964). Subsequently, empathy scales shifted toward emotional empathy, in which self-report items were concerned with respondents' reactions to the emotions of others. Eventually, some researchers (Davis, 1983; Hogan, 1975) became concerned with how empathy affected social roles. Up to this juncture, then, empathy research had been primarily concerned with one of two topics: how empathy – frequently defined as empathy by Q-sorts – functions in the therapy situation, and what scales can be used to measure empathic capacity.

There has, however, been another approach to the concept of empathy in psychoanalytic psychotherapy (Kohut, 1959, 1971, 1977, 1980, 1984). Although Kohut's work has not greatly influenced academic psychology, his impact on modern psychoanalysis and psychoanalytic theory has been considerable. For our purposes, what seems to be important about his work is not his definition of empathy, but his probing analysis of the role of empathy in the acquisition of psychological information. Although his writings do not provide a clear definition of empathy, it is possible to construct one. To Kohut (1959), empathy seems to be the process whereby "we think ourselves into his place" and take by "vicarious introspection," or empathy, the experience of another "as if it were our own and thus revive inner experiences" in order to arrive at "an appreciation of the meaning'' (p. 461). There is little to quarrel with in this description of empathy. However, Kohut (1959) also proposed that introspection and empathy were the most important aspects – the "essential aspects" – of psychoanalytic observation. Eventually, Kohut's insistence that the "limits of psychoanalysis are defined by the potential limits of introspection and empathy" (1959, p. 482) was taken to indicate his departure from classical analysis. In his subsequent studies, Kohut explored further the limits of empathy and the nature of the psychological states to which it could gain privileged access. In this connection, he wrote that empathy is the "mode of cognition which is specifically attuned to the perception of complex psychological configurations" (1971, p. 300). He reaffirmed this position later (1980), noting that empathy is for the "acquisition of objective knowledge about the inner life of another person" (p. 485). Kohut had received his medical degree from the University of Vienna and therefore was probably familiar with the works of phenomenologists who were making a similar point. Stein (1964), for example, wrote, "Empathy . . . is the experience of foreign consciousness in general, . . . This is how man grasps the psychic life of his fellow man" (p. 11). Both Kohut and Stein maintained that empathy was a basic human endowment. Stein (1964) wrote, "Just as our own individual is announced in our own perceived experiences, so the foreign individual is announced in empathized ones" (p. 33). And Kohut (1977) made clear that "the empathic understanding of the experience of other human beings is as basic an endowment of man as his vision, hearing, touch, taste, and smell" (p. 144). In other words, Kohut and Stein both argued that empathy provides people with capacity to know about the psychological states of other human beings, and that this capacity is innate.

However, there are certain things that empathy is not. Empathy is not infallible. Empathy "as a process or operation can lead us to either correct or incorrect, accurate or inaccurate results (Kohut, 1980, p. 485). Empathy is not sympathy or compassion.

> Empathy is surely a necessary precondition for our ability to experience compassion; and compassionate acts, in order to be effective, must be guided by the accurate empathic assessment of the recipient's needs. But the same can also be said with regard to many of our hostile – destructive feelings; in order to be effective, certain destructive actions . . . must be guided by the accurate empathic assessment of the victim's sensitivities. (1980, p. 483)

Empathy also is not intuition.

> What we call intuition is, therefore, in principle, resolvable into speedily performed mental activities which, in and of themselves, are not different from those mental activities which do not strike us as unusual in this particular sense. . . . Talent, training, and experience will at times combine to produce results . . . which strike us as intuitive. . . . On the other hand, slow and painstaking

nonintuitive mental processes are not restricted to the nonempathic scrutiny of
the physical world, but may also be used in empathic observation. (1971, pp.
302–303)

Thus, we must distinguish "empathy from the result to which empathic operation leads" (1980, p. 485). Empathy is not infallible, it is not necessarily compassionate, it does not cure as if by love, it is not by itself therapeutic (1984,
p. 85), and it is not an intuitive process.

On the other hand, Kohut wrote that empathy is "a value-neutral mode of
observation" and it should itself be evaluated within an empirical context (1984,
p. 84). For example, empathy as an "information-gathering activity" (1984,
p. 84) declines "the more dissimilar the observed is to the observer" (1971, p.
37). Insofar as other people's behaviors, desires, and values "are similar to our
own, we are enabled to empathize with them on the basis of clues that may seem
insignificant to people from different backgrounds" (1959, p. 463). As the cus-
toms of others become more remote, accurate empathy becomes more difficult.
But the goal of empathy is to remain objectively neutral. Empathy is a tool for
gathering data; it is not used in the service of theory construction (1980, pp. 483–
484), although the information gathered by empathic means can then be integrated with theory in order to give the patient "a dynamic or genetic interpretation" (1980, pp. 483–484). Kohut frequently made the interesting point that
"psychoanalysis gathers its data in order to explain them" (1977, p. 306), and
this observation seems equally appropriate to Rogerian psychotherapy.

Built into Kohut's phenomenological position is the delineation of the kinds
of scientific activities in which empathy would be appropriate. Some sciences,
he wrote, "base themselves on "introspection and vicarious extrospection,"
whereas others base themselves on "introspection and vicarious introspection
(empathy). To the first category belong the physical and biological sciences, to
the second the psychological sciences, par excellence psychoanalysis, the science of complex mental states" (1980, p. 457). There must always remain a
certain arbitrariness about these kinds of distinctions. Kohut (1959, p. 460) defines psychological phenomena in terms of introspective and empathic observation, so there is some circularity here. But this enables him to make the important
point (from his point of view) that without empathic observation we record

> only the physical fact of movement. We can measure the upward deviation of
> the skin above the eye to the minutest fraction of an inch, yet it is only through
> introspection and empathy that we understand the shades of meaning of aston-
> ishment and disapproval that are contained in the raising of the eyebrow. . . .
> The mere fact that we see a pattern of movements leading to a specific end does
> not, by itself, define a psychological act. . . . If there is conscious or uncon-
> scious intent with which we can empathize, we speak of a psychological act
> . . . ; if no such intent is present, we think of a cause-and-effect chain of phys-
> ical events. . . . A phenomenon is "somatic," "behavioristic," or "social" if

our methods of observation do not predominantly include introspection and empathy. (1959, pp. 461–462)

This is, of course, an old problem in psychology, which goes back to Franz Brentano (1874/1924), but it is an important issue for the concept of empathy. If one can go beyond the terms of the argument, itself, which now has an anachronistic ring, Kohut is maintaining a kind of cognitive psychology, a psychology wherein we consider attitudes and values as well as behaviors. His point, actually, is that empathy brings us closer to an understanding of these attitudes and values, which is close to Titchener's (1909) original intent.

Empathy, therefore, is not only "a mode of cognition . . . attuned to the perception of complex psychological facts" (Kohut, 1971, p. 300); for Kohut it is also a method of gathering data for scientific purposes. However, empathy is also "a powerful emotional bond between people" (1984, p. 84) – just as Titchener had said (1915, 1924). And, finally, although Kohut had earlier argued that empathy, by itself, was not curative, in his last published work he noted that "empathy per se, the mere presence of empathy, has also a beneficial, in a broad sense, a therapeutic effect – both in the clinical setting and in human life in general" (1984, p. 85).

Empathy in social and developmental psychology

The concept of empathy is becoming increasingly important in social and developmental psychology, but such has not always been the case. Moreover, empathy has been a latecomer to experimental social psychology. This may come as a surprise to some, so let us look briefly at the historical evidence. Most psychologists would say that modern social psychology began with McDougall's (1908/1912) *An Introduction to Social Psychology;* although less often recognized, H. F. Allport's (1924) *Social Psychology* was also important. McDougall's instinct theory integrated the topics by which the field of social psychology was to be defined for many years. McDougall's book was reprinted more than any other book in social psychology and its influence was great. Allport (1924) translated many of McDougall's topics into conditioning terms and made social psychology more acceptable to American psychology at that time. His book is a classic of its kind, but, like McDougall's, it does not mention empathy. After World War II, interest in social psychology burgeoned again. Under the influence of men like G. W. Allport, Kurt Lewin, and Edward Tolman, social psychologists became interested in cognition. Then three important and very different texts appeared (Asch, 1952; Heider, 1958; Krech & Crutchfield, 1948) that became required reading for everyone, especially graduate students in social psychology. Empathy was not mentioned by Asch or Heider, although both were fluent in German, and Krech and Crutchfield used it only once – in connection with the perceived similarity between the perceiver and the object (1948, p. 9). So much for the concept of empathy in social psychology up to the 1960s.

The 1960s saw a tremendous increase in studies of positive forms of social behavior (Wispé, 1981). Although the early studies (Berkowitz & Daniels, 1963; Darly & Latané, 1968) did not invoke the concept of empathy, they reintroduced different kinds of dependent variables: helping, giving, intervening, and so on. To explain these dependent variables, the authors used a whole host of motivational constructs, among them altruism (Wilson, 1975), dependence (Schopler & Batson, 1965), moods (Cialdini, Kenrick, & Bauman, 1982; Wispé, 1980), and empathy (Batson & Coke, 1981; Hoffman, 1981; Krebs, 1975). For example, in a careful and complicated study, Krebs (1975) combined a vicarious instigation technique and a manipulation of similarity with a dependent measure of altruism that appeared to have more face validity than most so-called measures. Krebs also obtained a number of psychophysiological measures that he considered to be related to empathy. Krebs found that similarity was related to certain physiological responses and, in fact, to his measure of altruism.

In one of the most sustained investigations of empathy, Batson and his colleagues (Batson, Duncan, Ackerman, Buckley, & Birch, 1981; Coke, Batson, & McDavis, 1978; Toi & Batson, 1982) used an ingenious manipulation of false feedback and placebo effects to arouse what they called "personal arousal" and "empathy," both of which were measured by carefully constructed scales. These investigators did indeed find that their empathy scale (with items like "sympathetic," "tender," "warm," etc.) discriminated a helping response to a woman's taped message of distress.

Despite the honest differences of opinion on the definition of empathy in current social psychology (Wispé, 1986), the concept has been used to explain a wide variety of altruistic behaviors (Hoffman, 1981). What is more important than the terminological controversies, however, is that a number of research programs are now investigating parameters of empathy.

Empathy had a somewhat different history in developmental psychology. As has already been noted, Baldwin (1897) used the term *ejective consciousness* to refer to something like empathy in children's moral development. Much later, Susan Isaacs and Lois Murphy observed children's social behavior with an eye to identifying something like empathy, although neither used that term. Isaacs (1946) studied children in a school setting, using a psychoanalytic orientation. Lois Murphy (1937) analyzed the social behavior of two- to four-year-old children in a nursery and found that children's social behavior could be recorded quite reliably. Somewhat later, Feshbach and Roe (1968) and their colleagues developed a test for empathy in children that is still widely used. Sex differences in empathy became a natural concern in developmental psychology and led to a great deal of interesting research that pointed out the difficulties in analyzing the concept of empathy empirically (e.g., Eisenberg & Lennon, 1983; Hoffman & Levine, 1976; Mussen & Eisenberg, 1977). Thus, in developmental psychology, as in social psychology, the concept of empathy was widely used to explain such things as affective empathy and sex and age differences in empathic capacity.

Conclusion

It has been exciting to trace the history of the concept of empathy. What are our conclusions? Perhaps we can offer the following:

1. The idea of *Einfühlung* goes back more than a century, although the term *empathy* is of comparatively recent origin, having been coined by Titchener (1909).
2. The idea of *Einfühlung*/empathy has seen service in psychology in aesthetics, personality theory, and psychotherapy of quite different persuasions.
3. The hard-core meaning of *Einfühlung*/empathy has always been the process whereby one person "feels her/himself into" the consciousness of another person. The term has always conveyed the idea of knowing about the awareness of another. Sometimes this is referred to as a projection of one's self into, or onto, another person or thing. This occurs with either social or nonsocial objects of perception.
4. This capacity is usually regarded as innate.
5. This innate capacity enables one person to perceive the existence of another person. This is the capacity by which one person obtains knowledge of the subjective side of another person. Just as my sense tells me who *I* am, this capacity allows me to learn about the difference in the "foreign" other. I know that I am not he, because my experience of *him* is different from my experience of *me*.
6. Empathy is not the only concept to refer to this peculiar capacity of human beings to "take the role of the other."
7. One cannot explain empathy, any more than one can explain memory or imagination, although one can investigate its parameters.
8. Currently much of this work is being done in social, developmental, and clinical psychology – wherein the future of the concept of empathy may lie.

References

Allport, F. H. (1924). *Social psychology.* Boston: Houghton Mifflin.

Allport, G. W. (1937). *Personality; a psychological interpretation.* New York: Henry Holt.

Allport, G. (1961). *Pattern and growth in personality.* New York: Holt, Rinehart & Winston.

Allport, G. (1968). The historical background of modern social psychology. In G. Lindzey & E. Aronson (Eds.), *Handbook of social psychology* (2d ed.). Reading, MA: Addison-Wesley.

Asch, S. (1952). *Social psychology.* New York: Prentice-Hall.

Baldwin, J. (1897). *Social and ethical interpretations in mental development.* London: Macmillan.

Batson, C. D., & Coke, J. (1981). Empathy: A source of altruistic motivation for helping. In J. Rushton & R. Sorrentino (Eds.), *Altruism and helping behavior.* Hillsdale, NJ: Erlbaum.

Batson, C. D., Duncan, C., Ackerman, P., Buckley, T., & Birch, K. (1981). Is empathic emotion a source of altruistic motivation? *Journal of Personality and Social Psychology, 40,* 290–302.

Bender, I., & Hastorf, A. (1953). On measuring generalized empathic ability (social sensitivity). *Journal of Abnormal and Social Psychology, 48,* 503–506.

Berkowitz, L., & Daniels, L. (1963). Responsibility and dependency. *Journal of Abnormal and Social Psychology, 66,* 429–436.

Boring, E. (1950). *A history of experimental psychology.* New York: Appleton-Century-Croft.

Brentano, F. (1924). *Psychologie vom empirischesan Standpunkte.* Leipzig: Meiner (original work published 1874).

Cialdini, R., Kendrick, D., & Bauman, D. (1982). Effects of mood on prosocial behavior in children and adults. In N. Eisenberg (Ed.), *The development of prosocial behavior.* (New York: Academic Press.

Coke, J., Batson, C. D., & McDavis, K. (1978). Empathic mediation of helping: A two-stage model. *Journal of Personality and Social Psychology, 36,* 752–766.

Cooley, C. (1902). *Human nature and the social order.* New York: Chas. Scribner's Sons.

Cottrell, L. (1950). Some neglected problems in social psychology. *American Sociological Review, 15,* 705–712.

Darley, J., & Latané, B. (1968). Bystander intervention in emergencies: Diffusion of responsibility. *Journal of Personality and Social Psychology, 8,* 377–383.

Davis, M. (1983). Measuring individual differences in empathy; Evidence for a multidimensional approach. *Journal of Personality and Social Psychology, 44,* 113–126.

Dollard, J., & Miller, N. (1950). *Personality and psychotherapy.* New York: McGraw-Hill.

Downey, J. (1929). *Creative imagination.* New York: Harcourt, Brace.

Dymond, R. (1949). A scale for the measurement of empathy ability. *Journal of Consulting Psychology, 13,* 127–133.

Eisenberg, N., & Lennon, R. (1983). Sex differences in empathy and related capacities. *Psychological Bulletin, 94,* 100–131.

Feshbach, N., & Roe, K. (1968). Empathy in six and seven year olds. *Child Development, 39,* 133–145.

Freud, S. (1949). *Group psychology and the analysis of the ego.* New York: Liveright (original work published 1921).

Freud, S. (1960). *Jokes and their relations to the unconscious.* London: Routledge & Kegan Paul (original work published 1905).

Gage, N., & Cronbach, L. (1955). Conceptual and methodological problems in interpersonal perception. *Psychological Review, 62,* 411–422.

Groos, K. (1892). *Einleitung in die Asthetik.* Giessen: J. Ricker.

Hastorf, A., & Bender, I. (1952). A caution respecting the measurement of empathic ability. *Journal of Abnormal and Social Psychology, 47,* 574–576.

Heider, F. (1958). *Psychology of interpersonal relations.* New York: Wiley.

Hobart, C., & Fahlberg, N. (1965). The measurement of empathy. *The American Journal of Sociology, 70,* 595–603.

Hoffman, M. (1981). Is altruism a part of human nature? *Journal of Personality and Social Psychology, 40,* 121–137.

Hoffman, M., & Levine, L. (1976). Early sex differences in empathy. *Developmental Psychology, 6,* 557–558.

Hogan, R. (1975). Empathy: A conceptual and psychometric analysis. *Counseling Psychologist, 5,* 14–18.

Isaacs, S. (1946) *Social development in young children.* London: Routledge & Sons.

Kahn, E. (1985). Heinz Kohut and Carl Rogers. *American Psychologist, 40,* 893–904.

Kohut, H. (1959). Introspection, empathy, and psychoanalysis. *Journal of the American Psychoanalytic Association, 7,* 459–483.

Kohut, H. (1971). *The analysis of the self.* New York: International Universities Press.

Kohut, H. (1977). *The restoration of the self.* New York: International Universities Press.

Kohut, H. (1980). Reflections. In A. Goldberg (Ed.), *Advances in self psychology.* (pp. 473–554). New York: International Universities Press.

Kohut, H. (1984). Introspection, empathy, and the semicircle of mental health. In J. Lichtenberg, M. Bornstein, D. Silver (Eds.), *Empathy* (Vol. 1, pp. 81–100). Hillsdale, NJ: Erlbaum.

Kovach, F. (1974). *Philosophy of beauty.* Norman: University of Oklahoma Press.

Krebs, D. (1975). Empathy and altruism. *Journal of Personality and Social Psychology, 32,* 1134–1146.

Krech, D., & Crutchfield, R. (1948). *Theory and problems of social psychology.* New York: McGraw-Hill.

Lipps, T. (1903). Einfühlung, inner Nachahmung, und Organ-empfindungen. *Archiv für die gesamte Psychologie, 2,* 185–204.

Lipps, T. (1905). Das Wissen von fremden Ichen. *Psychologische Untersuchungen, 4,* 694–722.

McDougall, W. (1912). *An introduction to social psychology.* Boston: Methuen (original work published 1908).

Marwell, G. (1964). Problems of operational definitions of "empathy," "identification" and related concepts. *Journal of Social Psychology, 63,* 87–102.

Mead, G. (1934). *Mind, self and society from the standpoint of a social behaviorist.* Chicago: University of Chicago Press.

Murphy, G. (1947). *Personality: A biosocial approach to origins and structure.* New York: Harper.

Murphy, L. (1937). *Social behavior and child personality.* New York: Columbia University Press.

Mussen, P., & Eisenberg, N. (1977). *Roots of caring, sharing, and helping.* San Francisco: Freeman & Co.

Piaget, J., & Inhelder, B. (1963). *The child's conception of space.* London: Routledge & Kegan Paul.

Prandtl, A. (1910). *Die Einfühlung.* Leipzig: Johann Barth.

Rogers, C. (1942). *Counseling and psychotherapy.* Boston: Houghton Mifflin.

Rogers, C. (1951). *Client-centered therapy.* Boston: Houghton Mifflin.

Rogers, C. (1957). Necessary and sufficient conditions of therapeutic personality change. *Journal of Consulting Psychology, 21,* 95–103.

Rogers, C. (1959). A theory of therapy, personality, and interpersonal relationships as developed in the client-centered framework. In J. S. Koch (Ed.), *Psychology: a study of a science: Vol 3. Formulations of the person in the social context* (pp. 184–256.) New York: McGraw-Hill.

Rogers, C. (1975). Empathic: An unappreciated way of being. *The Counseling Psychologist, 2,* 2–10.

Scheler, P. (1954). *The nature of sympathy* (P. Heath, trans.). London: Routledge & Kegan Paul. (original work published 1912).

Schopler, J., & Batson, N. (1965). The power of dependency. *Journal of Personality and Social Psychology, 2,* 247–254.

Stein, E. (1964). *On the problem of empathy.* The Hague: Martinus Nijhoff.

Sullivan, H. (1953). *The interpersonal theory of psychiatry.* New York: W. W. Norton.

Titchener, E. (1909). *Experimental psychology of the thought processes.* New York: Macmillan.

Titchener, E. (1915). *A beginner's psychology.* New York: Macmillan.

Titchener, E. (1924). *A textbook of psychology.* New York: Macmillan.

Toi, M., & Batson, C. D. (1982). More evidence that empathy is a source of altruistic motivation. *Journal of Personality and Social Psychology, 18,* 281–292.

Underwood, B., & Moore, B. (1982). Perspective-taking and altruism. *Psychological Bulletin, 91,* 143–173.

Washburn, M. (1932). Ejective consciousness as a fundamental factor in social psychology. *Psychological Bulletin, 39,* 395–402.

Wellek, R. (1970). *Discriminations: Further concepts of criticism.* New Haven: Yale University Press.

Wilson, E. (1975). *Sociobiology: The new synthesis.* Cambridge: Harvard University Press.

Wind, E. (1963). *Art and anarchy.* London: Faber and Faber.

Wispé, L. (1980). The role of moods in helping behavior. *Representative Research in Social Psychology, 11,* 2–15.

Wispé, L. (1981). Research on positive and negative social behavior. *Social Behavior and Personality, 9,* 203–209.

Wispé, L. (1986). The distinction between sympathy and empathy: To call forth a concept a word is needed. *Journal of Personality and Social Psychology, 50,* 314–321.

Woodworth, R. (1938). *Experimental psychology.* New York: Holt.

3   Evolutionary bases of empathy

Robert Plutchik

Empathy has been defined as "the capacity for participating in, or a vicarious experiencing of another's feelings, volitions, or ideas and sometimes another's movements to the point of executing bodily movements resembling his" (*Webster's Third New International Dictionary,* 1971). This definition has several implications. First, it suggests that empathy is an internal state or experience similar to an emotion. Second, it implies that this emotional state can sometimes be recognized through imitative bodily movements. A further implication is that empathy is a complex state, the existence of which is judged on the basis of indirect evidence. Such evidence would include verbal reports of feelings or volitions, overt behavior indicative of imitation, and other clues. Empathy is thus an inference. Note that "empathy" comes from the Greek word *empatheia,* meaning "affection or passion." English words that are most similar in meaning to empathy are *agreement, understanding, harmony,* and *sympathy.*

Given this brief phenomenological description of empathy, in what sense can the concept be related to biological and evolutionary issues? What does it mean to seek an evolutionary basis for fear, aggression, courtship, or love. From an evolutionary perspective, two basic questions of interest are (1) Do animals exhibit behavior patterns that are homologous to empathy in humans? (2) What survival function does empathy serve?

Empathy in animals

That some behaviors homologous to empathy can be found in animals is evident from the descriptions of comparative psychologists and ethologists. In 1927, Wolfgang Kohler, in describing his work with chimpanzees, wrote: "Chimpanzees understand 'between themselves' not only the expression of subjective moods and emotional states, but also of definitive desires and urges" (p. 307).

A vivid description of a process suggestive of empathy is given by the

38

van Lawicks (1971) in portraying the initiation of mass hunting by African wild dogs.

> Old Genghis trotted over to where Havoc, Swift and Baskerville lay together. At his approach they jumped up and all four began nosing and licking each other's lips, their tails up and wagging, their squeaks gradually changing to frenzied twittering. In a moment all the adult dogs had joined them and soon the pack was swirling round and round in the greeting ceremony. . . . And then, as suddenly as it had begun, the wild flurry of activity subsided and the pack started to trot away from the den on its evening hunt. (p. 58)

Still another example of empathylike behavior in an animal is provided by the experiences of Harry Raven, a former curator of the American Museum of Nattural History in New York (see Preston, 1981). In 1930, during a trip to Africa, he bought a baby chimpanzee whose mother had been killed. Eventually he took the chimp, who he named Meshie Mungkut, to his home in America and raised her as a member of his family. When Meshie was six years old she became sexually mature and difficult to handle; as a result, she was placed in a zoo in Chicago. About a year later Raven visited the zoo and went to see Meshie. ''The zookeeper didn't want to let Raven into the cage but he insisted. When he went in, Meshie rushed into his arms and clung to him tightly. Tears were streaming down her face.'' The implication of this incident is that both Harry Raven and Meshie Mungkut shared a strong affectionate bond which their separation had not diminished.

What appears to be common to the three examples cited is the implied idea of *understanding, likemindedness, sympathy, concordance,* and *reciprocation,* all terms that *Roget's Thesaurus* gives as synonyms for empathy. These are complex emotional states whose existence can only be inferred on the basis of indirect signs and symptoms. The kind of evidence we use to infer the existence of empathy in an animal is the same general type of evidence we use to infer the existence of any emotion in an animal. These types of evidence are summarized briefly here (for more details, see Plutchik, 1980). In order to identify a particular emotion, we examine an organism's choices, its goal-directed behaviors, the consequence of such behaviors, the consistency over time of certain stimulus–response relations, and the nature of peer reactions to the behaviors. This is essentially what ethologists do in studying such phenomena as aggression, defense, and courtship.

Some hypotheses about empathy in animals

I suggest that empathy is a widespread phenomenon in the animal world and is implied by a wide variety of behavior patterns. These include schooling behavior of fish, flocking and mobbing behavior of birds, and herding behavior of mammals. All such behaviors involve mimicry (or allelomimetic behavior as defined by Scott, 1980) and affective communication.

Marler (1984) has described a series of studies dealing with animal affective communication. He has demonstrated that alarm calls in vervet monkeys are not diffuse expressions of anxiety, but provide fairly specific signals of particular types of predators that in turn influence the behaviors of an animal's conspecifics. Using recorded playback of vervet alarm calls, Marler found that at least three different alarms produce differential responses, even in the absence of a real predator. Leopard-alarm calls (loud, short, repeated tonal sounds) caused vervets to run up into trees. Eagle-alarm calls (low-pitched staccato grunts) caused vervets to run into dense cover and to look up into the sky. Snake-alarm calls (high-pitched chutters) caused the monkeys to look down onto the ground and to stand on their hind legs to get a better view in the tall grass (Seyfarth, Cheney, & Marler, 1980a,b) These findings strongly suggest the presence of empathy: Alarm experiences of one animal are transmitted to other animals through specialized signals. The transmission of such signals leads to similar behavior in the two animals; for example, both may climb a tree to avoid a leopard.

Two important questions arise about such affective signaling. As noted earlier, a basic question of evolutionary interest is whether or not the behavior pattern has survival value. In the case of the vervet monkeys, these animals are endangered by several different predators. A response that may increase the chances of survival with one predator may increase risk with another. In Kenya, for example, leopards hunt by ambush and capture monkeys that stray into dense underbrush. To avoid leopards, the vervet monkey needs to climb into the thin, high branches of a tree. Such behavior, however, increases the risk that the monkey will be seized by a hunting eagle. Therefore, to increase the chances of survival, vervet alarm calls must specify the type of threat that is present so that appropriate escape behavior may result.

The second question concerns the ontogenetic origins of such affective empathic signaling. In the same studies carried out with infant monkeys, some differential signaling did occur, but more mistakes were made. The young monkeys acted as if their brains already contained some schemata for classifying predatory animals. It is thus likely that alarm signals, as well as many other emotional responses, have a genetic component, as might be expected from an evolutionary perspective (Plutchik, 1980, 1985).

The essence of the empathic response is the communication of an emotional state from one organism to another. This state, as is true of all affects, is a complex event, a hypothetical construct, whose presence can only be established on the basis of various kinds of indirect evidence.

Survival value of group behavior

Ethologists have demonstrated that group behavior contributes to inclusive fitness (i.e., the likelihood of genetic representation in future generations). Social grouping provides increased defense against predators. Birds in flocks have higher chances of survival than solitary birds. For example, many birds – including starlings, blackbirds, jays, and finches – show mobbing behavior, such as group harassment of predators such as hawks or owls (Wilson, 1975). In addition, the chemical defenses that many organisms (such as beetles and butterflies) use against predators become more potent in group formation.

Another advantage is that the herd or school can use scent and visual aids to detect predators in all directions and more quickly than can a solitary animal. Furthermore, if a herd or school is attacked, predators can consume only a fixed average number of prey at each encounter; thus, the larger the group, the less the relative risk of death.

Still another advantage of group formation is its effect on the synchronization of the reproductive cycle. In most animals, breeding activity tends to peak at the same approximate time, so that the young are born into a relatively stable protected environment.

If group behavior is to function in an organized way, there must be communication between the members of the group. In particular, there must be empathic signaling of emotional states so that survival-related actions can be taken in concert. Thus, empathy, in this evolutionary sense, contributes to the adaptive patterning of group behavior and increases the chances of individual survival.

Imitation as a mode of empathy

As already mentioned, empathy implies imitation or mimicry. Animals exhibit various forms of imitative behavior. True imitation has been observed in Japanese macaques, where the initiation of potato washing by a single individual was imitated by others and has become a social norm in some groups. Social facilitation of eating has been observed in many animals. A review of this phenomenon, in which ordinary behavior is increased in pace or frequency by the actions of other individuals, has been reviewed by Zajonc (1965).

Observational (imitative) learning has various benefits for survival. It can lead an individual to new food sources, and it can ensure safer exploration of new foods. In harsh environments where food occurs in irregular, unpredictable patches, imitative and flocking behavior greatly increases the chances of locating food as well as defense against predators. Flocks are more adept at finding food than are single individuals, and they harvest it more efficiently. Wilson (1975) refers to such imitative behavior as "empathic learning."

Empathic behavior also occurs in the context of play. Play is restricted to the higher vertebrates. It is not seen in social insects or cold-blooded vertebrates, but is found in all mammals. Play behavior generally involves aggressive, sexual, and affectionate interactions between young animals of a species. So that play behavior will not be misinterpreted as "real" aggression or sex, a meta-message that both animals can recognize has to be expressed about the context. Such mutual affective signaling can be interpreted as empathy. An example of metacommunication in Old World monkeys is the use of a "play-face" or "relaxed open-mouth display" as an invitation to play instead of to fight (Wilson, 1975).

Display signals as triggers of empathy

Earlier in this chapter it was suggested that empathy may be induced by an alarm signal. The receiver of the alarm signal presumably experiences some of the same feelings as the sender and reacts behaviorally in a similar way. One may now generalize this idea. In fact, humans and animals exhibit many types of displays that are related to specific types of interactions. Displays may be thought of as enhanced signals that are related to motivationally important events. Examples of such displays include

1. Greeting or recognition displays
2. Courtship displays
3. Mating displays
4. Dominance displays
5. Submissiveness displays
6. Alarm displays
7. Challenge displays
8. Distress displays
9. Feeding displays
10. Food-begging displays.

What all these displays have in common is a high probability of inducing similar feelings and behaviors in the individuals sending and receiving the displays. In connection with courtship, for example, we recognize that many animals breed only during a specific time of the year, or only in particular locations. Successful mating depends on a synchrony of certain physiological processes in males and females. Therefore, courtship displays act to bring animals together at appropriate times and places and initiate processes connected with the release of ova and sperm. Courtship displays also create a mating mood designed to overcome aggressive and fearful barriers that might normally exist between the males and the females. Another function of displays is to prevent attempts at cross mating. In many animals, courtship consists largely of identity checks between the male and female; fertilization occurs only after females have identified males of their own species. Evidently courtship displays induce empathic responses in a male and female that have value for inclusive fitness.

Empathy is thus not a separate emotion by itself, but a kind of induction process by which emotions, both positive and negative, are shared, and which increase the chances of similar behavior in the participants. Thus, two individuals may empathically share feelings of love or affection, feelings of danger, or feelings of outrage and hostility. If there is a common element in these diverse situations, it is the presence of an important emotion related to survival and the ability of each participant to *accept* an emotional message, whatever its form.

Empathy and bonding

One other important aspect of empathy in an evolutionary context is that it serves to bond individuals to one another, especially mothers to infants. From an evolutionary point of view, the organism is most vulnerable to the vicissitudes of the environment, including predation, when it is newborn. For this reason, various signals, displays, communication patterns, and behaviors that increase the chances of survival are found in immature organisms and are present at or shortly after birth. Because survival is a problem from the moment of birth, certain mechanisms must exist both in the child and in the mother or caretaker to help ensure survival. If young organisms had to wait until the infant learned how to attract its mother's attention and support, and if the mother had to learn how to provide it, the chances of species survival would be small. Communication patterns have to work the first time they are used. Thus emotions emitted by the infant function in part as communication signals that have various adaptive consequences for survival (Plutchik, 1983), for example, by attracting a nurturing adult to a hungry or lost infant.

There is considerable evidence indicating that parents strongly influence the behavior of infants. Less well recognized is the fact that infants have a powerful effect on their parents. Hofer (1983), for example, has presented evidence that mother–child attachment has developed from primitive biologically based approach tendencies that have homeostatic, regulatory functions in the autonomic, endocrine, and neurochemical systems of both parents and offspring. From a review of the recent literature, Trevarthen (1984) concludes that very young infants can imitate (emphathize with) facial expressions of adults and that the patterns of speech mothers exhibit to infants reveal empathic sensitivity to the subtle variations in facial expression of the infant. Trevarthen (1984) notes that "infant expressions may have a profound emotive effect on adults – they are felt as emotional. Moreover, these same movements are exquisitely sensitive to the affectional quality of the responses they elicit from adults. . . . The expressions (between the two feeling subjects) become manifestations of an empathic awareness and mutual control'' (p. 150).

In a study that reveals the impact of the infant on its caretakers (Frodi et al., 1978), a group of mothers and fathers of newborn infants looked at videotape presentations of an infant. Some of the parents were shown a crying baby and others were shown a smiling baby. The parents were asked to rate their moods on seeing the infants, and at the same time the parents' blood pressure and skin conductance were recorded.

The parents who viewed the crying baby reported feeling more annoyed, irritated, distressed, disturbed, indifferent, and less attentive and less happy than the parents who viewed the smiling infant. These results were obtained for both mothers and fathers, although the mothers' ratings tended to be more extreme. When parents viewed the crying infant, their diastolic blood pressures rose significantly, but no blood pressure changes occurred during their observation of the smiling child. Skin conductance increased while the subjects were viewing the crying infant, but it was unaffected when they saw a smiling infant.

The authors concluded that crying and smiling infants elicit different empathic emotional and physiological reactions from parents. They suggest that crying is perceived as aversive and that parents have a strong desire to terminate this aversive signal from an infant. A smiling infant produces pleasant feelings with little or no arousal. However, the feelings elicited by both crying and smiling incline the parents to move close to the infant, in one case to stop the crying, and in the other to prolong the smiling. Such closeness tends to have survival value in an evolutionary sense.

This study by Frodi et al. (1978) strongly supports the view that infants have a powerful effect on the emotional states of their parents. It also implies that empathic sharing of emotions provides the fundamental basis for social bonding between parents and children.

Overview

In this chapter, empathy is considered a process whereby emotionally significant experiences are shared by two or more individuals. The emotions involved in such sharing can be either positive or negative. The process appears to be widely distributed in the animal kingdom and is illustrated by such phenomena as schooling, flocking, mobbing, and herding behaviors in fish, birds, and mammals. It may even be seen in the social insects.

Empathy may also be thought of as a component of affective signaling or communication and is triggered by the large number of display behaviors seen in animals. The available evidence suggests that empathy can be inferred in both young and mature animals and that it is probably based on innate schemata that are genetically determined. As with all behaviors that have genetic components, there is reason to believe that experience and learning may also influence the intensity and frequency of empathic behaviors.

From an evolutionary point of view, empathy has important survival value and contributes to inclusive fitness. It assists individuals in gathering and hunting for food, detecting predators, courtship, and ensuring reproductive success. Considering the variety of contexts in which it is relevant, empathy is not a simple, observable behavior per se, but a complex inferred state whose properties can be determined only on the basis of various kinds of indirect evidence.

Finally, empathy involves the sharing or mutual induction of emotional states and should thus be considered in the context of a general theory of emotion. I suggest that empathy relates most directly to my psychoevolutionary theory of emotion (Plutchik, 1980), which assumes that emotions are communication and survival mechanisms that all organisms use in the struggle for survival. The theory also hypothesizes that emotions are complex chains of events with stabilizing feedback loops, are hypothetical constructs, have a genetic basis, can be best represented by a three-dimensional model, and are related to various other conceptual domains. Evidence for these assumptions has been presented in various studies, all of which point to the importance of empathy in the general study of emotions.

References

Frodi, A. N., Lamb, M. E., Leavitt, L. A., Donovan, W. L., Neff, C., & Sherry, D. (1978). Fathers and mother's responses to the faces and cries of normal and premature infants. *Developmental Psychology, 14,* 190–198.

Hofer, M. A. (1983). On the relationship between attachment and separation processes in infancy. In R. Plutchik and H. Kellerman (Eds.), *Emotions in early development.* New York: Academic Press.

Kohler, W. (1927) *The mentality of apes.* London: Kegan Paul, Trench, and Trubner.

Lawick, H. van, & Lawick-Goodall, J. (1971). *Innocent killers.* Boston: Houghton Mifflin.

Marler, P. (1984). Animal communication: Affect or cognition? In K. R. Scherer, and P. Ekman (Eds.), *Approaches to emotion.* Hillsdale, NJ: Erlbaum.

Plutchik, R. (1983). Emotions in early development: A psychoevolutionary approach. In R. Plutchik and H. Kellerman (Eds.), *Emotions in early development* (vol. 2). New York: Academic Press.

Plutchik, R. (1980). *Emotion: A psychoevolutionary synthesis.* New York: Harper and Row.

Plutchik, R. (1985). Emotion and temperament. Paper presented at the symposium "Biology and Temperament" at the meeting of the American Psychological Association in Los Angeles, August 1985.

Preston, D. J. (1981). Meshe Mungkut. *Natural History,* October 1, 74–76.

Scott, J. P. (1980). The function of emotions in behavioral systems: A systems theory analysis. In

R. Plutchik and H. Kellerman (Eds.), *Theories of emotion* (Vol. 1). New York: Academic Press.

Seyfarth, R. M., Cheney, D. L., & Marler, P. (1980a). Vervet monkey alarm calls: Semantic communication in a free-ranging primate. *Animal Behavior, 28,* 1070–1094.

Seyfarth, R. M., Cheney, D. L., & Marler, P. (1980b). Monkey responses to three different alarm calls: Evidence of predator classification and semantic communication. *Science, 210,* 801–803.

Trevarthen, C. (1984). Emotions in infancy: Regulators of contact and relationships with persons. In K. R. Scherer and P. Ekman (Eds.), *Approaches to emotion.* Hillsdale, NJ: Erlbaum.

Wilson, E. O. (1975). *Sociobiology: The new synthesis.* Cambridge, MA: Belknap.

Zajonc, R. B. (1965). Social facilitation. *Science, 149,* 269–274.

4   The contribution of empathy to justice and moral judgment

Martin L. Hoffman

Few psychologists or philosophers can agree as to whether any moral principles are universal. Three broadly held principles, however, are often viewed as universal:

1. the principle of justice or fairness, essentially distributive justice and written about extensively by Immanuel Kant and his followers, which states that society's resources (rewards, punishments) should be allocated according to a standard equally applicable to all;
2. the principle of impartial benevolence, associated mainly with writers in the Utilitarian tradition, especially David Hume and Adam Smith, which states a moral act is one that takes into account all people likely to be affected by it – at the face-to-face level this has become a principle of caring about the well-being of others, including their need for self-respect, dignity, and avoidance of pain; and
3. the principle of maintaining the social order, derived largely from Hobbes's view that, without society, the individual would be constantly embattled, hence nothing.

The advocates of one principle do not deny the importance of the other two, but view them as subordinate.[1]

I think of these principles not as mutually exclusive precepts, but as "ideal types," any or all of which may be relevant in a given situation. When more than one are applicable, they are usually compatible – caring and justice, for example, reinforce each other in the case of honest, hard-working farmers who lose their farms because of economic forces beyond their control. However, these principles may be incompatible in some situations, as in voting for tenure when a candidate's performance is not quite up to the expected standard. If one likes the candidate and knows that one of his/her children is chronically ill, caring may move one to vote in his/her favor. At the same time, justice, may argue for a negative vote, or one might vote negatively to affirm one's commitment to the tenure system. One might even see the relevance of all three princi-

47

ples and be confused about how to vote, the issue finally turning on the intensity of one's feeling for the candidate and one's commitment to caring as a principle, versus one's commitment to distributive justice and to the tenure system.

Many psychologists have been concerned with justice/fairness and caring/consideration. Notions of justice are at the heart of Kohlberg's moral theory, which has been criticized for being overly cognitive and ignoring affect. Caring has been the focus of people like me who are interested in affect, especially empathy. The notion of maintaining the social order has been virtually ignored by psychologists, and I will say nothing more about it.

I have long been working on a scheme for the development of empathy, which I define as an affective response more appropriate to someone else's situation than to one's own.[2] I have described the scheme in detail (Hoffman, 1984); summarized evidence for empathy's status as a moral motive, that is, in contributing to prosocial behavior (Hoffman, 1978); theorized about empathy's role in moral internalization (Hoffman, 1983); traced empathy's roots in Western philosophy (Hoffman, 1982c); and speculated on its biological evolutionary beginnings (Hoffman, 1981). I have also investigated sex differences and the contribution of female sex–role socialization to empathy and to an empathy-based, humanistic moral orientation (Hoffman, 1970, 1975b, 1977). I believe that empathy as elaborated in my developmental scheme may provide the basis for a comprehensive moral theory, although to formulate such a theory one would have to expand the scheme in several directions. This chapter is a beginning attempt at such an expansion.

First, I briefly describe the scheme to pave the way for my argument, ending with five empathy-based moral affects: empathic distress, sympathetic distress, guilt, empathic anger, and empathic injustice. I then discuss how these affects may contribute to caring and justice principles, the role they may play in moral judgment and decision making, and the problem of empathic bias and how to reduce it. Finally, I speculate about the stabilizing effect that moral principles, as "hot cognitions," may have on empathy. Although I have long suggested a link between empathy, moral principles, and judgment (Hoffman, 1970, 1980, 1982b, 1984b), this is my first attempt to argue systematically for such a link.

Development of empathic moral affect

The scheme for empathic distress, an empathic affective response to another person's distress, starts with a simple innocent-bystander model – in which one encounters someone in pain, danger, or deprivation – and generates five empathic affects that are mediated by social cognitive development and various causal attributions or inferences.

The scheme includes five hypothesized modes of empathic affect arousal (I.A–E in Table 4.1), which have been described in detail and documented elsewhere (Hoffman, 1984a). I make four points about them here. First, they do not form a strict sequence of stages in the sense of subsequent modes encompassing and replacing preceding modes. The first mode typically drops out after infancy, owing to controls against crying; however, adults may feel sad when they hear a cry and some adults may even feel like crying themselves, although they usually control it. The fifth mode, being deliberate, may be relatively infrequent – for example, it may be used by parents and therapists who believe they can be more effective if they experience some of their child's or patient's feelings. The intermediate three modes enter at various points in development and may continue to operate throughout life.

Second, the existence of five arousal modes suggests that empathy may be overdetermined and hence may be a reliable affective response to another's distress. Thus, if only expressive cues (facial, vocal, postural) from someone in distress are provided, mimicry is available to arouse empathic distress in observers. If only situational cues are provided, conditioning and association are available. Ordinarily, the victim is present and all modes may be brought into play, which mode is dominant depending on which cues are salient. Even if the victim is not present, information about his or her distress communicated by someone else can produce empathy in an observer (through arousal modes I.D–E in Table 4.1).

Third, empathy may be self-reinforcing. Every time we empathize with someone in distress, the resulting cooccurrence of our own distress and distress cues from the other may increase the strength of the connection between cues of another's distress and our own empathic response and thus increase the likelihood that future distress in others will be accompanied by empathic distress in ourselves.

Fourth, most arousal modes require rather shallow levels of cognitive processing (e.g., sensory registration, simple pattern matching, conditioning) and are largely involuntary. Thus it should not be surprising that empathy appears to be a universal, largely involuntary response – if one attends to the relevant cues one responds empathically – that may have had survival value in human evolution (Hoffman, 1981).

Although empathy may usually be aroused by these simple involuntary mechanisms, its subjective experience is rather complex. Mature empathizers know the affect aroused in them is due to stimulus events impinging on someone else, and they have an idea of what that person is feeling. Young children who lack the self–other distinction may be empathically aroused without this knowledge. This suggests that the development of empathic distress corresponds to the de-

Table 4.1. *Scheme for the development and transformation of empathic distress*

I. Modes of empathic affect arousal; operate singly or in combinations

   (Automatic – nonvoluntary)
   A. Primary circular reaction; neonate cries to sound of another's cry
   B. Mimicry; automatic imitation plus afferent feedback
   C. Conditioning and direct association

   (Higher-level cognitive)
   D. Language-mediated association
   E. Putting self in other's place; other-focused and self-focused

II. Development of a cognitive sense of others

   A. Self–other fusion
   B. Object permanence; other is physical entity distinct from self
   C. Perspective taking; other has independent internal states
   D. Personal identity; other has experiences beyond the immediate situation, own history, and identity

III. Developmental levels of empathy (coalescence of I and II)

   A. Global empathy
   B. "Egocentric" empathy
   C. Empathy for another's feelings
   D. Empathy for another's experiences beyond the immediate situation, general condition, future prospects
      1. Empathy for an entire group

IV. Partial transformation of empathic into sympathetic distress

   Begins to occur in transition from III.A to III.B; subsequently, one's affective response to another's distress has a pure empathic component and a sympathetic component

V. Causal attribution and shaping of empathy into related moral affects

   A. If victim is cause of distress, he/she may no longer be seen as a victim, so basis for empathy is removed.
   B. *Sympathetic distress:* Victim has no control over cause of victim's distress
   C. *Guilt:* Observer is cause of victim's distress
      Guilt over inaction: Observer, though not the cause, does nothing and therefore views self as responsible for continuation of victim's distress
      Guilt by association: Observer's group is cause of victim's distress (observer's or group's relative advantage may increase guilt further)
   D. *Empathic anger:* Someone else is cause of victim's distress
      1. Empathic anger may be reduced and/or turned toward victim, depending on context (e.g., if culprit was previously harmed by victim)
      2. If culprit represents society, empathic anger may lead to social criticism and moral/political ideology
   E. *Empathic injustice:* Contrast between victim's plight and character

velopment of a cognitive sense of others, the four broad stages of which are indicated in II.A–D in Table 4.1 (see Hoffman, 1975a, for evidence for these stages):

1. fusion, or at least a lack of clear separation between the self and the other;
2. awareness that others are physical entities distinct from the self;
3. awareness that others have feelings and other internal states independent of one's own; and
4. awareness that others have experiences beyond the immediate situation and their own history and identity as individuals.

Empathic affect is presumably experienced differently as the child progresses through these stages.

The resulting coalescence of empathic affect and social–cognitive development yields four levels of empathic distress (III.A–D in Table 4.1), which I now describe briefly (see Hoffman, 1984a, for details).

1. *Global empathy.* Infants may experience empathic distress through the simplest arousal modes (I.A–C in Table 4.1) long before they acquire a sense of others as physical entities distinct from the self. For most of the first year, then, witnessing someone in distress may result in a global empathic distress response. Distress cues from the dimly perceived other are confounded with unpleasant feelings empathically aroused in the self. Consequently, infants may at times act as though what happened to the other happened to themselves. An 11-month-old girl, on seeing a child fall and cry, looked as though she was about to cry herself, then put her thumb in her mouth and buried her head in her mother's lap, as she does when she herself is hurt. (For other examples, see Hoffman, 1975a; Kaplan, 1977; and Zahn-Waxler, Radke-Yarrow, and King, 1979.)

2. *"Egocentric" empathy.* With object permanence and the gradual emergence of a sense of the other as physically distinct from the self, the affective portion of the child's global empathic distress may be transferred to the separate image-of-self and image-of-other that emerge. The child may now be aware that another person and not the self is in distress, but the other's internal states remain unknown and may be assumed to be the same as one's own. An 18-month-old boy fetched his own mother to comfort a crying friend although the friend's mother was also present – a behavior that, although confused, is not entirely egocentric because it indicates that the child is responding with appropriate empathic affect.

3. *Empathy for another's feelings.* With the onset of role taking, at about 2–3 years, one becomes aware that other people's feelings may differ from one's own and are based on their own needs and interpretations of events; consequently one becomes more responsive to cues about what the other is actually feeling.

Furthermore, as language is acquired, children become capable of empathizing with a wide range of increasingly complex emotions. Empathizing with a victim's distress, children may also eventually become capable of empathizing with the victim's anxiety about the loss of self-esteem, hence with the desire *not* to be helped. Finally, children can be empathically aroused by information about someone's distress even in that person's absence. This leads to the fourth, most advanced level.

4. *Empathy for another's life condition.* By late childhood, owing to the emerging conception of oneself and others as continuing people with separate histories and identities, one becomes aware that others feel pleasure and pain, not only in the immediate situation but also in their larger life experience. Consequently, although one still responds empathically to another's immediate distress, one's empathic response may be intensified when one realizes that the other's distress is not transitory but chronic. Thus, one's empathically aroused affect is combined with a mental representation of another's general level of distress or deprivation. As one acquires the ability to form social concepts, one's empathic distress may also be combined with a mental representation of the plight of an entire group or class of people (e.g., the poor, oppressed, outcast, or retarded). (This empathic level can provide a motive base, especially in adolescence, for the development of certain moral and political ideologies that are centered around alleviation of the plight of unfortunate groups; see Hoffman, 1980, in press.)

When one has advanced through these four levels and encounters someone in pain, danger, or distress, one is exposed to a network of information about the other's condition. The network may include verbal and nonverbal expressive cues from the victim, situational cues, and one's knowledge about the victim's life beyond the immediate situation. These sources of information are processed differently: Empathy aroused by nonverbal and situational cues can be mediated by largely involuntary, cognitively shallow processing modes (mimicry; conditioning). Empathy aroused by verbal messages from the victim or by one's knowledge about the victim requires more complex processing, such as language-mediated association or putting oneself in the other's place.

The various cues, arousal modes, and processing levels usually contribute to the same affect, but contradictions may occur – for example, between different expressive cues, such as facial expression and tone of voice, or between expressive and situational cues. If one's knowledge of the other's life condition conflicts with the other's immediate expressive cues, the expressive cues may lose much of their force for an observer who knows they reflect only a transitory state. Imagine someone who does not know that he or she has a terminal illness laughing and having a good time. A young child might respond with empathic joy, whereas a mature observer might experience empathic sadness or a mingling of sidness and joy. Similarly, a mature observer's empathic distress (but not a child's) might decrease if the other person is known to have a generally happy life and the immediate distress is a short-lived exception. Clearly, the most advanced empathic level involves some distancing – responding partly to one's mental image of the other rather than only to the others' immediate stimulus value. (See Hoffman, 1986, for a more general discussion of the interaction of sensory, perceptual, and higher-order cognitive processes in generating affect.) This fits my definition of empathy, not as an exact match of another's feelings, but as an affective response that is more appropriate to the other's situation than to one's own.

Partial transformation of empathic into sympathetic distress

The transition from global to "egocentric" empathy (IV in Table 4.1) may involve an important qualitative shift in feeling: Once children are aware that others are distinct from themselves, their own empathic distress, which is a parallel response – a more or less exact replication of the victim's presumed feeling of distress – may be transformed, at least in part, into reciprocal concern for the victim. That is, they may continue to respond in a purely empathic manner – feeling uncomfortable and highly distressed themselves – but they may also experience a feeling of compassion, or "sympathetic distress," for the victim, along with a conscious desire to help, because they feel sorry for the victim, not just to relieve their own empathic distress.

Evidence for this shift comes from observational research (Murphy, 1937; Zahn-Waxler et al., 1979) and from anecdotes such as those cited earlier, which show that: (1) children progress developmentally, first responding to someone's distress by seeking comfort for the self and later trying to help the victim rather than the self; and (2) a transitional stage, in which children feel sad and comfort both the victim and the self, seems to occur at about the same time that they first become aware that others are distinct from themselves.

What developmental processes account for this shift? I suggested earlier that the unpleasant, vicarious affect that is experienced as a part of the child's initial global, undifferentiated self is transferred to the separate image-of-self and image-of-other that emerge during the self–other differentiation process. It seems likely that the wish, which is not necessarily conscious, to terminate the unpleasant affect is also similarly transferred to the emerging image-of-other and image-of-self. (See Hoffman, 1984a, for a more detailed discussion.) Consequently, the child's empathic response now includes two components: a wish to terminate the other's distress – the sympathetic distress component – and a more purely empathic wish to terminate distress in the self. The last three empathy development levels (III.B–D) may therefore describe the development of an affective response that has both an empathic distress and a sympathetic distress component.

A question may arise as to whether the pure empathic component is egoistic rather than prosocial. I have argued that it is both and may therefore be an important bridge between these two personality dimensions (Hoffman, 1981). In any case, it functions prosocially, because the other's distress must be alleviated if one's own distress is to end; this component must therefore be distinguished from the usual, primarily self-serving egoistic motives. The sympathetic distress component is obviously prosocial.

Causal attribution, empathy, and related moral affects

People are always making causal attributions, and there is evidence that they do this spontaneously (Weiner, 1985). It therefore seems reasonable to suppose that, when one encounters someone in distress, one will often make attributions about the cause, and the particular attribution made may determine how empathic affect is experienced. Consider now some causal attributions and the resulting affects (V.A–D in Table 4.1).

Sympathetic distress. One may respond to another's distress without making a causal attribution when the other's plight is salient, there are no causal situational cues powerful enough to draw one's attention from the other's plight, and one has no prior information about the cause. These conditions often exist when young children witness someone in distress, and were therefore assumed in my discussion of early developmental levels of empathy and its transformation into sympathetic distress. One may also feel sympathetic distress when there are cues or one has information indicating that victims have no control over their plight, as in serious illness or accidental injury. Sympathetic distress in mature observers may also be part of a complex ambivalent response, as when one condemns a man in the electric chair for his crimes while sympathizing with him because of information indicating that early experiences over which he had no control played an important role in his life.

Empathic anger. If the cues indicate that someone else caused the victim's plight, one's attention may to some extent be diverted from the victims to the culprit. One may feel anger at the culprit, partly because one sympathizes with the victim and partly because one empathizes with the victim and feels oneself vicariously attacked.[3] One's feelings may also alternate between empathic and sympathetic distress and empathic anger; or empathic anger may crowd out one's empathic and sympathetic distress entirely. Note that John Stuart Mill (1861/1979) suggested that empathic anger, which he described as "the natural feeling of retaliation . . . rendered by intellect and sympathy applicable to . . . those hurts which wound us through wounding others [serves as the] guardian of justice.'' A simple example of empathic anger is that of the 17-month-old boy in the doctor's office who, on seeing another child receive an injection, responds by hitting the doctor in anger.[4]

Empathic anger may also occur in complex contexts in which it is shifted from one target to another, along with the accompanying empathic and sympathetic distress. For example, if one discovers the victim did harm to the culprit on an earlier occasion, one's empathy for the victim may decrease, and one may begin to feel empathic and sympathetic distress for the culprit because of the hurt that led to the culprit's aggression in the first place; one may even empathize with the culprit's anger. Alternatively, one might discover that the victim has a history of being mistreated in his or her relationship with the culprit. In this case, one may assume the victim had a choice (why else would he or she continue the relationship?) and is therefore responsible for his or her own plight and thus is not a victim. One's empathic and sympathetic distress for the victim and empathic anger at the culprit may then decrease sharply. The empathic anger of young children is apt to miss these nuances, and if children's perceptions are confined to the immediate situation, they may respond in all these situations with simple empathic anger directed at the visible culprit.

A particularly relevant case here is one in which the observer blames the victim's plight – say, extreme poverty – on someone who is absent, especially when that someone represents the larger society or a powerful group within it. For example, one may see the victim's basic material needs as not being met because of society's neglect or the lack of an adequate "safety net." One may then feel empathic and sympathetic distress for the victim and empathic anger toward the powerful group or society as a whole.

Guilt feeling. The observer thus far in our analysis is an innocent bystander. If one is not innocent but the cause of the other's distress, the conditions may be ripe for feeling guilty,[5] that is, for a combination of empathic and sympathetic distress and a self-blame attribution. I have suggested that this combination may originate in discipline encounters in which parents point up the harmful consequences of the child's actions for others (Hoffman, 1983). Blaming oneself for another's distress may often result in empathic anger that is directed toward the self and thus may intensify the guilt feeling. Even if one is an innocent bystander but for some reason does not help, one may feel guilty because one blames oneself, not for *causing* the other's plight, but for contributing to its continuation by not intervening to help – the guilt is over inaction.

When one reaches the most advanced level of empathy development, one can not only categorize victims into groups but one can also categorize oneself as a member of a group. One may than have a feeling of guilt by association if one's group is seen as causing the victim's distress or benefiting from the same social system that disadvantages the victim. And, finally, I have suggested elsewhere (Hoffman, 1980) that one may feel guilty if one simply sees oneself as being in a relatively advantaged position vis-à-vis the victim. I call this "existential guilt" because one has done nothing wrong but feels culpable owing to life circumstances beyond one's control.

Empathic injustice. Other information beside that pertaining to the cause of the victim's distress may shape one's empathic response. I just mentioned that the contrast between the victim's plight and one's own good fortune may produce guilt feelings. Other contrasts are possible, such as that between the victim's plight and other people's good fortune. If one observes highly disadvantaged people in a context in which the extravagant life-style of others is salient, one may feel empathic injustice. Perhaps more important for our present purposes is the contrast between the victim's plight and his or her own general conduct or character. Thus if the victim is viewed as bad, immoral, or lazy one may conclude that his or her fate was deserved, and one's empathic and sympathetic distress might decrease. If the victim is viewed as basically good, however, or at least not bad, immoral, or lazy, one might view his or her fate as undeserved or unfair. One's empathic distress (or sympathetic distress, guilt, or empathic anger – whichever is appropriate) might then be expected to increase. Furthermore, the empathic affect may be transformed in part into a feeling that has elements in common with guilt and empathic anger but appears subtly different enough to be given a new name: empathic injustice.

An example of empathic injustice is found in the case of the 14-year-old Southern male "redneck" described by Coles (1986). After several weeks of joining his friends in harassing black children trying to integrate his school, this boy, a popular athlete,

> . . . began to see a kid, not a nigger – a guy who knew how to smile when it was rough going, and who walked straight and tall, and was polite. I told my parents, "It's a real shame that someone like him has to pay for the trouble caused by all those federal judges."
> Then it happened. I saw a few people cuss at him. "The dirty nigger," they kept on calling him and soon they were pushing him in a corner, and it looked like trouble, bad trouble. I went over and broke it up. . . . They all looked at me as if I was crazy. . . . Before [everyone] left I spoke to the nigger . . . I didn't mean to. . . . It just came out of my mouth. I was surprised to hear the words myself: "I'm sorry." (pp. 27–28)

After this incident, he began talking to the black youth, championing him personally, while still decrying integration. Finally, he became the black youth's friend and began advocating "an end to the whole lousy business of segregation." When pressed by Coles to explain his shift, he attributed it to being in school that year and seeing "that kid behave himself, no matter what we called him, and seeing him insulted so bad, so real bad. Something in me just drew the line, and something in me began to change, I think" (pp. 28).

The boy clearly seemed to experience sympathetic distress, empathic anger, and guilt. But what really seemed to move him was the contrast between the black youth's admirable conduct and the way he was being treated – it was as if the boy felt that this was a fine person who deserved better. Empathic injustice may be important because it seems closer than other empathic affects to bridging the gap between simple empathic distress and moral principle.

Complex combinations. Here is an example of the complex combination of empathic affects possible in moral encounters: A shabbily dressed man is observed robbing an obviously affluent person on the street. A young child might feel empathic and sympathetic distress for the victim and anger at the immediate, visible culprit. Mature observers might have these same feelings, but a variety of other empathic affects as well. They might feel guilty over not helping the victim. If they are ideologically liberal, they might empathize and sympathize not only with the victim but also with the culprit because of his poverty. The observers might view the culprit as a victim of society and feel empathic anger toward society. Furthermore, if the observers are affluent as well as liberal, they might feel guilty over being relatively advantaged persons who benefit from the same society. Ideologically conservative observers might not sympathize with the culprit but might respond with unalloyed empathic anger instead. They might also feel empathic anger toward society, but in this case because they view the victim, not the culprit, as a victim of society (because of inadequate law enforcement and citizen protection).

To summarize, the empathic reaction to someone's distress produces two basic affects: empathic distress and sympathetic distress. In addition – depending on various causal and other attributions – empathic anger, several types of guilt, and a feeling of empathic injustice may be generated. There is considerable research evidence that empathic and sympathetic distress (the research does not separate them) and guilt feelings function as motives for moral action (Hoffman, 1978, 1982b). Empathic anger has not yet been researched, but it seems reasonable to suppose that such anger includes a disposition to intervene and protect the victim in some way (although egoistic motives like fear may result in inaction). Also, since anger has long been known to "mobilize one's energy and make one capable of defending oneself with great vigor and strength" (Izard,

1977, p. 333), it seems reasonable to expect empathic anger to be an energizer of moral action, as suggested in this quotation from a letter to the *New York Times:*

> The pictures of starving children in Ethiopia are heartwrenching but feeling sad isn't enough . . . we send a check, the pictures disappear from TV screens, and soon we forget that millions are dying. . . . Instead we should feel outraged that in a world of plenty hunger still exists. Outrage produces action . . . etc. (February, 1985)

Research is needed to see if the letter writer is correct, not only in stating that empathic anger leads to action but that empathic anger is more likely to lead to action than is sympathetic distress.

Thus far, I have presented a scheme for empathy and empathy-related moral affects that may be aroused when the instigating stimulus is someone in pain or an otherwise distressing situation. If this scheme is to provide the basis for a comprehensive moral theory, these empathic affects, though generated by a by-stander model, must be arousable in other types of moral encounters as well. Furthermore, these empathic affects must be congruent with the major moral principles. That is, the feelings, thoughts, and action tendencies associated with the affects must fit in with a principle's meaning and intent. Under these conditions, it would be reasonable to suppose that in the course of a person's development empathic affects will become meaningfully associated with moral principles, so that when empathic affect is aroused in a moral encounter this will activate the moral principles. The principles, along with the empathic affect, might then help guide the individual's moral judgment, decision making, and action. In some instances, the sequence might be reversed – the principle might be activated first and then its associated empathic affect elicited. The remainder of this chapter is concerned with these issues.

Empathic arousal in moral encounters

Empathic affects may be aroused not only in bystander situations but also in most other types of moral encounters. The reasons are as follows:

1. Human beings have the capacity for representation, and represented events can evoke affect, as shown in the voluminous mood-induction research in which all manner of affects are generated by imagining oneself in a relevant situation that one experienced in the past or simply made up (e.g., Harris & Siebel, 1975).
2. Human beings are capable of transposing stimuli and of imagining that stimuli impinging on someone else are impinging on oneself, and trans-posed stimuli can evoke empathic affect (Stotland, 1969).

3. The semantic meanings of events can become conditioned stimuli for autonomic arousal and therefore, presumably, for affect (Razran, 1971; Zanna, Kiesler & Pilkonis, 1970).

Thus, empathic affects should be arousable through the mediation of language and role taking (I.D–E in Table 4.1). The victim need not be present; one need only be informed about the victim.

Consequently, the bystander model can be intended to include instances in which one hears about victims second- or thirdhand – from parents, teachers, newspapers, or television. The model's essential features may also obtain when one is talking, arguing, or merely thinking about contemporary moral issues such as racial segregation, abortion, whether doctors should tell people how seriously ill they are, whether doctors should terminate life-support systems for brain-dead people, or how society should distribute its resources. If, in the course of these activities, relevant victims come to mind or are pointed up by others, one is then in the bystander's position of observing or imagining someone in distress. These situations are often more complex than the simple bystander model. At times they include competing principles and conflicting motives as well as pragmatic concerns, and the complexity may limit the vividness and salience of the imagined event, hence the intensity of empathic affects aroused. Nonetheless, these affects may still influence the moral judgments made in the situation.

Potential victims may also come to mind or be suggested by others when one is not in the bystander position but is contemplating an action that may directly or indirectly affect the welfare of others, with or without one's knowledge. One may be thinking of ways to resolve a conflict, break bad news to someone, go back on a promise, or simply satisfy some material need that at first may seem to have no bearing on the concerns of others. Or, one may be engaged in a task that clearly and explicitly requires making a moral judgment and decision. Consider the task of writing a recommendation for tenure. The instigating stimulus for engaging in the task is not the distress of someone, but a request from a colleague in another university. One might simply write a letter indicating, as objectively as possible, one's judgment of the candidate's competence. On the other hand, one might think about the candidate, imagining how he or she would feel and what would happen if tenure were denied, or one might imagine how one would feel if one were in the candidate's place. The empathic and sympathetic distress (or, more strictly, the anticipatory empathic and sympathetic distress) that one might feel as a result of this role taking might then influence the tone and content of the letter.

Writing tenure letters is one of many moral encounters that may be readily transformed into situations involving victims or potential victims. Indeed, it is difficult to imagine moral encounters in everyday life that do *not* involve potential victims and therefore are not likely to be so transformed. The likelihood that one's actions will affect someone's welfare is another important reason – along with the human tendency to react empathically to victims, whether physically present or imagined – for expecting empathy to play a significant role in a comprehensive moral theory. I now discuss a third reason: the congruence between empathy and the principles of caring and of justice.

Congruence between empathy and moral principles

Moral principles are often presented as abstractions. When they are concretized in actual life events, however, the victims and potential victims often stand out, and empathic affects become relevant.

Empathy and caring

The link between empathic affects, especially sympathetic distress, and the caring principle appears rather direct and obvious: The empathic affects and caring operate in the same direction – that is, toward considering the welfare of others. This link appears to be reflected in the empathic moral reasoning that often accompanies people's behavior when they encounter someone in distress. Consider this example from the book *Uncle Tom's Cabin,* reported by Kaplan (in press), in which an affluent, politically uninvolved housewife whose empathy for slaves she knew, who "have been abused and oppressed all their lives," leads her to oppose a newly passed law against giving food, clothes, or shelter to escaping slaves. Arguing with her husband, who supports the law on pragmatic and legal grounds, she verbalizes what amounts to a general principle of caring – "the Bible says we should feed the hungry, clothe the naked, and comfort the desolate," adding that "people don't run away when they're happy, but out of suffering." She becomes so intensely opposed to that "shameful, wicked, abominable" law that she vows to break it at the earliest opportunity.

This episode is reminiscent of Huckleberry Finn's moral conflict between his empathic feeling for Miss Watson's slave Jim, whom he helped escape, and both Missouri law and church teaching at the time, which strongly opposed helping slaves escape. In a famous passage, Huck first writes a letter exposing Jim's hiding place, but then, after a great deal of agonizing soul-searching in which his moral thinking is driven by conflicting moral feelings – sympathetic distress and guilt over the consequences for Jim if he is exposed, and the feeling of how awful a "sin" it would be to keep Jim's whereabouts a secret – he tears the letter up and says to himself, "All right then, I'll *go* to hell." As powerful as that passage is, the episode from *Uncle Tom's Cabin* goes beyond it for our purposes because it indicates that empathy may lead to a response that transcends the immediate, individual victim. More specifically, the episode suggests that the combination of empathic and sympathetic distress and empathic anger in a particular situation may provide the motive for affirming a general caring principle, which may then serve as a premise for the moral judgment that laws violating it are morally wrong.

Empathy and distributive justice

Although the link between empathy and justice is less obvious and less direct than that between empathy and caring, it does exist, as I hope to show in this section. To begin, there are at least three distinct, and seemingly mutually exclusive, principles of distributive justice:

1. *Need* – Society's resources should be allocated according to what people need: Those who need more should receive more; those who need less should receive less.
2. *Equality* – Each person has the same intrinsic worth, in some larger religious or philosophical sense (e.g., in the sense of Bentham's principle, ''Everyone to count for one and nobody for more than one''), and therefore society's resources should be divided equally.
3. *Equity* – People should be rewarded according to how much they produce (their output) or according to how much effort they expend.

It seems obvious that choosing one of these abstract principles of justice becomes transformed into an empathy-relevant task as soon as one imagines the consequences of various distribution systems for certain people. If one imagines the consequences and empathizes with poor people, one may conclude that any truly moral distribution system must guarantee everyone at least a minimal level of well-being and may end up affirming the principle of need or of equality. In other words, need and equality appear to have a caring component that may be activated when one empathizes with people whose welfare may be adversely affected by a distribution system, thus transforming the distributive justice issue, in part, into a caring issue.

Alternatively, one might empathize with the needs and expectations of people who work hard and save for their families, and as a result one might affirm the principle of distributing resources according to *effort*. Consider this response of a 13-year-old male research subject to the question, ''Why is it wrong to steal from a store?'' ''Because the people who own the store work hard for their money and they deserve to be able to spend it for their family. It's not fair; they sacrifice a lot and they make plans and then they lost it all because somebody who didn't work for it goes in and takes it.'' In this response, the subject has transformed an abstract moral question into an empathy-relevant one by imagining a particular victim. The response has a clear empathic-identification component: One empathizes with the other's effort, sacrifice, plans, and expectations about enjoying the fruits of his or her labor and with the other's disappointment and loss. There also appears to be an empathic-anger component, as well as a feeling of empathic injustice. The response thus suggests that effort, like need and equality, has a caring component, which in this case may be activated when one empathizes with people who work hard. Empathic affect may thus contribute to one's receptivity to the principle of equity based on effort. The size of the contribution depends on the extent of one's tendency to empathize with hardworking people rather than to derogate or compete with them or to empathize with the poor instead. Only research can provide the answer.

The principle of equity based on *output* is a different matter. Distributing resources on the basis of output seems to imply that the individual's welfare and internal state are irrelevant considerations. This would seem to rule out a direct link between empathy and output. There are at least two possible indirect links, however:

1. If output is assumed to reflect effort, as it often is, then my argument about the contribution of empathy to effort may also apply to output.
2. If distribution systems based on output motivate people to produce more, as many people believe, then there is more to go around and everyone benefits, including the poor (this reflects the trickle-down idea).[6]

It may thus be possible for empathic identification with the poor to lead one to affirm equity of output as a moral principle, but the route is circuitous and it seems far more likely that empathic identification with the poor will incline one toward the need or equality principles. A recent study of adults by Montada, Schmitt, & Dalbert (1986) supports this expectation. They found a positive correlation between a questionnaire measure of empathy and a preference for need, and a negative correlation between empathy and equity based on output. I found the same thing in an unpublished study of college students. When the subjects were asked to explain their choices, the high-empathy subjects tended to give explanations that included a concern for those who might be disadvantaged under other systems.

Need, equality, and equity are not mutually exclusive and may occur in different combinations. One principle may be dominant, the others playing a constraining role, as exemplified by the moral philosopher Rashdall (1907), who insisted that "equality is the right rule for distributive justice in the absence of any special reason for inequality" (p. 225); among the "special reasons" are need, output, and effort. Alternatively, a distribution system may be based on equity of output but may be regulated so that no one suffers if low output is due to forces beyond one's control (effort); no one, regardless of output, is excessively deprived (need); and vast discrepancies in wealth are not permitted (equality).

As an example of complexity, consider the first two drafts of the "Bishops Pastoral Letter on Catholic Social Teaching and the U.S. Economy" (1984, 1985). The analysis of the American economy in these documents appears to have been transformed into a situation relevant to empathic distress by imagining the economy's consequences for poor people. Thus the documents proclaim the Church's "tradition of compassion for the poor." Included are numerous statements describing in eloquent detail and empathic tone the plight of the poor – their "homelessness," "feelings of despair," "vulnerability," "the daily assaults on their dignity." The statement concludes that "gross inequalities are morally unjustifiable, particularly when millions lack even the basic necessities of life," and it characterizes present levels of unemployment and poverty as "morally unacceptable." In other words, the bishops' statement is an argument that starts with the expression of empathy and the compassion for the suffering poor. It attributes that suffering to the country's system of distributing resources. It then affirms need as a principle of justice and argues that the system is morally wrong because it is insensitive to so many people's needs. However, the statement also notes that absolute equality in distribution of resources, or distribution strictly according to need, is not necessary. In the end, it supports the principle of equity, pleads that equity be tempered with need and equality. The statement thus illustrates an important point: Empathy is more likely to operate in combination with other factors (economic, political, pragmatic) in deriving the complex moral prin' ples pertaining to distributive justice in modern society.

To summarize, in contemplating how society's resources should be distributed, one might focus on the implications for oneself and on the implications for others. For highly egoistic people, their own welfare is paramount and they are apt to be most receptive to distributive justice principles that coincide with their own condition: equity based on output if one is a higher producer, need or equality if one produces little. For empathic people, the welfare of others may be important and they may opt for need or equality even if they are high producers. Or, as seems more likely, a person's egoistic and empathic proclivities may both operate, the result being a distributive-justice orientation that combines the two – output tempered by need and equality, for example.

I have used the term *link* and suggested that empathic people opt for certain principles, but what exactly is the nature of the relation between empathy and moral principles and when and how does it become established? I comment only briefly on these matters. First, it seems obvious that, developmentally, empathic affects become part of most people's affective and motivational structures long before moral principles are seriously considered. At some point in late childhood or adolescence the individual is exposed to various moral principles, usually in a loose, scattered fashion. The "cafeteria" model seems appropriate here: The more empathic one is, the more receptive one should be to caring, need, equality, and perhaps effort.

Apart from this *developmental receptivity* to moral principles there is also the *activation* of moral principles already in one's repertoire. I have suggested that empathic affect arousal may activate related moral principles. It also seems likely that because of the congruence between empathy and principle discussed earlier, the two may be elicited independently. Either way, the resulting cooccurrence of empathy and principle may be expected to strengthen the bond between them, increasing the likelihood that both will be operative and will affect moral judgment in future situations. The influence of principles on moral judgment has been taken for granted (e.g., Kohlberg, 1969). Consider now the impact of empathic affects.

Empathy and moral judgment

Empathy's potential contribution to moral judgment is more complex than its contribution to principles, because here the relationship is mediated by complex reasoning in particular moral encounters. This reasoning is presumably based on moral principles, and it would simplify matters if there were a universal moral principle from which to derive the logically correct moral judgment for each situation. But, as I noted earlier, there are no universally accepted moral principles. We must therefore ask not only how people derive judgments from principles, but what determines which principle, if any, one chooses in the first place, that is, which principle is activated in a situation; and, when two principles are in conflict, what determines which one wins out. My thesis is that empathy plays a key role in all these situations.

David Hume (1751/1957) suggested more than 200 years ago that moral judgment ultimately depends on empathy. That is, moral judgment is based on feelings of satisfaction, pain, uneasiness, or disgust that result from the observer's empathy with the feelings of the person whose action is being appraised and with the feelings of those who are affected by this action. Hume's argument is as follows: First, it is obvious that we all applaud acts that further our own well-being and condemn acts that may harm us. Therefore, if we empathize with others we should applaud or condemn acts that help or harm others; and, unless we are abnormally callous, we will feel indignant (empathic anger) when someone willfully inflicts suffering on others. Empathy may thus guide the moral judgments we make about others. Furthermore, since people may be presumed to respond empathically to similar events in similar ways, empathy may thus provide the common informational input that impartial observers need to reach a consensus on moral judgments. Finally, Hume points out, we talk to one another about these events and respond empathically to each other's descriptions of the relevant acts and their consequences; these empathic responses provide further help in our efforts to reach a consensus. Although Hume does not discuss justice, my notion of empathic injustice can be used to apply Hume's argument to justice: We obviously feel indignant when we do not receive what we deserve because of our efforts or our output; it follows that, if we empathize with others, we should feel indignant when someone else does not receive what he or she deserves because of their effort or output.

Hume's view that empathy provides a reliable basis for consensus in moral judgment has been criticized by Rawls (1971), who argues that empathy lacks the situational sensitivity necessary for achieving a rational consensus. My own empathy scheme, summarized earlier, may solve this problem in part by assuming that at the most advanced empathic level one processes a network of cues that includes a knowledge of the other's life condition beyond the immediate situation. Mature empathy thus reflects a sensitivity to subtle differences in the severity and quality of the consequences that different actions might have for different people. It thus seems clear that empathy can contribute to informed moral judgments. Hume's claim that empathy provides the ultimate basis for reaching *consensus* on moral judgments is another matter, one that requires empirical testing.

Empathy's contribution to moral judgment can be illustrated by anecdotes and hypothetical illustrations. The examples I cited earlier are cases in point. The woman in *Uncle Tom's Cabin* not only affirmed a general caring principle but also used it as the basis for making the moral judgment that a law that violates this principle is morally wrong. The Bishops' Pastoral Letter not only affirmed a justice principle that incorporated need and appears to have been a direct outcome of empathic reasoning based on identification with the poor, but it also used that principle as the basis for the moral judgment that the country's allocation system is morally wrong because it creates many victims. Furthermore, the white Southern schoolboy incident not only illustrates empathic injustice, but also shows how empathic identification with a particular victim can, over time, foster a change in attitude toward a previously accepted social institution – racial segregation – with the result that one now judges that the institution is wrong.

In the research on moral judgment and decision making, subjects are typically asked how someone facing a particular moral dilemma should act and why such action would be better or worse than other actions. Or they may be asked to identify the moral issue in the dilemma. The situation is different in real life. To be sure, some occupations may require people to make judgments of others and decide whether they should receive certain punishments or rewards (such as a promotion or pay increase). For the most part, however, people's moral encounters do not begin with such a cognitive task. More likely, one's moral precepts are apt to be activated when one encounters someone in danger or distress and feels a conflict between the desire to help that individual and the desire to continue to pursue one's own goals of the moment; when one feels outraged by someone's inhumane or unjust treatment of another; when one discovers that one's actions have harmed another or that one's contemplated action may harm someone; when one realizes that one's contemplated action on behalf of someone may operate to the detriment of someone else; when one is tempted, or under external pressure, to act in a way that violates another's reasonable expectations (e.g., by breaking a promise, violating a trust, telling a lie).[7] Culture plays a role in all this, as does history. Deciding whether to have an abortion has recently become a moral dilemma (in which personal needs are placed against the violent consequences to the fetus) for some people who in the past might have considered it a moral dilemma (in which personal needs are placed against the physical danger to oneself). Advances in medical technology have added an element of moral complexity to the medical practitioner's former, relatively simple goal of prolonging life: Organ transplants save lives, but cost–benefit analysis may show that more lives could be saved if the money were spent differently.

There are many variations on these themes. What impresses me is that most moral dilemmas seem to involve victims or potential victims (and beneficiaries) of one's own actions. This means that in the course of thinking about what to do in these situations one may often be confronted with the image, or idea, of someone being helped or harmed by one's own action. This appears to be true even when one is not the actor but is compelled to judge or evaluate the action of others. It follows that empathy may often be aroused in moral judgment and decision making in life; and the empathy aroused, if my previous argument for a link between empathy and moral principles is correct, may not only have a direct effect on moral judgment and reasoning, but may also serve to activate one's moral principles and bring them to bear in the moral reasoning process, more or less along the lines indicated in the examples cited throughout this chapter.

In sum, I am arguing that most moral dilemmas in life may arouse empathy because they involve victims – seen or unseen, present or future. Since empathy is closely related to most moral principles, the arousal of empathy should activate moral principles, and thus – directly, and indirectly through these principles – have an effect on moral judgment and reasoning. This may also be true of moral reasoning in abstract situations, such as Kohlberg's moral dilemmas, provided the person making the judgment empathically identifies with relevant characters in them. Here are some examples of subjects' responses to moral questions that seem to reflect empathic identification operating in the service of moral judgment (Hoffman, 1970). The moral dilemma is an adaptation of Kohlberg's story about two men – Al, who broke into a store and stole $500, and Joe, who lied to a known benefactor about needing $500 for an operation. The subjects were asked who did worse, and why. Most answers, as expected, pertained to the need for law and order, the Ten Commandments, and the possibilities of getting caught. Although the item did not highlight a victim, one quarter of the subjects, who ranged from 11 years to middle age, seemed to transform it into one involving empathic identification with a victim – either an immediate victim of one of the men's actions or potential future victims.

For example, Joe's action was said to be worse because he made the benefactor feel betrayed by someone he trusted, because he made the benefactor lose faith in people and become bitter, because he misused the benefactor's faith and pity, or because people who really needed help would no longer be able to get it. Al's action was said to be worse because the storeowner worked hard for the money, saved for his family, and needed the money – this is the kind of response I described in discussing equity of effort. Note that these empathic-identification responses more than doubled in frequency when the focus of the question changed from the actor ("Who did worse?") to the observer ("Which would make you feel worse, if you did it?"). The empathic-identification responses in which Joe's act was deemed worse might appear to reflect a simple liking for the kind benefactor – a personal bias or halo effect rather than a moral judgment – but this is not the case. When asked "what kind of person" the benefactor was, the subjects who gave these empathic-identification responses were as likely as the other subjects to criticize him for being foolish or naive. In other words, they empathized with him and felt it was wrong to deceive him, although they were critical of him. These responses are more convincing as *moral* judgments because they transcend personal feeling for the person harmed.

Empathic bias and how to reduce it

The case for empathy thus far looks rather strong. There are problems, however, that might appear to limit empathy's contribution to all but the simplest of situations. One is that empathy may be biased in several ways. First, there is research evidence that observers are more empathic to victims who are familiar and similar to themselves than to victims who are different, although, I hasten to add, they are usually empathic to victims who are different – just less so (Feshbach & Roe, 1968; Klein, 1971; Krebs, 1970). Second, it seems that people are more apt to be empathically aroused by someone's distress in the immediate situation than by distress that they know is being experienced by someone somewhere else or that is likely to be experienced in the future. There is no empirical evidence for such a here-and-now bias, but it seems likely in view of the fact that several of the arousal processes noted in Table 4.1, especially the involuntary processes (conditioning, association, mimicry) are dependent on immediate situational and personal cues. These cues are absent when someone's distress occurs somewhere else or when it is likely to occur in the future.

These biases constitute a flow in empathic morality and raise questions about its applicability in situations involving conflicting moral claims, that is, situations in which one must make a moral judgment and decision and the welfare of several people or groups depends on one's action, but only some of these people are familiar or present in the immediate situation. First, is it a fatal flaw? The answer depends on two things: whether there is an alternative morality that is bias-free, and whether the bias in empathic morality can be eliminated or minimized. Regarding the first point, the most likely alternative is cognitive morality in the Kohlberg tradition, which states that one can solve moral dilemmas by applying the universal principle of justice to the particular situation and by reasoning out the solution. There are problems with this formulation. As I noted, it is unlikely that justice can be considered universal; in any case, there are several other principles beside justice, and justice itself has several variants. The question that follows is what determines which of these principles is chosen, or activated, in a particular moral dilemma? One's socialization into a particular culture or subgroup would seem to be a reasonable answer, as would one's needs and predilections of the moment, contextual cues, and perhaps the empathic affect that may be aroused along the lines I suggested. The principle chosen may also serve as a rationalization, not necessarily conscious, for one's own interests, as long suggested by philosophers in the tradition of emotive theory (Ayer, 1936; Brandt, 1979; Edwards, 1955).

Aside from these biases in choosing a moral principle, decades of research on ethnic and racial prejudice suggest that one's principles may be applied differentially to members of one's own group and members of other groups. Within one's group, one's moral principles are likely to be applied differentially to people who are present or absent, as I suggested may also be true of empathy. Moreover, the reasoning process, too, is open to question. There is considerable evidence that reasoning based on factual knowledge about the physical world is often unreliable, partly because of the human tendency to employ "availability" and other error-producing heuristics (Tversky & Kahneman, 1973). Surely the same must be true of reasoning in the moral domain. Thus, although this notion may seem counterintuitive, there are no a priori grounds for assuming that cognitive morality is any freer of bias than empathic morality. Whether it is freer of bias is an empirical question that awaits research.

The second question about the applicability of empathic morality is whether empathic bias can be reduced to a manageable level. The answer here is more complex. First, a correction for bias toward the here and now is built into my empathy scheme, as I illustrated earlier with the terminally ill person who is happy in the immediate situation. However, in order to be able to empathize with the victim's plight beyond the immediate situation, the observer requires information about the victim's condition in other situations, and this information must enter the observer's consciousness at the appropriate time. If the observer lacks the necessary information, it must be given to him or her; if the observer has it stored in memory, something in the situation must prime it so that it will be recalled. Furthermore, the observer must be sufficiently advanced developmentally to be able to process the information and realize that it may be a more compelling index of the victim's welfare than the victim's contradictory current behavior.

This brings us to the question of the role of moral education in reducing empathic bias, which I can only comment on briefly here. One thing moral education can do is teach people a simple rule of thumb: Look beyond the immediate situation and ask questions such as "What kind of experiences does the other person have in various situations beyond the immediate one?" "How will my action affect him or her, not only now but in the future?" and "Are there other people, present or absent, who might be affected by my actions?" If children learn to ask these questions, they should be able to enhance their awareness of all those who may be affected by their actions, whether present or not. In addition, to compensate for the here-and-now bias in intensity of empathic affect, children might be encouraged to imagine how they would feel in the place of those others. And, finally, a positive value might be placed on spatial and temporal impartiality, and children might be encouraged, insofar as possible, to give equal consideration to all of those who may be affected by their actions. Children cannot be expected to engage in this laborious process all the time (nor can adults), but with such moral education their empathic responses should at least be less exclusively confined to the here and now and should more closely approach the ideal of spatial and temporal neutrality.

As for the familiarity–similarity bias, Hume (1751/1957) declared that it was perfectly natural for people to empathize more with their kin than with strangers and that doing this was not necessarily incompatible with being moral. He also said that efforts must be made to minimize this bias and suggested that society can be organized so as to minimize it: People, each having a particular bias and knowing about their own and the other's bias, can devise systems of social rules that minimize bias and encourage impartiality. To this I would add a moral education curriculum that stresses the common humanity of all people and includes efforts to raise people's levels of empathy for outgroup members. Such efforts might include direct face-to-face cultural contact and training in role-taking procedures that are vivid enough to generate empathic feeling for people in circumstances that are different from their own. The combination of rule systems and empathy-enhancing moral education should expand the range of people to whom individuals can respond empathically, thus reducing familiarity–similarity bias.

How empathic bias may be reduced in life can be illustrated in the task of writing a letter of recommendation for a former student. When composing such a letter, we may empathize with the student, to whom we feel close. Thus when negative things about the student come to mind, we may experience a moral conflict in trying to decide whether to include this negative information and hurt his chances or withhold it and violate both our standards of honesty and our commitment to the collegial system of evaluating job applications. Our empathy for the student may lead us to withhold the information and tolerate the resulting guilt feeling. Or, we may also empathize with our peer colleagues, who need the information and are counting on us to be objective and tell the truth. Obviously the moral conflict would be more complex if in addition one had to consider whether one might be betraying the trust of these unseen colleagues.[8] We may even go one step further and empathize with people whom we do not know at all and who will probably never see our letter but whose welfare may nevertheless be affected by it, namely, the other applicants for the job. This situation would further complicate the moral conflict. Regardless of our final decision, the multiple empathizing, which clearly contributes to the moral conflict, may also reduce the potency of our initial empathic bias in favor of the particular student.

Here is an even more complex example adapted from an illustration used by Noddings (1984). In considering whether to sponsor a favorite graduate student's research proposal that requires deception, a professor might empathize with the student's pride in a well-written proposal, the student's fear that months of work will be wasted if the professor rejects the proposal, and the student's eagerness to get on with the job. This empathy for the student may be strong enough to motivate the professor to sponsor the proposal. So far, there appears to be no moral conflict. But the situation may be transformed into a moral conflict if the professor's belief that deception is wrong is activated. Deception may be too abstract a concept to elicit enough affect to compete with the professor's empathy for the student. But if the professor is aware of this fact and also of his or her empathic bias, he or she may try to compensate for the bias and penetrate the abstractness by thinking about subjects being harmed by the research – by imagining how a hypothetical subject, perhaps a person he or she cares about very much, might respond to the experimental manipulation. If the danger perceived is great enough, the professor's anticipatory empathic distress may be so intense that despite his or her empathy for the graduate student (and the fact that the proposal is otherwise satisfactory), the professor might refuse to sponsor the student's research. The professor's empathic revulsion might even be so great as to compel him or her to propose guidelines for the control of all research requiring deception. This example illustrates how the combination of biases – for the familiar and the here and now, all favoring the student – may be overcome by a more or less deliberate effort to empathize with exemplars of other people whose welfare may be affected by one's action.

As in the letter-of-recommendation example, the professor might go a step further and empathize with people who are unseen and perhaps unknown but whose welfare may be indirectly at stake – namely, other researchers whose careers might be jeopardized by excessive constraints on research or other people who may ultimately benefit from the research. As a result of this multiple empathizing, the professor might refuse to sponsor the student's research but might refrain from making rules that will bind other investigators. The outcome may be entirely different, of course, but whatever it is, the process illustrates, first, how one's initial empathic response may be biased toward familiar individuals and toward the here and now, and second, how the effects of that bias may be counteracted by empathizing with people who are not present but whose welfare may nevertheless be affected by one's actions.

This all sounds like traditional utilitarian moral reasoning: Consider the future as well as immediate consequences of one's action for people who are absent as well as present. But we should not lose sight of the role of empathy in providing both substantive input and motivation at various points in the reasoning process. In any case, it seems reasonable to conclude that although empathic morality may be flawed because of certain biases, it may be no more flawed than the most apparent alternative, cognitive morality in the Kohlberg tradition. Furthermore, empathic bias appears to be controllable, although to control it one may have to add a cognitive perspective that attempts to give equal weight to all people whose welfare may be affected by one's actions. With this perspective, empathy may not only contribute to moral principles but may also play a constructive role in complex moral judgments and decision making.

Moral principles as "hot cognitions"

I have suggested that empathy contributes to caring and most principles of justice through empathic identification with victims and potential victims of society and its institutions. What are the circumstances in which this process occurs? One possibility is that it occurs in the normal course of development in children who have been socialized to be empathic. Empathic socialization begins in early childhood (Hoffman, 1982b), but it is not until late childhood or early adolescence that children are able to comprehend the meaning of moral principles. It follows from my previous argument, then, that, to the degree that children are empathic, they should be receptive to the principles of caring, need-based justice, equality, and perhaps effort-based justice. In this cafeteria model, people are disposed to select from the moral principles available in society, those that fit their empathic dispositions. One internalizes the principles with little external pressure, because they are in keeping with one's empathic leanings.

The moral encounters one has through life may also play a significant role, because of the empathic affects often aroused. These empathic affects are most likely to be aroused in bystander situations in which victims are salient from the start. But they may also be aroused, as I suggested, in other situations in which victims do not become apparently until later on (e.g., when writing a letter of recommendation). In either case, the empathic affects may dispose one to act on the victim's behalf; such a response would be in opposition to one's egoistic motives in the situation and thus would instigate one type of moral conflict.[9]

A moral conflict is essentially a conflict between alternative courses of action. Therefore it seems reasonable to assume that, when one experiences a moral conflict, one inevitably wonders what to do, considers alternative actions, and anticipates consequences for others. Such thoughts may not only bring to mind victims and potential victims, thus arousing empathic affects, but may also bring to mind the guidelines to action, including relevant moral principles (caring, need, etc.) and associated norms to which one has been previously exposed and that have been stored in memory. The empathic affect and moral principles may be evoked independently, or empathic affect may be aroused first and then may prime the moral principles. Either way, the cooccurrence of a principle and empathic affect should produce a bond between them (or strengthen any existing bond). The result may be that the principle, even if learned initially in a "cool," didactic context (e.g., abstract intellectual discourse in which victims are not salient), acquires an affective charge. An interesting reversed sequence may then become possible: In future cool contexts, for example, in answering moral judgment research questions, the abstract principle may be activated first and this may trigger empathic affect. Such a sequence may explain the emotionality in my subject's explanation of why it is wrong to steal (see the section Empathy and distributive justice). In other words, as a consequence of being coupled with empathic affect in moral encounters, a moral principle may be encoded and stored as an affectively charged representation – as a "hot" cognition or category.

What exactly is represented in such a "hot" category? Probably anything that has been associated with the principle and its accompanying empathic affects in life, including verbal descriptions of the principle's content, as well as events in which the principle is violated – events involving victims, culprits, and actions that conform or violate the principle. These representations are apt to be charged with the empathic affects associated with them in one's experiences; and when one subsequently encounters an instance fitting one of these representations, one may be expected to respond to it with the category's affect (as is assumed to occur in general when hot categories are activated; see Fiske, 1982; Hoffman,

1986). Empirical evidence that moral principles are encoded as hot categories is lacking, but a study by Arsenio and Ford (1985) suggests that single instances of the violation of a moral principle may be so encoded. The findings – young children experienced negative affect when told stories in which a child acts inconsiderately toward another, and their later recall of these stories was aided by the induction of negative affect – suggest that violations of particular principles may be encoded as hot cognitions. Perhaps the same is true of categories of violations.

A potentially important implication of all this is that a person's affective and cognitive responses in moral encounters are due not only to the immediate stimulus event (cues from the situation and from the victim), but also to the affectively charged moral principles that one's action and other aspects of the stimulus event may activate. The empathic affect elicited in moral encounters may thus have a stimulus-driven component and a component driven by the activated, affectively charged principle. This may have important implications for prosocial action. In some situations, for example, the empathic affect elicited by the stimulus event alone may be too weak, perhaps because of a paucity of relevant cues from victims, to override the egoistic motives that may also be operating. But if one's caring principle were activated, its associated empathic affect might be released. This category-driven component, alone or in combination with the stimulus-driven component, may be powerful enough to exceed the threshold needed to override the egoistic motives. Activating one's moral principles may thus provide an additional source of empathic affect, with a resulting increase in one's overall motivation for moral action. The obverse side to this should also be mentioned. In some situations, the empathic affect elicited by the stimulus event alone may be so intense that it produces the disruptive effects of "empathic overarousal" (Hoffman, 1978). In these cases, if one's caring principle were activated and the stimulus event assimilated to it, the category-driven component might *reduce* empathic affect intensity to a more manageable level. Thus, the activation of an affectively charged moral principle may have a heightening or leveling effect and in general might function to stabilize one's level of empathic affect arousal in different situations.

In sum, empathy may play a significant role in determining whether one becomes committed to a moral principle by giving the principle an affective base. But once the principle is in place, activating it in future moral encounters may increase or decrease the intensity of one's empathic affective response. Moral principles may thus make it more likely that moral conflict will lead to effective moral action.

The hot-cognition concept also has implications for memory, as there is reason to believe that both affect and cognition contribute to memory. Recent research suggests that affect in general is an extremely powerful retrieval cue (Bower,

1981). In addition, I have argued that empathic affect associated with moral concepts acquired in early discipline encounters contributes to remembering (and internalizing) these moral concepts (Hoffman, 1983). The Arsenio and Ford (1985) study supports this view. On the cognitive side, a moral principle is, in part, a semantically organized category of knowledge (or prototype). Like other categories, it encompasses many instances and is shaped and made more complex over time in the process of accommodating to new instances. The fact that categorical knowledge is highly enduring in memory, for reasons spelled out by Tulving (1972), should therefore apply to moral principles. Thus, both the affective and cognitive components of a moral principle should help maintain it in memory, keeping it available for activation in future moral encounters.

Concluding remarks

My aim in this chapter has been to demonstrate the possible role of empathy in a comprehensive moral theory. To this end I have argued as follows:

1. When one witnesses someone in distress, one may respond empathically, that is, with affect more appropriate to the other's situations than to one's own. The most likely response is empathic or sympathetic distress, but, depending on the available cues and one's prior knowledge about the victim, one may make certain causal and other attributions that may transform these feelings into empathic anger, guilt, and empathic injustice.

2. The essential features of this bystander model, including the five empathic affects it can generate, do not require a victim to be physically present because human beings have the capacity for representation and represented events have the power to evoke empathic as well as direct affect. What is required is that a victim or potential victim be imagined, as may occur when one is told or reads about someone's plight, is engaged in conversation or argument about moral issues, or even makes moral judgments about hypothetical situations in a research project. Occasions like these, though cognitively and motivationally more complex than most bystander situations, may arouse empathic affects in a similar way. In other situations, one's own actions are at issue, and when one acts or contemplates acting in a way that may affect other people's welfare, imagining the consequences for them may be expected to arouse empathic affect. Thus many, perhaps most, moral encounters appear to involve victims and potential victims (and beneficiaries, although I focus on victims) and can be counted on to evoke empathic affects.

3. Empathic affects are by and large congruent with caring and most forms of justice. These are the prevailing moral principles in Western society and may be assumed to be the part of people's knowledge structures that are most often brought to bear in moral encounters. The content of these principles also makes

them relevant, in varying degrees, to issues involving victims. The moral principles may therefore be activated either by the empathic affects aroused in a moral encounter or by the relevance of their content to the victim dimension of the moral encounter. Either way, the resulting cooccurrence of the empathic affect and moral principle creates a bond between them that is strengthened in subsequent cooccurrences. Moral principles, even when initially learned in "cool" didactic contexts, may in this way acquire an affective charge and take on the characteristics of a hot cognition.

4. An important implication of the hot-cognition concept is that when a moral principle is subsequently activated even in didactic or research contexts, empathic affect may be aroused. Another implication is that empathic affects aroused in moral encounters may have a stimulus-driven and a category-driven component. The category-driven component may have a heightening or leveling effect on the intensity of the stimulus-driven component in any given moral encounter. The overall result may be to help stabilize the individual's level of empathic affective reactions in different situations over time.

5. Empathic affect may also make important contributions to moral judgment and decision making. The contribution may be direct, or it may be mediated by the moral principles activated by the affects. In either case, the contribution may be limited by empathic bias toward the familiar or toward the here and now. However, these biases may be reduced by socialization that highlights the commonalities among human groups, places high value on impartiality, and trains people in the techniques of multiple empathizing, that is, empathizing not only with people in the vicinity who may be affected by one's actions, but also with people who are absent.

A neglected question in morality research is that of why a person applies one principle and not another in a moral encounter. Cognitive moral theories have difficulty answering this question because they lack affective and motivational concepts. My suggestion that empathic affect may shed some light on this question may seem counter intuitive. Why should affect influence the selection of a principle? This is not a simple, unadorned affect, however, as I hope I have made clear, but an empathic affect informed by one's cognitive sense of others, one's relevant causal attributions, and, in the ideal case, one's knowledge of the importance of being impartial. Furthermore, the affects may be subject to conscious efforts to correct their characteristic biases, efforts such as empathically identifying with people who are absent as well as present, which may provide a number of relevant empathic affective inputs that are then worked into the moral reasoning and judgment process. These inputs, when congruent with one another, may lead directly to the final moral judgment or decision. When the inputs are contradictory (e.g., empathic joy on contemplating an action that will make someone who is present happy versus empathic distress on recognizing that the same action may harm someone who is absent), one must somehow weigh the relative importance of each. This may be a cognitive weighing, or one may base one's moral judgment on the input that includes the most intense affect, as in my example of the professor whose empathic concern for future research subjects finally outweighed his empathic concern for his graduate student.

My theoretical argument does not extend to this final phase of the moral reasoning process in which the importance of various inputs is weighed – not only empathic inputs but also moral principles and pragmatic considerations. Rather, my objective is to make sure that all relevant inputs, including empathy-based inputs, are taken into account. In this sense, my approach, as noted earlier, fits squarely in the long Utilitarian tradition in Western philosophy, which states that what is good is what benefits most people. Utilitarians often say that in any moral encounter one should consider the potential harm or benefit an action might have for all people – present or absent. I suggest that empathic affect makes an important contribution toward this end.

Before concluding, I want to correct a statement I made at the beginning of the chapter. There *is* an overriding principle on which there may be close to universal agreement, at least in Western philosophy. However, it has no particular content, but simply states that, whatever one's moral principle it must be applied impartially – to strangers as well as kin, to people who are absent as well as present, and to the future as well as the present implications of action.[10] This principle has been implicit throughout my argument.

Finally, I am *not* saying that empathic affects are an adequate substitute for moral principles or that actions guided by empathic affects automatically qualify as moral actions, as Blum (1980) and Gilligan (1982) seem to imply. According to Gilligan, an empathy-based caring morality is equal, and in many ways superior, to an equal-rights-based justice morality – even though justice morality proceeds from the premise that everyone should be treated the same, whereas caring morality does not require such impartiality. Gilligan's examples of caring do not reflect the complexities of having to care for two or more people, when one can only care for one and must make a choice, nor does she deal with familiarity and here-and-now-biases. Consider a doctor who cares for and goes out of the way to give all of his or her consulting time to a particular patient, but neglects others who are equally in need of attention. This doctor is obviously empathic and cares a lot, to the point of setting aside personal needs, but I would have difficulty calling this moral behavior. On the other hand, I do not go as far as Kohlberg and others, who seem to consider acts moral only if they derive from moral principles. The issue is complex, and I do not have an answer except to suggest a development criterion. The doctor in question may not be acting morally, but a young child, who, out of sympathetic distress, goes out of his or her way to help someone, may be acting morally.

I *am* saying that empathic affect may contribute to acceptance of moral principles in relevant situations and to the motivation to act in accordance with moral principles. Empathic affects may also contribute inputs to moral reasoning based on principles, and thus to moral decision making and moral judgment. My argument is not foolproof, as it is based mainly on anecdotal and hypothetical examples showing that people's moral reasoning and judgment sometimes have a quality of personal concern for others that seems to reflect an underlying empathic identification with them. There is also the research mentioned earlier showing that empathy correlates positively with a preference for need-based equity and negatively with a preference for output-based equity as principles of distributive justice. This research is encouraging but limited in applicability because causal inferences cannot be made (although empathy obviously predates moral principles developmentally and may therefore be the more likely antecedent). Furthermore, the research says nothing about process. We need experimental studies of how empathic and sympathetic distress, guilt, and empathic anger affect one's receptivity to certain moral principles as well as the moral reasoning and judgment used in applying these principles. Longitudinal research is also needed to explain how these empathic affects contribute developmentally to an internalized commitment to moral principles and to the moral reasoning and judgments based on them.

Notes

1. Utilitarians, for example, may view both justice and the social order as subprinciples instrumental in attaining impartial benevolence.
2. This definition differs from others, which require a close match between the affective response of the target person and that of the observer. The advantages of my definition have been discussed elsewhere (Hoffman, 1982a).
3. Empathic anger should be distinguished from the type of self-righteous indignation that serves to tout one's own moral superiority.
4. I thank Inge Bretherton for this example.
5. This type of guilt feeling should be distinguished from Freudian guilt, which results not from awareness of harming someone in the present, but from activation of early repressed childhood anxieties about losing parental love; it is often unconscious and may be experienced when no one else is involved (masturbation guilt).
6. There is reason to question this assumption. Though output-oriented societies apparently produce more than other societies, such comparisons may ignore important uncontrolled variables. Experimental research by Deutsch (1985), in which relevant variables were controlled, raises serious questions about whether distribution of resources on the basis of output actually does produce greater overall output. If it does not, is there any other reason for considering output equity a justice principle?
7. We may feel guilty about violating the expectations of others intentionally, or unwittingly, owing to our normal habits. We are apt to feel far guiltier, however, about breaking an actual promise, because in this case we not only violate another's expectations but we are responsible for having created those expectations in the first place. (We may, of course, feel an obligation

to keep a promise even if no one will be injured if we don't; this type of moral feeling appears to fall outside the domain of empathic morality.)

8. I stress the role of empathy in all of these examples, but we may be concerned about honesty and fairness without empathizing.
9. Other types of moral conflict involve opposition between principles, in which one's egoistic needs may not be an issue.
10. A contemporary Western philosopher who plays down the importance of impartiality is Blum (1980), who argues that it is morally appropriate to favor one's friends.

References

Arsenio, W. F., & Ford, M. E. (1985). The role of affective information in social–cognitive development: Children's differentiation of moral and conventional events. *Merrill–Palmer Quarterly, 31,* 1–17.

Ayer, A. J. (1936). *Language, truth and logic.* London: Gollancz.

Bishops' pastoral letter on Catholic social teaching and the U.S. economy: First draft (1984). *Origins, 14,* Nos. 22, 23.

Bishops' pastoral letter on Catholic social teaching and the U.S. economy: Second draft (1985). *Origins, 15,* No. 17.

Blum, L. A. (1980). *Friendship, altruism and morality.* London: Routledge & Kegan Paul.

Bower, G. H. (1981). Mood and memory. *American Psychologist, 36,* 129–148.

Brandt, R. A. (1979). *A theory of the good and the right.* New York: Oxford University Press.

Coles, R. (1986). *The moral life of children.* Boston: Atlantic Monthly Press.

Deutsch, M. (1985). *Distributive justice: A social psychological perspective.* New Haven, CT: Yale University Press.

Edwards, P. (1955). *The logic of moral discourse.* New York: Free Press.

Feshbach, N. D., & Roe, K. (1968). Empathy in six- and seven-year olds. *Child Development, 39,* 133–145.

Fiske, S. T. (1982). Schema-triggered affect: Applications to social perception. In S. Fiske and M. Clark (Eds.), *Cognition and affect: The Carnegie-Mellon Symposium* (pp. 55–78). Hillsdale, NJ: Erlbaum.

Gilligan, C. (1982). *In a different voice.* Cambridge MA: Harvard University Press.

Harris, M. B., & Siebel, C. E. (1975). Affect, aggression, and altruism. *Developmental Psychology, 11,* 623–627.

Hoffman, M. L. (1970). Conscience, personality, and socialization techniques. *Human Development, 13,* 90–126.

Hoffman, M. L. (1975a). Developmental synthesis of affect and cognition and its implications for altruistic motivation. *Developmental Psychology, 11,* 607–622.

Hoffman, M. L. (1975b). Sex differences in moral internalization. *Journal of Personality and Social Psychology, 32,* 720–729.

Hoffman, M. L. (1977). Sex differences in empathy and related behaviors. *Psychological Bulletin, 84,* 712–722.

Hoffman, M. L. (1978). Empathy, its development and prosocial implications. In C. B. Keasey (Ed.), *Nebraska Symposium on Motivation* (Vol. 25, pp. 169–218). Lincoln: University of Nebraska Press.

Hoffman, M. L. (1980). Moral development in adolescence. In J. Adelson (Ed.), *Handbook of adolescent psychology,* (pp. 295–343). New York: John Wiley & Sons.

Hoffman, M. L. (1981). Is altruism part of human nature? *Journal of Personality and Social Psychology, 40,* 121–137.

Hoffman, M. L. (1982a). Measurement of empathy. In C. Izard (Ed.), *Measurement of emotions in infants and children* (pp. 279–296). New York: Cambridge University Press.

Hoffman, M. L. (1982b). Development of prosocial motivation: Empathy and guilt. In N. Eisenberg, (Ed.), *Development of prosocial behavior* (pp. 281–313). New York: Academic Press.

Hoffman, M. L. (1982c). Affect and moral development. In D. Cicchetti (Ed.), *New directions in child development* (pp. 83–103). San Francisco: Jossey-Bass.

Hoffman, M. L. (1983). Affective and cognitive processes in moral internalization: An information processing approach. In E. T. Higgins, D. Ruble, & W. Hartup (Eds.), *Social cognition and social development: A socio-cultural perspective* (pp. 236–274). New York: Cambridge University Press.

Hoffman, M. L. (1984a). Interaction of affect and cognition in empathy. In C. Izard, J. Kagan, & R. Zajonc (Eds.), *Emotions, cognition, and behavior* (pp. 103–131). New York: Cambridge University Press.

Hoffman, M. L. (1984b). Empathy, its limitations, and its role in a comprehensive moral theory. In J. Gewirtz & W. Kurtines (Eds.), *Morality, moral development, and moral behavior* (pp. 283–302). New York: John Wiley.

Hoffman, M. L. (1986). Affect, cognition, and motivation. In R. M. Sorrentino and E. T. Higgins (Eds.), *Handbook of motivation and cognition: Foundations of social behavior* (pp. 244–275). New York: Guilford.

Hoffman, M. L. (in press). Empathy and prosocial activism. In N. Eisenberg, J. Reykowski, & E. Staub (Eds.), *Social and moral values*. Hillsdale, NJ: Erlbaum.

Hume, D. (1957). *An inquiry concerning the principle of morals* (Vol. 4). New York: Liberal Arts Press. (Original work published 1751).

Izard, C. E. (1977). *Human emotions*. New York: Plenum Press.

Kaplan, E. A. (in press). Women, morality, and social change: A historical perspective. In N. Eisenberg, J. Reykowski, & E. Staub (Eds.) *Social and moral values*. Hillsdale, NJ: Erlbaum.

Kaplan, L. J. (1977). The basic dialogue and the capacity of empathy. In N. Freedman & S. Grand (Eds.), *Communicative structures and psychic structures*. New York: Plenum.

Klein, R. (1971). Some factors influencing empathy in six- and seven-year-old children varying in ethnic background (Doctoral dissertation, University of California, Los Angeles, 1970). *Dissertation Abstracts International, 31,* 3960A. (University Microfilms No. 71-3862)

Kohlberg, L. (1969). The cognitive developmental approach. In D. A. Goslin (Ed.), *Handbook of socialization theory and research*. Chicago: Rand McNally.

Krebs, D. L. (1970). Altruism: An examination of the concept and a review of the literature. *Psychological Bulletin, 73,* 258–303.

Mill, J. S. (1979). *Utilitarianism*. Cambridge, MA: Hackett (original work published 1861).

Montada, L., Schmitt, M., & Dalbert, C. (1986). Thinking about justice and dealing with one's privileges; A study on existential guilt. In H. W. Bierhoff, R. Cohen, & J. Greenberg (Eds.), *Justice in social relations*. New York: Plenum Press.

Murphy, L. B. (1937). *Social behavior and child personality*. New York: Columbia University Press.

Noddings, N. (1984). *Caring*. Berkeley: University of California Press.

Rashdall, H. (1907). *The theory of good and evil*. New York: Oxford University Press.

Rawls, J. A. (1971). *A theory of justice*. Cambridge, MA: Harvard University Press.

Razran, G. (1971). *Mind in evolution*. Boston: Houghton Mifflin.

Stotland, E. (1969). Exploratory investigations of empathy. In L. Berkowitz (Ed.), *Advances in experimental social psychology* (Vol. 4). New York: Academic Press.

Tulving, E. (1972). Episodic and semantic memory. In E. Tulving & W. Donaldson (Eds.), *Organization of memory*. New York: Academic Press.

Tversky, A. & Kahneman, D. (1973). Availability: A heuristic for judging frequency and probability. *Cognitive Psychology, 5,* 207–232.

Weiner, B. (1985). "Spontaneous" causal thinking. *Psychological Bulletin, 97,* 74–84.
Zahn-Waxler, C., Radke-Yarrow, M., & King, R. A. (1979). Childrearing and children's prosocial initiations towards victims of distress. *Child Development, 50,* 319–330.
Zanna, M. P., Kiesler, C. A., & Pilkonis, P. A. (1970). Positive and negative affect established by classical conditioning. *Journal of Personality and Social Psychology, 14,* 321–328.

5   Empathy and psychotherapy

James Marcia

Empathy and psychotherapy within a developmental context

One way to study the function of empathy in psychotherapy is to survey psychotherapies in order to determine whether and how each of them considers empathy. I do not think that we would learn much from that approach. Hence, I have adopted a different, more perilous, course, but one that may give us some new directions for thinking about empathy and psychotherapy. I discuss both psychotherapy and empathy within a developmental context. *Developmental* here refers to a point of view similar to the genetic aspect of psychoanalytic theory, that is, to understanding adult personality in terms of the conditions of childhood.

In the first part of the chapter, I define psychotherapy and empathy and briefly examine their relationship in general terms. Next, I discuss empathy within the context of the following personality developmental theories: Freudian, Sullivanian, object-relations, client-centered, and behavioral. I then describe the role of empathy more specifically within the psychotherapies related to the above theories, including bioenergetics. I conclude with some personal observations on empathy drawn from the general practice of psychotherapy within an ego psychoanalytic framework.

Psychotherapy

Psychotherapy, viewed developmentally, is not a protagonist-rescuing deus ex machina, but a kind of psychological dietary supplement in an ongoing ego developmental process involving an interaction between a more or less nourishing environment and a more or less adapted individual. Hartmann (1964) and Erikson (1950) have discussed the "epigenetic principle" – an assertion that a ground plan for the development of ego skills exists at birth and will be manifested in the more or less successful resolution of a series of age (stage)-specific crises, given an "average expectable environment." The exact constituents of that average expectable environment depend upon the particular theorist's view of the nature and psychological requirements of childhood. However, average expectable environment is taken here to mean societal conditions ("institutions" and "rituals"; Erikson, 1982) that make demands and furnish rewards in mutuality with the growing individual's abilities and needs. When this environment–individual relationship is asynchronous, an ego developmental (psychosocial) stage is resolved toward the negative pole (e.g., at infancy, the resolution reflects more mistrust than basic trust). Psychotherapy enters this developmental relationship as the provision of *better-than-average* expectable environment. The psychotherapist's task, seen from this perspective, is to aid the individual in remediating previous negatively resolved issues concerning stages of the life cycle as well as coping with the current salient issue. (Counseling, by contrast, might be seen as helping the individual to cope only with the issue of the current stage.) Psychotherapy is thus the provision by "the world" of developmental remediation.

Psychotherapy developmentally construed is not psychotherapy defined. Everything from psychological rebirth and spiritual transcendence to the cosmetic removal of unappealing personal habits (such as nail biting and snake phobias) has been called psychotherapy. Because no one comprehensive definition is universally accepted, I offer one that is useful for the purposes of this discussion. Essentially, psychotherapy involves methods employed by one party in the service of ameliorating the psychological condition of a second party. Usually the second party requests this amelioration and can expect either a decrease in pain or an increase in the meaningfulness of that pain, or, if extraordinarily fortunate, both. The goal of the relationship is that it be terminated. Both the provider and recipient are participants in the therapeutic process, although the relationship is tilted toward the recipient-participant in terms of attention and psychological benefit, and tilted toward the provider-participant in terms of compensation for services and extent of influence. Hence, psychotherapy is not as egalitarian as friendship or as one-sided as surgery. Almost all psychotherapy involves communicational contact between at least two persons in order that the helper can understand the helped one sufficiently to proceed along a treatment path. It is at this communicational junction that empathy enters into psychotherapy.

Empathy

That empathy can be understood developmentally is the theme of this book. Just what empathy has to do with personality development and how this relates to psychotherapy, construed as a developmental aid, is the subject of this chapter. Empathy essentially requires an attitude or a stance of openness to another's experience. The definition of empathy to be adopted here is one that permits discussion of its relationship to psychotherapy. The psychotherapist Theodore Reik (1949) has described four aspects of the empathy process in psychotherapy:

1. *Identification* – paying attention to another and allowing oneself to become absorbed in contemplation of that person
2. *Incorporation* – making the other's experience one's own via internalizing the other
3. *Reverberation* – experiencing the other's experience while simultaneously attending to one's own cognitive and affective associations to that experience
4. *Detachment* – moving back from the merged inner relationship to a position of separate identity, which permits a response to be made that reflects both understanding of others as well as separateness from them.

Clearly, this definition refers to both cognitive and affective aspects of empathy.

Some aspects of this definition warrant discussion. The first has to do with the voluntariness of empathy. In psychotherapy, the therapist can set him/herself to function in an empathic mode. However, he/she must also be certain that the temporary regression involved in this lowering of ego boundaries remains "regression in the service of the ego" (Kris, 1952). In the original empathic situation, that of a mother[1] and an infant, empathy is initiated with little conscious control. However, both psychotherapy and effective mothering require that the merger aspect of the relationship be temporary.

Another factor to consider is the onset of empathy in psychotherapy. In a therapeutic session, the therapist's empathic process coexists with the patient's ongoing production of material. Patients don't stop experiencing (or talking) while therapists empathize. New verbal material and affective states are continually being produced, so that the therapist, in order to be accurately empathic in a timely sense, cannot just "do" empathy, but must "be" in an empathic state. It is with respect to this issue of timeliness that the intuitive function (Jung, 1946) enters the process of empathy in psychotherapy. Intuition, the ability to know *D*, given *A*, without going through steps *B* and *C*, probably aids the therapist in keeping up with a patient (or sometimes being ahead), while remaining in an empathic state.

The other aspect of Reik's definition that I discuss has to do with communication. As Goldstein and Michaels (1985) make clear, client-centered (Rogerian) psychotherapists believe that communication is a necessary part of any definition of empathy (see Keefe, 1976, 1979). However, empathy can exist in a psychotherapeutic session without being communicated. Three examples come to mind.

First, a therapist can empathize with a patient and choose to do nothing with the information. For example, sometimes it is wise to "play dumb" in order to encourage and teach patients to become more expressive, both to themselves and others, about their inner states; sharing one's empathic understanding can forestall this process. Second, a therapist may empathize with a patient, but formulate a nonempathic interpretation. That is, the interpretation may bear little similarity to the patient's current conscious internal state and yet be therapeutically useful by redirecting attention to important issues or by providing cognitive structure. Finally, a therapist may communicate empathy, but this communication may not necessarily be received by a patient, particularly by a very disturbed patient. In any case, there is no particular reason why empathy *must* be defined as having a communicational aspect, nor why empathy must be communicated in order for psychotherapy to be effective. This leaves open the possibility that if it *is* communicated, therapy will be effective. That is, there may be something so developmentally facilitative about empathy that, when it is provided in psychotherapy, the therapy is almost always effective.

Empathy and the development of personality

In contrast to other chapters in this book, this one is concerned less with the development of empathy than with the effects of empathy on personality development. The hypothesized importance of empathy for personality development, just as the hypothesized function of empathy in psychotherapy, varies with the theorist. On an even more basic level, one's theory of personality development, of psychotherapy, and of the function of empathy reflects one's fundamental assumptions about human nature. Greenberg and Mitchell (1983), in an indispensable text on object-relations theory within psychoanalysis, have said it well: "Only by analysis of an analyst's vision of human experience can his theoretical position be accurately assessed (p. 348)." From the beginning, one knows almost instinctively that empathy is going to be more important to a Rousseau-based theory than to a Hobbesian one, more important within a Kantian than a Lockean framework (Rychlak, 1981), and more important to Rogers than to Skinner.

S. Freud and H. S. Sullivan

Sullivan's developmental views can be understood best by juxtaposing them with Freud's. For Freud, the essential problem of infancy could be described as taming. The infant, a drive(id)-dominated creature, more animal than human, has to be judiciously gratified and frustrated so that he/she can eventually

learn to delay gratification and to develop adaptive skills in order to more or less
fend for him/herself in a world that is, at best, indifferent, at worst, antagonistic.
Freud considers drives to come first and relationships to follow. That is, some
"objects" are experienced as regularly drive-gratifying entities and are ca-
thected. (Objects, here, refer to persons or to aspects of persons.) There is a
certain interchangeability among objects, and the focus is primarily in the struggle between impulse and control in the individual and on the mental structures
that come to be formed out of this struggle.

Sullivan (1962) differs from Freud. For Sullivan, infants seek objects, not just
gratifications, from the beginning. Although Sullivan also speaks of needs (for
satisfaction and for security), these are not as zonally specific as Freud's, nor
necessarily oriented toward libidinal pleasure of tension reduction in organ systems; and they are thoroughly interpersonally based. Even the more biologically
toned satisfaction needs include, in infants, "need for contact," and, in adults,
the need for increasingly complex intimate interactions with others.

Empathy is central in Sullivan's theory. It is by means of primitive empathy,
described as a prototaxically experienced flow of feeling between mother and
infant, that the mother's anxiety is, in Sullivan's terms, "prehended" (sensed
below the level of awareness) by the infant. It is this inescapable anxiety that
occasions the infant's development of a self (to avoid anxiety) and of different
personifications of the self ("good me," "bad me," "not me") and others ("good
mother," "bad mother," etc). Personality itself, then, comes to consist solely
of interpersonal interactions with internal and external personifications. In Freud's
view, personality resides *within* the individual taken as an object of observation;
in Sullivan's view, it resides *between* persons as interacting subjects. According
to Freud, tensions arising from body zones drive individuals into interaction with
others; according to Sullivan, body zones are vehicles through which more basic
interpersonal needs are expressed. For Freud, anxiety stems primarily from internal conflict (ego–superego, ego–id); for Sullivan, anxiety is always interpersonal.

For Sullivan and Sullivanians in general, empathy is fundamental to human
development (see Fromm-Reichmann, 1950); it is an important ingredient in
their perception of therapy as a *relationship* based upon *participant* observation.
This is not just an increase in therapeutic democracy; it affects the nature and
meaning of interpretations. Within a strictly Freudian analytic model, interpretations are the curative aspect of therapy, and empathy, if employed, is in the
service of making an accurate interpretation. Gedo (1981), in fact, warned *against*
the frequent use of empathy in psychoanalysis:

> Although introspection and empathy are indeed vital tools in the performance
> of psychoanalysis, emphasis on the use of these unique, subjective observa-
> tional pathways must not lead us to overlook the fact that the most common

intellectual activity of the analyst is actually the matching of sets of primary data to (more or less familiar) patterns or schemata. (p. 176)

He further stated: "The less we have to rely on empathy in psychoanalytic work, the fewer therapeutic errors will follow" (p. 184).

Beginning with Sullivan, and extending to the other theorists to be discussed, the situation is just reversed. Instead of seeing empathy as only one tool in the service of the curative interpretation, these theorists see the interpretive activity as a vehicle for the expression of empathic concern. Within the strict psychoanalytic drive-based model, interpretations must be correct to be fully therapeutic; within the relational–interpersonal model, interpretations can be tentative and even faulty at times if they are made within the empathic curative relationship. If one were to split empathy into its cognitive and affective components, Freudians would emphasize the cognitive aspects, and Sullivanians, the affective.

Object-relations theorists

Neither Freud nor Sullivan saw many children in psychotherapy. It remained for other psychoanalytic therapists (Bowlby, 1969, 1980; Klein, 1948; Mahler, Pine, & Bergman, 1975; Winnicott, 1965), whose practices consisted primarily of children, to confirm the importance of the interactional process between the mothering one and the child, as well as the significance of empathy as a mediator in this process. Two important issues concerning empathy are highlighted in the discussion of these theorists: the importance of drives versus relationships (object relations) in child development; and the assumed presence or absence of an autonomous, developing self.

The classical Freudian position is that personality structure grows out of an individual's characteristic way of gratifying biologically based drives, initially in the face of external scarcity and sanctions and eventually in the face of internal controls. The notion of a self was a late development in Freud's thinking and was treated as an epiphenomenon – a representation of the ego. In contrast, object-relations theorists emphasize the formation of relationship-based structures rather than drive-based structures, and some of these theorists posit an autonomous developing self. Following are the views of some representative object-relations theorists. Although empathy may not be specifically discussed by each theorist, the importance of empathy in both developmental theory and psychotherapy increases with increased emphasis on interpersonal interaction and the formation of a self.

Melanie Klein. What the object relations theorists did was to locate the formation of definite, nonnarcissistic object relations in the child's development earlier than the classical Freudian oedipal period. The initial, and in some ways the most radical, departure from Freud's position was Melanie Klein's (1948). In almost Jungian fashion, she proposed that innate prefigurations of knowledge of objects were prior to and separate from actual experience. Although she maintained a drive orientation, she combined objects *with* drives: "Drives for her are not discrete quantities of energy arising from specific body tensions, but passionate feelings of love and hate directed toward others and utilizing the body as a vehicle of expression. *Drives, for Klein, are relationships"* (Greenberg & Mitchell, 1983, p. 146; italics in original).

W. R. D. Fairbairn. Fairbairn (1952), departing further from Freud than Klein, saw body zones as the means to object contact. The mouth, for example, is not important because it is, a priori, a site of libido concentration; rather it *becomes* an important zone because it leads to contact with the breast. What is basic is not an oral drive, but breast seeking. Developmental progression, for Fairbairn, is not based upon shifting areas of libido concentration, but upon progressively maturing modes of relations with others. One of the clearest differences between Fairbairn and Klein is their differing location of the fundamental source of developmental difficulties. According to Klein, the basic issue is the inner, instinctual self-destructiveness of the child. According to Fairbairn, the issue lies in the realm of the mother–child relationship; he saw maternal deprivation, not the child's self-destructive fantasies, as the factor impeding development. Like Sullivan, Fairbairn focuses less on the internal workings of the psyche and more on the observable interaction between persons. Hence, empathy plays a larger part in Fairbairn's than in Klein's theory.

D. W. Winnicott. Winnicott (1965) helped to introduce the concept of self into psychoanalytic theory, not as a perceptual by-product of the ego's reflecting on the synthesized id–ego–superego mental structure, but as an autonomous and developing aspect of personality. For Winnicott, it is not egos that interact, but persons (selves). The mother's role in the formation of the self is to provide a "holding environment" within which the integrating infant can be contained: "An infant who has had no one person to gather his bits together starts with a handicap in his own self-intergrating task" (Winnicott, 1945, p. 150, cited in Greenberg & Mitchell, 1983, p. 191). In a theme repeated by Kohut (1971), Winnicott views the mother as a kind of mirror that serves both to reflect and to organize the infant's initially scattered, but gradually integrating, sense of self. Empathy enters this process in that the "good enough mother" is "able to resonate with the baby's wants and needs, [so that] the latter becomes attuned to his own bodily functions and impulses, which become the basis for his slowly evolving sense of self" (Greenberg & Mitchell, 1983, p. 193). It is the gradual diminution in the mother's finely attuned responding (decreasing empathy) that contributes to the child's later sense of separateness and individuality. Consistent with the trend set by Sullivan, and in contrast with Freud, Winnicott described early infancy, not in terms of the individual baby, but in terms of the relational field between infant and caretakers, a field that has much more to do with psychological than with physiological nurturance.

Margaret Mahler. Margaret Mahler (Mahler et al. 1975) aligns herself with Hartmann's (1964) ego psychoanalytic theory and attempts to achieve an accommodation between an object-relational approach and classical psychoanalytic theory. Hartmann recast "object relations" as part of his "average expectable environment," whose function is to meet individual needs; remember, however, that these needs have now expanded from Freud's original tissue-tension-based drives to include ego needs. Hartmann's focus on adaptation to reality, although a move to the "left" of Freud in terms of ego orientation, was still to the "right" of the object-relations theorists in that a self was not posited (except as a representation), and the focus for him, as for Sigmund and Anna Freud, was on the *individual's* adaptation to the world and not on an interactional progression of more differentiated and mature object relations. Consistent with an ego psychoanalytic outlook, Mahler (1946, p. 47, quoted in Greenberg & Mitchell, 1983, p. 273), states that the function of parents is to "give the child the object-related opportunity for channelization; i.e., utilization and amalgamation of his love and aggressive tendencies." However, when Mahler begins discussing the concept of individuation as the endpoint of the symbiosis, differentiation, practicing, and rapprochement subphases of development, she departs significantly from the classical Freudian emphasis on the Oedipal period as the crucial one for personality development, and she begins to sound increasingly like a self theorist on the order of Winnicott and Kohut. However, to quote Greenberg and Mitchell, where "Winnicott's 'personhood' is an innate given which is encouraged by the 'facilitating environment,' Mahler's 'personhood' is *achieved* through, among other factors, adaptation to the environment" (see Greenberg & Mitchell, 1983, p. 285). Nevertheless, that environment, as personified by the mother, is one in which the infant is *embedded* during the subphase preceding differentiation and the mode of communication is still characterized by the empathic "contagion" of affect described by Sullivan. Thus, although Mahler strives to maintain the classical drive-oriented perspective of Freudian theory, the thrust of her work seems to move her inexorably toward a self-development, object-relations point of view, and, hence, toward an increasing emphasis on the significance of the affective component of empathy in personality development and psychotherapy.

Client-centered and self theory

Ordinarily, one would expect a discussion of object-relations theorists to close with a description of Heinz Kohut's self theory. However, in order to highlight the surprising similarity between Kohut's psychoanalytically derived theory and Roger's phenomenologically based theory with respect to the issue of empathy and personality development, Rogers is discussed first, followed by Kohut.

Carl Rogers. Rogers (1951, 1959) takes a phenomenological approach in which no assumption is made of an "essential" reality in the form of mental structures (Gedo's "patterns and schemata"; see section Freud and Sullivan). Rather, it is the individual, not the therapist, who is the legitimate arbiter of reality; thus, in client-centered therapy, neither interpretations nor diagnoses are made. Rogers assumes a built-in tendency to "actualize the organism"; hence, in the atmosphere of an accepting environment, an individual will automatically flourish, guided by a kind of internal gyroscope oriented toward organismic enhancement. This tendency toward growth goes off course when the child fails to receive "positive regard" from his or her caretakers and comes to restrict awareness of experiences to those that are positively regarded, and distorts or denies nonpositively regarded experiences. The circumstances under which the child receives external positive regard are called "conditions of worth."[2] Because the child is assumed, by Rogers, to have an innate need for positive regard, it adopts these conditions of worth as its own, and the conditions of worth are externally imposed. Hence, a conflict is engendered between these *social* prescriptions and the *organism's* valuing tendency. In short, what the child as an organism experiences as good conflicts with what the child as a socialized individual experiences as good. So that positive regard will be maximized, experience is truncated, and tension exists between what could be experienced (originating from the organism) and what actually is experienced in awareness. In therapy, conditions of worth can be "undone" by the therapist's unconditional positive regard for *all* of the client's experiences, thereby permitting previously blocked thoughts and feelings to enter awareness. The province of the self (that part of the individual's phenomenal field labeled "me" or "I") is enlarged by aligning it with the organismic valuing tendency rather than conditions of worth.

In essence, Rogers conceives of the human infant entering the world as a good and growing organism within which a healthy self can develop whose boundaries are coterminus with those of the organism. This self becomes experientially constricted, however, as the individual avoids experiences that violate learned conditions of worth. The aim of therapy is to expand (the boundaries of) the self to include as much of the ongoing organismic experience as possible and to rein-state the organismic valuing tendency.

Heinz Kohut. Kohut's (1971) conclusions about human nature are surprisingly close to those of Rogers, although the two theorists come from very different orientations. (Kohut was president of the American Psychoanalytic Association from 1964 to 1965.) Kohut, like Rogers, grants the self a functional role in personality. The conditions for its development are very similar to Rogers's "un-conditional positive regard." Those "others" who constitute the most important figures in the infant's world are termed *selfobjects* by Kohut, and his description of the child's relationship to them could almost stand as a definition of empathy:

> The child's rudimentary psyche participates in the selfobjects' highly developed psychic organization; the child experiences the feeling states of the selfobject – they are transmitted to the child via touch and tone of voice and perhaps by still other means – as if they were his own. (1977, p. 86; quoted in Greenberg & Mitchell, 1983, p. 353)

Kohut's concept of mirroring refers to the abiding, positive reflection of the infant's growing self by both the mother and the father. It includes positive responses to the infant's grandiosity, general empathy, constancy, nurturance, respect, idealization, and sharing – in short, mirroring is unconditional positive regard. Hence, although the psychoanalytically committed Kohut presumes a much higher degree of internal structure than does the phenomenologically ori-ented Rogers, they converge to a remarkable degree in their assumptions about infancy and their prescriptions for optimal personality development.

Behaviorism

Behavioristic theorists, in addition to psychoanalytic, object-relational, and client-centered theorists, have been concerned with the conditions of child-hood. However, until the more recent work of Bandura (1977, 1978) on social learning, the notions of relationship and empathy did not seem very important within their approaches. The fundamental assumption made by learning theorists is that behavior can be modified through variations in the fundamental processes of reinforcement and extinction (and, more recently, imitation: "reinforcement-free" learning). There may be "nothing" inside the organism of significance for understanding behavior (Skinner) or there may be innate hierarchies of response (Hull); whatever the case, the primary source of variability in the formation and understanding of behavior lies with the environment. Starting with Watson's famous statement, "Give me a dozen healthy infants," behaviorists have been more concerned with the technology of change than with the process of development. Hence, the interpersonal world is construed in a rather discrete fashion so that it can be modified, and the learning process takes precedence over personality *content* (see Dollard & Miller, 1950). Behavior is thought to be built up of discrete units that take on an "organismic" appearance only when viewed from a distance, like a Seurat painting. Whatever behavior an infant displays, aside from the running-off reflexive responses, is a function of selective reinforcement. In one sense, learning theorists and classical psychoanalysts are similar; both believe that development proceeds from a bodily, drive-oriented, base.

Bandura (1977) departs from the classical learning theory position in somewhat the same way object-relations theorists' depart from classical analytic theory. With the introduction of concepts of learning by imitation and modeling, Bandura approaches the possibility of a relationship-oriented stance; and with the concept of efficacy, at least a descriptive, if not a structural, notion of self is introduced into the theory. Now that more attention is being paid to cognitive factors in behavior modification, to behavior acquired independently of reinforcement, and to the concept of self, it seems fair to state that behaviorism can move in the direction of a more internalized and relationship-oriented position. However, directional movement is not arrival.

Empathy in psychotherapy

The foregoing positions have been discussed because they pertain to the conditions of childhood and, hence, make potential contributions to ideas about the effects of empathy on child development. Given my view of psychotherapy as an event occurring within a developmental context, these effects of empathy in child development are assumed to be important for discussing empathy and psychotherapy. I propose that the more importance a theorist attaches to the effect of empathy on early childhood development, the more stress he/she will place on it in psychotherapy. What follows, then, is a discussion of the role of empathy within specific psychotherapeutic approaches.

Classical psychoanalysis

In classic psychoanalysis, empathy is not emphasized except as it may be useful in formulating accurate interpretations. Gedo (1981), arguing from an orthodox perspective, takes the Kohutians to task for advocating the replacement of the psychoanalytic ambience that they perceive as "cold and critical" with "a warmly accepting atmosphere"; an atmosphere that Gedo thinks "few clinicians . . . can create without going out of their way" (p. 286). It is especially the affective aspect of empathy to which orthodox analysts object, although Gedo is not particularly enthusiastic about empathy's cognitive contribution, either.

"Evenly hovering attention" is acceptable, but relying upon "the healing power of empathy" is not. "Because it is a scientific enterprise, the primary purpose of psychoanalysis is the acquisition of knowledge. Even in the treatment setting, to subordinate this purpose to any other goal is tendentious and counter-productive; only the analysand may appropriately wish to improve his lot" (Gedo, 1981, p. 369). For Gedo, cognitive reliance on empathy is intellectually and technically sloppy, and affective reliance on it is counter transferential. Blum (1980 p. 47), although less vehement, concurs with Gedo's position: "Analytic 'cure' is primarily effected through insight and not through empathy, acceptance, tolerance, etc."

In general, it is any notion of cure through love to which most classical analysts object. But empathy is not love, any more than transitory identification with a patient is counter transference. If the affective connotations surrounding empathy were removed, then only the most regression-phobic of the classical analysts would likely oppose its use. For example, when Arlow (1980), a classical analyst, discusses the nature of the analyst's experience during the process of analyzing, his description (pp. 200–203) parallels almost exactly the definition of the empathic process (with a more cognitive slant) described by Reik at the beginning of this chapter.

Psychoanalytic psychotherapy

Consistent with differences in their goals and techniques (Paolino, 1981, 1984), psychoanalytic psychotherapists differ from psychoanalysts in the importance they attach to empathy. Psychoanalysis gives first priority to increasing self-knowledge, the alleviation of suffering being secondary; psychoanalytic psychotherapy reverses these priorities. Whereas psychoanalysis has definite technical parameters, psychoanalytic psychotherapy is more flexible in this respect. For example, in psychoanalytic psychotherapy, transference can be used to promote positive changes, not just "analyzed." Both approaches adhere to psychoanalytic theory as a way of construing personality development and psychotherapy.

One implication of the flexibility of technique that is characteristic of psychoanalytic psychotherapy is that the therapeutic relationship, itself, becomes an important treatment component, and, with it, empathy, in both its cognitive and affective aspects, assumes more importance than in classical analysis. Hence, one finds Herron and Rouslin (1982) cautioning against empathy *deficit* in therapy as a result of the therapist's unresolved narcissistic needs. Paolino (1981) described empathy as "the capacity of the therapist to reach down into his most intimate inner self and to listen with his own mental and physical being in order to grasp fully and share the message that the patient is trying to communicate"

(p. 11). He cites empathy as one of the seven necessary criteria for becoming a psychoanalytic psychotherapist. Clearly, the psychoanalytic psychotherapists emphasize the importance of empathy in both its cognitive and affective aspects.

Object-relations therapy

As one might expect, object-relations theorists also emphasize the importance of both the cognitive and affective aspects of empathy. Ekstein (1978) cites both Winnicott and Mahler in discussing the interrelationship of the mother's empathy, the child's feeling loved, and the child's developing capacity to reason. He then draws a parallel to psychotherapy wherein empathy helps the patient feel understood and become more reasonable about his/her life. Ekstein seems to be saying that affective empathy promotes cognitive development – an interesting reversal of the position that empathy is a purely cognitive variable (i.e., role taking).

Sullivan's emphasis on the interpersonal interactional nature of psychotherapy has already been noted. His work with male schizophrenics illustrates his attempts to establish developmentally remedial therapeutic contexts. "Sullivan's goal was to employ healthy human relations between staff and patients as a therapeutic procedure, reasoning that schizophrenia had its origin in initially unhealthy interpersonal relations . . . his special ward at Sheppard–Pratt was, in a sense, a corrective, pre-adolescent society" (Monte, 1980, p. 364). From both his writings and those of Fromm-Reichmann (1950), it is clear that Sullivanians emphasize both cognitive and affective aspects of empathy, although they place somewhat more emphasis on the latter, consistent with an emphasis on the therapeutic relationship itself as a therapeutic ingredient.

Kernberg (1980) and Kramer (1980) discuss the importance of empathy in understanding the complex nature of transference within the object-relations approach. In addition to being perceived transferentially as single, separate objects, as in the classical analytic approach, therapists, according to object-relations theory, may also be viewed as part objects. Moreover, transference of one object relation to the therapist can be used defensively by the patient to avoid awareness of another, more threatening internal object. In this complex situation, empathy is especially important as a cognitive tool.

> The analyst, while empathizing by means of a transitory or trial identification with the patient's experience of himself and his object representations, also explores empathically the object relation that is currently predominant in the interactive or non verbal aspects of the transference, and, in this context, the nature of the self- or object representation that the patient is projecting onto him. (Kernberg, 1980, p. 212)

Because personality is seen by object-relations theorists as being organized at pre-oedipal levels, transferences and interpretations occur at a more oral level. Concepts such as Winnicott's "holding environment" and Mahler's "attachment-separation-individuation" sequence, which are applicable to the mothering situations described earlier, can also apply to psychotherapeutic ones. Although these theorists consider empathy to be more important for cognitive, interpretive purposes, they also find it useful affectively, for establishing the general therapeutic context of object-relational therapy. Kernberg (1970) refers to the therapeutic applicability of Winnicott's concept of the "holding" function of the analyst: "his ongoing emotional availability to the patient at points of severe regression" (p. 229). However, he makes it quite clear that, although important for psychological growth in therapy, "empathy is a prerequisite for interpretive work, not its replacement" (p. 232). Mahler et al. (1975), Loewald (1970), and Kramer (1980) all consider empathy important as an analytic tool *in the service of insight and interpretation.* Hence, it is not to these object-relations theorists that one can look for a predominant emphasis on the positive effects of empathy's affective component.

As one moves on to Winnicott, Guntrip (1971), and, of course, Kohut, the therapeutic relationship itself, apart from interpretations, becomes increasingly important, as does the affective component of empathy. "Winnicott sees the curative factor in psychoanalysis not in its interpretive function, but in the manner in which the analytic setting provides missing parental provisions and fills early developmental needs" (Greenberg & Mitchell, 1983, p. 201). Both Winnicott and Guntrip see psychotherapy as an essentially maternal relationship, replacing defensive attachments with more gratifying and realistic ones, one of which can be the therapist. Kohut is the most explicit about the importance of both the affective aspect of empathy in establishing the ambience of the therapeutic relationship. Via empathy, the therapist creates a positive interpersonal field, in which he/she becomes a self-object that the patient can internalize and that then becomes the core of a compensatory self-structure. "This provides a kind of developmental second chance" (Greenberg & Mitchell, 1983, p. 356). Again, "characterological change does not take place through interpretation, but through experience, 'microinternalization' of the analyst's function as a self-object" (Greenberg & Mitchell, 1983, p. 357).

A summary of the role of empathy in psychodynamic psychotherapy, including both the classical analytic and object-relational approach follows. Classical psychoanalysis is primarily drive-oriented and considers relationship factors to be secondary to individual ones. The analyst's responsibility is to maintain some psychological distance between patient and therapist and to make accurate interpretations. Empathy is useful, cognitively, to the extent that it enhances the accuracy and timing of interpretations; however, its affective aspect is suspected of being counter transferential, and extensive reliance on it, even as a cognitive tool, is to be avoided. For psychoanalytic psychotherapy, empathy is cognitively and affectively useful, although in the sense of a rather nonspecific "ambience of the relationship." Object-relations theorists are divided between those who see empathy as useful only to the interpretive process, as in classical analysis, and those who see it as a major curative ingredient in itself, similar to client-centered therapy. The former, although they emphasize a positive therapeutic relationship more than do classical analysts, prefer to use empathy as a cognitive tool. The latter, who explicitly emphasize the therapeutic nature of the relationship itself, consider empathy to be an essential cognitive and affective component of treatment, and place particular emphasis on the latter aspect.

Client-centered therapy

Empathy plays a key role in client-centered therapy. If the therapist were allowed to do only one thing, Rogerians would likely choose to communicate empathic understanding. The rationale for this is clear from their theory of the development of psychopathology. Individuals get into emotional trouble because they constrict their experience to conform to internalized conditions of worth. In order to suspend conditions of worth and to restore the organismic valuing tendency, the therapist must establish an atmosphere of positive regard, free of conditions. Hence, he/she must attend to the client, permit the client's recognized and unrecognized feelings to enter the therapist's awareness, gain some sense of the client's internal world, and then reflect this knowledge back to the client accurately and in an emotionally understandable way. This empathic process encourages the client to regard previously shunned experiences positively.

At this juncture it is important to explain what unconditional positive regard is *not*. It is *not* niceness and love. It is nonjudgmental attention paid to all of another's experiences (not necessarily his/her behavior) within a generally accepting interpersonal context. Empathy helps to broaden and deepen the attention paid to the client's experiences and to ensure that the ensuing communication of understanding will be received accurately. Note that *communication* of empathy is assumed to be important in the psychotherapeutic process; in fact, it is sufficiently important that Rogerian therapists would like to make it part of the definition of empathy itself.

It is greatly to the credit of the Rogerians, that, of all the psychotherapeutic orientations (save the behaviorists), they have been the most willing to subject their presumed effective psychotherapeutic ingredients to experimental testing. Goldstein and Michaels (1985) have reviewed this research extensively and summarize it as follows:

Early psychotherapy research (client-centered) too sweepingly concluded that high levels of therapist empathy enhanced therapeutic outcome whoever the patient and therapist were, and whatever the therapy was. Subsequent investigation and reflection led to a more moderate view, one that saw therapist empathy being facilitative in some instances, not in others. Empathy-in-psychotherapy research has entered a prescriptive phase. A beginning has been made at pointing toward therapist, patient, relationship, and to a lesser extent, treatment variables as prescriptive markers. (pp. 142–143)

As a result of the extensive experimental and experiential evidence that has been accumulated to support the centrality of empathy in effective interpersonal interaction, empathy training programs have been undertaken, not only for therapists, but also for parents and teachers. It appears that Rogerians have realized, to some extent, their social vision. Empathy has infiltrated the home and the school. Parent, teacher, and therapist training programs and research into their outcomes are all reviewed in Goldstein and Michaels (1985).

Some questions remain about these training programs, however. Empathy may be seen as a normal human capability having a definable developmental sequence, and, hence, as a skill that most adults could be expected to possess. Why, then, should empathy training be necessary? Perhaps individuals who really *need* empathy training (to make up for a developmental deficit) are engaging in their own psychotherapy. There would be nothing particularly wrong with that if the training was sufficiently "psychotherapeutic" to produce significant personality change. However, most empathy training programs are not individually tailored or thoroughgoing enough to accomplish this and could be more accurately labeled empathy enhancement. In this vein, Goldstein and Michaels's (1985) suggestion that trainees should be preselected (for "average expectable empathy levels") is well taken.

Bioenergetics

The issue of therapist empathy enhancement brings us to the interesting point raised by Davis (1985), who argued that a relationship exists between empathy viewed as motor mimicry and empathy training. The historical precedence for this point is found in Lipps (1926) who conceived of empathy as the motoric (kinesthetic) re-creation of one person's state in another so that one replicated in oneself the same physical cues that gave rise to thoughts and feelings in another. Most writers seem to consider motor mimicry at least one part of the empathic process. Thus, a factor that may make individuals *un*empathic is a lack of awareness of their own internal physiological states. Wilhelm Reich (1949) and bioenergetic therapists following him (e.g., Lowen, 1975) have suggested that characteristic body postures are developed in response to fear and guilt. One "holds" and "holds in" one's body in such a way as to protect oneself against psychological pain consequent on acting on forbidden impulses. The body then becomes armored in specific ways so that even the perception of these impulses is blocked. The way to unblock chronically armored areas is to manipulate the body directly, for example, by means of bioenergetics, Rolfing, or Feldenkrais techniques. Whereas Freud attempted to get at the body via the mind (free association and catharsis in conversion reactions), bioenergetics therapists aim to get at the mind (psychic conflicts) via the body. To the extent that empathy depends upon motor mimicry and motor mimicry depends upon a "freely resonating" physiological structure, it might seem reasonable to include bodywork as part of any empathy training program for potential psychotherapists.[3]

Behavioral therapy

What is one to say of empathy in behavior therapy? Not much. What certainly is the case across behavior therapies, from systematic desensitization and implosive techniques to operant conditioning procedures, is that behavior therapists are extraordinarily scrupulous both in defining the parameters of symptoms and in eliciting discriminative environmental stimuli. In order to do this, they must frequently consult the patient, sometimes in exquisite detail (as in the construction of a fear hierarchy for systematic desensitization). As suggested at the beginning of this chapter, any time there is communicational contact between therapist and patient, an opportunity for empathy arises. However, empathy is not seen as an important ingredient in behavior therapy. In fact, orthodox behavior therapists are as chary about empathy as are orthodox analysts; again, it seems to be the affective connotation of warmth (disparaged as "touchy-feely") that is upsetting. Yet, empathy still seems to make its appearance. Lazarus's (1971) description of training in emotional freedom ("the recognition and appropriate expression of each and every affective state," p. 318) seems to include an empathic component. Similarly, the imaginative scenes used in Stampfl's implosion therapy (Stampfl & Levis, 1967) have the therapist acquiring a detailed cognitive and affective account of the dimensions of a patient's phobia.

Even when empathy is not directly implicated in a treatment procedure, interpersonal behavior therapy gives rise to interactions in which the *opportunity* for empathy exists. Following are three such examples. The first is from Davison (1968), who reports on the use of counterconditioning in the treatment of a sadistic fantasy. One procedure used was the " 'older brother' type of relationship which the therapist established in talking with Mr. M. about conventional sex. . . . Much time was spent in deliberately provocative 'locker-room talk' " (p. 394). The second example shows how a severe anorexic was treated with operant techniques, namely, controlled regimen in which, unknown to the patient, activities enjoyable to her were made contingent upon eating behavior (Bachrach,

Erwin, & Mohr, 1968). One aspect of the treatment was that this institutionalized and likely *interpersonally* starved woman was accompanied at all three daily meals by one of the three male therapists: her psychiatric resident, a staff research psychologist, and a medical student. Finally, Wisocki (1973), in an epilogue to her discussion of the treatment of a heroin addict by covert conditioning (imaginal) techniques, stated:

> I certainly do not deny the value of nontechnical aspects of therapy. In fact, when performing behavior therapy I deliberately try to operationalize warmth, interest, motivation, and so on to enhance the efficacy of the procedures themselves. For instance, twice I took the client out for a beer after the therapy hour to encourage him to sample the life style of his peers. Once I gave him a puppy ("someone who would always love him" in his words). I expressed personal disappointment in him when he failed to practice his assignments and was elated when he did. I was available by phone whenever he wished and did not confine the discussion of his problems to the office. (p. 340)

To say that empathy occurred in the above three examples may be stretching the point a bit. However, the types of interpersonal situations described certainly provided the *opportunity* for an empathic connection between therapist and patient, even if they were eschewed as a therapeutic technique by the therapists involved.

Personal observations

I close this chapter with some observations based on my own 20 years of experience in the "general practice" of psychodynamic psychotherapy. There are some patients with whom it is difficult to empathize. Hysterics make it easy; they are "feeling machines." Obsessive–compulsives make it difficult; they are nit-picking, cold, and stingy with their feelings. Ordinarily, one does best by attempting to empathize with their *struggles for control* over their aggressive and sexual feelings rather than their aggressive and sexual feelings, per se. In addition, there are some patients with whom it is downright toxic to empathize. Even the most dedicatedly masochistic therapist quails at the prospect of experiencing directly (internalizing) the primitive and wildly shifting emotions that a borderline patient can traverse in a single session: clinging infantile dependence, towering rage, blatant seductiveness, and cringing self-abasement.

Empathy, like Bettleheim's (1960) "love," is "not enough" to see a psychotherapist through the range of patients and pathologies likely to be encountered in the general practice of psychotherapy. But, to the extent that it is our most thoroughgoing way of apprehending the world of another, I see empathy as at least a necessary (although not sufficient) therapeutic skill for effective treatment. I think that it is clear from the foregoing discussion about the receptive nature of empathy and its function in child rearing and psychotherapy, that it comprises the "feminine" communal aspect of therapy, as contrasted with the "masculine" agentic aspect. In this light, it would be interesting to investigate the relation between therapists' sex-role orientation and their relative emphasis on empathy in psychology.

Are there no caveats concerning empathy in psychotherapy? Is being on the receiving end always the positive experience that Rogerians would have us believe? There is probably a sufficient narcissistic component in most of us that basks in the accurate reflection of our inner states by another – but not in all of us all of the time. It should be remembered that empathy can be experienced as a kind of invasion or penetration; being understood by another can be painful. The song "Killing Me Softly," popularized by Roberta Flack, tells of feeling feverish, embarrassed, viewed as though transparent, and known "in all my black despair" when a certain singer was performing. As D. H. Lawrence writes in "Image-making Love,"

> Always
> at the core of me
> burns the small flame of anger, gnawing
> from trespassed contact, from red-hot finger
> bruises, on my inward flesh,
> from hot, digging-in fingers of love.*

It might be argued that the foregoing do not fit Reik's definition of empathy used in this chapter. In the case of the singer, there may have been no intention to empathize, and the communicated understanding may have been fortuitous. In the second case, the poet may have been the target of an incomplete empathic process, the goal of which was to give the empathizer emotional control. In both cases, "being known" is experienced unpleasantly as "being intruded upon." Whereas empathy, viewed only as a skill, could be used, with or without awareness, in the service of the subject as well as of the object, real empathy would have to take into account *all* of the feelings of the other. Hence, in both of the above cases, the most accurately empathic response would be silence; the empathizer would know not only the other's feelings but also his/her feelings about being known.

In any case, some patients, like the member of the singer's audience and the intrusively loved poet, would prefer to be spared the therapist's penetrating insights. It is a wise therapist who is sufficiently empathic not to consider a patient's wish to "keep his/her own counsel" as resistance in every case.

Any possible negative consequences for patients of therapists' empathy are

---

*From *The Complete Poems of D. H. Lawrence,* edited by Vivian de Sola Pinto and F. Warren Roberts. Copyright © 1964, 1971 by Angelo Ravagli and C. M. Weekley, Executors of the Estate of Frieda Lawrence Ravagli. Reprinted by permission of Viking Penguin Inc.

less likely and less severe than the effects that prolonged empathic responding can have on therapists themselves. The first three aspects of Reik's description of the empathic process are identification, incorporation, and reverberation. Consider the effects on the individual of engaging in this process on a daily basis. To empathize consistently with a number of different people, most of whom are in some kind of psychological pain, is to live, vicariously, as many painful lives as the number of patients one sees. Aside from the psychological toll this takes, it also sets the psychotherapist apart from most other members of society, for he/she lives not only his/her individual life, but, via empathy, the lives of many others.

Summary

In this chapter I have discussed empathy and its role in child development and psychotherapy from a developmental perspective. Those theorists who are most concerned with the conditions of childhood (that is, psychodynamic, client-centered, and behavioral theorists) have been described in terms of the function they ascribe to empathy in the development of personality and in the process of psychotherapy. Empathy emerges as a variable of differing importance in psychotherapy according to the theorist's emphasis on the drive-versus-relationship aspect of development, on an epiphenomenal versus an autonomous self, and on interpretive activity versus interpersonal–interactive activity as an essential therapeutic ingredient.

Notes

1. Mothering is considered to be an activity that can be engaged in by persons of different genders and ages. The term *mothering* is used instead of *parenting* because the former emphasizes nurturance and attachment in early infancy. The term *mother* will be used generically to refer to the person who fills this role for the infant. Clearly, fathers, in this sense, can be mothers.
2. "Conditions of worth" are actually circumscribing contingencies; that is, the *fewer* the conditions of worth, the more of the child's experiences are positively regarded.
3. Could bodywork become the training equivalent for client-centered therapists that didactic analysis is for psychoanalysts?

References

Arlow, J. A. (1980). The genesis of interpretation. In Blum (1980).

Bachrach, A. J., Erwin, W. J., & Mohr, J. P. (1968). The control of eating behavior in an anorexic by Gestalt conditioning technique. In Morse and Watson (1977, pp. 363–376).

Bandura, A. (1977). *Social learning theory*. Englewood Cliffs, NJ: Prentice-Hall.

Bandura, A. (1978). The self-systems in reciprocal determinism. *American Psychologist, 33*, 344–358.

Bettleheim, Bruno. (1960). *Love i‑ not enough*. New York: Basic Books.

Blum, H. P. (1980). Curative and creative as parts of insight. In Blum (1980, pp. 41–71).

Blum, H. P. (Ed.) (1980). *Psychoanalytic explanations of technique: Discussion in the theory of therapy.* New York: International Universities Press.

Bowlby, J. (1969). *Attachment and loss* (Vol. 1).

Bowlby, J. (1980). *Attachment and loss* (Vol. 2).

Davis, M. R. (1985). Perceptual and affective reverberation components. In A. P. Goldstein and C. J. Michaels (1985).

Davison, G. C. (1968). Elimination of a sadistic fantasy by a client-controlled counter-conditioning technique: A case study. In Morse and Watson (1977, pp. 390–399).

Dollard, J., & Miller, N. (1950). *Personality and psychotherapy: an analysis in terms of learning, thinking, and culture.* New Haven: Yale University Press.

Ekstein, R. (1978) Psychoanalysis, sympathy, and altruism. In L. Wispé (Ed.), *Altruism, sympathy and helping.* New York: Academic Press.

Erikson, E. H. (1950). *Childhood and society.* New York: Norton.

Erikson, E. H. (1982). *The life cycle completed: A review.* New York: W. W. Norton.

Fairbairn, W. R. D. (1952). *An object-relations theory of the personality.* New York: Basic Books.

Freud, A. (1974). Four lectures on child analysis. In *The writings of Anna Freud* (Vol. 1). New York: International Universities Press.

Fromm-Reichmann, F. (1950). *Principles of intensive psychotherapy.* Chicago: University of Chicago Press.

Gedo, J. E. (1981). *Advances in clinical psychoanalysis.* New York: International Universities Press.

Goldstein, A. P., & Michaels, C. J. (1985). *Empathy: Development, training, and consequences.* Hillsdale, NJ: Erlbaum.

Greenberg, J. R., & Mitchell, S. A. (1983). *Object relations in psychoanalytic theory.* Cambridge, MA: Harvard University Press.

Guntrip, H. (1971). *Psychoanalytic theory, therapy and the self.* New York: Basic Books.

Hartmann, H. (1964). *Essays on ego psychology.* New York: International Universities Press.

Herron, W. G., & Rouslin, S. (1982). *Issues in psychotherapy.* Bowie, MD: Brady.

Jung, C. G. (1946). *Psychological types.* New York: Harcourt Brace.

Keefe, T. (1976). Empathy: The critical skill. *Social Work, 21,* 10–14.

Keefe, T. (1979). The development of empathic skill. *Journal of Education for Social Work, 15,* 30–37.

Kernberg, O. F. (1980). Some implications of object relations theory for psychoanalytic technique. In Blum (1980).

Klein, M. (1948). *Contributions to psycho-analysis, 1921–1945.* London: Hogarth Press.

Kohut, H. (1971). *The analysis of the self.* New York: International Universities Press.

Kramer, S. (1980). The technical significance and practical application of Mahler's separation and individuation theory. In Blum (1980).

Kris, E. (1958). *Psychoanalytic explorations in art.* New York: International Universities Press.

Lazarus, A. A. (1971). Acquiring habits of emotional freedom. In Morse and Watson (1977, pp. 317–324).

Lipps, T. (1926). *Psychological studies.* Baltimore, MD: Williams and Wilkins.

Loewald, H. (1970). Psychoanalytic theory and the psychoanalytic process. In Ruth S. Eissler et al. (Eds.), *The psychoanalytic study of the child* (Vol. 25, pp. 45–68). New York: International Universities Press.

Lowen, A. (1975). *Bioenergetics.* New York: Coward, McCann and Geoghegan.

Mahler, M., Pine, F., & Bergman, A. (1975). *The psychological birth of the human infant.* New York: Basic Books.

Monte, C. F. (1980). *Beneath the mask* (2nd ed.). New York: Holt, Rinehart & Winston.

Morse, S. J., and Watson, R. I. (1977). *Psychotherapies: A comparative casebook.* New York: Holt, Rinehart & Winston.

Paolino. T. J. (1981). *Psychoanalytic psychotherapy: Theory, technique, therapeutic relationships and treatability.* New York: Bruner/Mazel.

Reich, W. (1949). *Character analysis* (3rd ed.; T. P. Wolfe, Trans.). New York: Farrar, Straus & Giroux.

Reik, T. (1948). *Listening with the third ear: The inner experience of the psychoanalyst.* New York: Grove.

Rogers, C. R. (1951). *Client-centered therapy.* Boston: Houghton Mifflin.

Rogers, C. R. (1959). A theory of therapy, personality and interpersonal relationships as developed in the client-centered framework. In S. Koch (Ed.), *Psychology: A study of a science. Study I. Conceptual and systematic. Vol. 3.: Formulations of the person in the social context* (pp. 184–256). New York: McGraw-Hill.

Rychlak, Joseph F. (1981). *An introduction to personality and psychotherapy: A theory-construction approach* (2nd ed.). Boston: Houghton Mifflin.

Stampfl, T. G., & Levis, D. J. (1967). Essentials of implosive therapy: A learning theory – based psychodynamic behavioral therapy. *Journal of Abnormal Psychology, 72,* 496–503.

Sullivan, H. S. (1962). *Schizophrenia as a human process.* New York: Norton & Norton.

Winnicott, D. W. (1965). *The maturational process and the facilitating environment.* New York: International Universities Press.

Wisocki, P. A. (1973). The successful treatment of a heroin addict by convert conditioning techniques: An updated report with afterthoughts. In Morse and Watson (1977, pp. 333–341).

Commentary on Part I

Ervin Staub

In reading the valuable chapters in this first, theoretical section of the book, I was struck by the bewildering array of explicit and implicit meanings of the term *empathy*. Distinctions among the various meanings are insufficiently drawn, both here and in the literature. It is no wonder that authors of articles on empathy usually start with their own definition. They must identify which of the multiplicity of meanings they use.

Substantial portions of these four chapters deal with the definition of empathy. I believe that I can be of the most service in my comments by differentiating among the varied types of empathy and offering a classification that others might find useful in the future. I will comment on the four chapters as I distinguish among the types of empathy.

These chapters also discuss the functions of empathy. Here, again, it may be both a valuable service and a useful guide in commenting on the papers to identify the various functions of empathy, from its important role in parent–child relations and the development of the child's personality to its role in motivating a person to help a needy other.

Other significant aspects of the study of empathy

Before I examine the definitions and functions discussed in these chapters, I want to comment on two significant issues in the study of empathy that the chapters deal with only peripherally: how empathy develops and how it is generated.

With regard to development, Plutchik (chapter 3) suggests that empathy, which can be inferred in both young and mature animals, "is probably based on innate schemata that are genetically determined." He acknowledges that experience and learning affect empathy, at least, its intensity and frequency. Hoffman (chapter 4) briefly reviews his well-known model of the development of empathy. His primary concern is empathic distress, a response to another's distress. In his conception, empathy is an affective response more appropriate to someone else's situation than one's own, and it evolves with the evolving cognitive sense of the other: that is, with the sense of increasing separateness between self and other and with increased appreciation of the identity of the other. Beyond these comments, there are no new formulations of how empathy evolves. There is no discussion of the experiences and socializing influences that might allow the genetic potential for empathy to evolve in particular persons.

There is limited discussion of how empathy is generated as a function of circumstances or the characteristics of the persons involved. Plutchik notes that various "displays" and other behaviors of animals generate empathy. Hoffman proposes that empathic distress combined with specific attributions about others' distress – whether the victim is thought to be blameless, or the self is blamed, or a third party is considered to be at fault – generates different empathic feelings: sympathetic distress, guilt feelings, or empathic anger. This is a worthwhile beginning. Empathy is certainly generated in an interactive fashion by circumstances (such as the condition of another, surrounding events, social influences such as verbal communications that provide an "imagine him/her," or an objectifying observational set) and by various personal characteristics, including the attributional tendencies of an observer. The development of a theory of how empathy is generated is an important task for the future.

The meanings of empathy: a classification schema

It is evident from Wispé's thorough review (chapter 2) that the concept of empathy has had many uses and has evolved and become transformed in many ways. Wispé also shows that a number of the paths in this evolution have made little contribution to our current usage. In the following paragraphs I differentiate types of empathy and point out their contemporary relevance and use. Even though each type has its own definition, a general (and therefore inaccurate) definition of empathy might be *apprehending another's inner world and joining the other in his or her feelings.*

Cognitive empathy

A basic aspect of empathy is an awareness, an understanding, a knowing of another's state or condition or consciousness, or how another might be affected by something that is happening to him or her. Some people refer to this as role taking, or as perspective taking, others as empathy. This appears to be the most basic meaning of the term in these theoretical chapters, in that this *cognitive empathy,* as I shall call it, is a precondition for the other kinds. I have long thought that it would be best to use the term *role taking* for this meaning, and reserve *empathy* for other uses. However, reading these chapters, with the reviews of large bodies of literature that they contain, has convinced me that this meaning of the term is irreversibly embedded in the literature.

Participatory empathy

The term is also used to mean what I call *participatory empathy,* particularly in Wispé's and Marcia's chapters. Much of the empathy in psychotherapy, as reflected in these authors' discussions, is participatory. Participatory empathy is probably the most common type in everyday experience. A person enters the world of another, tunes in to the other, feels with the other, participates in the other's ongoing experience, but usually without strong emotion or intense feeling of his or her own. It is a *psychic participation* – a term Wispé quotes from Downey – with a connection in feeling inherent in it. The participation will normally go beyond both knowing or understanding the other and reproducing his or her thoughts and feelings in oneself (parallel empathy): It is frequently reactive, with thoughts and feelings that arise *in response* to the other's experience, but is rooted in and responsive to the other's experience (see the discussion of parallel and reactive empathy later in this commentary).

An important issue to consider here, in the words of Downey, as quoted by Wispé (chapter 2), is the use of the concept of empathy to denote the "projection of all self-experiences into the object." This projection of the self into others (which is appropriate in the case of aesthetic appreciation, where, according to Wispé, the concept originated) can result in *false empathy.* The other's experience is not accurately perceived: Instead, what one would experience under the circumstances of the other is attributed to the other. In contrast to *accurate empathy,* false empathy is not a joining of the other, and it is unlikely to have the positive consequences that usually result from accurate empathy.

Marcia (chapter 5) and Wispé both suggest that therapists who have an empathic connection with their clients, and for whom empathy goes beyond knowing and might be therapeutic in itself, must experience participatory empathy. Such empathy can have a reverberating quality, whereby one person's experience of another's state expresses itself in ways that are perceived and experienced by the other. That is, the expression of empathy, although it can be shaped or inhibited, may be a natural, intrinsic part of participatory empathy. The reverberation can generate a cycle of mutual empathic experiencing, an empathic connection between people. I am using the term *reverberating* in a different way from Marcia, who uses it to describe a person experiencing another's experience and attending to his or her own associations with it.

Because the affective intensity of participatory empathy is not high, it is possible for people to step back from the empathic connection. Therapists, in particular, must be able to "move back from the merged inner relationship to a position of separate identity" (Marcia, chapter 5). Actually, we must all be able to do this in the course of ordinary experience, so that we won't lose ourselves in others, so that we can return to our own identity.

Cognitive empathy is neutral, it can be a tool of both caring and hostility. It is directly involved in gathering information and accurately knowing another person. In participatory empathy there is a positive quality, a caring by one person for another, a joining of the other.

Affective empathy

The feelings or condition of a person or persons can generate strong vicarious emotion in others. The emotion is vicarious in that neither the conditions that affect the person who is the object of empathy nor his or her emotions have any direct effect on the empathizing person. This type of empathy is of interest to those concerned with prosocial behavior, because it is considered an important motivator of it. This is the type of empathy that Hoffman is primarily concerned with.

Neither Wispé's informative review of the history of the empathy concept nor Marcia's discussion of empathy in personality development and psychotherapy mentions this type of empathy. Their focus is on what I call cognitive and participatory empathy. The reason for this may be either that there is no difference between participatory and affective empathy, or that, without a classification system to differentiate among types of empathy, valid and potentially useful distinctions are lost.

I am suggesting that the empathy experienced by a person who witnesses the pain or intense distress of another (or perhaps another's intense joy) is frequently different in a variety of components – greater in intensity, frequently less in the sensitivity required from the person and in the depth of cognitive empathy that must preceded it – from the participatory empathy I discussed before. The differences in components might be quantitative, in that affective empathy can involve in-depth cognitive processing of another's condition or consciousness. They often add up to a functionally and perhaps also qualitatively different state, however. Affective empathy may have greater motivational force and may be more focused or delineated, whereas participatory empathy may be more differentiated and complex.

Empathic joining

In his discussion of empathy among animals, Plutchik seems to refer to affective empathy. However, in many of his examples, one organism joins another in a shared feeling. The feeling starts with one, but the second one's emotion is not vicarious. Although the stimulus is the emotion of the first organism, this emotion generates the full experience of the same (or a reactive) emotion in the other organism(s). *It is a sharing of emotion,* not in a participatory way, by entering another's experience, but by *the other's experience generating the same experience in oneself.* Frequently, a precondition for this empathic joining is a cognitive empathy, an understanding of the cues that others provide. At times, an additional source of empathic joining is shared goals, as in the schooling behavior of fish.

One of Plutchik's examples of empathy – the response by birds to another's alarm signal – seems to me debatable. As a precondition for proper response, the signal must be understood. However, in the case of referential communication, in which a person tells another that something he/she is looking for is on the table, an ability to read the cues provided by the other is not required. *Table* has a common, shared meaning. The same may be true of the alarm signal. Moreover, the emotion generated by the alarm signal, and the resulting behavior, are not vicarious: They are responses to the meaning of the stimulus for the responding organism.

On the whole, the developmental levels of empathy suggested by Hoffman (see his Table 4.1) apply to each of the types of empathy, especially to participatory and affective empathy. They do not apply completely, however. Certainly, cognitive empathy could not have the form of "global empathy." Egocentric empathy is inconsistent with participatory empathy. It is possible to delineate how Hoffman's developmental levels apply to the different types of empathy.

Parallel and reactive empathy

As part of our classification we must take into account the quality of emotion in empathy and the relation of empathy to sympathy. Strictly speaking, empathy might involve a matching, a reproduction of another's experience in one's own experience. But such a reproduction is a limited form of empathy.

I have proposed the terms *parallel empathy* and *reactive empathy* (Staub, 1979; Staub & Feinberg, 1980) to describe, respectively, a *matching* or *reproduction* of another's feelings and an *empathic reaction* to the other's state, condition, consciousness or emotion. Under many conditions it is less developmentally advanced to experience parallel empathy, which is a lower-level, relatively more *self-related* than *other-related* empathic response. For example, in a study in which we identified these two different empathic responses in second- to fourth-grade children, boys who had higher parallel empathic responses on a test were the recipients of somewhat fewer positive behaviors from their peers in their everyday interactions (Staub & Feinberg, 1980). The reactive empathy scores of girls (who were the only ones to show reactive empathy in this study, perhaps because of a developmental difference) were positively related to their positive behaviors toward peers – such as helping, sharing, and cooperation – and were substantially positively related to peers acting positively toward them in the course of daily interactions.

Reactive empathy – for example, children feeling sad or angry upon seeing a presumably hungry, young black boy standing in front of an empty, grungy looking refrigerator – requires a perception of the other's state (cognitive empathy) and a caring about the other's need. Truly participatory empathy will be reactive; it will be a sensitive and joining response, rather than a simple reproduction of another's feelings. Affective empathy can be either parallel or reactive.

The research findings of Batson and his associates (1981, 1983) consistently show that people who themselves experience distress when exposed to another's distress will help the other mainly when there are external reasons to do so, whereas people who report feeling sympathetic, moved, compassionate, tender, warm, and softhearted in response to others' distress will provide help under a wider range of conditions. They will help even when they can escape continuing exposure to the other's distress. The former response appears parallel, the latter reactive.

If children with reactive empathy are more sensitive and caring, this explains the behavior of their peers toward them. In contrast, children who lean toward parallel empathy may focus more on the self. Reactive empathy encompasses *sympathy,* a caring and compassionate response to the state of others, as discussed by Hoffman in chapter 4 and in the work of others (see Batson, Duncan, Ackerman, Buckley & Birch, 1981; Batson, O'Quin, Fultz, Vanderplus, & Isen, 1983; Staub, 1986; Staub & Feinberg, 1980). Wispé (1986, p. 318) defines sympathy as a "heightened awareness of the suffering of another person as something to be alleviated." This important concept intimates the desire to *reach out* to another, at least in feeling if not in action. However, reactive empathy is a category that is broader than sympathy, as it is usually defined: Reactive empathy is a reaction centered in caring for another – it is other related – but its forms may be more varied. For example, it includes anger about the suffering of the other. Sympathetic distress, guilt (if it is based on empathy rather than on deviation from rules), and empathic anger, which are discussed by Hoffman, can all be considered reactive empathic emotions.

To sum up, in this section I have identified several types of empathy: cognitive, participatory, affective, and empathic joining. I have also differentiated between parallel and reactive empathy, and between false and accurate empathy. Such distinctions may help us to understand the relationships among different types of empathy, and the communalities and differences in their origins, in how they are generated, and in the behaviors that follow them.

The functions of empathy

Empathy serves profoundly important functions. Not surprisingly, these functions are a primary concern of the chapters in Part I. In some, the functions are spelled out, in others, they are implied. In describing them, I will comment on the chapters by adding my own thoughts about functions.

The role of empathy in survival

Plutchik focuses on the survival value, or the evolutionary significance of empathy. In his view, empathy increases the inclusive fitness of organisms: First, group behavior, which requires empathy, enhances survival in a variety of ways, for example, by providing increased defense against predators. Second, "emotional empathy serves to bond individuals to one another, especially mothers to infants" (chapter 3), and enhances the care that mothers provide for infants and the pair's tendency to seek proximity. In these and other ways, empathy contributes to survival. Another aspect of this function is that empathy in humans makes group life possible. Without the positive emotional connections of which empathy is basic source and building block, people could only live together if their relations were completely defined and delimited by rules that inhibited them from harming others and prescribed ways to cooperate.

Given its survival value, empathy must be genetically coded. In animals, this genetic potential would normally become actualized. However, human infants live under tremendously varied conditions. Thus it is important to specify the experiences that will promote or retard the development of this genetic potential that result or do not result in the developmental course of empathy that Hoffman has discussed (see Hoffman, 1976; Staub, 1985, 1986).

The role of empathy in the development of persons

Who we are, who we become, is greatly affected by empathy and processes that are based on empathy. Plutchik and Marcia both stress the role of empathy in the development of organisms. This is the focus of Marcia's entire chapter, which asks whether the development occurs in the context of the socialization of the child, or in psychotherapy, which serves to remediate "previously negatively resolved life cycle stage issues" as well as help the client cope with "the current salient issues" (chapter 5). Empathy is frequently a spontaneous process, involuntary or nonvoluntary, but, as Marcia notes, therapists can "set" themselves to function in an empathic mode. Research on empathic sets has shown that people can also influence, set, or elicit in others an empathic mode (see, for example, Regan & Totten, 1975). Obviously, as shown by research and experience, people can also set themselves or lead others to a nonempathic mode. Many therapists and researchers (some of whom are referred to by Marcia, Plutchik, and Wispé) have noted the role of empathy in development. What are some major aspects of this role?

Empathy as a means to positive modes of relating. Empathy is a source of connection between people that leads to a positive mode of relating to others. In time this can result in positive feelings toward human beings in general. If caretakers respond with participatory or affective empathy to the infant, and the infant responds in positive ways, a transactional system of positive (in contrast to negative) ways of relating can evolve. The infant can also initiate the empathic connection, for example, by imitating the facial expressions of adults. This begins at an early age and might stimulate empathic joining. When accurate empathy guides the caretaker's behavior, the infant's needs will be best fulfilled. Both the gratification of needs and the perception in another of empathy with oneself are likely to be reinforcing. Progressively, the child is likely to develop stable positive feelings toward those with whom he or she has empathic connection, which generalize to other human beings.

Empathy as a source of the self-concept and of self-expansion. Empathy, in Sullivan's interpersonal theory, is fundamental to human development. The infant prehends the mother's positive and negative emotions, which affect the development in the infant of the perception of "good me," "bad me," and "not me." In Fairbairn's view, the "good enough mother" is "able to resonate with the baby's wants and needs, (so that) the latter becomes attuned to his own bodily functions and impulses, which becomes the basis for his slowly evolving self" (see Marcia, chapter 5). Thus, the infant's empathic experience of the mother's feelings and the mother's empathic responses to the infant help to initiate and organize the infant's experience of self.

Wispé notes that other writers, such as Mead, Cooley, and Baldwin, have focused on how we evolve and define ourselves by seeing ourselves in others' reflections of us. Most of these reflections must be empathically perceived by us. It is even possible that, *as we empathically join others in the feelings and reactions that we evoke in them,* as we thus share with them their feelings about us, we proceed to experience and then to conceptualize and define ourselves.

Empathy in therapy can contribute to the development of the self. It plays a less intensive but nonetheless essential role in helping the therapist know, understand, and gather information about a client beyond what is provided by him or her in direct communication. In the view of Carl Rogers, as described by both Wispé and Marcia, empathy plays an essential role in helping a client become aware of and accept parts of himself or herself that were formerly unacceptable owing to prior experience, especially with parents. As a result, some portion of the totality of the person's experiences were not conceptualized, did not become part of the self-concept. They exert a destructive influence. The therapist's acceptance of the client, which both requires empathy and is expressed and thus communicated to the client through empathy, is essential if the client is to perceive and accept these experiences and feelings in himself or herself. Only then can they become part of the self-concept. Thus, empathy in therapy is crucial in helping clients gain self-awareness, self-acceptance, and a self-concept that accurately expresses their total being.

Wispé cites passages from both Downey and Freud that indicate empathy plays an important role in our understanding and in our taking in from others what is not part of us, what is alien to us. We can break the limitations of our selves and expand beyond our direct experience, beyond our identity, by empathizing with others. This requires an advanced capacity for empathy. To perceive in others, even if not fully but accurately, what is not a part of us, to participate in their experience that goes beyond ours, we must have not only the capacity for empathy, but also an openness to experience. This can only be developed by relying on partial and fragmentary experiences that we ourselves have had, and on undeveloped parts of ourselves in perceiving or prehending and empathically responding to others. An interesting point to consider is the limit of such empathy. That is to say, how unfamiliar can the territory of self and experience be into which people can still move empathically?

Empathy as a source of moral principles

The contribution of empathy to caring and to principles of justice, as well as to moral judgment, is the central subject of Hoffman's chapter. Here I want to note the essential role of empathy in the development of such moral principles, or what I call moral value orientations (Staub, 1985, 1986). Elsewhere, Hoffman (1983) has focused on the role of empathy in moral internalization. In chapter 4 he reviews his previous theorizing (Hoffman, 1984) about the development of empathy-based moral affects.

Empathy makes a special contribution to the development of what Hoffman calls the principle of caring, which is similar to Gilligan's morality of care and responsibility and my "prosocial orientation" or prosocial value orientation (Staub, 1978, 1980, 1985, 1986). The experience of empathic connection – in both participatory empathy and empathic joining – and of others' empathy with ourselves is crucial if we are to create a bond between self and others. This is a source of positive evaluation of human beings and a caring about their welfare, which are the basic components of a prosocial orientation. Without empathy, people might develop moral principles that focus on rules and on maintaining the social order, which I have called a rule orientation, but it is unlikely that they would feel genuine connection to and caring for others.

Empathy as a component of moral principles and an influence on moral judgment

The exploration of this role is a significant contribution of Hoffman's chapter, which he sees as a "beginning attempt" to expand his conception of the development of empathy into a comprehensive moral theory.

Hoffman notes that empathy is an important source or component of the "principle of caring" as well as the "principle of justice," particularly when the focus of the justice principle is people's need or effort expanded. He also suggests that empathy affects what principle people select in making moral judgments. Thus, empathy may have a "direct effect on moral judgment and reasoning" (chapter 4), owing to the connection between empathy and moral principles, as well as an activating effect. Moreover, the cooccurrence of moral principles and empathic affect in a moral conflict situation will result in "an affective charge being acquired by the principle," which comes to be encoded as a "hot cognition."

With the advances of the past 20 years in moral theory and research, the time is ripe to offer a comprehensive model of morality. My own attempt to formulate a general theory of morality, which focuses on motivation and moral action (especially prosocial behavior and aggression) and on the development of personal characteristics that contribute to moral action (see Staub, 1985, 1986), suggests some alternative considerations with regard to these issues.

First, moral principles, rules, and standards are inherently motivating; to follow them is inherently rewarding and to deviate from them is inherently (and affectively) aversive. In my own perspective, moral value orientations such as the prosocial and rule orientations are themselves motivational or goal orientations that are related to the realm of others' welfare. They are characterized by desires or preferences for classes of outcomes or end states and by associated cognitive networks. Thus, to the extent that we focus on them as cognitions, when they become active motivations, they will be hot cognitions. They can become even "hotter," or can change in quality, when joined by empathy. Over time, moral principles can fuse with empathy and be jointly coded. Our "prosocial orientation," for example, may well be the outcome of such fusion (Staub, 1985, 1986).

Second, empathy functions as a motive, and as such it is likely to be involved in the activation and selection of moral principles, as Hoffman suggests. It might also be worthwhile to consider the selection of moral principles or the level of moral reasoning that enters into moral judgment in the framework of a comprehensive motivational system, so that we can examine the role of both moral and nonmoral motivation in selection. I have discussed the "activating potential of the environment" for motives, especially personal goals. Circumstances can activate many different motives, both morally relevant and self-related ones, sometimes at the same time. The motives that become active, whether self-related (as is the desire for achievement or for power) or other-related (as is empathy), will influence the principle or type of reasoning that is chosen. There will be a tendency to avoid conflict and maximize gain by the "choice" of moral principle or level of reasoning that allows the person to satisfy his or her active motive or goal (see Staub, 1985; Eisenberg, 1986). A theoretically more accurate statement may be the following: Moral value orientations are themselves goal orientations that can be activated by morally relevant circumstances. Sometimes they will be jointly activated with other goals, so that there will be a compromise in the type and level of moral reasoning that is used, in the choice of outcomes, and in the resulting action.

The influence of empathy on moral behavior

Plutchik's discussion in chapter 3 is concerned with *how empathy affects behavior*. Hoffman briefly refers to his strong interest in empathy as a motive for prosocial action. In his view, empathy is also likely to affect other types of moral behaviors.

My own abiding interest has been in the development of a theory that helps us understand and predict moral action (Staub 1978, 1980, 1986). Even to consider whether empathy will or will not arise in a particular instance or why it sometimes does and at other times does not, we must have a theory that specifies the situational conditions and personal characteristics that contribute to empathy, and that indicates how these varied influences interact. In particular, a general theory is needed to shed light on prosocial and moral action. Even if empathy with a sufferer does arise, it will not necessarily lead to helpful action. Circumstances can activate more than one motive, and another motive may predominate. Even if empathy is the dominant motive, "supporting characteristics" such as skills and competencies will affect whether empathy is expressed in action. Such characteristics also influence whether empathy will arise: The knowledge of one's total inability to help a suffering victim may make empathy with a sufferer aversive, and thus it may be less likely to arise in such circumstances.

Empathy as a source of separation, antagonism, and aggression

The authors of the preceding chapters and I agree that empathy is a source of connection among a people. However, being connected to some may mean being separated from others. An imperfect analogy for this is the appearance of stranger anxiety about the time that infants become attached to caretakers.

Empathic connections among people can join with hostility toward others, an outgroup, in solidifying a group and fulfilling the members' need for connection. The *contagion of emotion* within a group, its spread among the members, requires cognitive empathy and is a form of empathic joining. It often appears when a group turns against others, for example, during a lynching or some other form of mob behavior.

The complex relationship between empathy and aggression, although important, is seldom discussed in the current literature. Empathy probably has an important role in diminishing aggression (Feshbach & Feshbach, 1969; Staub, 1978, 1986). As yet, we do not know whether people who have a greater capacity for certain kinds of empathy tend, when angry, to behave less aggressively than do other people as a consequence of their various experiencing of another's suffering. The alternative is that such people, because of their capacity to experience another's pain, find their aggression against others to be highly satisfying. If the latter happens and conditions are right, some varieties of empathy may increase aggression.

The uses of "nonempathy"

An important contribution of Marcia's chapter is his discussion of when and how empathy or the expression of empathy can have harmful rather than beneficial effects. Sometimes, by not communicating his or her empathic understanding, the therapist helps the client more than by communicating it. To empathize with some patients can be ''toxic'' or destructive for the client. In the mother–child relationship, it is the ''gradual diminution in the mother's finely tuned responding (decreasing communicated empathy) that contributes to the child's later sense of separateness and individuality'' (chapter 5).

All this can be generalized to other relationships and contexts. The empathic perception of a child's pain and hurt must often be communicated with the greatest sensitivity, and sometimes not at all. A direct communication is often nonempathic and hurtful. And, just as ''both psychotherapy and effective mothering require that the merger aspect of the relationship be temporary'' (chapter 5), so it is essential for the healthy development or functioning of parties in most empathic connections that their ''merging'' be temporary. Although empathy is an essential source of human connection, and connecting identities can be beneficial in many ways, losing identities can be disastrous.

References

Batson, C. D., Duncan, B. D., Ackerman, P., Buckley, T., & Birch, K. (1981). Is empathic emotion a source of altruistic motivation? *Journal of Personality and Social Psychology, 40,* 290–302.

Batson, C. D., O'Quin, K., Fultz, J., Vanderplus, M., & Isen, A. M. (1983). Influence of self-reported distress and empathy on egoistic versus altruistic motivation to help. *Journal of Personality and Social Psychology, 45,* 706–718.

Eisenberg, N. (1986). *Altruistic emotion, cognition and behavior.* Hillsdale, NJ: Erlbaum.

Feshbach, N. D., & Feshbach, S. (1969). The relationship between empathy and aggression in two age groups. *Developmental Psychology, 1,* 102–107.

Hoffman, M. L. (1976). Empathy, roletaking, guilt, and development of altruistic motives. In T. Lickona (Ed.), *Moral development and behavior* (pp. 124–143). New York: Holt.

Hoffman, M. L. (1983). Affective and cognitive processes in moral internalization: An information processing approach. In E. T. Higgins, D. Ruble, & W. Hartup (Eds.), *Social Cognition and Social Development: A Socio-Cultural Perspective* (pp. 236–274). New York: Cambridge University Press.

Hoffman, M. L. (1984). Interaction of affect and cognition in empathy. In C. Izard, J. Kagan, and R. Zajonc (Eds.), *Emotions, cognition, and behavior* (pp. 103–131). New York: Cambridge University Press.

Regan, D., & Totten, J. (1975). Empathy and attribution: Turning observers into actors. *Journal of Personality and Social Psychology, 32,* 850–856.

Staub, E. (1978). *Positive social behavior and morality: Vol. 1. Social and personal influences.* New York: Academic Press.

Staub, E. (1979). *Positive social behavior and morality, Vol. 2. Socialization and development.* New York: Academic Press.

Staub, E. (1980). Social and prosocial behavior: Personal and situational influences and their interactions. In E. Staub (Ed.), *Personality: Basic aspects and current research* (pp. 236–294). Englewood Cliffs, NJ: Prentice-Hall.

Staub, E. (1985). Social behavior and moral conduct: A personal goal theory account of people benefiting and harming others. Unpublished manuscript, University of Massachusetts, Amherst.

Staub, E. (1986). A conception of the determinants and development of altruism and aggression: Motives, the self, the environment. In Zahn-Waxler, C. (Ed.), *Altruism and aggression: Social and biological origins* (pp. 135–164). New York: Cambridge University Press.

Staub, E., & Feinberg, H. K. (1980). *Regularities in peer interaction, empathy, and sensitivity to others.* Paper presented at the Annual Meeting of the American Psychological Association, Montreal.

Wispé, L. (1986). The distinction between sympathy and empathy: To call forth a concept, a word is needed. *Journal of Personality and Social psychology, 50,* 314–322.

Part II

Empathy across the life span

6 Empathy and emotional understanding: the early development of empathy

Ross A. Thompson

Consider the following observations:

> At 14 months, S observed a crying 6-month-old baby; she watched; tears welled in her eyes; she began to cry; she looked to her mother. (Zahn-Waxler, Radke-Yarrow, & King, 1977, p. 2)

> At nine months, Hope had already demonstrated strong sympathetic responses to other children's distress. Characteristically, she did not turn away from these distress scenes though they apparently touched off distress in herself. Hope would stare intently, her eyes welling up with tears if another child fell, hurt themselves or cried. At that time, she was overwhelmed with her emotions. She would end up crying herself and crawling quickly to her mother for comfort. (Kaplan, 1977, p. 95)

> In the second incident, Michael, aged 15 months, and his friend Paul were fighting over a toy and Paul started to cry. Michael appeared disturbed and let go, but Paul still cried. Michael paused, then brought his teddy bear to Paul but to no avail. Michael paused again, and then finally succeeded in stopping Paul's crying by fetching Paul's security blanket from an adjoining room. (Hoffman, 1975, p. 612)

How do we explain such behavior in very young children? Are the infant and toddlers in these vignettes fundamentally egocentric? What is the significance of others' distressed expressions to them, and how does this change with the growth of emotional understanding? Are their own distress responses empathic in quality, or can they be attributed to a startle reaction, projection, or self-concern?

The purpose of this chapter is to consider emerging perspectives concerning the development of empathic responding in the early years. Interest in the development of empathy has a long history, and recent years have witnessed a burgeoning research interest in empathy and its correlates in childhood and at later ages. However, there has been comparatively little research on empathy in the early years, perhaps because of theoretical assumptions that children this young

I am grateful for the valuable research assistance of Amy Thompson in this project. Helen Buchsbaum's and Diana Etchison's comments on an earlier draft of this chapter are also appreciated.

lack the cognitive abilities required to respond vicariously to others' emotions. One goal of this chapter, therefore, is to review critically recent research relating to these assumptions, and to suggest that a fully developmental approach to empathy must begin with the study of empathic and quasi-empathic phenomena in very young children. This view underscores the developmental relationship between empathy and emotional understanding in the early years and offers a number of directions for further study.

The chapter opens with a review of definitional issues and theoretical perspectives on empathy and their implications for the study of empathy in early development. This is followed by a discussion of research focused on the young child's emerging abilities to interpret and respond appropriately to the emotional expressions of others, and the implications of this research for the development of empathy. In the next section, several broader research issues are outlined, followed by a concluding summary of new perspectives on empathy and emotional understanding in the early years.

Theoretical perspectives and definitional issues

Generally speaking, three theoretical perspectives can be applied to the study of empathy development in the early years. The first consists of psychoanalytic and neoanalytic theories that portray the emergence of empathy in the context of the emotional intimacy shared by mother and infant (e.g., Burlingham, 1967; Freud, 1964; Kaplan, 1977; Spitz, 1965; Stern, Barnett, & Spieker, 1983; Sullivan, 1953). Owing to the infant's dependence on the mother and the early symbiotic relation between them, from this perspective the child is viewed as being highly sensitive to variations in maternal affect and moods that may be transmitted nonconsciously and in subtle ways. The baby is vulnerable to these influences since a clear sense of self–other differentiation is thought to be lacking in early object relations. This resonant emotional response to maternal affect has been viewed by some as an autonomous ego function (Stern et al., 1983). In any case, the child's capacity for empathy increases in sophistication and scope with the growth of object relations and the development of psychological individuation early in the second year (see Kaplan, 1977; Mahler, Pine, & Bergman, 1975). This account of the emergence of empathy in the context of the mother–infant bond has been used to explain not only the infant's sharing of transient moods and emotions (e.g., anxiety), but also of longer-term dispositions and personality characteristics of the mother (e.g., Spitz, 1965). Although heuristically interesting, this formulation has failed to generate a substantial body of research concerning early empathy, perhaps because of the strong influence of cognitive-developmental theory on empathy research.

It is worth noting, however, that Hoffman (1977) has proposed a reformulation of the analytic view in conditioning terms. That is, the mother's emotional state may be transmitted to the baby through the quality of her physical handling of the infant, which may elicit discomfort or upset in the child. This is accompanied, of course, by her vocal and facial expressions of emotion, and subsequently these emotional cues may themselves become conditioned stimuli evoking distress in the baby, which may result in a primitive kind of pseudo-empathy. It remains to be seen whether this reformulation of the analytic view offers a more viable explanation of early vicarious responding, since this approach has also not yet generated much empirical research.

A second perspective with much greater influence on the developmental study of empathy is reflected in the work of social-cognitive researchers stimulated by Piaget's developmental theory. In this view, a capacity for empathic responsiveness is contingent on the development of certain cognitive reasoning abilities, including person permanence, the ability to differentiate the psychological attributes of oneself and others, and rudimentary ability to assume the psychological role of another (e.g., Deutsch & Madle, 1975; Feshbach, 1978; Greenspan, Barenboim, & Chandler, 1976; Shantz, 1975). Although this approach has stimulated considerable research linking empathy to these cognitive-developmental prerequisites, it has also directed attention away from the study of empathy in the early years, since infants and toddlers are viewed as lacking the role-taking capacities required for empathy. In contrast to the analytic view, genuine empathy is unlikely to occur prior to the late preschool years, according to the cognitive-developmental view.

This conclusion may be premature, however, since recent evidence suggests an emerging awareness of internal psychological conditions and rudimentary forms of self–other differentiation very early on. A number of researchers (Bretherton & Beeghly, 1982; Bretherton, McNew, & Beeghly-Smith, 1981; Dunn & Kendrick, 1982a,b) have documented that after age 2 there is a burgeoning of spontaneous child utterances concerning the internal experiences of self and others that reflects a growing appreciation of the emotional, volitional, and cognitive states that individuals can experience. This evidence also suggests an implicit awareness that one's own psychological condition can differ from that of another (e.g., "Mommy, is Tara mad at me?" at 25 months; Bretherton et al., 1981). This elementary kind of self–other differentiation in verbal behavior probably builds on earlier, nonverbal kinds of differentiated self–other awareness in toddlers' social behavior (see, for example, Lempers, Flavell, & Flavell, 1977). Thus, even young children do not seem to exhibit substantial confusion between the internal states of others and their own in everyday circumstances, especially when the other's condition is clear and salient to the child. Although young children's inferences of others' psychological experiences are much less robust in more complex or subtle role-taking situations, these simple kinds of psychological inferences may be fully adequate in many naturally occurring situations that call forth an empathic response.

A third perspective to the study of empathy is reflected in recent research on early socioemotional development (e.g., Campos, Barrett, Lamb, Goldsmith, & Stenberg, 1983; Sroufe, 1979), which portrays the infant and young child as a highly motivated and responsive social partner for whom emotions (of the self and others) play a significant motivational and organizational role. An important contribution to this emergent viewpoint is the ethological perspective to early development (e.g., Bowlby, 1969; Hinde, 1974). According to this view, infants are fundamentally predisposed from birth to emit socioemotional signals and respond to others' socioemotional cues – especially those from caregivers – because such behaviors are survival enhancing. The child's emotional reactions play an important role not only as potent proximity-eliciting signals to the social surround (e.g., cries, smiles), but also in the appraisal processes by which the young child's reactions to environmental events are organized, regulated, and monitored (see Bowlby, 1969, chap. 7; Sroufe, 1979). Similarly, the emotional behavior of others is viewed as providing the child with important informational cues that have motivational consequences for children in their ongoing transactions with the environment.

This viewpoint has several implications for researchers who are interested in the young child's responses to the emotions of others. It suggests that the socioemotional signals of others may be early and prepotent elicitors of attention and arousal, especially those conveying alarm or distress (i.e., signals that are relevant to the infant's safety and security). Emotional expressions are especially important because of their potent signaling quality and because they can be recognized from a very early age (Oster, 1981). Such expressions are thus important early sources of social information and have motivational consequences for infants as they regulate how infants react to diverse aspects of the social environment. Their motivational character may derive, in part, from the arousal of resonant emotion in the child.

Thus, contrary to the portrayal of infants as fundamentally egocentric organisms, this perspective portrays infants as being highly responsive in nonegocentric ways to the socioemotional expressions of others, and are motivated to use these expressions in their ongoing transactions with the surround. Although this theoretical view has not been systematically applied to the study of empathy, an early capacity for vicarious arousal is consistent with this formulation and would serve similar informational and motivational purposes.[1] This viewpoint thus raises important questions concerning how very young children are affected by the emotional expressions of others and the motivational consequences – questions that are clearly pertinent to the early development of empathy. Such questions form the starting point for our review of relevant research on early empathy.

What is empathy?

The nature of empathy and its origins can be defined in different ways. Several issues seem to be at the heart of these definitional differences.

First, is empathy primarily affective or cognitive in quality? Although most researchers agree that empathic responding entails *both* cognitive and affective components, they differ in their relative emphasis on each. Some (e.g., Hoffman, 1981b; Murphy, 1937; and most psychoanalytic writers) emphasize the affective arousal in empathic reactions and place less emphasis on cognitive inferences concerning the other person's emotion. From this perspective, therefore, certain forms of empathy (qua affective contagion) could be observed in very young children under certain conditions. Other theorists place greater emphasis on the cognitive components of empathy, usually in terms of an ability to cognitively assume the psychological role of another (e.g., Deutsch & Madle, 1975; Feshbach, 1978; Greenspan et al., 1976). The latter approach is developmentally more demanding and suggests that true empathic responding is unlikely prior to the achievement of a certain criterion of nonegocentric thought. This view, however, may limit researchers' appreciation of simpler forms of vicarious arousal at earlier ages.

Second, does an empathic response directly match the emotion experienced by the other person, or is it merely similar in valence? An emphasis on emotional matching (e.g., Feshbach & Roe, 1968) is perhaps theoretically more rigorous, but requires a high level of perceptual discrimination and cognitive sophistication that may be beyond the capabilities of most young children. Thus, many children may inappropriately be deemed nonempathic owing to their limited ability to discriminate expressions of more subtle emotions or their inadequate understanding of certain emotional experiences. A definition of empathy that requires an exact match of emotion is also inappropriate for young children because it requires the use of verbal self-report measures in order to assess confidently the veridicality of the observer's response. Finally, defining empathy in terms of affective matching seems contrary to the theoretical role of empathy as a motivator of prosocial behavior. Observers who vicariously experience the same emotion as another in distress may, at times, be prevented from offering assistance when the vicarious distress is immobilizing (e.g., empathic fear or panic). Usually, we assume that observers are motivated to help by sharing a more generalized distress reaction. For these reasons, therefore, a definition of empathy that requires an observer to share the general emotional tone of another – whether or not there is a direct emotional match – seems appropriate for most purposes.

Third, to which cues concerning another's experience does an empathic observer respond? In everyday circumstances, observers can usually draw on multiple cues providing redundant information (Murphy, 1937). Vicarious responding is easier and may be apparent at younger ages when children can observe clear, direct expressions of another's emotion that are consistent with that person's situation. When such direct cues are not available or are inconsistent, inferences must be drawn from indirect sources; therefore greater demands will be placed on a child's cognitive and role-taking capabilities and there will be less likelihood of an empathic response. This is important since many studies of children's empathy use abstract story narratives (often with dissonant situational and expressive cues) that place greater demands on empathic responding than commonly occur in everyday circumstances. Thus, evidence for empathy may depend, in part, on the kind of direct or indirect information that is available concerning another's emotional experience.

Taken together, these definitional issues concerning (1) the affective and cognitive bases of empathic responding, (2) the veridicality of the observer's response, and (3) the kinds of cues to which the person responds are largely concerned with the degree of *inference* required in an observer's empathic response to another. On one hand, children as well as adults experience the direct, almost involuntary pull of another's emotional expressions in accident settings and other situations eliciting strong affect in others. This kind of emotional contagion requires minimal inference from an observer because these powerful emotional cues seem reflexively to call forth a resonant emotional response. On the other hand, other situations require much greater inferential role taking and, at times, a sophisticated interpretation of another's affective cues, such as when we interpret socially constrained emotional displays. These occasions make much greater cognitive demands on the potential empathizer, and empathic responding is not necessarily automatic.

It seems most appropriate to regard *both* kinds of empathic responding as anchorpoints on a continuum of empathy. Such a view affirms the similarity of the empathic experiences of young children and adults when faced with another's compelling emotional cues. It also fosters developmental study by raising important questions about how the experience of empathy is affected by different situational conditions and the growth of certain age-related abilities. The latter include the development of emotional understanding (e.g., knowledge concerning the instigators of emotion, display rules, etc.), the broadening of the child's own background of emotional experiences, and capacity for self-reflection, and increasing cognitive and role-taking skills. From this perspective, one can look for evidence of early expressions of empathy in situations involving direct and compelling cues from another, even though young children lack the cognitive skills required for more sophisticated, inferential kinds of empathic responding. With this portrayal of gradations of empathic responding in mind, we now turn to research that is relevant to the development of empathic responding in the early years of life.

Emotional resonance and empathic responding in the early years

Although the everyday observations of parents attest to the sensitivity of young children to the emotions of others, systematic study of this phenomenon has begun only recently. Consequently, much of the research reviewed in this section was not concerned with empathy per se, but rather with processes related to the young child's emotional reactions to direct expressions of affect from another. Their application to early empathy is sometimes conjectural but, when taken together, these findings converge on two important observations that are pertinent to the developmental study of empathy. First, it is clear that from early in the first year, infants are capable of emotional resonance or contagion – that is, of sharing the same emotion as a consequence of another's emotional display. Although these responses are not empathic in quality since they do not derive from knowledge of the other's situation or condition, they are probably important precursors of empathy. Second, responses to another's arousal that are more clearly empathic in quality begin to appear midway through the second year of life. We now turn to the relevant research.

Reactive crying in newborns

The phenomenon of neonatal crying in reaction to the distress cries of other newborns had long been reported informally by parents and practitioners, but was not systematically investigated until the work of Simner (1971). In a series of studies, Simner presented 2- to 4-day-old newborn infants with 6 minute tapes of various auditory stimuli:

1. spontaneous crying by a 5-day-old neonate,
2. spontaneous crying by a 5½-month-old,
3. a computer-synthesized replication of a newborn cry,
4. the baby's own spontaneous crying (recorded on an earlier occasion), and
5. white noise that was equivalent in sound intensity.

Simner found that the sound of neonatal crying produced significantly more re-active crying in newborns than did either white noise, the 5½-month-old cry, or the synthetic cry. There were some indications that newborns showed more arousal to the sound of their *own* cry than to the neonatal cry, but this finding was not reliable.

These findings were largely replicated by two groups of investigators. Using Simner's tapes, Sagi and Hoffman (1976) found that the neonatal cry evoked significantly more fussing than did the synthetic cry or a silent control condition. Martin and Clark (1982) tested 1-day-olds with 4-minute tapes of neonatal crying, the crying of an 11-month-old, and the newborn's own crying (recorded earlier) and found that the sound of another newborn's crying was the most potent cry-eliciting stimulus. In contrast to the results reported by Simner, the sound of the newborn's *own* prior crying seemed to elicit attention and interest rather than distress but also indicated a differentiation of the two stimuli. However, these findings are difficult to interpret because the cry tapes probably differed in sound intensity: The newborn's own cry was spontaneous, whereas the audio tape of another newborn infant was obtained during a "painful injection." Thus, it is unclear whether differences in infants' responsiveness were due to whether the cry was self-produced or to the intensity of the stimulus, and further research is needed.

Although neonatal reactive crying has been described as "a rudimentary empathic distress reaction at birth" (Sagi & Hoffman, 1976), other explanations also merit consideration. These include the possibility that crying is the outcome of a conditioned distress response to auditory cues resembling the infant's own cry (Hoffman, 1982b) and that crying is a primitive form of reproductive assimilation (Piaget, 1951). The problem with both alternatives is that each relies on the perceived similarity between another's cry and the child's own cry. The findings of Martin and Clark (1982) seem to belie this assumption, but until the reliability of their results is established these interpretations will remain difficult to evaluate. It is important to note that researchers have consistently found that reactive crying is clearest for the crying of infants of approximately the same age, as seems consistent with conditioning and reproductive assimilation explanations, and may reflect a constraint on the range of stimuli evoking neonatal reactive crying. In sum, it is probably more appropriate to regard such crying as a primitive kind of emotional contagion evoked, in part, by the similarity of the cry to the newborn's own distress sound. Since it is clearly not a response to another's situation, reactive crying cannot be called empathic.

This kind of emotional contagion is apparent at somewhat older ages also. Hay, Hash, and Pedersen (1981) observed pairs of 6-month-olds together with their mothers during 10-minute play trials and noted the effects of one child's naturally occurring distress on the partner. They found that a model of cumulative influence accounted for a child's reactions to a partner's distress, and that the child's upset was more likely to occur the longer the partner cried. Children were highly likely to become upset, for example, when the partner had fussed continuously for 2 minutes or longer. Since neonatal reactive crying also occurred after a 1- to 2-minute latency (Simner, 1971), these findings are concordant with this research and warrant further investigation of reactive crying at a range of different ages in the first year.

Affective synchrony in mother–infant play

Students of early socioemotional development have devoted considerable attention to mother–infant face-to-face play, which begins to occur regularly when infants are 2 to 3 months of age (e.g., Brazelton, Tronick, Adamson,
Als, & Wise, 1975; Malatesta & Haviland, 1982; Stern, 1977). This activity is
unique because it is purely social in quality: Unlike other contexts for mother–
infant interaction, there are no routine caregiving activities to compete for attention, and consequently they are regarded by researchers as important contexts
for the early development of social skills and social expectations. Moreover,
these play episodes entail a sharing of affect between mother and baby that may
provide an important foundation for the development of empathy.

According to researchers, each partner contributes to these play exchanges
through a repertoire of interactive behavior, and it is the synchrony and alterna-
tion of maternal and infant behavior that has led some researchers to characterize
these exchanges as a "nonverbal conversation" or "behavioral dialogue." The
hypothesized goal of these exchanges is *positive affective synchrony* between
mother and baby – that is, the mutual sharing of positive arousal during which
infants manifest the excited, engaged sociability that adults find rewarding (Brazelton et al., 1975; Stern, 1977). Much of the responsibility for this falls on the
mother who, through her animated play behavior and contingent responding to
the infant's social cues, contributes most to the achievement of affective synchrony (Thompson & Lamb, 1983).

These affective dynamics are illustrated in recent studies by Malatesta and
Haviland (1982) and Malatesta (1985). In each, bouts of mother–infant face-to-
face play were videotaped, and microanalyses of maternal and infant facial
expressions of emotion were subsequently conducted. These researchers found
that mothers were highly likely to imitate infant expressions of enjoyment and
interest (which occurred most frequently), as well as expressions of surprise,
sadness, and anger when they occurred, although mothers rarely displayed negative emotions to the baby. Thus infant–mother dyads exhibited considerable
positive affective synchrony, partly as a consequence of the mother's contingent
matching of positive infant emotional expressions. Over the course of the first
year, infants showed increasing rates of positive expressions in play, which were
a function, in part, of maternal contingent responding to infant affect (Malatesta,
1985).

These reports suggest that mothers were seeking to accentuate and enlarge the
infant's positive emotional responses by contingently imitating positive displays
and maintaining a generally positive expressive demeanor. Such positive "affective attunement" (Stern, Hofer, Haft, & Dore, 1985) not only engages the infant

emotionally, but may also contribute to the development of a resonant emotional response by the baby. That is, if the mother responds to the infant's smiles with imitative smiling and also with other exuberant initiatives, the infant's own positive arousal is likely to be heightened as a result. Over time, the association of maternal smiling and other social initiatives with the infant's own excitement may make the mother's expressions themselves potent cues for the baby's own positive expressions. This kind of emotional contagion or resonance may, in fact, constitute the infant's major contribution to the establishment of affective synchrony during episodes of mother–infant play.

Although the possibility of emotional resonance on the part of the baby in face-to-face play may contribute to an understanding of the dyad's affective synchrony, it is doubtful that the baby's response can be called empathic since it does not derive from a clear appreciation of the mother's situation or experience. It is, instead, a form of classical conditioning involving the frequent cooccurrence of maternal and infantile expressions of delight. But because it entails a much more sophisticated response to a partner's affect compared to the reactive crying of neonates, this early experience of emotional resonance in mother–infant play may provide an important foundation for more sophisticated forms of empathy in mother–infant interaction later in the first year.

Interpreting facial cues of emotion: the onset of social referencing

The studies of mother–infant face-to-face play indicate that, early in the first year, infants respond affectively to the mother in ways that suggest resonant emotion. But it is unclear from these studies *how* this kind of emotional communication takes place, because the infant is reacting to a combination of maternal emotional cues in the face, vocal tone, and body movement (Stern, 1977). The infant's capacity to interpret signals in each specific modality is of obvious relevance to the early development of empathy, as is evidence of the infant's emotional responses to these expressions in others.

A number of studies have dealt with the development of infants' abilities to discriminate among different facial expressions of emotion and to interpret them as emotional signals (see reviews by Klinnert, Campos, Sorce, Emde, & Svejda, 1983; Oster, 1981). Infants are capable of organized facial scanning at 2 months of age (Haith, Bergman, & Moore, 1977), and from 2 to 5 months of age they develop the capacity to discriminate among facial expressions of happiness, anger, surprise, and other emotions (e.g., Barrera & Maurer, 1981; LaBarbara, Izard, Vietze, & Parisi, 1976; Young-Browne, Rosenfeld, & Horowitz, 1977). However, the discriminations occurring at this time are probably not due to the emotional meaning of different facial expressions, but rather to their variant stimulus properties. For example, Oster and Ewy (reported in Oster, 1981) found that 4-

month-olds could discriminate a "toothy" grin from a sad expression, but could not discriminate a closed-mouth grin from the sad expression, probably because there were fewer discriminable stimulus differences in the latter comparison.

When do infants begin to attribute emotional meaning to different facial expressions? On this question, the evidence is more sparse. Kreutzer and Charlesworth (1973) presented live portrayals of angry, sad, happy, and neutral facial expressions (accompanied by vocal and gestural cues) to infants at 4, 6, 8, and 10 months of age. They reported that although the youngest infants responded indiscriminately to these emotional displays, at 6 months and older infants showed more negative affect to the negative expressions. Although much additional research is needed (including studies that present facial cues apart from vocal and gestural cues), this finding offers suggestive evidence that infants begin to interpret facial expressions as emotional cues sometime in the second half of the first year.

Once facial expressions are imbued with emotional meaning, what effect does this have on the infant's responding to others? Students of early development have recently begun exploring how infants use such cues, especially from an adult, when faced with uncertain or ambiguous situations. In unfamiliar laboratory conditions, for example, toddlers will devote considerable effort to remaining within the mother's viewing range, even when she is physically present but merely turned away (Carr, Dabbs, & Carr, 1975). They will also display inhibited play and subdued affect when she is present but preoccupied (Sorce & Emde, 1981). And by the end of the first year, infants begin "checking back" visually when faced with uncertain circumstances, such as the presence of a loud toy or the approach of an unfamiliar adult (e.g., Rheingold & Eckerman, 1973). This pehnomenon has been called "social referencing" (Campos & Stenberg, 1981; Feinman, 1982; Klinnert, Campos, Sorce, Emde, & Svejda, 1983), and it reflects an active effort by infants to obtain emotional cues from others to assist in their own assessment of an uncertain situation.

Social referencing has been observed in infants as young as 7 months old (Sorce, Emde, & Frank, 1982), but it is more commonly observed beginning at about 10 to 12 months of age (Klinnert, Campos, Sorce, Emde, & Svejda, 1983). A number of investigators have demonstrated the important effects a mother's posed emotional cues can have on an infant's tendency to approach or avoid an unusual person or object. For example, Klinnert (1981) presented 12- and 18-month old infants with novel and somewhat forbidding toys in a laboratory playroom in the mother's presence, and instructed mothers to pose facial expressions conveying either fear, joy, or neutral emotion. For those infants who regularly referenced the mother, maternal facial expressions had a profound effect: Infants were significantly more likely to move away from mother to approach the toy when the mother was smiling, but to retreat to the mother when she was displaying fear. Although it is clear that a stimulus event must be ambiguous in order to elicit referencing (Gunnar & Stone, 1984; Sorce, Emde, Campos, & Klinnert, 1985) – since distinctly pleasant or aversive events require little assistance in the baby's appraisal – studies of social referencing indicate that maternal emotional expressions significantly influence infants' responses to these events by the end of the first year. Furthermore, indications that infants will reference a familiarized adult who is present in the room along with the mother (Klinnert, Emde, & Butterfield, 1983) reflect some generality to the referencing phenomenon.

Why do the mother's emotional expressions have such an effect? The efficacy of these signals may be due, in part, to the arousal of resonant emotion within the child. That is, a mother's clear display of negative emotion may arouse wariness in a child, which fosters behavioral inhibition, whereas maternal expressions of positive affect produce resonant feelings of well-being that facilitate approach and exploration. Support for this view has been found by several researchers who have noted that negative affect was evident in infants after they referenced mothers displaying fearful expressions (see Klinnert, Campos, Sorce, Emde, & Svejda, 1983; Sorce et al., 1985). Thus it appears that, soon after infants have attributed emotional meaning to facial expressions, these expressions play a role in behavioral regulation, probably through the arousal of a resonant emotional reaction in the child that mediates subsequent approach or avoidance of uncertain events. It is difficult to say, however, whether the child's referencing is genuinely empathic, since the purpose of social referencing is presumably to assess one's *own* circumstances rather than another's. Nevertheless, referencing phenomena clearly point to the importance of others' emotional expressions as salient informational cues and as sources of resonant arousal in infants as young as 10 to 12 months of age. Further research is needed to evaluate the nature of social referencing in naturalistic as well as laboratory conditions – and referencing involving other expressive modalities – in order to assess the generality of this phenomenon.

Emotional sharing and prosocial motivation

In studies of social referencing, the child's derivative emotional reaction is an outcome of self- rather than other-concern, since researchers believe the purpose of such referencing is to better appraise one's own current circumstances. There is, however, growing evidence that after infants become capable of attributing emotional meaning to emotional expressions, they also begin to respond vicariously to these expressions, and that in the second year this may motivate rudimentary forms of helpgiving. Support for this conclusion comes from a report by Main, Weston, and Wakeling (1979), who observed the "concerned attention" (i.e., attention and knit eyebrows) of 12-month-olds to an adult actor who displayed distress in a laboratory playroom. Infants who displayed "concerned attention" were reported by mothers to behave helpfully and prosocially at home.

More substantive evidence comes from an ambitious cross-sequential home-observational study by Zahn-Waxler, Radke-Yarrow, and their colleagues (Cummings, Zahn-Waxler, & Radke-Yarrow, 1981, 1984; Zahn-Waxler & Radke-Yarrow, 1979, 1982; Zahn-Waxler, Radke-Yarrow, & King, 1977, 1979). These researchers devised a unique methodology to record young children's responses to naturally occurring expressions of emotion around them: Twenty-four mothers were trained to observe critically and record such incidents soon after they occurred at home over a 9-month period. The sample was divided into three cohorts: those who began the study (1) when the child was 10 months old ($N = 8$), (2) when the child was 15 months old ($N = 9$), and (3) when the child was 20 months old ($N = 7$).

The findings yielded by these maternal reports were striking. Among even the youngest children in the sample, the distress of others elicited orienting and, in nearly one third of the 10- to 14-month-olds, distress crying (Zahn-Waxler & Radke-Yarrow, 1982). At these ages, few infants could act constructively to relieve another's distress, so their arousal was unaccompanied by instrumental behavior. With increasing age, however, constructive initiatives (e.g., helpgiving, seeking an adult) increased significantly, and the child's own resonant distress declined (perhaps as a consequence). Children at this age also increasingly imitated the distress cues of the other, as if "trying on" their emotional expressions to comprehend them better (Zahn-Waxler et al., 1977). Such a phenomenon resembles the process of "motor mimicry" hypothesized by Hoffman (1982b) to be an important mechanism of empathic arousal. Thus, the major developmental change in children's reactions to others' distress was a shift from a global resonant distress reaction to greater other-directed instrumental behavior midway through the second year (Zahn-Waxler & Radke-Yarrow, 1979, 1982). This developmental trend was evident not only in the maternal narratives, but also during simulations of distressed behavior conducted when research assistants visited the home.

Does this behavior reflect empathic responding in toddlers? Certainly these findings provide the strongest evidence to date for vicarious arousal at this age. On the other hand, it is often difficult to eliminate competing hypotheses for the children's responses on the basis of the narrative accounts provided by the mothers. For example, a young child's sober expression of "concerned attention" may reflect an orienting response or efforts to interpret or understand another's emotional outburst rather than empathy. At times, reactive distress may be the outcome of having been startled by another's sudden, intense crying. In addition, a young child's self-concern may be aroused by the sight of another in distress, which may cause the child's own upset. It should also be noted that instances of resonant distress were not common at these ages (nor in the study by Dunn and Kendrick reported in the next section), and many children simply ignored the distress of others. Thus, vicarious responding was not pervasive nor always clearcut in children of this age, and individual differences predominated in these studies.

Part of what makes this evidence so interesting is the early link between resonant distress and prosocial initiatives suggested in the maternal narratives. Whereas the earliest initiatives at about 1 year of age consisted of positive physical contact such as touching or patting, older children exhibited verbal reassurance, acts of sharing, defense of the victim, and other instrumental acts (Zahn-Waxler & Radke-Yarrow, 1982). In addition, the self-punitive behavior that was evident when the child had caused another's distress – and also when the child was *not* responsible – may reflect an apparent confusion in the child's understanding of causality for another's upset, and perhaps an early link between vicarious distress and guilt (see Thompson & Hoffman, 1980). Zahn-Waxler, Radke-Yarrow, and King (1979) also reported that maternal child-rearing techniques were related to children's prosocial initiatives in the two older cohorts. The children of mothers who used emotionally assertive statements to explain the distress the child caused another were more likely to act reparatively when they hurt another and altruistically when they were bystanders to another's distress. In these cases, the combination of inductive discipline with a psychologically "power-assertive" emotional tone may have focused young children's attention on the distress of another and its causes, as well as emphasized the human dimension of the child's actions.

Thus it is the growing tendency of toddlers to combine their "concerned attention" with prosocial initiatives that argues for the empathic basis of the child's resonant emotional reaction. If such distress was due primarily to a startle reaction or orienting, it would be unlikely to motivate helpgiving at this early age, prior to the internalization of social norms concerning helpgiving. This transition to instrumental assistance is probably related to the broadening of the toddler's behavioral repertoire as well as a growing psychological understanding of others (see Bretherton et al., 1981). Indeed, it may be their growing capacity to act instrumentally that results in a decline, with age, in children's global distress reactions to another's upset.

Is there evidence that children at these ages respond vicariously to other kinds of emotional experiences they observe at home? Cummings, Zahn-Waxler, and Radke-Yarrow (1981, 1984) focused on maternal reports concerning anger and affection observed by the child. Not surprisingly, they found that when toddlers witnessed affectionate episodes at home, they responded with positive emotion and affectionate initiatives of their own. When anger was observed, however, distress and anger (e.g., scolding or hitting one of the participants) were the most frequent responses. These investigators reported that toddlers' anger responses had a distinctly punitive quality and did not simply mimic the anger they observed and thus suggested that a contagion of affect rather than simple imitative behavior had occurred. To be sure, there are alternative explanations: Witnessing an angry encounter involving a parent could increase a toddler's *self*-concern and foster heightened distress, and anger could also result from efforts to defend the family member who was being attacked. Similarly, observing affection could induce pleasure through the child's expectation of sharing in this experience. Thus the empathic origins of these responses are not always clear, although these findings rather clearly indicate how much children are affected by diverse emotional expressions at home.

Somewhat clearer findings have been reported in an experimental study by Cummings, Iannotti, and Zahn-Waxler (1985) with an independent group of 2-year-olds. In this study, the aggressive behavior of toddlers toward a peer increased following exposure to a 5-minute period of simulated angry adult conflict. As in the earlier study, angry behavior was not imitative in quality, but appeared to reflect a sharing of the angry mood that had previously been observed – and was directed this time toward an innocent partner.

Taken together, these findings provide the strongest evidence to date for the emergence of empathic responding midway through the second year and its role as a motivator of prosocial initiatives. To be sure, the reliance on maternal reports, while providing important and unique insights into children's reactions to others' naturally occurring emotional expressions, may have certain disadvantages, despite these researchers' efforts to foster clear and unbiased narrative accounts. For example, since mothers of children at this age are concerned with encouraging empathy and prosocial behavior in their offspring (Kagan, 1984), this may have influenced their descriptive accounts of their children's reactions. But the weight of the evidence clearly points to the sensitivity of children this young to the emotional expressions of others, not only for information concerning the child's status (i.e., social referencing), but as the basis for more genuine other-directed concern motivating early prosocial behavior. There are also clear indications that empathy underlies this motivational system.

Vicarious responding in early sibling relationships

Somewhat similar conclusions may be drawn from an extensive longitudinal study of early sibling relationships by Dunn and Kendrick (1982a,b). The focus of this study was the emerging relationship between an older sibling (the majority were between 18 and 23 months old at the time of the sibling's birth) and the infant brother or sister. These investigators conducted interviews with mothers and two hour-long home observations of family interaction on each of four occasions: during the mother's pregnancy and when the second child was 1, 8, and 14 months old.

Not surprisingly, the arrival and presence of the sibling was an extremely salient experience to the older child, provoking a great deal of interest, concern, and scrutiny. This was reflected also in the older child's prosocial initiatives toward the younger. Even when the younger child was 1 month old, the majority of mothers reported that the older sibling sought to comfort the younger child when the latter was distressed. By the time the younger child was 8 months old, Dunn and Kendrick (1982a) reported that in 40 percent of the families the older child was observed showing empathic concern for the younger; the majority of these older children were under 30 months of age at the time. During the final observations, more than half (65%) of the older children displayed empathic responsiveness to the younger child, who was now 14 months old. Typically these behaviors were expressions of concern accompanied by simple acts of helping, such as offering toys or food when the younger child was crying. Even more impressive was evidence from maternal reports that the *younger* siblings were themselves responding vicariously to the distress of their older brothers and sisters by the time they were 14 months old. Thus, like the studies by Zahn-Waxler and her colleagues, this study of early sibling interaction suggests that a capacity for empathic responding emerges in the middle of the second year and is associated with toddlers' prosocial initiatives. Since this study entailed substantial periods of direct observation of sibling behavior as well as maternal reports, the evidence may be somewhat more reliable, although few details were provided about how empathy was evaluated in children's behavior.

In all, these observations and interview reports suggest that sibling interactions may be a special arena for the development of empathic responding, with the clearest evidence for empathy apparent late in the second year. There are several reasons why siblings may be especially responsive to the emotional expressions of the other child (Dunn, 1983). Siblings share a common world of relationships and experiences (especially if they are close in age or are the same sex), and thus the events that arouse emotion in one child are likely to be easily understood by the other. In other words, affective role taking is facilitated by the similarity in their age, setting, and experiences, and this may increase a child's emotional responsiveness to a younger or older sibling. However, their shared perspective may also foster self-concern in an older sibling when the younger child is hurt (especially when the older sib feels responsible), as well as the envy and rivalry that are also a part of sibling relationships (Dunn & Kendrick, 1982a,b). Thus, empathic tendencies are part of a matrix of competing motives owing to the unique relationship shared by siblings. Nevertheless, sibling interaction appears to provide fertile ground for the study of early empathy and merits further study by developmentalists.

Summary

The strong conclusion that emerges from the research reviewed in this section is that infants and toddlers are neither indifferent to the emotional experiences of others nor incapable of understanding them. Contrary to views that emphasize a young child's difficulty with maintaining self–other differentiation and sharply curtailed role-taking capabilities, the reports of these studies reveal that children can understand others' emotional experiences by the time of their first birthday. The affective behavior of others provides important sources of information in evaluating uncertain or ambiguous situations, and there is some evidence for vicarious responding to the distress of others, even though it may initially be unaccompanied by instrumental acts of helping. By the middle of the second year, toddlers have become more sophisticated in reacting to others' emotional experiences with a range of prosocial initiatives, often accompanied by verbal expressions of sympathy. To be sure, these behaviors are not uniformly evident across all children in the second year (as is true at any age), and several studies indicate that maternal child-rearing practices are influential in these variations in empathic responding and prosocial motivation (see also Buchsbaum, 1986). Individual differences in empathic responding may also be influenced by temperamental variability on dimensions such as fearfulness and sociability (Buchsbaum, 1985). But the weight of the evidence suggests that a *capacity* for empathy develops by the middle of the second year, as reflected in the kinds of naturally occurring situations tapped in these studies.

Describing *how* empathy develops over this period is a more speculative task, partly because most of the available research was not explicitly designed to study the early emergence of empathy. However, these studies suggest important links between the development of empathy and the growth of social and emotional understanding in the child. In the first half-year of life there is little evidence that facial expressions have emotional meaning for infants apart from other cues, and thus there is little clear evidence for empathic responding based on such expressions. At the same time, the experience of reactive distress to newborn crying and, somewhat later, the affective synchrony experienced in mother–infant play may provide an important foundation of resonant emotional sharing of another's affective experience, a capacity that may have evolutionary bases.[1] It is not until the second half of the first year, however, that infants begin to attribute emotional meaning to facial expressions; moreover, their discrimination of vocal indicators of emotion (about which we know rather little; see Svejda & Campos,

1982) and other expressive modalities and the integration of multiple modes of emotional communication probably contribute to the child's growing ability to "read" others' expressions appropriately. Once the child imbues emotional expressions (facial, vocal, etc.) with emotional meaning, a capacity to respond vicariously to the emotions of others seems to follow soon afterward. The experience of social referencing may, in fact, be an important pathway to the growth of genuinely empathic responding, which seems to occur during the second half of the second year. In other words, the toddler's increasingly deliberate use of others' emotional expressions as information sources for the self – combined with the arousal of a resonant emotional response – may provide the basis for the child's use of these expressions to learn about the *other's* condition as well, and to feel vicariously another's affect.

Clearly, an important transition in empathic responsiveness occurs when the child becomes aware that others have internal, subjective states that are distinct from her own and that merit attention in social interaction. As noted earlier, this likely occurs earlier than most cognitive-developmental theorists have claimed. In this regard, Trevarthen's (1982; Trevarthen & Hubley, 1978) concept of "secondary intersubjectivity" suggests that a rudimentary awareness of the subjective states of others may appear as early as 1 year of age. In his studies of early referential communication and linguistic and protolinguistic development, Trevarthen argues that when infants and toddlers make efforts to achieve joint intentionality with another by trying to direct another's attention (e.g., pointing to an object and looking and vocalizing), acquire assistance (e.g., pulling at mother's hand), obey simple requests, or return affectionate gestures, they are exhibiting an understanding that the subjective states of individuals differ and can potentially be shared. This understanding, according to Trevarthen, provokes an interest in mutual or shared subjectivity that is the basis for the development of a variety of communicative and cooperative behaviors in subsequent months. If this is true, it suggests that once children have imbued emotional signals with emotional meaning, the development of "secondary intersubjectivity" fosters the mutual sharing of emotional conditions. This can occur when, for example, toddlers seek comfort from a caregiver, or when they sympathize with the distress of another.

Although this account is somewhat speculative, it suggests a number of important new directions for much-needed future research on empathy and its early development. Indeed, after a long hiatus of interest in empathic responding by very young children – owing to their presumed cognitive limitations – the research reviewed in this section suggests that a resurgence in this area is clearly warranted. A number of new research directions have been outlined in the preceding pages. The next section outlines several general issues for future study.

Key issues in future research

Targets of the empathic response

Although researchers commonly assume that empathy can be evoked by the emotional expressions of any individual, this may not be true, especially in early development. From a theoretical standpoint, psychoanalytic theorists regard the infant's mother as a prepotent target of vicarious arousal, whereas individuals with an ethological perspective emphasize responsiveness to biologically related conspecifics (especially caregivers), in accord with the concerns of human adaptation. Moreover, in the research reviewed earlier, there are suggestions of differential vicarious responding to the distress of others. For example, researchers have found that the distress cries of same-age peers evoked significantly more distress in newborns than did the crying of an older baby. Toddlers were more likely to respond vicariously to maternal simulations of distress and laughter (and to react prosocially in the former case) than when a stranger enacted these emotions (Zahn-Waxler & Radke-Yarrow, 1982; see also Buchsbaum, 1985). However, children of this age were also more likely to react with crying to the sound of another child's crying than to an adult's crying (Zahn-Waxler, Iannotti, & Chapman, 1982).

Differentiations in the degree of early empathic responding merit further study because of their relevance to our understanding of the early bases of vicarious arousal. Students of empathy in older children have long been aware of the fact that perceived similarity between the child and the distressed other heightens the probability of vicarious responding (Shantz, 1975), and this may be especially true of younger children. In view of their cognitive and role-taking limitations, affective sharing may occur more easily for very young children who are witnessing events they can easily understand (such as physical distress) occurring to individuals who are likely to be similar to themselves (such as peers and siblings). Indeed, in her early study of sympathy in young preschoolers, Murphy (1937) found that previous personal experience with a peer's upsetting situation was an important contributor to sympathetic responding. Consistent with this, Hoffman (1981b, 1982b) has suggested that vicarious arousal may occur through the child's association of another's distress cues with similar personal experiences. Thus peers, siblings, and parents may be especially potent targets of early empathic responding because their similarity to the child, a background of shared experiences, and the child's emotional attachments to family members facilitate emotional sharing with partners such as these.

In view of this, to what extent do instances of early empathic responding reflect projection of the child's own feelings to distressed individuals or reflect a veridical emotional response which is self-concerned (see Chandler, 1977)? As noted above, many of the examples of early empathy presented in previous research are subject to these alternative interpretations although these processes seem much less likely to occur in other situations. Consider, for example, a child who witnesses another child fall down and cry. Strictly speaking, projection in such a situation would require that the observer attribute his/her own feelings of well-being to the distressed accident victim, since the observer was not involved in the accident. Sometimes, however, critics argue that the observer's distress may actually derive from *imagining* how he/she would feel in that situation, rather than responding directly to the victim's distress cues. In this case, "projection" results from a form of cognitive role taking, and the observer's affective reaction derives, in part, from identifying with the distressed victim. Given the confluence of these affective and cognitive role-taking aspects of an observer's response to a distressed victim (in adults as well as children), dubbing the latter component a form of projection seems unnecessarily reductionistic. To summarize, even when the target of a young child's empathic response is one who is very similar to the child, projection may not be an alternative explanation for early empathic behavior as commonly as some have assumed.

Modality of empathic arousal

One of the reasons that the evidence for early empathy from recent research may be so surprising is that developmental researchers usually have not studied empathy in the context of naturally occurring events involving another's distress. More commonly, they have used abstract story situations involving pictures and narratives that impose much greater demands on a young child's cognitive capacities. Such assessments probably underestimate early empathic responding because they omit most of the compelling distress cues that often call forth a vicarious response in naturalistic settings. Thus, it is not surprising that young children perform poorly on such tasks, since these procedures require greater interpretation and inference than is needed in everyday circumstances involving another's direct emotional expressions.

By contrast, in naturalistic situations young children are faced with highly salient emotional cues from others. Among the variety of available cues, the vocal component – anguished crying, angry shouting, loud laughter, and so forth – may be the most arousing because its intensity compels attention. Viewed developmentally, vocal cues of emotion may be prepotent early elicitors of vicarious arousal since it is not until relatively late in the first year that facial expressions are imbued with emotional meaning by infants. Consistent with this, the earliest exemplar of emotional resonance – neonatal reactive crying – depends exclusively on vocal cues, and such cues may also be involved in the establishment of affective synchrony in mother–infant play.

In short, different modalities of emotional expression may be differentially effective in eliciting empathy, and auditory cues may assume early importance because of their salience. Facial expressions of emotion require visual attention and therefore can be ignored or unattended, but vocal expressions are difficult to disregard. Unfortunately, although we have some information concerning non-linguistic vocal indicators of emotion in the human voice (e.g., Scherer, 1979), we have little understanding of how these indicators are understood by children at different ages (Svejda & Campos, 1982). Such a task provides an important research agenda for students of emotional development and empathy, especially those who are interested in understanding the many expressive modalities by which potential empathizers can respond to another's distress.

Emotional tone of the empathic response

Like most of the research on empathy with older children, studies of early expressions of empathy primarily concern young children's responses to the distress of others, although there is evidence that young children can also vicariously enjoy another's positive emotional experience. There is reason to believe, however, that adults as well as young children are more likely to respond empathically to salient expressions of negative emotion in others. The hypothesized functions of empathic arousal in human adaptation (e.g., to foster altruistic actions; see Hoffman, 1981a) enlist empathy primarily in response to others' distress cues. Similarly, from the ethological perspective, human infants are thought to be highly sensitive to social cues that are relevant to protection from threat, and this is more likely to entail distress signals. For these reasons, distress cues may be more salient and compelling than cues of positive emotionality throughout the life span. However, this hypothesis requires empirical testing since there has been little research on the vicarious experience of positive emotion in young children or adults.

Construct versus index

There is a long-standing theoretical tradition linking empathy to prosocial behavior dating back several centuries (Hoffman, 1977), and it is a reflection of the influence of this tradition that empathy is sometimes indexed by the occurrence of helping behavior. Another reason for this is that prosocial initiatives can be more easily and clearly observed than can a person's emotional reaction to someone in distress. But the wisdom of this operationalization is debatable, given empathy may not always foster prosocial initiatives, and helping behavior is influenced by many factors beside empathy. This is especially true in the case of early empathy, when limitations on toddlers' social knowledge and constraints on the behavioral repertoire may restrict the kinds of helping behavior they can produce, independent of their vicarious emotional response to another's distress. Indeed, very young children may respond in a variety of ways to the discomfort produced by witnessing another's upset – for example, they may seek to escape from the situation and may even attack the victim (Dunn, personal communication, 1985; Zahn-Waxler et al., 1979). Consequently it is important to ensure that the *index* of empathic responding accurately reflects the theoretical *construct:* the arousal of emotion in an observer that is more appropriate to another's situations than to one's own (Hoffman, 1982a). Prosocial initiatives may be independent of this.

Consistent with this view, Buchsbaum (1985) recently observed thirty-three 18-month-olds during home visits in which distress was simulated by the mother and an adult stranger. Independent measures of "affective empathy" (which was focused on the child's emotional response) and "behavioral empathy" (which concerned the child's prosocial initiatives) were obtained. Affective and behavioral indices of empathy were significantly correlated only with respect to the mother; they were uncorrelated when the interviewer was upset. These indices were also correlated differently with measures of the child's temperament and of mother–child interaction. These findings are not surprising since offering help to an adult stranger makes different demands on a young child compared with offering support to the mother, but they indicate that affective empathy may be independent of prosocial behavior in many cases.

Both Dunn and Kendrick (1982a) and Hoffman (1982b) have commented on the tendency to infer empathy in very young children on the basis of the quality of their prosocial initiatives. For example, it is easy to label "egocentric" a one-year-old who watches another child fall and cry, then begins to whimper herself and turns to her mother for comfort. Similarly, a toddler who responds to an adult's sadness by offering a pacifier or a beloved doll might also be deemed egocentric. Clearly, in instances like these it is the child's *prosocial initiative* that is absent or that reflects egocentric thinking and not the child's *empathic response,* since in each case the child responds with emotion that is more appropriate to another's plight than to the child's own circumstances. Furthermore, it is unclear whether the child's initiative is, in fact, necessarily egocentric instead of simply ignorant, since very young children have limited social knowledge about the behavior that can alleviate another's upset. As Dunn and Kendrick (1982a) have noted, adults as well as children are sometimes uncertain about how best to assist another and, in these situations, adults often resort to those interventions that they would find comforting. Thus, offering a victim a teddy bear may be a reasonably thoughtful effort by a toddler. And if prosocial initiatives of any kind cannot be devised, seeking self-comfort may be the next best recourse. The important point is that the young child's allegedly egocentric helping behavior may, in fact, reflect deficiencies in social understanding. However, the *instigation* to act helpfully, with whatever degree of sophistication, may still derive from a genuinely empathic response to another's distress. With this in mind, future students of early empathy should use indices of empathy that closely reflect the construct under study.

Conclusion

The study of empathy is a difficult and challenging enterprise, especially in its earliest manifestations. Motivated by an awareness of the importance of vicarious responding to many aspects of human sociability, researchers nevertheless find the construct to be both conceptually and empirically elusive. Indeed, many might be inclined to agree with Sullivan (1953):

> So although empathy may sound mysterious, remember that there is much that sounds mysterious in the universe, only you have got used to it; and perhaps you will get used to empathy. (pp. 41–42)

Such a statement is especially relevant to the earliest manifestations of emotional resonance and empathy, since it is more difficult for researchers to "get into the head" of children of this age than at any other. Partly for this reason, and because of the limitations of the relevant research, the present account is, at times, uncomfortably speculative. Despite these limitations, however, the weight of the evidence calls into question the assumption that very young children are too egocentric to understand the emotional experiences of others, and it suggests that a basic capacity for empathic responding begins to emerge by the middle of the second year with the growth of emotional understanding in toddlers. The earliest manifestations of empathy are, in turn, preceded by experiences of emotional resonance (as in social referencing) that may be important precursors to genuinely empathic arousal. Taken together, these findings warrant renewed theoretical and research attention to empathy in the early years, and raise interesting and provocative new questions concerning the socialization of vicarious responding. The early emergence of individual differences in empathic responsiveness – which is distinct from a normative *capacity* for empathy – has not been the focus of this review, but also merits substantial research attention. In all, it is time for a broadened view of empathy – one that takes into consideration multiple developmental contributors to vicarious arousal. In so doing, future research efforts are more likely to yield a richer and more fully developmental perspective to empathy.

Note

1. Although arguments that empathy may be an outcome of natural selection (e.g., Hoffman, 1981a,b) offer a useful beginning to the application of ideas from ethology and evolutionary biology to this area, recent work in behavioral ecology (Krebs & Davies, 1981) and evolutionary biology (Trivers, 1985) indicates a number of more specific issues that must be considered in hypothesizing a role for empathy in human evolution. These include: (1) The multiple possible functions of empathy in human adaptation, including its role as a motivator of altruism, in caregiving behavior (viewed in terms of both adult and offspring behavior), in mate selection, and in other functions. Each entails a different cost–benefit ratio for reproductive success as well as having different implications for the ontogenesis of empathy – whether empathy is viewed primarily as a juvenile adaptation (i.e., a trait that aids individuals through their youth) or as a developmental adaptation (i.e., a trait that fosters lifetime reproductive success). (2) The multiple possible targets of empathic responsiveness, ranging from biologically related kin (who are most relevant to inclusive fitness considerations) to familiar conspecifics to unfamiliar conspecifics. Again, each has different implications for reproductive success. (3) The multiple possible situations in which empathy could be aroused and its consequences for reproductive success. Since natural selection probably functions in terms of conditional behavioral strategies (rather than behavioral stereotypies) that depend on ecological demands, it seems likely that appraisal processes (concerning the relatedness of the recipient, alternative options available, the costliness of vicarious arousal and derivative behaviors, and other factors) would have evolved enabling humans to distinguish situations in which empathic responding would serve fitness purposes from those in which it would not. In short, a capacity for empathy as a global, generalized response is probably an oversimplification of its role in human adaptation, and thus it is probably more useful to view empathy as a graded response to different targets and ecological conditions.

References

Barrera, M. E., & Maurer, D. (1981). The perception of facial expressions by the three-month-old. *Child Development, 52,* 203–206.

Bowlby, J. (1969). *Attachment and loss: Vol. 1. Attachment.* New York: Basic Books.

Brazelton, T. B., Tronick, E., Adamson, L, Als, H., & Wise, S. (1975). Early mother–infant reciprocity. In *Parent–infant interaction* (CIBA Foundation Symposium 33). Amsterdam: Elsevier.

Bretherton, I., & Beeghly, M. (1982). Talking about internal states: The acquisition of an explicit theory of mind. *Developmental Psychology, 18,* 906–921.

Bretherton, I., McNew, S., & Beeghly-Smith, M. (1981). Early person knowledge as expressed in gestural and verbal communication: When do infants acquire a ''theory of mind''? In M. E. Lamb & L. R. Sherrod (Eds.), *Infant social cognition.* Hillsdale, NJ: Erlbaum.

Buchsbaum, H. (1985, April). *Is an easy baby always nice?* Paper presented at the meeting of the Society for Research in Child Development, Toronto, Ontario, Canada.

Buchsbaum, H. (1986, April). *Parent–child interactions and empathy among 18–36 month olds.* Paper presented at the meeting of the International Conference on Infant Studies, Los Angeles, CA.

Burlingham, D. (1967). Empathy between infant and mother. *Journal of the American Psychoanalytic Association, 15,* 764–780.

Campos, J. J., Barrett, K. C., Lamb, M. E., Goldsmith, H. H., & Stenberg, C. (1983). Socioemotional development. In P. H. Mussen (Ed.), *Handbook of child psychology: Vol. II. Infancy and developmental psychobiology* (M. M. Haith and J. J. Campos, Eds.). New York: Wiley.

Campos, J. J., & Stenberg, C. R. (1981). Perception, appraisal and emotion: The onset of social referencing. In M. E. Lamb & L. R. Sherrod (Eds.), *Infant social cognition*. Hillsdale, NJ: Erlbaum.

Carr, S., Dabbs, J., & Carr, T. (1975). Mother–infant attachment: The importance of the mother's visual field. *Child Development, 46,* 331–338.

Chandler, M. J. (1977). social cognition: A selective review of current research. In W. F. Overton & J. M. Gallagher (Eds.), *Knowledge and development* (Vol. 1). New York: Plenum.

Cummings, E. M., Iannotti, R. J., & Zahn-Waxler, C. (1985). Influence of conflict between adults on the emotions and aggression of young children. *Developmental Psychology. 21,* 495–507.

Cummings, E. M., Zahn-Waxler, C., & Radke-Yarrow, M. (1981). Young children's responses to expressions of anger and affection by others in the family. *Child Development, 52,* 1274–1282.

Cummings, E. M., Zahn-Waxler, C., & Radke-Yarrow, M. (1984). Developmental changes in children's reactions to anger in the home. *Journal of Child Psychology and Psychiatry, 25,* 63–74.

Deutsch, F., & Madle, R. A. (1975). Empathy: Historic and current conceptualizations, measurement, and a cognitive theoretical perspective. *Human Development, 18,* 267–287.

Dunn, J. (1983). Sibling relationships in early childhood. *Child Development, 54,* 787–811.

Dunn, J., & Kendrick, C. (1982a). *Siblings: Love, envy, and understanding.* Cambridge: Harvard University Press.

Dunn, J., & Kendrick, C. (1982b). Siblings and their mothers: Developing relationships within the family. In M. E. Lamb & B. Sutton-Smith (Eds.), *Sibling relationships.* Hillsdale, NJ: Erlbaum.

Feinman, S. (1982). Social referencing in infancy. *Merrill–Palmer Quarterly, 28,* 445–470.

Feshbach, N. D. (1978). Studies of empathic behavior in children. In B. A. Maher (Ed.), *Progress in experimental personality research* (Vol. 8). New York: Academic Press.

Feshbach, N. D., & Roe, K. (1968). Empathy in six- and seven-year-olds. *Child Development, 39,* 133–145.

Freud, S. (1964). *An outline of psychoanalysis.* London: Hogarth.

Greenspan, S., Barenboim, C., & Chandler, M. J. (1976). Empathy and pseudo-empathy: The affective judgments of first- and third-graders. *Journal of Genetic Psychology, 129,* 77–88.

Gunnar, M. R., & Stone, C. (1984). The effects of positive maternal affect on infant responses to pleasant, ambiguous, and fear-provoking toys. *Child Development, 55,* 1231–1236.

Haith, M., Bergman, T., & Moore, M. (1977). Eye contact and face scanning in early infancy. *Science, 198,* 853–855.

Hay, D. F., Nash, A., & Pedersen, J. (1981). Responses of six-month-olds to the distress of their peers. *Child Development, 52,* 1071–1075.

Hinde, R. A. (1974). *Biological bases of human social behavior.* New York: McGraw-Hill.

Hoffman, M. L. (1975). Developmental synthesis of affect and cognition and its implications for altruistic motivation. *Developmental Psychology, 11,* 607–622.

Hoffman, M. L. (1977). Empathy, its development and prosocial implications. In C. B. Keasey (Ed.), *Nebraska Symposium on Motivation.* (Vol. 25). Lincoln: University of Nebraska Press.

Hoffman, M. L. (1981a). Is altruism part of human nature? *Journal of Personality and Social Psychology, 40,* 121–137.

Hoffman, M. L. (1981b). The development of empathy. In J. P. Rushton & R. M. Sorrentino (Eds.), *Altruism and helping behavior.* Hillsdale, NJ: Erlbaum.

Hoffman, M. L. (1982a). The measurement of empathy. In C. E. Izard (Ed.), *Measuring emotions in infants and children.* Cambridge: Cambridge University Press.

Hoffman, M. L. (1982b). Development of prosocial motivation: Empathy and guilt. In N. Eisenberg (Ed.), *The development of prosocial behavior.* New York: Academic Press.

Kagan, J. (1984). *The nature of the child.* New York: Basic Books.

Kaplan, L. J. (1977). The basic dialogue and the capacity for empathy. In N. Freedman & S. Grand (Eds.), *Communicative structures and psychic structures.* New York: Plenum.

Klinnert, M. (1981, April). *Infants' use of mothers' facial expressions for regulating their own behavior*. Paper presented to the meeting of the Society for Research in Child Development, Boston.

Klinnert, M. D., Campos, J. J., Sorce, J. F., Emde, R. N., & Svejda, M. (1983). Emotions as behavior regulators: Social referencing in infancy. In R. Plutchik & H. Kellerman (Eds.), *Emotion: Theory, research, and experience: Vol. 2. Emotions in early development*. New York: Academic Press.

Klinnert, M. D., Emde, R. N., & Butterfield, P. (1983, April). *Social referencing: The infant's use of emotional signals from a friendly adult with mother present*. Paper presented to the meeting of the Society for Research in Child Development, Detroit.

Krebs, J. R., & Davies, N. B. (1981). *An introduction to behavioural ecology*. Oxford: Blackwell Scientific Publications.

Kreutzer, M. A., & Charlesworth, W. R. (1973, March). *Infants' reactions to different expressions of emotion*. Paper presented to the meeting of the Society for Research in Child Development, Philadelphia.

LaBarbara, J., Izard, C. E., Vietze, P., & Parisi, S. (1976). Four- and six-month-old infants' visual responses to joy, anger, and neutral expressions. *Child Development, 47*, 535–538.

Lempers, J. D., Flavell, E. R., & Flavell, J. H. (1977). The development in very young children of tacit knowledge concerning visual perception. *Genetic Psychology Monographs, 95*, 3–53.

Mahler, M. S., Pine, F., & Bergman, A. (1975). *The psychological birth of the human infant*. New York: Basic Books.

Main, M., Weston, D., & Wakeling, S. (1979, March). *"Concerned attention" to the crying of an adult actor in infancy*. Paper presented to the meeting of the Society for Research in Child Development, San Francisco.

Malatesta, C. Z. (1985, April). Facial expressions of infants and mothers during early interaction. In T. Field (Chair), *Emotional expressions in infants and young children*. Symposium conducted at the Meeting of the Society for Research in Child Development, Toronto, Canada.

Malatesta, C. Z., & Haviland, J. M. (1982). Learning display rules: The socialization of emotional expression in infancy. *Child Development, 53*, 991–1003.

Martin, G. B., & Clark, R. D. (1982). Distress crying in neonates: Species and peer specificity. *Developmental Psychology, 18*, 3–9.

Murphy, L. B. (1937). *Social behavior and child personality: An exploratory study of some roots of sympathy*. New York: Columbia University Press.

Oster, H. (1981). "Recognition" of emotional expression in infancy? In M. E. Lamb & L. R. Sherrod (Eds.), *Infant social cognition*. Hillsdale, NJ: Erlbaum.

Piaget, J. (1951). *Play, dreams and imitation in childhood*. New York: Norton.

Rheingold, H., & Eckerman, C. (1973). Fear of the stranger: A critical review. In H. W. Reese (Ed.), *Advances in child development and behavior* (Vol. 8). New York: Academic Press.

Sagi, A., & Hoffman, M. L. (1976). Empathic distress in the newborn. *Developmental Psychology, 12*, 175–176.

Scherer, K. R. (1979). Nonlinguistic vocal indicators of emotion and psychopathology. In C. E. Izard (Ed.), *Emotions in personality and psychopathology*. New York: Plenum.

Shantz, C. U. (1975). The development of social cognition. In E. M. Hetherington (Ed.), *Review of child development research* (Vol. 5). Chicago: University of Chicago Press.

Simner, M. L. (1971). Newborn's response to the cry of another infant. *Developmental Psychology, 5*, 136–150.

Sorce, J. F., & Emde, R. N. (1981). Mother's presence is not enough: Effect of emotional availability on infant exploration. *Developmental Psychology, 17*, 737–745.

Sorce, J. F., Emde, R. N., Campos, J., & Klinnert, M. D. (1985). Maternal emotional signaling: Its effect on the visual cliff behavior of 1-year-olds. *Developmental Psychology, 21*, 195–200.

Sorce, J. F., Emde, R. N., & Frank, M. (1982). Maternal referencing in normal and Down's syndrome infants: A longitudinal analysis. In R. N. Emde & R. Harmon (Eds.), *The development of attachment and affiliative systems*. New York: Plenum.

Spitz, R. A. (1965). *The first year of life*. New York: International Universities Press.

Sroufe, L. A. (1979). Socioemotional development. In J. D. Osofsky (Ed.), *Handbook of infant development*. New York: Wiley.

Stern, D. N. (1977). *The first relationship*. Cambridge: Harvard University Press.

Stern, D. N., Barnett, R. K., & Spieker, S. (1983). Early transmission of affect: Some research issues. In J. D. Call, E. Galenson, & R. L. Tyson (Ed.), *Frontiers of infant psychiatry*. New York: Basic Books.

Stern, D. N., Hofer, L., Haft, W., & Dore, J. (1985). Affect attunement: The sharing of feeling states between mother and infant by means of inter-modal fluency. In T. M. Field & N. A. Fox (Eds.), *Social perception in infants*. Norwood, NJ: Ablex.

Sullivan, H. S. (1953). *The interpersonal theory of psychiatry*. New York: Norton.

Svejda, M. J., & Campos, J. J. (1982, March). *Mother's vocal expression of emotion as a behavior regulator*. Paper presented at the meeting of the International Conference on Infant Studies, Austin, TX.

Thompson, R. A., & Hoffman, M. L. (1980). Empathy and the development of guilt in children. *Developmental Psychology, 16*, 155–156.

Thompson, R. A., & Lamb, M. E. (1983). Individual differences in dimensions of socioemotional development in the second year. In R. Plutchik & H. Kellerman (Eds.), *Emotion: Theory, research, and experience: Vol. 2. Emotions in early development*. New York: Academic Press.

Trevarthen, C. (1982). The primary motives for cooperative understanding. In G. Butterworth & P. Light (Eds.), *Social cognition: Studies in the development of understanding*. Chicago: University of Chicago Press.

Trevarthen, C., & Hubley, P. (1978). Secondary intersubjectivity: Confidence, confiding and acts of meaning in the first year. In A. Lock (Ed.), *Action, gesture and symbol: The emergence of language*. New York: Academic Press.

Trivers, R. (1985). *Social evolution*. Menlo Park, CA: Benjamin Cummings.

Young-Browne, G., Rosenfeld, H., & Horowitz, F. (1977). Infant discrimination of facial expressions. *Child Development, 48*, 555–562.

Zahn-Waxler, C., Iannotti, R., & Chapman, M. (1982). Peers and prosocial development. In K. H. Rubin & H. S. Ross (Eds.), *Peer relationships and social skills in childhood*. New York: Springer-Verlag.

Zahn-Waxler, C., & Radke-Yarrow, M. (1979, March). *A developmental analysis of children's responses to emotions in others*. Paper presented to the meeting of the Society for Research in Child Development, San Francisco.

Zahn-Waxler, C., & Radke-Yarrow, M. (1982). The development of altruism: Alternative research strategies. In N. Eisenberg (Ed.), *The development of prosocial behavior*. New York: Academic.

Zahn-Waxler, C., Radke-Yarrow, M., & King, R. A. (1977, March). *The impact of the affective environment on young children*. Paper presented to the meeting of the Society for Research in Child Development, New Orleans.

Zahn-Waxler, C., Radke-Yarrow, M., & King, R. A. (1979). Child rearing and children's prosocial initiations toward victims of distress. *Child Development, 50*, 319–330.

7   Empathy and related responses in children

Mark A. Barnett

The concept of empathy

The concept of empathy, like many others in psychology, has meant different things to different people. The central issue in the conceptual debate has been the extent to which empathy encompasses an affective, as well as a cognitive, component. Some writers and researchers (Borke, 1971, 1973; Buckley, Siegel, & Ness, 1979; Greenspan, Barenboim, & Chandler, 1976) have defined empathy as the cognitive ability to recognize and understand the thoughts, perspectives, and feelings of another individual. A contrasting view (Batson & Coke, 1981; Feshbach, 1978; Hoffman, 1975a, 1982; Sawin, 1979; Staub, 1978; Stotland, 1969), and the one adopted in this chapter, is that empathy denotes the vicarious experiencing of an emotion that is congruent with, but not necessarily identical to, the emotion of another individual. Since the sharing of another's emotion can result from either direct contact with the affective cues transmitted by the other or from one's knowledge of another's state, the role of cognition in one's empathic arousal is expected to vary considerably from situation to situation.

The integration of cognitive and affective components is highlighted in models of the expression and development of empathy in children. According to Feshbach's (1978) three-component model, an empathic response requires (1) the ability to discriminate and identify the emotional states of another, (2) the capacity to take the perspective or role of the other, and (3) the evocation of a shared affective response. To Feshbach, the cognitive (1, 2) and affective (3) components of empathy are complexly intertwined and critical ingredients in a child's enactment of positive social behaviors. Hoffman's (1975a, 1977a, 1981, 1982) model attempts to explain how cognitive and affective factors play changing and interactive roles in the child's social and moral development. According to Hoffman, the child's emerging capacity to understand the distinction between self and other and the growing awareness that other individuals have internal states and feelings independent from one's own lay the foundation for higher levels of

146

empathic responding. Thus, the circumstances that will elicit empathic emotional arousal are believed to change and broaden with the child's increasing experiences and cognitive growth.

The empathy–prosocial behavior connection[1]

Although empathy has occasionally been construed as a prosocial response, in and of itself, it has more frequently been considered a mediator of other interpersonal responses (Barnett, 1982; Feshbach, 1982; Hoffman, 1977a). The mediation topic that has received the greatest attention from developmental researchers is the association between empathy and prosocial behavior.

Studies of the relationship between the young child's empathic disposition and prosocial behavior have frequently used the Feshbach Affective Situation Test of Empathy (FASTE; Feshbach & Roe, 1968) as the measure of empathy. This measure consists of four pairs of narrated slide sequences showing children in situations designed to elicit happiness, sadness, anger, and fear. Following each slide sequence the child is asked, "How do you feel?" Each response is rated on the degree to which it matches the affect of the child featured in a slide sequence. Although some positive results have been reported (Feshbach, 1973; Marcus, Telleen, & Roke, 1979), the majority of studies have indicated that scores on the FASTE, or modified versions of it, are unrelated to scores on various prosocial indices (see reviews in Radke-Yarrow, Zahn-Waxler, & Chapman, 1983; Underwood & Moore, 1982).

The use of nonverbal indices of emotional arousal in studies of the empathy–prosocial behavior relation is becoming more widespread, and these studies have yielded some encouraging findings (Howard, 1983; Leiman, 1978; Main, Weston, & Wakeling, 1979; Marcus, Roke, & Bruner, 1985; Peraino & Sawin, 1981; Sawin, 1979). For example, Leiman (1978) reported that 5- and 6-year-old children who were rated as displaying empathic facial expressions upon seeing a same-sex actor lose a favored marble collection subsequently worked harder on a task (the "marble donation machine") to replace the actor's play materials than did children whose facial expressions had been rated as neutral and nonempathic.

Additional support for the association between empathy and prosocial behavior comes from training studies with children (Feshbach, 1979, 1982; Iannotti, 1978; Staub, 1971). In general, these studies have demonstrated that structured experiences promoting role taking and sensitivity to the feelings of others can facilitate the expression of helping and sharing in children.

The pattern of results emerging from these studies indicates that the arousal of empathy may be associated with heightened prosocial behavior in children. However, there are certainly numerous qualifiers of this relation. For example, children who perceive little personal responsibility to help or who feel incompetent to intervene effectively (Aronfreed, 1968) and children who become over-aroused by empathic distress (Hoffman, 1982) may be unable to translate their emotional arousal into appropriate prosocial behavior. Thus, although the experience of empathic arousal may increase the likelihood of a helpful response, it does not ensure that a helpful response will be enacted.

Although the empathy–prosocial behavior relation has been of primary concern in the developmental literature, theorists and researchers have begun to consider empathy (involving negative and positive emotions) within the broader framework of affective and interpersonal development (Barnett, 1982; Bryant, 1982; Clark, 1980; Feshbach, 1982; Kurtz & Eisenberg, 1983; Strayer, 1980; Zahn-Waxler & Radke-Yarrow, 1979). Indeed, Feshbach (1982) suggests that there may be

> a broad range of possible effects mediated by empathy. These include social understanding; greater emotional competence; heightened compassion, caring, and related behaviors; regulation of aggression and other antisocial behaviors; increased self-awareness; enhanced communication skills; and greater cohesion between the cognitive, affective, and interpersonal aspects of the child's behavior. (p. 320)

Although other emotions and social skills undoubtedly play an important part in these and other related areas, the extent of the child's empathic responsiveness to the diverse feelings of others will likely be found to occupy a central role in the individual's social-emotional development.

Regularity and individual differences in the development of empathy

A basic assumption of Hoffman's (1982) developmental model of empathy is that age-related changes in the experience of empathy reflect underlying changes in the individual's evolving cognitive sense of the other. As Hoffman's theory suggests, there does seem to be some developmental consistency among children, at least very early on, in their emotional sensitivity and responsiveness to the needs of others. For example, whereas 1- to 1½-year-old children often respond to another's distress by orienting to the other, showing distress (e.g., crying or whimpering), and perhaps seeking out their own caretaker, the 2-year-old is much more likely to attempt to intervene effectively on behalf of the victim of distress (Radke-Yarrow & Zahn-Waxler, 1984; Zahn-Waxler & Radke-Yarrow, 1982). Certainly some modes of empathic arousal, such as those requiring advanced associative and perspective-taking skills, are beyond the capabilities of the very young child. As might be expected, older children have been found to be more likely than their younger counterparts to respond to abstract kinds of distress and subtle cues from others (Pearl, 1979; Radke-Yarrow, Zahn-Waxler, Cummings, Strope, & Sebris, 1981).

Although some regularity in the development and expression of empathy might be expected, there is also evidence that young children can differ markedly in their capacity or willingness to be sensitive and responsive to the feelings of others. For example, marked individual differences have been found in the extent to which children spontaneously match their own facial expressions to those of sad characters depicted in affect-laden slide or film presentations (Buck, 1975; Hamilton, 1973; Leiman, 1978). Zahn-Waxler and Radke-Yarrow (1979, 1982; see also Radke-Yarrow & Zahn-Waxler, 1984) have reported stable and patterned individual differences in empathic responses among 1- and 2-year-olds as well as individual continuity to age 7 in the child's intensity, complexity, and mode of response to others' emotions. With regard to the individual differences, it would appear that the affective and cognitive components of empathy have differing prominence in the responses of different children. Whereas the prosocial interactions of some children in these investigations were characterized as intensely emotional, other children tended to react to another's distress in an unemotional and analytical manner (e.g., inspecting, exploring, asking questions), in an aggressive manner (e.g., hitting a person who made a baby cry), or in an anxious and avoidant manner that suggested an intolerance to the emotional needs of others (e.g., turning and running away). About two-thirds of the children were reported to show a pattern of responding at 7 years of age that was similar to the pattern displayed at 2 years of age.

If such distinctive individual differences in responding to another's distress are already present at such an early age, then the early childhood years may be a particularly important time for parents and other socializing agents to attempt to either strengthen or modify the child's existing behavior. The following section reviews some of the socialization factors that may contribute to the development of empathy and related responses.

The socialization of empathy

During the first week of life, infants have been found to show distress and cry in response to the sound of another infant's cry; interestingly, no such response was made to a computer-simulated sound of equal intensity (Martin & Clark, 1982; Sagi & Hoffman, 1976; Simner, 1971). Hoffman (1977b) suggests that this affective orientation to other infants may represent a ''constitutionally based, early precursor of empathy'' (p. 299). Although the infant's primitive empathic response may suggest that humans have an inherent capacity to respond to obvious distress cues in others, early socialization experiences undoubtedly influence whether this capacity is suppressed or flourishes during childhood.

Before reviewing some of the potential antecedents of empathy, we should note the need for caution in three areas. First, little research available at present specifically focuses on the socialization of empathy and, therefore, any conclusions that may be drawn about a particular socialization experience must be considered speculative. Second, because the distinction between empathy and sympathy is often blurred in the individual (as well as in the literature), the socialization factors that serve to promote empathy and sympathy (and, indeed, any prosocial response having a prominent affective component) are expected to overlap considerably. Third, the following list of possible empathy-promoting socialization factors is intended to be neither exhaustive nor mutually exclusive. In fact, empathic responsiveness would be expected to develop most fully in an early socialization environment in which these factors operate together in a highly integrated manner.

Secure early attachment

One suspected early antecedent of empathy concerns the intense affective relationship between the caretaker and the infant. Sullivan (1940, 1953) proposed that the young child's empathic responsiveness to the feelings of others grows out of an early empathic involvement, or contagion of affect, with the mother's moods and emotions. In a similar vein, Mussen and Eisenberg-Berg (1977) concluded that ''strong early attachment appears to be a major antecedent of early interest in others and the latter may be a necessary precondition for the development of empathy'' (pp. 169–170). Mussen and Eisenberg-Berg reasoned that children with a strong sense of trust and security, derived from secure attachments to their parents, would be less preoccupied with satisfying their own needs and more responsive to the feelings and needs of others than less securely attached children.

Research addressing the role of early attachment in the development of responsiveness and sensitivity to others is scarce. Main (1977) reported that infants who were characterized as securely attached to their mothers at 12 months of age showed more interest in and reacted more positively to an adult playmate 9 months later than did infants who had been determined to be insecure in their maternal attachments. In a related study (Waters, Wippman, & Stroufe, 1979), children having a secure attachment at 15 months of age were rated as more sympathetic to peers' distress in the preschool at 3½ years of age than children who had been identified as having had an anxious attachment to their mothers.

These findings are suggestive of a link between the child's early attachment and emotional responsiveness. However, there undoubtedly are numerous factors that influence the extent to which a particular child is securely attached to his or her parents. Some of these factors, such as the degree of parental responsiveness to the child's cry and other expressions of distress, may have a predominant affective component and be highly relevant to the development of empathy. Other factors, such as those involving patterns of verbal interchange, may be less significant. Therefore, research designs that categorize parent–child relationships as secure or insecure likely obscure the contribution of particular interpersonal factors in the development of empathy and related responses. A more fine-grain analysis is needed.

Parental affection

A common ingredient in a secure early attachment is an abundance of love and nurturance. Not surprisingly, it has been suggested that parental affection, by satisfying the child's own emotional needs, also plays an important role in the development of empathy (Hoffman, 1982). Congruent with this notion, Eisenberg-Berg and Mussen (1978) found that mothers of highly empathic adolescent sons (as assessed by the emotional empathy measure devised by Mehrabian and Epstein, 1972) were reported as being more affectionate than were mothers of less empathic boys. The authors suggested that the failure to find a similar relationship for adolescent daughters was due to a ceiling effect on the daughters' empathy scores. In a subsequent study using the same empathy measure, Barnett, Howard, King, and Dino (1980) found that highly empathic undergraduates characterized their parents as having been more affectionate with them during childhood than did relatively less empathic undergraduates.

Although the results of these two studies indicate that parental affection may play an important role in the development of empathy, some caution must again be exercised in interpreting these data. Individuals differing in empathic disposition may tend to differentially distort or recall their parents' characteristics or socialization styles. A more comprehensive assessment of the role of parental affection in the development of empathy might incorporate naturalistic observations of the parent–child dyad by the caregiver and others (see Zahn-Waxler, Radke-Yarrow, & King, 1979). Nonetheless, in studies of the antecedents of empathy, the individual's own perceptions of his or her parents' characteristics and socialization practices would appear to be important information that cannot merely be replaced by the perceptions of others.

Availability of empathic models

There is a considerable amount of evidence, both from laboratory and naturalistic observations, that modeling and identification processes are major determinants of the acquisition, expression, and development of prosocial behaviors in children (see review in Mussen & Eisenberg-Berg, 1977). Unfortunately, little research has specifically examined the extent to which observing an empathic or sympathetic model influences the expression of similar responses in a young observer. Nonetheless, it seems reasonable to assume that the development of these responses would be enhanced during childhood by the availability of models who express sensitivity and compassion to the child and others.

With regard to the parent as model, Tomkins (1963) suggests that emotionally expressive parents who respond with sympathy and concern to their child's feelings of helplessness and distress are teaching their child to express distress without shame and to respond sympathetically to the distress of others. Some support for this notion comes from a study conducted by Zahn-Waxler et al. (1979). As part of a larger investigation, the authors assessed the degree to which mothers displayed empathic handling of their toddlers' needs and distress. Children whose mothers were rated high in empathic caregiving were found to be more emotionally responsive and helpful to persons in distress than were children of less empathic mothers. In another investigation (Barnett, King, Howard, & Dino, 1980), heightened empathy in 4- to 6-year-old girls (as assessed by the FASTE, described earlier) was found to be associated with a sex-stereotypic pattern of mother–father empathy (as assessed by the Mehrabian and Epstein [1972] measure). The authors speculated that when the mother is markedly more empathic than the father, empathy may be identified as distinctly gender appropriate for females, thereby enhancing its development in young girls. In this study, no relation was found between the boys' empathy scores and the empathy scores from either parent. Strayer (1983) reported that mothers', but not fathers', empathy scores on the Mehrabian and Epstein (1972) measure were significantly correlated with their children's scores on a similar self-report measure (Bryant, 1982).

The results of these and other studies (Eisenberg-Berg & Mussen, 1978; Feshbach, 1975) suggest that mothers may play a particularly important role in their child's development of empathy. However, fathers (as well as other important caregivers) have not always been included, or included as extensively as mothers, in studies of the child's social-emotional development. With many fathers becoming more actively involved in all aspects of child rearing, their contribution to their sons' and daughters' evolving capacities to empathize merits greater attention in the future.

Although parents are especially important models in their child's social-emotional development, the child's inclination to empathize may also be enhanced by exposure to and interaction with other sensitive and caring models, such as a special teacher, sibling, or playmate. In addition to the potential influence of various "live" models, children have been found to emulate television characters who display prosocial actions such as offering sympathy and assistance to needy others (see reviews in Mussen & Eisenberg-Berg, 1977; Rushton, 1979, 1981; Staub, 1979). In a typical study (Coates, Pusser, & Goodman, 1976), nursery-school children who watched segments of *Mister Rogers' Neighborhood* (a program containing many displays of cooperation, concern for feelings, and sympathy) subsequently showed more affectionate physical contact, sympathy, and emotional support for peers than did children who had watched segments of a program with less prosocial content.

In sum, experimental and naturalistic studies have indicated that children will imitate some forms of prosocial behaviors enacted by a model. However, as Radke-Yarrow et al. (1983) caution, "There is insufficient evidence from this research to say how modeling affects a broad range of prosocial responses, particularly affective responses, such as empathic feelings toward a victim" p. 504). Although it may be simpler methodologically to determine whether an observing child has imitated a model's action than affect, the additional cost to the researcher interested in the socialization of empathy would seem well worth the price.

Parental use of the inductive socialization technique

In those situations in which the child's actions have harmed another individual, Hoffman (1975b) contends that parental use of the inductive disciplinary technique, which calls attention to the victim's distress and encourages the child to imagine him/herself in the victim's place, is likely to "enlist the child's proclivities for empathy" (p. 234) and promote prosocial behavior.[2] Consistent with this notion, parents employing an inductive style of discipline have been found to have children who score higher on indices of generosity and consideration for others than parents practicing a predominately power-assertive disciplinary style (Dlugokinski & Firestone, 1974; Hoffman & Saltzstein, 1967). However, in these studies, as in experimental studies of induction and prosocial behavior (Eisenberg-Berg & Geisheker, 1979; Howard & Barnett, 1981), the child's emotional responsiveness to needy others was not specifically examined.

An investigation by Zahn-Waxler et al. (1979) has helped to clarify the role of parental disciplinary style in the development of children's sensitivity and responsiveness to the distress of others. In this study, the mothers of a 1½- to 2½-year-old children were extensively trained to record their child's reactions and their own behaviors in everyday encounters with expressions of distress in others. Heightened emotional responsiveness and prosocial behavior in young children were found to be associated with mothers who frequently (1) conveyed a clear cognitive message to the child (an explanation or a demonstration) of the consequences of his or her behavior for the victim, and (2) reinforced this message with a display of intense emotion and statements of principles and expectations for the child's behavior. Merely encouraging an awareness of the affective state of another person through the use of a calm and well-reasoned explanation was found to be insufficient to elicit the child's emotions and attempts to help. Indeed, Zahn-Waxler et al. (1979) argue that "the effective induction . . . is emotionally imposed, sometimes harshly and often forcefully" (p. 327). The mother's highly emotional reaction may indicate the importance of the situation to the child as well as model emotional responsiveness to the other's distress. The content of the induction may further define the meaning of her emotional response and provide additional information to the child about how to feel and act in the situation (Miller, 1984). Thus, it appears that in the caregiver's response to the child, as in the construct of empathy itself, the interaction of cognitive and affective components is essential.

Encouragement of the perception of similarity to others

Children have been found to respond more empathically to those who are perceived as similar to the self than to those who are perceived as dissimilar. This appears to be the case when similarity is defined either in terms of a shared characteristic, such as sex (Bryant, 1982, true for female subjects only; Feshbach & Roe, 1968) or race (Klein, 1971), or in terms of a shared personal experience (Aronfreed, 1968; Barnett, 1984b). Concerning the latter point, Barnett (1984b) found that a preschooler's empathy with an unhappy agemate (as assessed by a self-report measure and ratings of facial expression) was enhanced when the observing child had had a similar unpleasant experience (failing in a particular game.)

These findings would seem to suggest that encouraging a child to perceive others as similar to the self may contribute to the development and expression of empathy. However, since children are likely to base their perception of similarity to others on more abstract attributes as they mature, the encouragement, to be effective, must be made at an age-appropriate level of abstraction.

One way of enhancing children's perception of similarity to others might be to broaden their own basis for comparison with others. Hoffman (1976, 1982) contends that parents should allow their children to be exposed to a wide range of experiences and emotions so as to foster their sensitivity to the feelings of others. A child who has been shielded from particular distressful experiences, or discouraged from displaying overt expressions of distress, would presumably have a difficult time empathizing with a needy other whose predicament or emotional reaction is perceived as foreign and unfamiliar. Relevant to this notion is Lenrow's (1965) finding that nursery school children who showed relatively high levels of crying (encouraged, he believed, by a history of parental reinforcement of affect displays) tended to be more empathic than did agemates who cried less frequently. In a similar vein, Feshbach (1982) suggests that the empathic responsiveness and helpfulness of some individuals may be enhanced by having weathered a dysphoric experience, such as a serious familial illness or a loss. Although there is no direct research evidence for this interesting hypothesis, some tangential support comes from the world of show business. Comedians, whose autobiographical reports often include a childhood filled with difficult and trying experiences, seem to have the ability to make us laugh because of their unique insight into and sensitivity to the human condition – our failings, our perceptions, and our emotions.

The child's perception of similarity to others might also be promoted through the encouragement of universalistic beliefs and values that emphasize the connectedness among all people. Certainly, the information provided by parents, of both a religious and nonreligious sort, is likely to be critical in this regard. As Radke-Yarrow et al. (1983) conclude,

> Parents' cognitive structures in viewing persons and groups, in classifying others in society, and in placing the family in relation to these others should be important for children's prosocial behavior. About whom will the child feel similar or different? How large and inclusive or exclusive are the categories of commonalities that the child is taught? The content of the social information that is transmitted in the family would be expected to influence the child's feelings of empathy and the generality of such feelings. (p. 514)

Discouragement of excessive interpersonal competition

The encouragement of a highly competitive interpersonal orientation may generate heightened self-concern within a child and interfere with his or her inclination to respond to another individual's needs. Some support for this notion comes from studies of competitive dispositions in children as well as studies of the situational influences of competition.

Highly competitive boys have been found to be less generous (Rutherford & Mussen, 1968) and less empathic (Barnett, Matthews, & Howard, 1979) than their less competitive peers. A competitive goal structure, whether induced in the laboratory (Barnett & Bryan, 1974; Barnett, Matthews, & Corbin, 1979; Stendler, Damrin, & Hines, 1951) or assessed in the school (Johnson & Johnson, 1974) or home (Bryan & London, 1970), has been associated with lower levels of sharing and comforting than a noncompetitive or cooperative goal structure. Moreover, in an investigation of the antecedents of empathy, Feshbach (1975) reported that a paternal emphasis on competition was associated with low levels of empathy in sons (but not daughters).

The research support for the role of competitiveness/competition in the development of empathy is again tenuous and indirect. As is generally true for the other potential antecedents of empathy reviewed here, the evidence for this relation comes largely from correlational studies and from experiments in which the arousal of empathy must be inferred from some prosocial act that may or may not have a prominent affective component. To comprehend more fully the socialization of empathy, we clearly need to design experimental and naturalistic studies that incorporate assessments of the child's empathy and allow us to systematically examine the situational and personality variables that influence its expression (Barnett, 1984a).

Encouragement of a positive self-concept

Children who are encouraged to feel good about themselves may be more inclined to empathize with others than children who are preoccupied with personal inadequacies and other concerns about the self. Again, the research evidence for this notion is scant but suggestive. Strayer (1983) found empathy in 6-year-old children to be associated with a positive self-concept. In a discussion of her earlier study of "antecedents of empathy," Feshbach (1982) notes that "empathy in girls is associated with maternal antecedents that are likely to foster prosocial behavior and a positive self-image" (p. 332). Specifically, empathy in girls was found to be positively correlated with maternal tolerance and permissiveness and negatively correlated with maternal conflict, rejection, punitiveness, and excessive control. No such pattern was reported, however, for father–daughter, father–son, or mother–son dyads. In a naturalistic observation study of preschoolers conducted over an 8-week period (Strayer, 1980), children who were ranked high on displays of happy emotions (perhaps reflecting self-contentment) were also ranked high on empathic behavior toward peers. In contrast, children who were ranked high on displays of sad emotions were ranked low on empathy toward peers.

One aspect of a positive self-concept that may be particularly important in the development of empathy is the perception of oneself as an independent and competent helper (Barnett, Thompson, & Pfeifer, 1985). Children who are given the encouragement and opportunities to gain helping skills may be more inclined to empathize with a needy other than their less competent peers because they perceive that they have the capacity to alleviate the (now) mutually experienced distress. Similarly, Hoffman (1976) has stated that "providing the child with opportunities for role taking and for giving help and responsible care to others . . . should foster both sympathetic distress and awareness of the other's perspective, as well as the integration of the two" (p. 142). In a relevant cross-cultural comparison, Whiting and Whiting (1975) observed that assigning children specific caregiving responsibilities for their younger brothers and sisters tends to increase the children's overall level of sensitive caregiving to others.

Just as experiences that promote a positive self-concept and feelings of competence may encourage the development of empathy, children who are treated in a manner that is harsh, unloving, and damaging to a healthy sense of self would be expected to be less inclined to demonstrate an awareness of and sensitivity to the emotions of others. Some support for this notion comes from recent investigations involving abused children. In a study comparing the responses of 17 abused and 17 nonabused 3- to 6-year-olds, Camras, Grow, and Ribordy (1983) found that abused children were consistently less accurate than nonabused children in identifying facial expressions of emotion. Main and George (1985) observed the way in which abused and nonabused toddlers (1 to 3 years old) responded to distress in agemates in a day-care setting. Whereas the nonabused toddlers frequently responded with concern, empathy, and sadness to the distress that they witnessed, not one abused child showed any of these responses. Instead, the abused children tended to react with threats, anger, and physical attack to peers who expressed distress. By designing and comparing the effectiveness of various programs for remediating such early and marked deficits in interpersonal functioning, we stand to learn a great deal about the development of empathy in children.

Conclusion

Although the research support for any one suggested antecedent of empathy is rather weak, a clearer picture does emerge when all of the evidence is considered together. The development of empathy and related responses would appear to thrive in an environment that (1) satisfies the child's own emotional needs and discourages excessive self concern, thereby enabling the emotions and needs of others to become more salient, (2) encourages the child to identify, experience, and express a broad range of emotions, and (3) provides numerous opportunities for the child to observe and interact with others who, through their words and actions, encourage emotional sensitivity and responsiveness to others.

Research on the child's growing awareness of and responsiveness to the emotions of others is in its own infancy. By broadening our study of empathy, both in terms of the range of emotions and situations explored, we are likely to gain a greater understanding of the manner in which children come to experience, interpret, and respond to the various emotions in themselves and others. Because of their similarity and salience to one another, peers may prove to be especially influential socializing agents in the development of empathy and related responses. For example, Eisenberg, Lundy, Shell, and Roth (1985) suggest that although children are likely to use authority and punishment justifications to explain their compliance with adult requests, they are more inclined to attribute compliance to peer requests to their concern for the needs and desires of others. Therefore, Eisenberg et al. (1985) argue, the child's "performance of adult-initiated compliant acts may be less likely than peer-initiated actions to serve as a mechanism for the socialization of future internal or empathy-based prosocial tendencies'' (p. 326). On a more general level, Sullivan (1953) emphasized that peer interaction, and in particular an intimate friendship during childhood, helps the individual to develop a sense of humanity, interpersonal intimacy, and an emotional responsiveness to others' needs that extend beyond the particular peer or friend. An important goal of future research is to more clearly delineate the specific experiences among peers and friends that promote the development of empathy and concern for others.

A final note

In this, as in prior discussions of the topic, empathy has been considered a positive and socially adaptive response that should be nurtured in the child. Nonetheless, there may be occasions in which the expression of empathy and related responses is less than desirable. For example, in structured interpersonal competitions, such as an athletic contest or a classroom exam, excessive awareness of and concern about the feelings of others may prove counterproductive. Moreover, recent reports (Finkelhor, 1984; Wooden, 1984) indicate that, in addition to other deceptive ploys, child molesters may prey upon the child's empathic and helpful tendencies during the ''capture'' (e.g., a ''distressed'' adult may ask a small child to assist in finding a puppy that is said to be lost in the woods). Therefore, just as we encourage our children to be emotionally responsive to the needs of others, we must also teach them to discriminate those situations in which empathic responsiveness is appropriate and desirable from those situations in which it is inappropriate and potentially harmful.

Notes

1. For a more detailed discussion of the relation between empathy and prosocial behavior, see Eisenberg & Miller (Chapter 13).
2. Some authors (Singer, 1984; Stotland, 1969; Strayer, 1983) have suggested that a person's capacities to imagine and empathize may be related since both often involve some fantasized ''movement'' of the self into another individual's perspective or situation. Whether enhancing a child's imagination (for example, through involvement in a sociodramatic play training program) would have a positive effect on his or her tendency to empathize has yet to be determined.

References

Aronfreed, J. (1968). *Conduct and conscience: The socialization of internalized control over behavior*. New York: Academic Press.

Barnett, M. A. (1982). Empathy and prosocial behavior in children. In T. M. Field, A. Huston, H. C. Quay, L. Troll, & G. E. Finley (Eds.), *Review of human development*. New York: Wiley.

Barnett, M. A. (1984a). Empathy as a dependent variable. Paper presented at the meeting of the American Psychological Association, Toronto.

Barnett, M. A. (1984b). Similarity of experience and empathy in preschoolers. *Journal of Genetic Psychology, 145,* 241–250.

Barnett, M. A., & Bryan, J. H. (1974). Effects of competition with outcome feedback on children's helping behavior. *Developmental Psychology, 10*, 838–842.

Barnett, M. A., Howard, J. A., King, L. M., & Dino, G. A. (1980). Antecedents of empathy: Retrospective accounts of early socialization. *Personalty and Social Psychology Bulletin, 6*, 361–365.

Barnett, M. A., King, L. M., Howard, J. A., & Dino, G. A. (1980). Empathy in young children: Relation to parents' empathy, affection, and emphasis on the feelings of others. *Developmental Psychology, 16*, 243–244.

Barnett, M. A., Matthews, K. A., & Corbin, C. B. (1979). The effect of competitive and cooperative instructional sets on children's generosity. *Personality and Social Psychology Bulletin, 5*, 91–94.

Barnett, M. A., Matthews, K. A., & Howard, J. A. (1979). Relationship between competitiveness and empathy in 6- and 7-year-olds. *Developmental Psychology, 15*, 221–222.

Barnett, M. A., Thompson, M. A., & Pfeifer, J. R. (1985). Perceived competence to help and the arousal of empathy. *Journal of Social Psychology, 125*, 679–680.

Batson, C. D., & Coke, J. S. (1981). Empathy: A source of altruistic motivation for helping? In J. P. Rushton & R. M. Sorrentino (Eds.), *Altruism and helping behavior*. Hillsdale, NJ: Erlbaum.

Borke, H. (1971). Interpersonal perception of young children: Egocentrism or empathy? *Developmental Psychology, 5*, 263–269.

Borke, H. (1973). The development of empathy in Chinese and American children between three and six years of age: A cross-cultural study. *Developmental Psychology, 9*, 102–108.

Bryan, J. H., & London, P. (1970). Altruistic behavior by children. *Psychological Bulletin, 73*, 200–211.

Bryant, B. K. (1982). An index of empathy for children and adolescents. *Child Development, 53*, 413–425.

Buck, R. W. (1975). Nonverbal communication of affect in children. *Journal of Personality and Social Psychology, 31*, 644–653.

Buckley, N., Siegel, L. S., & Ness, S. (1979). Egocentrism, empathy and altruistic behavior in young children. *Developmental Psychology, 15*, 329–330.

Camras, L. A., Grow, J. G., & Ribordy, S. C. (1983). Recognition of emotional expression by abused children. *Journal of Clinical Child Psychology, 12*, 325–328.

Clark, K. B. (1980). Empathy: A neglected topic in psychological research. *American Psychologist, 35*, 187–190.

Coates, B., Pusser, H. E., & Goodman, I. (1976). The influence of "Sesame Street" and "Mister Rogers' Neighborhood" on children's social behavior in preschool. *Child Development, 47*, 138–144.

Dlugokinski, E. L., & Firestone, I. J. (1974). Other centeredness and susceptibility to charitable appeals: Effects of perceived discipline. *Developmental Psychology, 10*, 21–28.

Eisenberg, N., Lundy, T., Shell, R., & Roth, K. (1985). Children's justifications for their adult and peer-directed compliant (prosocial and nonprosocial) behaviors. *Developmental Psychology, 21*, 325–331.

Eisenberg-Berg, N., & Geisheker, E. (1979). Content of preachings and power of the model/preacher: The effect on children's generosity. *Developmental Psychology, 15*, 168–175.

Eisenberg-Berg, N., & Mussen, P. (1978). Empathy and moral development in adolescence. *Developmental Psychology, 14*, 185–186.

Feshbach, N. D. (1973). Empathy: An interpersonal process. Paper presented at the meeting of the American Psychological Association, Montreal.

Feshbach, N. D. (1975). The relationship of child-rearing factors to children's aggression, empathy and related positive and negative social behaviors. In J. DeWit & W. W. Hartup (Eds.), *Determinants and origins of aggressive behavior*. The Hague, Netherlands: Mouton.

Feshbach, N. D. (1978). Studies of empathic behavior in children. In B. A. Maher (Ed.), *Progress in experimental personality research* (Vol. 8). New York: Academic Press.

Feshbach, N. D. (1979). Empathy training: A field study in affective education. In S. Feshbach & A. Fraczek (Eds.), *Aggression and behavior change: Biological and social processes*. New York: Praeger.

Feshbach, N. D. (1982). Sex differences in empathy and social behavior in children. In N. Eisenberg (Ed.), *The development of prosocial behavior*. New York: Academic Press.

Feshbach, N. D., & Roe, K. (1968). Empathy in six- and seven-year-olds. *Child Development, 39,* 133–145.

Finkelhor, D. (1984). *Child sexual abuse: New theory and research*. New York: Free Press.

Greenspan, S., Barenboim, C., & Chandler, M. J. (1976). Empathy and pseudo-empathy: The affective judgments of first- and third-graders. *Journal of Genetic Psychology, 129,* 77–88.

Hamilton, M. L. (1973). Imitative behavior and expressive ability in facial expression of emotion. *Developmental Psychology, 8,* 138.

Hoffman, M. L. (1975a). Developmental synthesis of affect and cognition and its implications for altruistic motivation. *Developmental Psychology, 11,* 607–622.

Hoffman, M. L. (1975b). Moral internalization, parental power, and the nature of parent–child interaction. *Developmental Psychology, 11,* 228–239.

Hoffman, M. L. (1976). Empathy, role taking, guilt, and development of altruistic motives. In T. Lickona (Ed.), *Moral development and behavior: Theory, research, and social issues*. New York: Holt, Rinehart, & Winston.

Hoffman, M. L. (1977a). Empathy, its development and prosocial implications. In C. B. Keasey (Ed.), *Nebraska Symposium on Motivation* (Vol. 25). Lincoln: University of Nebraska Press.

Hoffman, M. L. (1977b). Personality and social development. *Annual Review of Psychology, 28,* 295–321.

Hoffman, M. L. (1981). The development of empathy. In J. P. Rushton & R. M. Sorrentino (Eds.), *Altruism and helping behavior*. Hillsdale, NJ: Erlbaum.

Hoffman, M. L. (1982). Development of prosocial motivation: Empathy and guilt. In N. Eisenberg (Ed.), *The development of prosocial behavior*. New York: Academic Press.

Hoffman, M. L., & Saltzstein, H. D. (1967). Parent discipline and the child's moral development. *Journal of Personality and Social Psychology, 5,* 45–57.

Howard, J. A. (1983). Preschoolers' dispositional empathy for specific affects: Differential relationships with naturally-occurring altruism and aggression. Paper presented at the meeting of the Society for Research in Child Development, Detroit.

Howard, J. A., & Barnett, M. A. (1981). Arousal of empathy and subsequent generosity in young children. *Journal of Genetic Psychology, 138,* 307–308.

Iannotti, R. J. (1978). Effect of role-taking experience on role taking, empathy, altruism, and aggression. *Developmental Psychology, 14,* 119–124.

Johnson, D. W., & Johnson, R. T. (1974). Instructional goal structure: Cooperative, competitive, or individualistic. *Review of Educational Research, 44,* 213–240.

Klein, R. S. (1971). Some factors influencing empathy in six- and seven-year-old children varying in ethnic background (Doctoral dissertation, University of California, Los Angeles, 1970). *Dissertation Abstracts International, 31,* 3960A. (University Microfilms No. 71-3862)

Kurtz, C. A., & Eisenberg, N. (1983). Role-taking, empathy, and resistance to deviation in children. *Journal of Genetic Psychology, 142,* 85–95.

Leiman, B. (1978). Affective empathy and subsequent altruism in kindergartners and first graders. Paper presented at the meeting of the American Psychological Association, Toronto.

Lenrow, P. B. (1965). Studies in sympathy. In S. S. Tomkins & C. E. Izard (Eds.), *Affect, cognition, and personality: Empirical studies*. New York: Springer.

Main, M. (1977). Analysis of a peculiar form of reunion behavior seen in some young daycare children. In R. A. Webb (Ed.), *Social development in daycare*. Baltimore, MD: Johns Hopkins University Press.

Main, M., & George, C. (1985). Responses of abused and disadvantaged toddlers to distress in agemates: A study in a day care setting. *Developmental Psychology, 21*, 407–412.

Main, M., Weston, D. R., & Wakeling, S. (1979). "Concerned attention" to the crying of an adult actor in infancy. Paper presented at the meeting of the Society for Research in Child Development, San Francisco.

Marcus, R. F., Roke, E. J., & Bruner, C. (1985). Verbal and nonverbal empathy and prediction of social behavior of young children. *Perceptual and Motor Skills, 60*, 299–309.

Marcus, R. F., Telleen, S., & Roke, E. J. (1979). Relation between cooperation and empathy in young children. *Developmental Psychology, 15*, 346–347.

Martin, G. B., & Clark, R. D. (1982). Distress crying in neonates: Species and peer specificity. *Developmental Psychology, 18*, 3–9.

Mehrabian, A., & Epstein, N. (1972). A measure of emotional empathy. *Journal of Personality, 40*, 525–543.

Miller, P. A. (1984). *Maternal childrearing practices and daughters' empathic response to peer distress*. Unpublished doctoral dissertation, University of Texas, Austin.

Mussen, P., & Eisenberg-Berg, N. (1977). *Roots of caring, sharing, and helping: the development of prosocial behavior in children*. San Francisco: W. H. Freeman.

Pearl, R. A. (1979). Developmental and situational influences on children's understanding of prosocial behavior. Paper presented at the meeting of the Society for Research in Child Development, San Francisco.

Peraino, J. M., & Sawin, D. B. (1981). Empathic distress: Measurement and relation to prosocial behavior. Paper presented at the meeting of the Society for Research in Child Development, Boston.

Radke-Yarrow, M., & Zahn-Waxler, C. (1984). Roots, motives, and patterns in children's prosocial behavior. In E. Staub, D. Bar-Tal, J. Karylowski, & J. Reykowski (Eds.), *The development and maintenance of prosocial behavior*. New York: Plenum.

Radke-Yarrow, M., Zahn-Waxler, C., & Chapman, M. (1983). Children's prosocial dispositions and behavior. In P. H. Mussen (Ed.), *Handbook of child psychology*. New York: Wiley.

Radke-Yarrow, M., Zahn-Waxler, C., Cummings, M., Strope, B., & Sebris, S. L. (1981). Continuities and change in the prosocial and aggressive behavior of young children. Paper presented at the meeting of the Society for Research in Child Development, Boston.

Rushton, J. P. (1979). Effects of prosocial television and film material on the behavior of viewers. In L. Berkowitz (Ed.), *Advances in experimental social psychology* (Vol. 12). New York: Academic Press.

Rushton, J. P. (1981). Television as a socializer. In J. P. Rushton & R. M. Sorrentino (Eds.), *Altruism and helping behavior: Social, personality, and developmental perspectives*. Hillsdale, NJ: Erlbaum.

Rutherford, E., & Mussen, P. H. (1968). Generosity in nursery school boys. *Child Development, 39*, 755–765.

Sagi, A., & Hoffman, M. L. (1976). Empathic distress in newborns. *Developmental Psychology, 12*, 175–176.

Sawin, D. (1979). Assessing empathy in children: A search for an elusive construct. Paper presented at the meeting of the Society for Research in Child Development, San Francisco.

Simner, M. L. (1971). Newborn's response to the cry of another infant. *Developmental Psychology, 5*, 136–150.

Singer, J. L. (1984). *The human personality*. New York: Harcourt Brace Jovanovich.

Staub, E. (1971). The use of role-playing and induction in children's learning of helping and sharing behavior. *Child Development, 42*, 805–816.

Staub, E. (1978). *Positive social behavior and morality: Social and personal influences* (Vol. 1). New York: Academic Press.

Staub, F. (1979). *Positive social behavior and morality: Socialization and development* (Vol. 2). New York: Academic Press.

Stendler, D., Damrin, D., & Hines, A. C. (1951). Studies in cooperation and competition: The effects of working for group and individual rewards on the social climate of children's groups. *Journal of Genetic Psychology, 79,* 173–197.

Stotland, E. (1969). Exploratory investigations of empathy. In L. Berkowitz (Ed.), *Advances in experimental social psychology* (Vol. 4). New York: Academic Press.

Strayer, J. (1980). A naturalistic study of empathic behaviors and their relation to affective states and perspective-taking skills in preschool children. *Child Development, 51,* 815–822.

Strayer, J. (1983). Affective and cognitive components of children's empathy. Paper presented at the meeting of the Society for Research in Child Development, Detroit.

Sullivan, H. S. (1940). *Conceptions of modern psychiatry.* London: Tavistock Press.

Sullivan, H. S. (1953). *The interpersonal theory of psychiatry.* New York: Norton.

Tomkins, S. S. (1963). *Affect, imagery, consciousness, Vol. 2: The negative affects.* New York: Springer.

Underwood, B., & Moore, B. (1982). Perspective-taking and altruism. *Psychological Bulletin, 91,* 143–173.

Waters, E., Wippman, J., & Sroufe, L. A. (1979). Attachment, positive affect, and competence in the peer group: Two studies in construct validation. *Child Development, 50,* 821–829.

Whiting, B. B., & Whiting, J. W. M. (1975). *Children of six cultures.* Cambridge: Harvard University Press.

Wooden, K. (1984). *Child lures.* Shelburne, VT: Child Lures, Inc.

Zahn-Waxler, C., & Radke-Yarrow, M. (1979). *A developmental analysis of children's responses to emotions in others.* Paper presented at the meeting of the Society for Research in Child Development, San Francisco.

Zahn-Waxler, C., & Radke-Yarrow, M. (1982). The development of altruism: Alternative research strategies. In N. Eisenberg (Ed.), *The development of prosocial behavior.* New York: Academic Press.

Zahn-Waxler, C., Radke-Yarrow, M., & King, R. A. (1979). Child rearing and children's prosocial initiations towards victims of distress. *Child Development, 50,* 319–330.

8 Adults' emotional reactions to the distress of others

C. Daniel Batson, Jim Fultz, and Patricia A. Schoenrade

You pick up a newspaper. One headline announces that thousands have lost their lives in an earthquake in Mexico; another introduces a story on drought victims dying of disease and starvation in Africa.

   Closer to home, a good friend comes to you in tears because she and her husband have just separated. Another friend is upset at learning that he will not get a hoped-for job offer.

What happens when we encounter people in distress? Often, we react emotionally. Often, too, we try to do something to alleviate their distress. But exactly what do we feel? Are the emotions we feel related to what we do? And if they are, how are they related? In this chapter, we attempt to answer these general questions concerning adults' emotional reactions to the distress of others – and the relation of these emotional reactions to prosocial motivation and behavior – by addressing five specific questions. The first three focus on the emotional reactions themselves: Do they exist? Are there different types? And if so, what accounts for the difference? The last two concern the relationship of the emotional reactions to the behavioral response: Is there such a relationship? And if so, what is the motivation underlying it?

   Concerning the emotional reactions themselves, we differentiate between two types: (1) feelings of empathy (sympathy) for another who is in distress and (2) feelings of personal distress that are produced by witnessing the other's distress.[1] In considering the associated behavioral response, we look at attempts to determine whether any motivation to help a distressed other could be altruistic (i.e., directed toward the ultimate goal of increasing the other's welfare). In general, modern psychological theories of motivation have assumed that the motivation underlying all behavior, including all prosocial behavior, is egoistic (i.e., directed toward the ultimate goal of increasing one's own welfare). But these theories may be wrong. Perhaps to some degree and under some circumstances, the

Preparation of this chapter was supported in part by University of Kansas General Research Fund Grant 3375-XO-0038, C. Daniel Batson, Principal Investigator; and by NSF Grant BNS-8507110, C. Daniel Batson, Principal Investigator.

163

motivation to help is actually other-centered rather than self-centered. Before we can consider such a possibility, however, we need to address some more basic questions.[2]

Do people react emotionally to the distress of others?

Without doubt, people often react emotionally to the perceived distress of someone else. Furthermore, their emotional reaction is often congruent with what they perceive the other's welfare to be. These assertions are based on studies of people witnessing target persons having an undesirable experience in which the stimuli causing the target's experience did not, and would not impinge on the observer.

In one of the first studies of this kind, Berger (1962) had people observe a target person performing a task. He led them to believe that following the onset of a visual signal the target person was either receiving electric shock or not, after which the target person either jerked his or her arm or did not. All observers were told that they themselves would not be shocked during the study.

Berger reasoned, first, that both a painful stimulus in the environment (shock) and a distress response (movement) were necessary for observers to infer that the target person was experiencing pain. He reasoned, second, that if observers were responding to the other's distress, they should display a physiological reaction to watching the target person only when they inferred that he or she was experiencing pain. Therefore, Berger predicted that participants who perceived both shock and movement would display more physiological arousal than participants for whom either the painful stimulus or the target's distress response, or both, were missing.

Berger's results patterned as predicted. Consistent with the assumption that people can experience emotion as a result of perceiving another in pain, participants in the shock-movement condition were more physiologically aroused while observing the target person than participants in the other three conditions. Subsequent research (Bandura & Rosenthal, 1966; Craig & Lowrey, 1969; Craig & Wood, 1969; Krebs, 1975; Lazarus, Opton, Nomikos, & Rankin, 1965; Stotland, 1969) has provided additional physiological evidence that people react emotionally as a result of perceiving another suffering an undesirable fate, even when these people are not, and will not be, suffering the same fate.

Perhaps, however, the increased arousal of observers in these studies was due not to an emotional reaction to the target's distress but to the observers' imagining how they would themselves react in the situation. If so, then their increased arousal would not really be evidence of one person reacting to another's distress. To examine this possibility, Steffan Hygge (1976) had participants observe a female target person as she was exposed to auditory tones delivered through headphones. Although all observers knew that they would not hear the tones themselves, some were led to believe that were they to hear the tones they would experience pain; others were led to believe that the tones would not cause them pain. Further, some of the observers were led to believe that the target person was experiencing pain when hearing the tones; others, that she was not. Hygge found that emotional arousal (assessed by a number of physiological measures) was greater for those who thought that the tones were causing the target pain. Observers' belief that they themselves would or would not find the tones painful did not affect emotional arousal.

Research has also provided evidence that the emotional reactions are often, although not always, congruent with the perceived welfare of target persons (Bandura & Rosenthal, 1966; Hygge, 1976; Krebs, 1975; Milgram, 1963; Staub, 1978; Stotland, 1969). For example, in a study by Stotland and Sherman (reported in Stotland, 1969), people who witnessed another person experiencing what they perceived to be pain reported their own emotional state to be one of increased tension and nervousness; they were also more likely than people in control conditions to report that they found participating in the study a relatively unpleasant experience. In contrast, people who witnessed another person experiencing what they perceived to be pleasure reported, relative to controls, that they found participating in the study to be a pleasant experience. Similarly, Krebs (1975) found that participants reported feeling relatively bad when watching someone whom they thought was about to receive an electric shock and relatively good when watching someone about to receive a reward.

Note that in both of these last two studies the reports of emotion coincided with evidence of increased emotional arousal on physiological measures. In control conditions, neither the physiological measures nor the self-reports provided evidence of an emotional response. This convergence of physiological and self-report data provides reasonably strong evidence that participants in these studies actually were experiencing emotions congruent with the perceived welfare of the other, and not simply saying so.

Are there differences in the types of emotional reactions to the distress of others?

Three different answers to this second question have been offered. First, in the early version of their arousal-reduction model, Piliavin and Piliavin (1973) implied a negative answer; they suggested that the various congruent emotional reactions to witnessing another's distress all contribute to a general level of aversive arousal. Second, in a revised version of the Piliavins' arousal-reduction model, Piliavin, Dovidio, Gaertner, and Clark (1981) proposed a *quantitative* distinction in emotional reaction: when the emotional reaction is of low magnitude (i.e., is assumed to occur in nonemergency situations), the emotion is experienced as empathy (sympathy); when the emotional response is of high magnitude (i.e., is assumed to occur in emergency situations), the emotion is experienced as personal distress. Third, Coke, Batson, and McDavis (1978) proposed a *qualitative* distinction between the emotional reactions of personal distress (e.g., feeling alarmed, upset, disturbed, and the like) and empathy (e.g., feeling sympathetic, compassionate, softhearted, tender, and the like). In contrast to Piliavin et al. (1981), Coke et al. assumed that either or both of these emotions might be experienced in nonemergency as well as emergency situations and when the emotional arousal was of low as well as high magnitude.[3]

Which of these three answers is correct? Do all congruent emotional reactions to the distress of others lie along a single dimension – with quantitative differentiation perhaps – or do they lie along qualitatively different dimensions? One way to try to answer this question is to factor-analyze individuals' self-reported emotional response to witnessing another's distress to see whether adjectives reflecting personal distress load on a different factor from adjectives reflecting empathy. This has been done in a series of studies, now six in number (Batson, Cowles, & Coke, 1979; Batson, O'Quin, Fultz, Vanderplas, & Isen, 1983; Coke, 1980; Coke et al., 1978; Fultz, 1982; Toi & Batson, 1982).

Evidence from factor analyses

Undergraduate participants in each of these six studies were asked to report on a 7-point scale (1 = not at all; 7 = extremely) how strongly they were feeling each emotion described in a list of emotion adjectives. The list included eight adjectives assumed to reflect the vicarious emotion of personal distress (*alarmed, grieved, upset, worried, disturbed, perturbed, distressed,* and *troubled*) and six adjectives assumed to reflect empathy (*sympathetic, moved, compassionate, tender, warm,* and *softhearted*). If distress and empathy are qualitatively distinct emotions, then subjects' ratings of the adjectives in these two sets should load on separate components in a principal-components factor analysis. Alternatively, if these emotions combine to form a single overall level of aversive arousal or are only differentiated quantitatively, then responses to all 14 adjectives should load on a single component. To provide a clear comparison of these alternatives it was important to ensure that different components were entirely unrelated, so an orthogonal rotation was used.

Before turning to the component analyses, it should be noted that the correlations of responses to the eight distress adjectives (averaged) with the six empathy adjectives (averaged) were positive in each of the six studies (the r's ranged from .44 to .75; all p's < .001). Although consistent with the possibility that adjectives of both types reflect a single dimension of emotional response, these correlations do not provide clear support for this possibility. There are at least three other reasons to expect subjects' reports of these emotions to be positively correlated. First, because both distress and empathy are emotions, they should be similarly affected by individual differences in general emotionality and in readiness to report emotions. Second, because both distress and empathy were evoked by perceiving a person in need, individual differences in perceptions of the magnitude of the need should have parallel effects on both. Third, in each of the six studies in this series, emotions were measured by self-reports on unidirectional adjective-rating scales, with adjectives reflecting distress and empathy intermixed. With this form of measurement, response-set biases could easily produce a positive correlation between reports of the two emotions.

Factor analysis can control for these potential confounds in the correlations, because factor analysis reflects systematic, independent patterns within and across individuals' responses. Accordingly, varimax-rotated principal-component factor analyses were performed on subjects' responses to the 14 emotion adjectives. These analyses revealed that a two-component solution included all components with eigenvalues above 1.0 in five of the six studies. (The one exception was the study by Batson et al., 1979, in which a third component had an eigenvalue exceeding 1.0.) The variance accounted for by the two-component solution ranged from 65% to 73% across the six studies. Furthermore, whereas the two-component solution included all components accounting for at least 10% of the total variance in all six studies, the one-component solution failed to meet this criterion in any study. Component loadings for each of the 14 emotion adjectives in the two-component solution are reported in Table 8.1.

As is apparent from Table 8.1, the loadings reveal a component structure that is highly consistent across studies; in each, the eight distress adjectives tend to load on one component, and the six empathy adjectives tend to load on a second, orthogonal component. The first component, which we have called the distress component, received high loadings (>.60) from *alarmed, upset, disturbed,* and *distressed* in all six studies, from *worried* and *perturbed* in five of the six, and from *grieved* and *troubled* in four of the six studies. The second component, which we have called the empathy component, received high loadings from *moved, compassionate, warm,* and *softhearted* in all six studies and from *sympathetic* and *tender* in four of five studies. (These last two adjectives were not used by Coke et al., 1978.)

The robustness of the finding that distress and empathy are qualitatively distinct emotional reactions is indicated by the consistency of the component structure across the six studies, which employed quite different need situations and elicited a range of magnitudes of distress and empathy. The first four studies employed relatively remote need situations, and participants consistently reported experiencing more empathy than distress (*t*'s for this difference ranged

Table 8.1. *Component loadings from varimax-rotated principal-components analysis of self-reported emotional responses to witnessing another in need (six studies)*[a]

	1 D	1 E	2 D	2 E	3 D	3 E	4 D	4 E	5 D	5 E	6 D	6 E
Distress adjectives												
Alarmed	.75*	.01	.72*	.49	.63*	.15	.72*	.34	.77*	.11	.80*	.19
Grieved	.51	.49	.65*	.48	.55	.58	.70*	.33	.68*	.42	.72*	.30
Upset	.84*	.39	.82*	.32	.74*	.38	.80*	.38	.87*	.17	.89*	.28
Worried	.40	.60*	.87*	.18	.67*	.35	.72*	.34	.78*	.18	.81*	.39
Disturbed	.83*	.35	.82*	.38	.76*	.20	.76*	.38	.89*	.18	.90*	.24
Perturbed	.84*	.17	.59	−.11	.76*	−.18	.69*	−.13	.82*	−.02	.68*	.11
Distressed	.62*	.56	.65*	.48	.81*	.32	.67*	.48	.87*	.25	.86*	.28
Troubled	.88*	.23	.58	.54	.80*	.22	.75*	.33	.59	.39	.87*	.32
Empathy adjectives												
Sympathetic	—	—	.58	.53	.23	.74*	.29	.69*	.04	.84*	.20	.82*
Moved	.31	.75*	.37	.78*	.41	.78*	.42	.74*	.31	.67*	.40	.72*
Compassionate	.25	.80*	.09	.82*	.40	.73*	.24	.80*	.14	.86*	.17	.90*
Tender	—	—	.66*	.32	.18	.86*	.28	.78*	.31	.78*	.36	.74*
Warm	.05	.82*	.23	.71*	−.03	.80*	.19	.80*	.20	.68*	.15	.66*
Softhearted	.12	.85*	.14	.73*	.11	.80*	.17	.86*	.05	.83*	.29	.86*

Note: D = distress component; E = empathy component; asterisk denotes loading >.60; —, Not applicable.
[a]Studies are as follows:

1. Coke, Batson, & McDavis (1978, experiment 2) – $N = 33$; females only
2. Batson, Cowles, & Coke (1979) – $N = 30$; females only
3. Coke (1980) – $N = 63$; females only
4. Toi & Batson (1982) – $N = 78$; females only
5. Fultz (1982) – $N = 61$; 26 males, 35 females
6. Batson, O'Quin, Fultz, Vanderplas, & Isen (1983) – $N = 88$; 39 males, 49 females

Source: Adapted from Batson (in press).

from 3.93 to 8.59, all p's < .001); the last two studies employed a more immediate need, and participants reported relatively high levels of both distress and empathy, with no reliable difference between the two (t's < 1.0). Yet the component structure in all six studies clearly supports the hypothesized independence of the emotional reactions of distress and empathy. (Further support for this independence comes from similar results reported by Archer, Diaz-Loving, Gollwitzer, Davis, & Foushee, 1981, and by Davis, 1983; but see also Shelton & Rogers, 1981).

The consistency of the two-component structure across this range of need situations and range of relative magnitudes of distress and empathy seems to indicate that these emotions are not the same. Specifically, it seems to contradict the suggestions (1) that feelings of distress and empathy are actually components of a single emotional reaction that is experienced as empathy in nonemergency situations and as distress in emergencies or (2) that distress and empathy are components of a single emotional reaction that is experienced as empathy at low levels of intensity and distress at high levels. Contrary to these two suggestions, the component analyses summarized in Table 8.1 reveal that people report personal distress and empathy as qualitatively distinct emotions in both low- and high-impact situations and when reporting both relatively low and high levels of distress and empathy.

This is not to say that the particular configurations of emotions experienced as distress and empathy, as well as the relationship between these configurations, will not differ in different need situations. As revealed in Table 8.1, *grieved* and *worried* were sometimes more closely associated with the empathy than the distress component, and in one study, both *sympathetic* and *tender* were more closely associated with the distress than the empathy component. In some need situations, for example, when an innocent child is suffering, it seems likely that distress and empathy will be closely intertwined. In other need situations, for example, when a peer is suffering, both may be present but more clearly differentiated. The clearer differentiation in the latter case might be expected owing to a greater tendency for observers to imagine themselves in the situation of a peer, sensing the distress they would themselves feel. In contrast, adult observers may be less likely to imagine themselves in a child's situation; as a result, the distress they feel may be prompted by a more other-oriented concern over the fact that the child is suffering rather than a self-oriented concern over how they would themselves react in the other's situation.

By itself, however, this evidence based on component analyses is far from conclusive. Some other discriminating feature of the two sets of adjectives might account for the consistent two-component solutions – for example, differences in social desirability of reporting distress and empathy. Corroborating evidence using other research strategies is needed.

Evidence from experimental manipulation

A second strategy for providing evidence of a qualitative distinction between distress and empathy would be to show that each of the emotions can be experimentally manipulated independently of the other. If the two emotions are *not* qualitatively distinct, then it should not be possible to affect the experience of one without also affecting the experience of the other.

Employing this logic, Batson, Duncan, Ackerman, Buckley, & Birch (1981, experiment 2) attempted to manipulate distress and empathy independently, using a misattribution technique. They had participants watch over closed-circuit television (actually a videotape) while a young woman, Elaine, received electric shocks. Her reactions made it clear that she found the shocks quite uncomfortable. To manipulate emotional response to watching Elaine, participants were given a drug capsule (actually a placebo) and were told either that, as a side effect, the drug would create a feeling of "warmth and sensitivity" or that it would create a feeling of "uneasiness and discomfort." Batson et al. reasoned that if these feelings were qualitatively distinct, then participants induced to misattribute feelings of warmth and sensitivity (empathic feelings) to the drug would perceive their emotional reaction to Elaine as predominantly personal distress. In contrast, participants induced to misattribute feelings of uneasiness and discomfort (distress feelings) to the drug would perceive their emotional reaction to Elaine as predominantly empathy.

Participants' responses to two items on a postexperimental questionnaire were quite consistent with this reasoning. Those told that the drug would make them feel warm and sensitive reported experiencing a relative predominance of uneasiness as a result of watching Elaine; those told that the drug would make them feel uneasy reported a relative predominance of warmth and sensitivity. This successful independent manipulation of perceived distress and empathy is entirely consistent with the suggestion that these emotional reactions are qualitatively distinct. Once again, it seems that there are differences in the types of emotional reactions to the distress of others. Moreover, these differences appear to be qualitative, not simply quantitative.

Evidence from motivational research

A third strategy for examining whether personal distress and empathy are qualitatively distinct emotional reactions is to look for evidence of motivational differences resulting from the two emotions. If the two emotions evoke recognizably different types of motivation, then they must be distinct. Before considering evidence for different motivational consequences of these emotional reactions, however, we must address two logically prior questions: What variables account for the quantitative and qualitative differences in emotional reactions that appear to exist? And, are these emotional reactions linked to behavioral responses to the distress of others?

What factors account for the quantitative and qualitative differences in emotional reactions to the distress of others?

Quantitative differences in emotional reactions to another's distress have most often been assumed to be related to the perceived clarity and severity of the other's distress. The qualitative difference between personal distress and empathy has most often been related to perspective taking and to individual differences in either ability or readiness to experience these emotions.

Quantitative differences in emotional reaction: effects of clarity and severity.

Although it seems intuitively plausible, there is only limited research evidence that the perceived clarity and severity of another's distress affect the magnitude of emotional reactions to that distress. We are aware of just two studies, both unpublished, that have tested this proposition directly (Byeff, 1970, and Sterling, 1977; see Dovidio, 1984, for a brief review). Both studies provide supportive evidence.

Additional, less direct evidence comes from the studies summarized in Table 8.1. The first four studies involved subjects hearing but not seeing the person in need; the victim and the need were relatively remote. In the last two studies, subjects saw as well as heard as the victim presumably received electric shocks in a nearby room. Only the luck of the (rigged) draw at the beginning of the study had prevented the subject from being the one receiving shocks. If perceived clarity affects the magnitude of the emotional reaction, then we might expect the increased proximity between subject and victim in these last two studies to increase the magnitude of the emotional response. This indeed seems to have occurred. Of the eight possible comparisons between the amount of self-reported empathy (average of the six empathy adjectives) reported by participants in one of the first four studies in Table 8.1 and the amount of empathy reported in one of the last two studies, all eight comparisons are in the predicted direction; seven of the eight are statistically reliable. As might be expected, the greater proximity in the last two studies also increased self-reported personal distress (average of the eight distress adjectives); for personal distress, all eight comparisons between one of the first four studies and one of the last two are highly significant. Given the consistency of this admittedly limited evidence, it seems reasonable tentatively to conclude that the perceived clarity and severity of another's need do affect the magnitude of emotional reactions.

Qualitative differences in emotional reaction: effects of perspective taking and dispositional empathy

Clarity and severity of need seem to increase reactions of both distress and empathy. What, then, determines whether a person will experience empathy in addition to or instead of personal distress? Perspective taking is the psychological variable most often assumed to be the antecedent of specifically empathic reactions to another's distress. In support of this assumption, there is considerable evidence that adopting the perspective of another who is suffering increases the empathic emotional reaction to witnessing that person suffer. Both Stotland (1969) and Krebs (1975) exposed people to target persons supposedly responding to painful, pleasurable, or neutral stimuli. In some studies Stotland manipulated perspective taking directly by instructing participants to imagine the target person's feelings, as opposed to observing the movements of the target person. In other studies he manipulated perspective taking indirectly by varying participants' perceived similarity to the target person, reasoning that among its other effects (e.g, increased liking) greater perceived similarity would lead to increased perspective taking. Krebs also manipulated perspective taking indirectly by varying perceived similarity.

Results of these studies support the hypothesis that taking another's perspective increases emotional reactions to that person's pleasure or pain. When observing a target presumed to be experiencing pain, persons instructed to take the target's perspective were more physiologically aroused than persons instructed to observe the target's movements. Those led to believe that they were similar to the target were also more physiologically aroused than those led to believe that they were dissimilar. Further, self-reports by participants in both Stotland's and Krebs's research indicated that arousal experienced under these conditions tended to be labeled in a manner congruent with the perceived state of the other. If the other was perceived to be in pain, participants tended to describe their own emotional state as one of tension, nervousness, and unpleasantness; if the other was perceived to be having a pleasurable experience, participants were likely to describe themselves as experiencing a good, pleasant emotional state.

This last observation raises the possibility that the emotional reaction to another's distress evoked by perspective taking might be personal distress rather than empathy. Toi and Batson (1982) conducted an experiment that examined this possibility. After receiving perspective-taking instructions modeled after those used by Stotland (1969), female undergraduates listened to a (bogus) radio broadcast in which another female introductory psychology student told of her problems trying to recover from an automobile accident. At the conclusion of the broadcast, participants reported their emotional response by rating a series of emotion adjectives that included both personal distress and empathy adjectives.

Results revealed that ratings of the empathy adjectives (averaged) were significantly higher for subjects instructed to take the perspective of the person in need than for subjects instructed to listen objectively to the broadcast, $p < .02$. Ratings of the distress adjectives did not differ reliably across perspective-taking conditions. Moreover, the perspective-taking instructions had a marginally significant effect on an index of predominant emotional response (empathy minus distress). In this experiment, then, the emotional reaction evoked by taking the perspective of the person in need appeared to be more one of empathy than of personal distress. Similar effects of perspective-taking instructions on self-reported empathy rather than distress were recently reported by Fultz, Batson, Fortenbach, McCarthy, and Varney (1986).

The combined results of these studies provide rather clear evidence that taking the perspective of a person in need increases empathic emotional reactions. Still, depending on the type of need situation (e.g., child versus adult in need) and wording of the instructions, it seems likely that perspective-taking instructions might produce an increase not only in empathy but also in personal distress.

Dispositional empathy

It has long been assumed that there are dispositional differences among individuals that affect both the quantity and quality of emotional reaction to others' distress. There is little agreement, however, about the exact nature of these dispositional differences. Some researchers suggest that the important differences lie in the ability to take another's perspective (Krebs & Russell, 1981) or in the readiness to do so (Davis, 1983; Stotland, 1969; Stotland, Matthews, Sherman, Hansson, & Richardson, 1978; Stotland, Sherman, & Shaver, 1971). Other researchers emphasize differences either in general emotionality or in the specific emotional reactions of empathy (e.g., Davis, 1983; Hoffman, 1977, 1981; Matthews, Batson, Horn, & Rosenman, 1981; Mehrabian & Epstein, 1972) and personal distress (Davis, 1983). There is even evidence that some of these individual differences might have a genetic origin (Hoffman, 1981; Matthews et al., 1981), perhaps with a sex linkage (Hoffman, 1977; but see also Eisenberg & Lennon, 1983).

At present, the two most popular measures of dispositional differences in emotional reactions to the distress of others are the Empathy Scale developed by Mehrabian and Epstein (1972) and the Interpersonal Reactivity Index developed by Davis (1983). The former seems to measure a tendency toward emotional arousability in a variety of situations – not only in response to seeing someone in distress, but in other situations as well – so one may question whether it is truly a measure of dispositional differences in empathic emotional reactions as distinct from differences in general emotionality (see Chlopan, McCain, Carbonell, & Hagen, 1985). The latter is a more differentiated measure. It includes four subscales designed to measure empathy fantasy (Stotland et al., 1978), perspective taking (Stotland, 1969), empathic concern (Coke et al., 1978), and personal distress (Coke et al., 1978). Although the multidimensionality and specificity of the Davis instrument is a potential improvement over the Mehrabian and Epstein scale, some recent evidence suggests that the Davis instrument is not problem-free.

It seems clear that the Davis (1983) scales can detect reliable individual differences in self-reports of a disposition to identify with fictional characters and to take the perspective of others, as well as differences in self-reports of a disposition to feel empathy or distress in response to witnessing others' distress. But it is far less clear what these individual differences in the self-reports mean. For example, take the statement, ''I often have tender, concerned feelings for other people less fortunate than me'' (from Davis's, 1983, Empathic Concern scale). What is the dispositional difference between persons who report that this statement describes themselves very well and persons who report that this statement describes themselves only moderately well? Do these different responses reflect a true difference in emotional reaction, a difference in what these persons are willing to report, or a difference in the way these persons want to be seen – either by themselves or by others?

Evidence is mounting that at least a substantial part of what is measured by self-report questionnaire measures of perspective taking and dispositional empathy like the Davis scales is an individual difference in self-presentation (see Archer et al., 1981; Batson, Bolen, Cross, & Neuringer-Benefiel, 1986; Fultz et al., 1986). It seems that these scales may tell us more about how respondents want to see themselves and to be seen by others than about how respondents actually react perceptually and emotionally when confronted with someone in distress. The respondent who says, yes, I try to take other people's perspective, or yes, I feel sorry for others who are suffering, is telling us something important about his or her self-concept and values. But the empirical evidence suggests that such assertions should not be taken at face value as accurate self-descriptions.

These self-presentation concerns may account for a substantial proportion of the observed sex differences on dispositional measures of distress and empathy. Although females consistently report more distress and empathy on self-report measures than do males, these sex differences tend to disappear when one takes less reactive measures (e.g., physiological measures) of emotional reactions to another's distress (Eisenberg & Lennon, 1983). This pattern of results suggests that the observed sex differences on self-report measures may be due, at least in part, to differences in sex-role norms that make it more appropriate for females to report both upset, anxious feelings, and tender, compassionate feelings. Whether there is a true sex difference in emotional reactions to the distress of others, as opposed to reports of these reactions, is not as yet clear.

In sum, although it seems entirely possible that individual differences in perspective taking, general emotionality, and the more specific emotional reactions of distress and empathy could affect the magnitude and type of emotional reaction to witnessing another person suffer, the evidence for such effects is far less clear than it might at first glance appear. What is clear is that we cannot assume an equivalence of the dispositional variables called perspective taking, empathy, and personal distress, with the perspective a person adopts or with that person's emotional response when actually confronted with someone in distress in some specific situation. The tendency to react emotionally when confronted with someone in distress and the tendency to report a disposition to react emotionally to the suffering of others are two quite distinct psychological phenomena. The relationship between them – or the lack of relationship – needs to be carefully examined, not assumed. Simply because researchers have used the same label to describe a dispositional and a situational variable does not mean that these variables are the same.

What is the relationship between emotional reactions to another's distress and behavioral response?

The most frequently hypothesized relationship between emotional reaction to another's distress and behavioral response is that the emotional reaction leads to action designed to reduce the other's distress, that is, to helping. To test this hypothesis, however, one cannot simply manipulate the strength of the painful stimulus impinging on a target person or the strength of the target's apparent distress. As the research reported above suggests, such manipulations should affect the strength of a bystander's emotional reactions, but these manipulations may also affect the bystander's perception of the magnitude of the target person's need. And perceived need might affect helping through psychological processes quite unrelated to emotion (such as the activation of norms stipulating that one should help more when a person is in greater need; see Berkowitz, 1972; Schwartz, 1977). Similarly, one cannot simply manipulate perspective taking and observe its effective on helping. As the research reported above suggests, perspective taking affects the strength of the emotional reaction, especially empathic emotion. But perspective taking might affect helping quite independently of its effect on emotions; so whatever emotion is caused by perspective taking might not be the cause of increased helping following perspective taking (see, Rubin & Schneider, 1973; Underwood & Moore, 1982).

To provide a clear test of the effect of emotional reactions on helping, it is necessary somehow to vary the level of emotion while exposing all participants to the same need situation and keeping constant their degree of perspective taking. In other words, it is necessary to vary the level of emotion directly, so that emotion is not confounded with other variables that might, by themselves, affect helping. With this criterion in mind, let us examine the research that has explored the relationship between emotional reactions – especially empathic reactions – and helping.

Studies by Aderman and Berkowitz (1970) and by Aronfreed and Paskal (cited in Aronfreed, 1968) provided results that are consistent with the hypothesis that empathic emotion leads to helping. But because these studies were not designed to test this specific hypothesis, they did not satisfy the criterion necessary to provide a clear test. Empathic emotion was neither directly manipulated nor even measured, so we cannot be sure that the manipulations actually increased empathy, or if they did, that empathy was the variable actually evoking the helping. An additional problem in interpreting the results of the study reported by Aderman and Berkowitz is that the participants were not given an opportunity to help the person whose suffering evoked their empathic response, but someone else. A priori it is not clear that empathy for one person should generalize to a second, unrelated person.

By taking physiological and self-report measures of empathy, Krebs (1975) provided more convincing evidence that a relationship exists between empathic emotion and helping. All participants in this study observed a target person exhibit the same sequence of behaviors. But some were given information about the target's situation that led them to believe that his or her experience was sometimes positive and sometimes negative (high-affect condition), others, that his or her experience was affectively neutral (low-affect condition). Participants were also led to believe they were either similar to the target person (similar condition) or that they were dissimilar (dissimilar condition).

Krebs found that, relative to people in the other three conditions, those in the high-affect–similar condition showed more physiological arousal while observing the target person, reported identifying with the target person to a greater extent, reported feeling worse while waiting for the target to experience pain, and gave more help to the target person. However, even Krebs's results did not demonstrate a causal relation between empathic emotion and helping – only that the two were affected similarly by the same independent variables. Moreover, the affect and similarity manipulations used to evoke empathy presumably also increased perceived need and perspective taking, variables that might themselves increase helping.

A study by Harris and Huang (1973) provided more direct evidence that emotional reaction to another's distress was related causally to helping. While participants were working on math problems, a confederate with a bandaged knee limped into the experimental room, tripped over a chair, and crying out in apparent pain, fell to the floor. Some participants were induced to misattribute arousal caused by this incident to an aversive noise; others were not. Harris and Huang based their predictions on Schachter's (1964) theory of emotions. If a bystander's emotional response is important in motivating helping, and if emotion consists of physiological arousal and a cognitive label, then leading people to attribute the arousal produced by witnessing the victim's distress to a stimulus other than the distress should reduce helping. Consistent with this prediction, participants induced to misattribute their arousal to the noise offered less help to the confederate than participants not so induced. Further, although it was not possible to measure perceived need in this study, there was no difference in reported emotional arousal between the two experimental conditions; there was only a difference in the degree to which the arousal was attributed to the noise. Harris and Huang interpreted their results as evidence that emotional reactions motivate helping.

Using misattribution to a drug rather than to noise, Gaertner and Dovidio (1977) provided a conceptual replication of Harris and Huang's study. In experiment 1, using a measure of heart rate, Gaertner and Dovidio confirmed that witnessing another person in distress produced increased cardiac activity. In experiment 2, they found that people induced to misattribute physiological arousal to a drug were slower to help than those not so induced. Moreover, the Gaertner and Dovidio procedure permitted a measure of the perceived severity of the distressed person's need, and no differences between the two drug conditions were reported. Sterling and Gaertner (1984) provided evidence that this misattribution process could be reversed. People physiologically aroused by doing push-ups who were then induced to misattribute this arousal to overhearing an accident were more likely to help the accident victim than people either not aroused by doing push-ups or not induced to misattribute this arousal.

The studies by Harris and Huang (1973), Gaertner and Dovidio (1977), and Sterling and Gaertner (1984) seem to meet the criterion for manipulating participants' self-perceived emotional reaction in a manner unconfounded with other variables that might affect helping, and the results of these studies consistently indicate that increased emotional reaction to another's distress can lead to increased motivation to help. But in none of these studies was there clear identification of the nature of the emotional arousal evoked in research participants when witnessing the target's distress. Participants in these experiments may have experienced feelings of empathy or of personal distress, either of which might have motivated helping.

To clarify this issue, Coke et al. (1978) conducted two experiments in which they attempted to manipulate the specific emotional reaction of empathy. In experiment 1 reported by Coke et al., participants listened to a tape recording of a radio newscast, which presented the situation of a young college senior, Katie Banks, who had recently lost her parents in a tragic automobile wreck. Employing Stotland's (1969) technique for manipulating perspective taking, Coke et al. instructed participants either to imagine how Katie felt about her situation (imagine her condition) or to observe the broadcasting techniques used in the newscast (observe condition). Just before participants heard the newscast, they were given a capsule in the context of another experiment. Half of the participants were told that the capsule – actually a placebo – would relax them (relax condition); the others were told that it would arouse them (arouse condition). After hearing the newscast, all participants were unexpectedly given an opportunity to help Katie by offering to run errands, care for her brother and sister, and so on.

Coke et al. (1978) reasoned that if perspective taking increases empathic emotional response, then people in the imagine condition should be more empathically aroused by the newscast than people in the observe condition. People in the imagine–arouse condition, however, should have a salient alternative explanation for this arousal; they had just taken a capsule that would arouse them. Only people in the imagine–relax condition were expected both to experience empathic arousal and cognitively to label that arousal as a response to Katie's plight. Therefore, following Schachter (1964), only these participants were expected to experience empathic emotion. Results revealed that, as predicted, people in the imagine–relax condition offered significantly more help to Katie than did people in any of the other three conditions. Nor could this difference be accounted for by differences in perceived need; participants in the imagine–relax condition actually perceived Katie's need to be slightly less than did participants in the other three conditions. These findings were entirely consistent with the hypothesis that empathic emotion is causally linked to helping.

In experiment 2, Coke et al. (1978) used a different strategy for manipulating empathic emotion; they artificially increased perceived empathy through the use of a false feedback of arousal paradigm (Valins, 1966). Participants listened to a tape-recorded pilot broadcast of a situation that was designed to be intrinsically unarousing: A graduate student in education was seeking volunteers to participate in her master's thesis research. All participants were instructed to imagine, while listening to the broadcast, how the graduate student felt about her situation. While listening, some participants received false physiological feedback indicating that they were not aroused (low-arousal condition); others received false feedback indicating that they were highly aroused (high-arousal condition). Prior to unexpectedly being confronted with an opportunity to help the graduate student, all participants were asked to indicate the degree to which they had experienced a number of emotions while listening to the broadcast.

Coke et al. (1978) predicted that people in the high-arousal condition would perceive themselves to be experiencing more empathy than people in the low-arousal condition, and that the greater empathy experienced by people in the high-arousal condition would lead to more helping. Results supported this prediction. Participants in the high-arousal condition indicated that they felt more empathic emotion but not more personal distress while listening to the broadcast than participants in the low-arousal condition; they also offered more help to the graduate student. Further, path analyses suggested that the effect of the false-feedback manipulation on helping was mediated by self-perceived empathic emotion and not by self-perceived personal distress. There was no evidence that any of these effects were due to differences in perceived need.

The Coke et al. experiments appear to have met the criterion for directly manipulating empathic emotion in a manner unconfounded with perceived need and perspective taking. Differences in perceived need could not account for the results of either experiment. Perspective-taking instructions were held constant in experiment 2. In experiment 1 they were manipulated, but by themselves did not increase helping; they did so only when participants attributed the arousal caused by perspective taking to the victim's plight. When people misattributed the arousal to a drug, perspective taking did not increase helping. But if the perspective-taking manipulation was not sufficient, by itself, to affect helping, neither was the attribution manipulation. People in the observe–relax condition did not offer more help than people in the observe–arouse condition. Apparently, without perspective taking there was no emotional arousal to label. In sum, the results reported by Coke et al., together with the results of other studies, provide consistent support for the suggestion that emotional reactions to another's distress – especially empathic emotional reactions – lead to helping.

But if an emotional reaction to another's distress is associated with an increased tendency to act to reduce that distress, what is the nature of the motivation underlying this relationship? Is the aroused individual motivated by an egoistic desire to reduce his or her own emotional arousal, or is he or she motivated by an altruistic desire to reduce the other's distress? These possibilities prompt our fifth question.

Are there qualitative differences in the nature of the motivation associated with different emotional reactions?

We propose an affirmative answer to this question. Specifically, we propose that those emotional reactions that fall under the general heading of personal distress (feeling alarmed, upset, disturbed, distressed, and the like) evoke egoistic motivation to have one's own emotional arousal reduced, whereas the emotional reactions that fall under the general heading of empathy (feeling sympathetic, compassionate, softhearted, tender, and the like) evoke altruistic motivation to have the other's need reduced.

This proposed answer is based on the results of a series of studies conducted by Batson et al. (1981), Toi and Batson (1982), and Batson et al. (1983). In these studies it was consistently found that when helping is moderately costly, research participants who experience a predominance of personal distress as a result of witnessing another person suffer are significantly less likely to help that person if they believe they will not continue to witness the person's suffering even if they do not help. This effect of the ease of escape from exposure to the other person's suffering suggests that subjects experiencing a relative predominance of distress are motivated by an egoistic desire to reduce their own distress. If they anticipate being freed from the stimulus causing their distress even if they do not help, then they are not likely to help. But if the only way they can escape the stimulus is by helping, then they are likely to do so.

Responses of research participants experiencing a relative predominance of empathy as a result of witnessing another person suffer are quite different. They are as likely to help that person when they believe they will not continue to witness the person's suffering as when they believe they will. Apparently, empathic emotion does not evoke egoistic motivation to reduce one's own emotional arousal. To the contrary, the finding that empathically aroused individuals are likely to help even when it would be easy to escape the empathy-inducing situation without helping suggests that they may be experiencing truly altruistic motivation. It appears that their ultimate goal may be, at least in part, to reduce the other person's distress rather than their own. (For more detailed reviews of this research, see Batson, in press; Batson, Fultz, & Schoenrade, 1987.)

Other egoistic interpretations of the motivation to help evoked by empathy

The suggestion that empathy evokes altruistic motivation to help has not, however, gone unchallenged. Archer et al. (1981), Cialdini, Schaller, Houlihan, Arps, Fultz, & Beaman (1987), Dovidio (1984), and Meindl and Lerner (1983) have all proposed alternative explanations for some or all of the evidence just summarized. In essence, the alternative explanations suggest that although empathy may not evoke motivation to reduce one's emotional arousal, as does personal distress, the motivation to help associated with empathy may still be egoistic. The empathically aroused individual may help in order to avoid anticipated punishments such as shame and guilt or to gain anticipated rewards such as enhanced self-esteem that arise specifically when a person is feeling empathy. Research is currently under way in several laboratories to test these alternative explanations.

Summary

There is clear evidence that people often react emotionally when confronted with others in distress. Moreover, it seems clear that there are qualitative as well as quantitative differences in these reactions. Seeing another in distress may cause us to experience personal distress. But to the degree that we take the perspective of the other, we are likely to experience a second, more other-oriented emotion; this emotion has been labeled empathy or sympathy. Finally, there is considerable evidence that the emotional response of personal distress evokes egoistic motivation to have one's own emotional arousal reduced, whereas empathic emotion does not. Whether the motivation to help associated with empathy is altruistic or simply a different form of egoistic motivation is not at present clear. A number of researchers are currently pursuing the answer to this question. The answer would seem to have wide-ranging theoretical and practical implications, for the question probes close to the heart of human nature.

Notes

1. We do not attempt to differentiate between the terms *empathy* and *sympathy* in this chapter; we use both to refer to other-oriented feelings of concern, compassion, and tenderness experienced as a result of witnessing another person's suffering.
2. Most of the research we discuss has been guided by a social psychological perspective rather than a developmental perspective; the concern has been to understand emotional reactions and their relation to behavior, not to trace changes in the reactions and behavior across the adult years. As a result, in virtually all of the studies considered in this chapter, the subjects were college students. To what extent can conclusions based on research with college students be generalized to adults in general? Given that most adults, including college students, are formal operational, one may not be too concerned that cognitive differences limit the generalizability. But one may remain legitimately concerned about sociocultural differences. To avoid clumsy hyphenated qualifiers, we simply speak of people's reactions, implying broad generality. But it is clear that many of these reactions would not occur in the same way among children (see chapters 6 and 7), and there may be other limits as well.
3. In some of his earlier writings, Hoffman (1975, 1976) made a distinction between empathic distress and sympathetic distress that parallels the Coke et al. (1978) distinction between personal distress and empathy. But in his more recent writings, Hoffman (1982) has tended to minimize this distinction, using the term *empathic distress* "generically" to refer to both empathic and sympathetic distress.

References

Aderman, D., & Berkowitz, L. (1970). Observational set, empathy, and helping. *Journal of Personality and Social Psychology, 14,* 141–148.

Archer, R. L., Diaz-Loving, R., Gollwitzer, P. M., Davis, M. H., & Foushee, H. C. (1981). The role of dispositional empathy and social evaluation in the empathic mediation of helping. *Journal of Personality and Social Psychology, 40,* 786–796.

Aronfreed, J. M. (1968). *Conduct and conscience: The socialization of internalized control over behavior.* New York: Academic Press.

Bandura, A., & Rosenthal, T. L. (1966). Vicarious classical conditioning as a function of arousal level. *Journal of Personality and Social Psychology, 3,* 54–62.

Batson, C. D. (in press). Prosocial motivation: Is it ever truly altruistic? In L. Berkowitz (Ed.), *Advances in experimental social psychology* (Vol. 20). New York: Academic Press.

Batson, C. D., Bolen, M. H., Cross, J. A., & Neuringer-Benefiel, H. E. (1986). Where is the altrusim in the altruistic personality? *Journal of Personality and Social Psychology, 50,* 212–220.

Batson, C. D., Cowles, C., & Coke, J. S. (1979). Empathic mediation of the response to a lady in distress: Egoistic or altruistic? Unpublished manuscript, University of Kansas.

Batson, C. D., Duncan, B. D., Ackerman, P., Buckey, T., & Birch, K. (1981). Is empathic emotion a source of altruistic motivation? *Journal of Personality and Social Psychology, 40,* 290–302.

Batson, C. D., Fultz, J., & Schoenrade, P. A. (1987). Distress and empathy: Two qualitatively distinct vicarious emotions with different motivational consequences. *Journal of Personality, 55,* 19–39.

Batson, C. D., O'Quin, K., Fultz, J., Vanderplas, M., & Isen, A. (1983). Self-reported distress and empathy and egoistic versus altruistic motivation for helping. *Journal of Personality and Social Psychology, 45,* 706–718.

Berger, S. M. (1962). Conditioning through vicarious instigation. *Psychological Review, 69,* 450–466.

Berkowitz, L. (1972). Social norms, feelings, and other components affecting helping and altruism. In L. Berkowitz (Ed.), *Advances in experimental social psychology* (Vol. 6). New York: Academic Press.

Byeff, P. (1970). Helping behavior in audio and audio-video conditions. Senior honors thesis, University of Pennsylvania.

Chlopan, B. E., McCain, M. L., Carbonell, J. L., & Hagen, R. L. (1985). Empathy: Review of available measures. *Journal of Personality and Social Psychology, 48,* 635–653.

Cialdini, R. B, Schaller, M., Houlihan, D., Arps, K., Fultz, J., & Beaman, A. (1987). Empathy-based helping: Is it selflessly or selfishly motivated? *Journal of Personality and Social Psychology. 52,* 749–758.

Coke, J. S. (1980). Empathic mediation of helping: Egoistic or altruistic? (Doctoral dissertation, University of Kansas, 1979). *Dissertation Abstracts International, 41,* 405B. (University Microfilms No. 8014371)

Coke, J. S., Batson, C. D., & McDavis, K. (1978). Empathic mediation of helping: A two-stage model. *Journal of Personality and Social Psychology, 36,* 752–766.

Craig, K. D., & Lowrey, J. H. (1969). Heart rate components of conditioned vicarious autonomic responses. *Journal of Personality and Social Psychology, 11,* 381–387.

Craig, K. D., & Wood, K. (1969). Psychophysiological differentiation of direct vicarious affective arousal. *Canadian Journal of Behavioural Science, 1,* 98–105.

Davis, M. H. (1983). The effects of dispositional empathy on emotional reactions and helping: A multidimensional approach. *Journal of Personality, 51,* 167–184.

Dovidio, J. F. (1984). Helping behavior and altruism: An empirical and conceptual overview. In L. Berkowitz (Ed.), *Advances in experimental social psychology* (Vol. 17). New York: Academic Press.

Eisenberg, N., & Lennon, R. (1983). Sex differences in empathy and related capacities. *Psychological Bulletin, 94,* 100–131.

Fultz, J. (1982). *Influence of potential for self-reward on egoistically and altruistically motivated helping.* Unpublished master's thesis, University of Kansas.

Fultz, J., Batson, C. D., Fortenbach, V. A., McCarthy, P. M., & Varney, L. L. (1986). Social evaluation and the empathy-altrusim hypothesis. *Journal of Personality and Social Psychology, 50,* 761–769.

Gaertner, S. L., & Dovidio, J. F. (1977). The subtlety of white racism, arousal, and helping behavior. *Journal of Personality and Social Psychology, 35,* 691–707.

Harris, M. B., & Huang, L. C. (1973). Helping and the attribution process. *Journal of Social Psychology, 90,* 291–297.

Hoffman, M. L. (1975). Developmental synthesis of affect and cognition and its implications for altruistic motivation. *Developmental Psychology, 11,* 607–622.

Hoffman, M. L. (1976). Empathy, role-taking, guilt, and development of altruistic motives. In T.

Lickona (Ed.), *Moral development and behavior: Theory, research, and social issues.* New York: Holt, Rinehart & Winston.

Hoffman, M. L. (1977). Sex differences in empathy and related behaviors. *Psychological Bulletin, 84,* 712–722.

Hoffman, M. L. (1981). Is altruism part of human nature? *Journal of Personality and Social Psychology, 40,* 121–137.

Hoffman, M. L. (1982). Development of prosocial motivation: Empathy and guilt. In N. Eisenberg (Ed.), *The development of prosocial behavior.* New York: Academic Press.

Hull, C. L. (1952). *A behavior system.* New Haven, CT: Yale University Press.

Hygge, S. (1976). Information about the model's unconditioned stimulus and response in vicarious classical conditioning. *Journal of Personality and Social Psychology, 33,* 764–771.

Krebs, D. L. (1975). Empathy and altruism. *Journal of Personality and Social Psychology, 32,* 1134–1146.

Krebs, D., & Russell, C. (1981). Role-taking and altruism: When you put yourself in the shoes of another will they take you to their owner's aid? In J. P. Rushton and R. M. Sorrentino (Eds.), *Altruism and helping behavior.* Hillsdale, NJ: Erlbaum.

Lazarus, R., Opton, E. M., Nomikos, M. S., & Rankin, N. O. (1965). The principle of shortcir-cuiting of threat: Further evidence. *Journal of Personality, 33,* 622–645.

Matthews, K. A., Batson, C. D., Horn, J., & Rosenman, R. H. (1981). "Principles in his nature which interest him in the fortune of others . . .": The heritability of empathic concern for others. *Journal of Personality, 49,* 237–247.

Mehrabian, A., & Epstein, N. (1972). A measure of emotional empathy. *Journal of Personality, 40,* 525–543.

Meindl, J. R., & Lerner, M. J. (1983). The heroic motive: Some experimental demonstrations. *Journal of Experimental Social Psychology 19,* 1–20.

Milgram, S. (1963). Behavioral study of obedience. *Journal of Abnormal and Social Psychology, 67,* 371–378.

Piliavin, J. A., Dovidio, J. F., Gaertner, S. L., & Clark, R. D. III. (1981). *Emergency intervention.* New York: Academic Press.

Piliavin, J. A., & Piliavin, I. M. (1973). The Good Samaritan: Why *does* he help? Unpublished manuscript, University of Wisconsin.

Rubin, K. H., & Schneider, F. W. (1973). The relationship between moral judgment, egocentrism, and altruistic behavior. *Child Development, 44,* 661–665.

Schachter, S. (1964). The interaction of cognitive and physiological determinants of emotional state. In L. Berkowitz (Ed.), *Advances in experimental social psychology* (Vol. 1). New York: Academic Press.

Schwartz, S. H. (1977). Normative influences on altrusim. In L. Berkowitz (Ed.), *Advances in experimental social psychology* (Vol. 10). New York: Academic Press.

Shelton, M. L., & Rogers, R. W. (1981). Fear-arousing and empathy-arousing appeals to help: The pathos of persuasion. *Journal of Applied Social Psychology, 11,* 366–378.

Staub, E. (1978). *Positive social behavior and morality* (Vol. 1). New York: Academic Press.

Sterling, B. (1977). The effects of anger, ambiguity, and arousal on helping behavior (Ph.D. dissertation, University of Delaware, 1977). *Dissertation Abstracts International, 38*(4), 1962.

Sterling, B., & Gaertner, S. L. (1984). The attribution of arousal and emergency helping: A bidirectional process. *Journal of Experimental Social Psychology, 20,* 586–596.

Stotland, E. (1969). Exploratory studies of empathy. In L. Berkowitz (Ed.), *Advances in experimental social psychology* (Vol. 4). New York: Academic Press.

Stotland, E., Matthews, K. E., Sherman, S. E., Hansson, R. O., & Richardson, B. Z. (1978). *Empathy, fantasy, and helping.* Beverly Hills, CA: Sage.

Stotland, E., Sherman, S. E., & Shaver, K. G. (1971). *Empathy and birth order: Some experimental explorations.* Lincoln: University of Nebraska Press.

Toi, M., & Batson, C. D. (1982). More evidence that empathy is a source of altruistic motivation. *Journal of Personality and Social Psychology, 43,* 281–292.

Underwood, B., & Moore, B. (1982). Perspective-taking and altruism. *Psychological Bulletin, 91,* 143–173.

Valins. S. (1966). Cognitive effects of false heart-rate feedback. *Journal of Personality and Social Psychology, 4,* 400–408.

Commentary on Part II

Paul Mussen

Each of the three interesting and informative chapters in Part II deals with a major segment of the life span and focuses on a few issues that are critical during that period. A substantial body of relevant research is reviewed, analyzed, and carefully evaluated in each chapter. Creative syntheses as well as challenging interpretations and insights are presented.

Readers who attempt to derive a comprehensive, or even normative, account of the course of development of empathy simply by integrating the information presented in these three chapters will be frustrated, however. This is true for several reasons. First, the chapters differ in focus, so that it is virtually impossible to integrate their contents. Thus, the principal issues vary from one period of life to another; what seems most relevant in infancy may not be important in adolescence. Also, the authors' conceptualizations of empathy vary. By and large, they agree that "empathy denotes the vicarious experiencing of an emotion that is congruent with . . . the emotion of another individual" (Barnett, chapter 7), and most regard empathy as a mediator between witnessing another's distress and actions that benefit the distressed individual. But beyond this they differ in their conceptualization of empathy as an emotion or a motivational state, and consequently, in how empathy is operationalized, measured, and investigated. For example, Thompson points out that the infant's primitive empathic responses (sometimes labeled "resonant emotional responses") cannot be defined or evaluated in terms of cognitive functions and/or verbal reports. In chapter 6, the earliest manifestations of empathy are viewed as joint products of the fundamental human predisposition to respond to social stimulation (presumably biologically determined), cognitive advances (specifically self–other distinctions, person permanence, and role-taking abilities), attachment to the mother, and caretaker–child interactions. In contrast, Barnett's chapter concentrates on individual differences in the strength and patterning of empathic reactions among children, and on variations in child-rearing techniques and interactions with siblings as explanatory principles. Batson et al. (chapter 8) have an entirely different agenda; they differentiate between the adult emotions of distress and empathy, delineate

185

conditions that are empathy eliciting, and demonstrate that empathy per se is associated with altruistic motivation. Their chapter is based primarily on laboratory research conducted in the model of experimental social psychology. Although Batson et al. report findings that have implications for understanding the *development* of empathy, these are not spelled out.

As is typical of fine integrative summaries of new domains of investigation, these chapters raise more questions than they answer. Any attempt to specify and discuss the many gaps in our knowledge of the development of empathy in this commentary would be preposterously ambitious and would require many more pages than are allotted. Instead, using these chapters as a launching pad, I attempt to delineate a few of the most significant unresolved issues and to suggest potentially fruitful approaches for investigating them.

In studying emotions, researchers often have well-established and relatively clear-cut criteria for assessment and theories that are the sources of testable hypotheses. Unfortunately, this is not true in the case of empathy, so it seems appropriate to make a brief digression here to speak of these matters before discussing specific issues in need of empirical study.

As readers of the three chapters in this section can detect, theory construction in the area of empathy has been very limited; no "grand" theory of structure and development exists. This is hardly surprising, for even casual introspection and observation provide compelling evidence that the phenomena constituting empathy – feelings, emotions, and concurrent overt reactions – are extraordinarily complicated and undoubtedly influenced by multiple interacting biological, sociocultural, and personal factors. Theories such as those of Hoffman and of Feshbach, mentioned at several points in this section, are suggestive and promising, but they do not purport to explain the complexity of empathy, its origins, or the changes it undergoes with age.

It is unlikely that an adequate, comprehensive theory of the development of empathy will be proposed in the near future. At present, the scientific study of this emotion is, in Kuhn's terms, in the preparadigmatic stage, and we cannot expect theory-driven research. Although an overarching model of the development of empathy over the life span is devoutly to be desired, researchers cannot wait until it is developed. Instead, they should designate questions for further research on the basis of what has already been discovered *plus* insightful psychological and social analyses of the ingredients of empathy.

Most of the research reported in this section makes use of a single measure of empathy, such as a test score or an index of concern. As phenomenological analysis and objective observation reveal, empathy may be manifested in many ways, including strong internal experiences of feeling as well as behavioral and physiological reactions such as facial expressions, gestures, and changes in heart rate and blood pressure. All these responses are potentially useful as indices of empathy, but no one criterion is entirely adequate in the study of the development of empathy. For example, self-reports can be employed only with older children or adults. The most fruitful measures may be those that are applicable over a wide time span, that is, physiological and or behavioral measures that can be reliably assessed in individuals of any age.

Measures of empathy used in research should be direct and unconfounded, that is, conceptually independent of variables that are assumed to be antecedents (such as maternal attachment) or consequents (such as prosocial action). Furthermore, since a single criterion is not likely to be a dependable index of the strength of the empathic response, multiple methods of measurement should be used wherever possible. This would enable researchers to determine the interrelationships or coherence among indices as well as the predictive value of any measure or combination of measures. Some measures may be powerful predictors of later empathy or of prosocial behavior at one period of development; others at other periods.

Let us turn now to the matter of the directions of future research. One fundamental unresolved issue centers on the nature of the *structure* (internal organization) of empathy. Which structure is characteristic: generalized empathic tendencies (predispositions to empathize with wide ranges of feelings and emotions) or areas or domains of empathy induced by only one or a few emotions (distress, for example) but not by others? Does the structure of empathy change with age, and if so, how? General awareness of *change* in others' emotional states – perhaps judged from facial or gestural cues – may precede understanding of specific emotional reactions, and intense dramatic emotional expressions may be capable of eliciting empathy before more subtle and subdued ones do. These and other structural questions can be answered only by careful, detailed observation, microanalyses, and intensive interviews of individuals across a wide age span. The fruitfulness of in-depth interviews, appropriate to the language and cognitive abilities of the interviewees, has been amply demonstrated (see, for example, the work of researchers such as Damon, Eisenberg, and Turiel). There is every reason to believe that such interviews could yield significant data on the dimensions and phenomenology of empathy, age, and individual differences in its structure, eliciting situations and events, as well as the conditions under which empathy generates, or fails to generate, prosocial activity.

From the point of view of *developmental* psychology, three fundamental (and interrelated) issues must be addressed:

1. the discovery and precise description of regularities in development and age transformations of empathy and its expression;
2. formulation and testing of explanatory hypotheses, that is, hypotheses about the processes underlying changes with age as well as about the

antecedents and consequences of individual levels of empathic responsiveness; and

3. determination of the degree of continuity of stability of empathy over time.

These issues require extensive, multifaceted, longitudinal studies. Unfortunately, the hardships and costs of such studies are enormous, but no satisfactory alternatives are available. Cross-sectional and/or experimental studies in themselves simply will not yield the necessary information.

Consider a small sample of the many questions raised in the chapters of this section that could be answered only by means of longitudinal study. Thompson notes that many neonatal infants make resonant emotional responses when they hear other infants crying but little is known about the biological, cognitive, or social antecedents of these responses. If the *capacity* for empathy is wired into the human organism, why do some infants fail to make these responses? Are those who react strongly and rapidly constitutionally more empathic than others? It hardly seems likely that these resonant emotional responses are necessary or sufficient conditions for the further development of empathy; certainly, those who do not manifest these infantile responses are not totally lacking in empathy later on. It is, of course, possible that those infants who make rapid and strong resonant emotional responses become more highly empathic adolescents and adults than those who show less empathy in infancy. At least, this is a hypothesis worth testing, and it can only be tested by longitudinal study.

Analogously, as Barnett reports, secure early attachment to the mother appears to be a major antecedent to high levels of empathic expression in young children. But it hardly seems likely that infants with insecure or ambivalent maternal attachments never develop empathic reactions; not is it probable that early secure attachments are the sources of some sort of reserve of security that invariably fosters the development of enduring high levels of empathy.

Barnett's chapter summarizes a small body of longitudinal research on continuity and change in empathic expression. In the study conducted by Zahn-Waxler and her associates, two thirds of the children showed stability in *patterns* of empathic response between the age of 2 and 7. It might therefore be concluded that early levels of empathy are *generally* good predictors of later responses, but the researchers also found many exceptions to this generalization; one third of the children studied shifted from one pattern of response to another during the 5-year span. What are the characteristics and experiences of individuals who manifest relatively stable levels of empathic responses, and how do these differ from those of individuals whose patterns change? Only longitudinal research can provide answers to questions about events or experiences that promote change or continuity in empathic responses.

Multivariate longitudinal research is required to discern the individual and interaction effects of the numerous biological, cognitive, and socialization factors that play roles in shaping empathy. Such research proceeds from an extensive and rich data base and thus makes it possible to explore a host of relevant questions. To illustrate, I mention a few; the reader can no doubt think of many more.

Thompson and Barnett have presented excellent summaries of extant information on general parent–child interactions (attachments, disciplinary techniques, parental modeling) that influence the child's empathic development. But, as Barnett suggests, more fine-grain analyses of the salient determinants are needed. What specific parental techniques enhance the development of empathy?

Intuition and everyday observations suggest that children's school experiences, cultural and/or ethnic background, as well as exposure to media have profound effects on the development of empathy. Yet these potential influences have not been the subject of systematic empirical research. Do the child's experiences at school or in the community at large reinforce and strengthen, or can they under some circumstances weaken, empathic tendencies acquired at home? Does the child reared in an empathy-fostering home environment become less empathic if he or she is enrolled in a competitive school? To what extent can characteristics of children's broader social world (exosystem) enhance or diminish the level of empathy attributable to experiences in their homes and schools (micro- or mesosystems)?

The high level of Chinese schoolchildren's empathy and their strong sense of consideration for others are impressive. When I asked an experienced school principal in China to explain these characteristics, she replied, ''In China the parents, the school, and the government all work together to promote the development of understanding and sympathy. In the United States a child may receive one message about sympathy at home and another kind of message from teachers or peers or from television.'' Although there is no evidence that the principal's conclusion is valid, the implication of her statement seems worthy of systematic examination.

Sociohistorical, cultural, and social organizational influences on empathy also need to be explored carefully. Do individuals reared in cultures that stress the unity of man and nature (Hopi, for example) have stronger empathic tendencies than those raised in other cultures? Analogously, are American children growing up in a historical period characterized by pervasive concern with the welfare of the poor and minority groups more empathic than children reared in a different ambience? What are the effects on empathy of membership in multiple cultural groups, especially if the groups have conflicting values and ideals?

Barnett notes Feshbach's highly plausible hypothesis that dysphoric personal experiences, such as the loss of a loved one, may enhance empathic reactions.

Some dysphoric experiences are unique, others are shared (for example, minority group status or victimization by flood or earthquake). Philip Hallie (1979) has written a moving account of the activities in a French Protestant village in the south of France during World War II when almost the entire population, at great risk to themselves, helped rescue Jews and other victims of the Holocaust. The author suggests that the unusual empathic and self-sacrificing responses of these villagers were attributable to their minority status in predominantly Catholic France, a status that made them unusually sensitive to the feelings of other victims of prejudice and discrimination.

The ultimate goal of all research on empathy is understanding real empathy as it occurs in the real world; this goal can be most readily achieved if investigators focus their attention on empathic reactions in natural settings, in real-life interactions. Contrived laboratory situations are not likely to elicit deeply felt empathic responses, and experimental manipulations cannot reproduce their numerous multifaceted, interacting antecedents. This is not to deny the value of laboratory studies, in the experimental social psychology model, such as those reported in Batson's chapter. Such studies are useful in testing specific hypotheses about empathic arousal and/or the relationship between empathy and prosocial acts such as helping and sharing. But there are real dangers in attempting to generalize the findings of such studies to real-life situations, dangers of oversimplifying the inherently complex phenomena encompassed in the concept of empathy, and of attributing cause to just one or a few of the effective antecedent variables. Thus, data from experimental studies reported by Batson demonstrate that high-arousal conditions are more empathy- and help-eliciting than low-arousal conditions, but tell us little about conditions that ordinarily induce high or low arousal or about individual differences in reaction to such conditions.

Inevitably, naturalistic study of the many interacting antecedents of empathy and the complicated (usually prosocial) consequences of empathy arousal will be extremely difficult and costly of time, energy, and money. In addition, such studies seem to be less rigorous than those done in the laboratory. However, in the long run they will contribute much more to our understanding of the development of empathy. Ample demonstrations of the feasibility and contributions of naturalistic studies are found in the research of Eisenberg and of Radke-Yarrow and their colleagues, cited in Barnett's chapter. In the research of Radke-Yarrow and colleagues, for example, mothers were trained to observe and record in detail instances of children's prosocial actions, the eliciting conditions, and the reactions of others present at the time. These records, together with information on child-rearing practices, provided an excellent basis for checking hypotheses about home conditions that facilitate (or inhibit) the development of prosocial behavior in children. Studies of this type, which include detailed and accurate reports by trained observers (especially those who had extensive contact with the participants in the study), could prove invaluable in exploring critical questions about the structure and development of empathy.

Reference

Haillie, P. *Lest innocent blood be shed*. New York: Harper & Row, 1979.

Part III

Current issues and empirical findings

9 Gender and age differences in empathy and sympathy

Randy Lennon and Nancy Eisenberg

The purpose of this chapter is to examine the literature concerning gender differences and age trends in empathy and sympathy. Owing to space limitations, we focus primarily on the empirical data; conceptual issues are considered only briefly. Additional discussion of changes with age can be found in chapter 7.

The topic of age trends in empathy has not received much attention from researchers. Although some investigators have explored changes in empathy with development (e.g., Adams, 1983; Radke-Yarrow & Zahn-Waxler, 1984), most have concentrated on cohorts within a narrow age span. In large part, this state of affairs is due to the lack of comparable measures for children, adolescents, and adults.

In contrast, gender differences in empathy have been widely investigated, although in most relevant studies, this has been a peripheral issue. We first examine the large corpus of information on gender differences in empathy and then review the research on age changes in empathy.

Gender differences in empathy

Many studies of gender differences in empathy have been motivated by the desire to test the widely held view that females are more empathic than males, a stereotype that is consistent with both sociological and psychological theory. For example, sociologists have attributed differences in the behavior of males and females to variations in the traditional social roles, in which males are expected to be concerned with tasks that allow the family and society to function, whereas females are expected to be concerned with harmony within the family unit (Parsons & Bales, 1955). From this perspective, nurturance and empathy are viewed as important characteristics for females because they enable females to carry out their role successfully. In contrast, such characteristics serve little purpose for males and therefore are not a focus of male socialization.

Psychoanalytic conceptualizations are also consistent with the assumed gender difference in empathy. Freud (1925/1950) asserted that because females do not

195

fear castration, they do not resolve the Oedipal complex as completely as males and develop weaker superegos. Therefore, females must rely more on primitive emotional capacities and less on moral capacities in their interactions with the world than do males. Specifically, females are viewed as being more concerned with inner space, more intuitive, and less concerned with the external world than are males (Deutsch, 1944; Erikson, 1975/1979).

There are also some empirical data to support the notion that girls are socialized to be more atuned to others' emotions than are boys. For example, Greif, Alvarez, and Ulman (1981) found that fathers (but not mothers) were much more likely to label emotions when telling a story to their 2- to 5-year-old girls than to boys. Moreover, Dunn, Bretherton, and Munn (1987) found that mothers made more references to feeling states in conversations with one- and two-year-old girls than with boys. However, data directly related to the issue of the socialization of gender differences in sympathy or empathy are extremely scarce. This is surprising, given the wealth of research concerning gender differences in prosocial behavior and empathy. Perhaps this dearth of research reflects the strength of many individuals' conviction that such differences in socialization are self-evident.

Previous reviews

There have already been four reviews of the work on gender differences in empathy, but the conclusions are inconsistent, in part because the reviewers defined empathy in different ways and examined different sets of studies. In two of these reviews (Block, 1979; Maccoby & Jacklin, 1974), empathy was defined broadly (i.e., as cognitive role taking, affective role taking, social sensitivity, and a vicarious emotional response to the affective state of another); moreover, the authors attempted to compare the findings of studies in which empathy was assessed in a number of different ways. Thus, it is not surprising that the reviewers concluded that there was no evidence of a consistent gender difference.

In a third review, Hoffman (1977) differentiated between studies in which empathy was defined as an emotional response and studies in which researchers measured role taking or social sensitivity. Eleven studies were included in his review (including 16 samples). Females scored higher on empathy in all studies, and in six samples this finding was significant or marginally significant. Therefore, Hoffman concluded that there was ample evidence to suggest that girls are more empathic than boys. However, most of the data Hoffman reviewed were obtained from samples of young children for whom a single measure of empathy (the Feshbach and Roe Affective Situations Test for Empathy or FASTE [1968]) was used.

Between the time of Hoffman's review and the last published review on gender differences in empathy (Eisenberg & Lennon, 1983), many new investigations of emotional empathy were undertaken and new methods to measure the construct were developed. In our 1983 review, we examined new as well as previously reviewed studies. To make sure that observed differences were due to sex and not to differences in method, we compared data from studies in which similar methods were employed to measure empathy. When there were enough data to warrant it, we performed meta-analyses to determine whether, and to what degree, gender differences existed. In addition, we computed the number of studies with null results necessary to reduce a finding below significance (the fail-safe number). When the data did not warrant a meta-analysis, we reported the overall trend of the results.

In the 1983 review, we found that gender differences in empathy appear to depend on how empathy is operationalized. For some measures of empathy (e.g., paper-and-pencil self-reports), we found large gender differences; for other measures (e.g., picture/story indices), we found small differences; for still other measures (e.g., facial/gestural and physiological measures), we found no gender differences.

Definitional issues

In some recent work, psychologists have been more precise than in the past in defining emotional empathy. Factor analyses (Batson, 1984; Davis, 1980) and some experimental work (Batson & Coke, 1983) have enabled researchers to identify various emotional reactions to the emotions or situation of another (especially negative emotions and situations):

1. *Personal distress* – An individual's vicarious experience of emotion may be experienced as a sense of self-concern. Because the focus of the emotion is on the self rather than on the other, this type of response is unlikely to generate concern for another or to mediate altruistic behavior.
2. *Emotional contagion* – This response refers to the vicarious experience of an affect that matches the emotion of another. It is measured by techniques in which empathy is operationalized as the degree of match between a subject's response and the emotion of another.
3. *Genuine concern for another or sympathy* – Batson (Batson & Coke, 1983) has called this reaction empathic or sympathetic concern. Here, the focus is on the other rather than the self, and there generally is not an exact match between the other's and one's own emotion.

Each of these emotional responses has been assessed with one or more of the current measures of empathy. Thus, the fact that gender differences in empathy differ dramatically across measures could be due to differences in the type of emotional reaction that is assessed with particular instruments. However, it is also possible that there are genuine gender differences for some types of emotional reactions labeled empathy but not for others. Thus, we distinguish when possible among various emotional reactions in our review of the literature.

In our previous review (Eisenberg & Lennon, 1983), we identified seven groupings of research on the basis of the specific measure of empathy used in each study. In this chapter, we use the same groupings to organize the findings concerning gender differences. In addition, we cover some new studies, as well as older studies that were not included in previous reviews.

Research on infants' reactions to another's crying

Our previous review included studies of the reflexive crying of infants in response to tape-recorded cries of other infants. If infants' reflexive crying is considered a primitive empathy response (an issue of debate), it seems reasonable to suggest that such crying reflects emotional contagion or personal distress. This is because infants appear to be limited in their ability to differentiate between their own and others' behaviors and internal states, and may interpret the cries of others as their own (Hoffman, 1984).

There have been three published reports on reflexive crying that include seven separate investigations (Martin & Clark, 1982; Sagi & Hoffman, 1976; Simner, 1971). We have been unable to locate any recent investigations. The pattern of gender differences in infant reflexive crying is consistent; in six of the investigations, females displayed more reflexive crying than did males ($p<.10$ in two of the six studies). However, a number of the studies concerning infant reflexive crying are flawed because the stimulus cry used to elicit responses was that of a female infant. Researchers have found that infants tend to cry more in response to cries that are similar (but not identical) to their own cries. When the sex of the stimulus cry was controlled, researchers found no gender differences in reflexive crying (Martin & Clark, 1982).

Picture/story techniques

Measures based on picture/story stimuli have been the most popular method of assessing empathy in young children. With this method, children are exposed to short stories and/or visual stimuli depicting a story and then are asked how they feel; one example of this technique is the FASTE (Feshbach & Roe, 1968). Empathy usually has been operationalized as the degree of match between self-report of emotion and the emotion appropriate to the protagonist in a given vignette.

In our 1983 review, we identified 21 studies in which the FASTE or derivative measures were employed. In seven of these studies, significant or marginally significant gender differences favored females (see Eisenberg & Lennon, 1983, for references); in three, the gender difference favored males; and in the remainder, there were no significant gender differences in empathy. According to the meta-analysis computed for these data, the pattern of gender differences favored females. However, the effect size was quite small (.10), and the number of studies reporting null findings needed to reduce the effect size to nonsignificance was less than 4.

Since 1983, we have located seven other investigations that were not included in our previous review in which the FASTE or similar measures were incorporated. Only one of these investigations (Cohen, 1974) reported a significant gender difference favoring females. The remaining six (Bazar, 1977; Freeman, 1984; Howard, 1983; Knudson & Kagan, 1982; Kuchenbecker, Feshbach, & Pletcher, 1974; Roe, 1980) reported no significant gender differences.

The overall pattern of results is consistent with our previous conclusion that evidence of a gender difference is quite weak when empathy is assessed with picture/story measures. If these types of measures do, in fact, reflect vicarious responsiveness, the type of reaction assessed could be emotional contagion, sympathy, or personal distress. Interestingly, the only investigators who clearly assessed sympathetic concern rather than emotional contagion or personal distress reported a significant gender difference favoring females (Staub & Feinberg, 1980). Perhaps personal distress or mere contagion is most likely to be assessed with picture/story indices, and there are no gender differences in these modes of emotional response.

Note that picture/story measures have been criticized by researchers who have suggested that demand characteristics in the assessment procedure may undermine the validity of this type of instrument (see Eisenberg & Lennon, 1983; Hoffman, 1982). Furthermore, Lennon, Eisenberg, and Carroll (1983) have found that gender differences in children's responses to the FASTE were influenced by the sex of the examiner. Equally important, it appears that by elementary school age, boys are more reluctant than girls to report experiencing sadness and fear in response to emotion-evoking stories (Brody, 1984). Thus, the validity of picture/story instruments is questionable, particularly with regard to identifying gender differences.

Self-report of empathy on questionnaire measures

Self-report questionnaire measures have been the most widely employed index of empathy in studies of school-age children and adults. The Mehrabian and Epstein (1972) scale has been the most frequently used measure of this type. It is designed to measure the trait (rather than state) of empathy. Other scales used in relevant research are the Davis (1980, 1983) scale of sympathetic concern, Bryant's (1982) modified version of the Mehrabian and Epstein scale for children, and the empathy subscale on the Junior Eysenck Personality Questionnaire (Eysenck, Easting, & Pearson, 1984). For all scales except Davis's sympathetic concern subscale, some items seem to measure emotional contagion, whereas other items appear to tap sympathetic concern, role taking, and general emotionality. Thus, it is likely that more than one type of emotional reaction usually is assessed with a given scale.

In all 16 studies covered in our 1983 review, females scored higher than males (see Eisenberg & Lennon, 1983, for references). We performed a meta-analysis on the data from these studies and obtained an effect size of .99; moreover, we found that it would take 2,541 studies reporting no significant effect to change the significance level of the effect size ($p < .00000001$) to $p > .05$. Since the 1983 review, we have located 13 additional studies. Consistent with previous results, females scored higher than males in 11 of these investigations (Adams, 1983; Asakawa & Shwalb, 1985; Bohlmeyer, Burke, & Helmstadter, 1985; Davis, 1980, 1983; Goldstein, 1985; Leftgoff-Sechooler, 1979; Rein, 1974; Rushton, Fulker, Neale, Blizard, & Eysenck, 1984; Vicente, Moriera, Moran, Comfort, & Finley, 1983; Watson, Grisham, Trotter, & Biderman, 1984). In one other study, no gender difference was obtained for a sample of medical students (Elizur & Rosenheim, 1982), whereas Strayer (1983) obtained a significant gender difference favoring females for 8-year-olds, but not for 6-year-olds or the children's parents. Finally, Marsh, Serafica, and Barenboim (1981) found that girls rated themselves as more sympathetic than did males on a single-item self-report measure.

These results can be interpreted in at least two ways. First, the gender difference favoring females may be due to biases in the self-reports. That is, because females are expected to be more concerned for others as well as more emotional than males, both males and females may respond in ways consistent with sex-role stereotypes when directly asked to report on sex-typed characteristics. However, it is also possible that, owing to different patterns of socialization, females are actually more likely to respond sympathetically or to experience personal distress or emotional contagion than are boys. Unfortunately, researchers have not controlled the demand characteristics associated with self-report questionnaires; nor have many differentiated among the various possible emotional responses that people may experience in reaction to another's affect. Thus, the reason for the large gender difference in responses to self-report empathy questionnaires is unclear, especially given the lack of such a large gender difference for other indices of empathy.

Self-report measures of empathy in simulated emotional situations

Researchers frequently have asked subjects about their emotional reactions after they have been exposed to an experimental situation designed to elicit a vicarious emotional response (e.g., videotapes or audiotapes of a person in need). In such investigations, participants frequently have been asked to report feelings of compassion or concern as well as, or instead of, simple dysphoric or euphoric reactions.

We have found 14 articles describing 17 studies in which such measures were employed (11 of these articles were included in our earlier review). In three of the four studies on children (Eisenberg, McCreath, & Ahn, 1985; Frodi & Lamb, 1978; Wilson & Cantor, 1985), no gender differences were obtained. In the other investigation (Zahn-Waxler, Friedman, and Cummings, 1983), girls reported more sympathetic reactions than did boys. In one of the studies on adults (Archer, Foushee, Davis, & Aderman, 1979), males reported significantly more empathy on one of two measures, whereas in six studies (Batson, O'Quin, Fultz, Vanderplus, & Isen, 1983, exp. 3; Craig & Lowery, 1969; Davis, 1983; Murray, 1978; Stotland, 1969; Wispé, Kiecolt, & Long, 1977), females reported more empathy. In two of these (Batson et al., 1983; Wispé et al., 1977), significant differences were found for only a subsample of dependent variables. For six other samples, no gender differences were reported (see Eisenberg & Lennon, 1983, for references). Thus, the overall pattern of findings is mixed; however, the reported differences favor females.

Facial/gestural and vocal measures of empathy

The use of facial/gestural or vocal measures of empathy has been a relatively recent development in the empirical literature. Some researchers (Hamilton, 1973; Leiman, 1978, Lennon, Eisenberg, & Carroll, 1986; Strayer, 1985; Zahn-Waxler et al., 1983) have rated children's facial and gestural responses while the children were observing films or enactments of others in affect-laden situations; other researchers have rated facial/gestural responses and vocal tone when children were being tested with picture/story indices (Howard, 1983; Marcus, Roke, & Brunner, 1985; Sawin, Underwood, Weaver, & Mostyn, 1981).

It is difficult to specify the type of vicarious reaction being assessed with these measures. Many investigators have examined the degree of congruence between a subject's emotional reaction and that of the stimulus person. In such instances, facial/gestural indices may assess emotional contagion because empathy is operationalized as emotional matching. However, in some cases the stimuli used to elicit an empathic response are children in distress situations. In these instances, observers are likely to experience sympathetic concern or personal distress, as well as emotional contagion.

Earlier we reviewed six studies in which facial/gestural and/or vocal measures of empathy were examined. Two findings emerged. First, no significant gender differences were found when empathy was assessed in response to the tape-recorded cries of an infant or in response to affect-laden videotaped stimuli of other children (Hamilton, 1973; Leiman, 1978; Lennon et al., 1984; Zahn-Waxler et al., 1983). In contrast, in studies in which facial/gestural or vocal responses were assessed while children were tested with the FASTE or similar indices, girls appeared to be more empathic than boys. Because of the aforementioned problems with picture/story indices, our overall conclusion was that there were no gender differences in empathy when facial gesture and/or vocal measures were employed.

We have located five recent investigations in which facial/gestural measures of empathy have been employed. In four of these, preschool and/or elementary school children's facial/gestural responses were rated while they watched film clips of other children in situations likely to elicit distress, fear, anger, or happiness. Three of the studies (Barnett, 1984; Eisenberg et al., 1985; Soloman, 1985) turned up no evidence of a gender difference. In another one (Strayer, 1985), girls appeared more likely to emit emotional displays than boys, and boys displayed fewer fearful vicarious responses than girls. However, for other affects such as anger and happiness, no significant gender differences were obtained. In the fifth study, Howard (1983) uncovered no gender difference in reactions to picture/story presentations.

The pattern of findings seems consistent with our prior conclusion that children do not display gender differences in empathy when empathy is assessed with facial/gestural or vocal measures. Although Strayer did obtain a gender difference in children's responses to fearful stimuli, she did not find a difference for others affects.

Physiological measures of empathy

As with measures of relexive crying, little information is available on gender differences in physiological indices of empathy. We located only eight studies on this topic (only the one by Wilson & Cantor [1985] had not been previously reviewed). Most of these investigations have been conducted with adults, although researchers have examined the responses of children in two studies (Frodi & Lamb, 1978; Wilson & Cantor, 1985).

Researchers reported no difference between the responses of males and females, except for Craig and Lowery (1969; see Eisenberg & Lennon, 1983), who found a gender difference favoring males. However, it appears that males in that study were generally more physiologically responsive in both the control and an empathic induction condition than were females. Thus, it is unlikely that the observed gender difference was related to empathy.

It is difficult to interpret physiological reactions to another's distress; such responses may represent a variety of reactions to another (e.g., personal distress to an aversive situation, irritation, emotional contagion, or sympathy). Nevertheless, the prevailing stereotypes lead one to expect females to exhibit greater physiological responsiveness, regardless of the exact nature of the emotional response. However, there is little empirical support for this expectation.

Teacher and peer-report measures

Few investigators have used other-report measures of empathy to assess gender differences in empathy. In our previous review, we cited two such investigations (Barnett, Howard, Melton, & Dino, 1982; Sawin et al., 1981). In both of these, teachers and/or peers rated females as more empathic than males. However, in another study located since 1983, teacher report of empathy was not significantly related to the sex of the child (Marsh et al., 1981). Nonetheless, overall, the data from other-report measures of empathy tend to be consistent with those from self-report indices in supporting the prevailing gender-role stereotypes.

Summary

The review of recent research concerning gender differences in empathy does not alter the conclusion of our 1983 review, namely, that gender differences in empathy may be an artifact of the method of measurement. When demand characteristics were high and participants had conscious control of their responses, gender differences were large; when demand characteristics were more subtle, gender differences were smaller. Finally, when demand characteristics were subtle and subjects were unlikely to exercise conscious control over their responding (e.g., physiological and somatic indices), no gender differences were obtained. However, an alternative interpretation is also possible. It may be that gender differences vary according to the type of vicarious emotion assessed. For example, when researchers used measures likely to assess emotional contagion or personal distress (e.g., reflexive crying, picture/story techniques; perhaps facial/gestural measures and physiological indices), there was little evidence of a gender difference in empathy. In contrast, when measures were more likely to tap sympathetic responding (e.g., self-reports in some simulated situations and other reports), females appeared to be more emotionally reactive than males.

However, as already mentioned, we do not yet know which types of emotional response tend to be elicited by which indices of empathy.

Perhaps what is most evident from reviewing the research concerning gender differences in empathy is the need for greater conceptual and methodological precision in future research. Research in which various vicarious emotional reactions are differentiated is sorely needed, as are reliable and valid indices of empathy. Only then will we be able to clarify the meaning of the pattern of gender differences in the empirical literature.

Age-related changes in empathy and sympathy

Few theorists or researchers believe that empathy and sympathy, in their full-blown or mature form, are present at birth. Indeed, although the role of empathy in the development of prosocial behaviors has interested psychologists for decades (e.g., Bathurst, 1933; Feshbach, 1978; Hoffman, 1976; Murphy, 1937), there has been surprisingly little theory or research directly pertaining to age changes in sympathy and empathy.

Theory

Although some psychologists have suggested that empathy has a genetic basis (e.g., Hoffman, 1981; Rushton, Russell, & Wells, 1984), the role of biology in the development of empathy has received little attention from theorists. Hoffman (1981) suggested that empathic arousal based on motor mimicry and classical conditioning may be a species-wide response and that early displays of empathy suggest a biological root to the development of empathy. However, the ways in which biology affects changes in the development of empathy in infancy and childhood have not been delineated.

In contrast, the roles of learning and cognitive development in the emergence of empathy and sympathy have received some, although insufficient, attention. For example, Aronfreed (1970) suggested that empathy is learned via a conditioning process in childhood. In his view, empathy develops by the repeated pairing of the child's own feelings of pleasure or distress (elicited by external stimuli) with cues of corresponding emotions in others. As a consequence, cues of others' emotions acquire the capacity to elicit corresponding emotions in the child. Moreover, because the child's emotional responses to affective cues in another become a conditioned response, the child learns that behaviors that make others happy or relieve another's distress are pleasurable for the child himself or herself. Thus, prosocial behaviors become self-reinforcing.

Aronfreed's (1970) theory focused more on the development of personal distress and prosocial action than on the development of sympathetic concern.

Moreover, his theory concerns only one possible mechanism for the development of empathy. In contrast, Hoffman (1976, 1984) has proposed a more detailed theoretical account in which empathy, sympathy, personal distress, and prosocial behavior are all discussed, although he does not necessarily use these terms. Hoffman's ideas are discussed in considerable detail in chapter 4, so that his conceptualizing regarding age changes in empathy is only briefly summarized here.

According to Hoffman (1984), children progress through four developmental levels of empathy. At the first level, infants are unable to perceive the self and other as distinct physical entities and consequently are unable to determine who is experiencing distress. Empathic distress is experienced through very simple arousal modes (e.g., conditioning, mimicry), and is involuntary and global. Hoffman identifies this type of reaction as empathy or as a precursor of empathy; we would call it vicarious contagion.

The transition to Hoffman's second level is heralded by the emergence of the ability to differentiate between self and other as physical entities. Early in this process of differentiation, children's awareness of the other as distinct from the self is viewed as tenuous, transitory, and vague; thus, the child probably reacts to another's distress as though the "dimly perceived 'self' and the dimly perceived 'other' were somehow simultaneously, or alternatively, in distress" (Hoffman, 1984, p. 112). However, with time, the child is able to differentiate clearly between another's and one's own distress.

With the onset of role-taking capabilities at about 2–3 years of age, Hoffman suggests that children become aware that others' feelings may differ from their own and that others' perspectives are based on their own needs and cognitive interpretation of events. Consequently, children are better able to respond appropriately to cues indicative of feelings in others and are believed capable of experiencing compassion or "sympathetic distress," although they may still respond to another's distress by being distressed themselves.

According to Hoffman, as children develop the concept of self and other as continuous beings with separate identities and histories, they become aware that others feel emotions not only in a given situation but also in relation to their larger life experience. Consequently, even if no immediate distress cues are available, individuals may sympathize as a result of imagining themselves having the experiences and feelings associated with another's life conditions.

In Hoffman's (1984) scheme, the child first experiences global emotional contagion or personal distress, and later, when the child develops an understanding of person permanence, is able to experience sympathy. Hoffman suggests that sympathetic distress includes a conscious desire to assist because one feels sorry for the victim. Some researchers believe that even the infant can differentiate between the self and another physical entity (e.g., Campos, pers. commun.,

April 1985); thus, Hoffman's view that the ability to distinguish between self and other is necessary for the emergence of sympathetic capabilities can be questioned. Nonetheless, his observations on the timing of the emergence of sympathy may be accurate.

The NIMH data

Longitudinal research conducted at the National Institute of Mental Health has provided considerable insight into the early development of empathy and sympathy. Marion Radke-Yarrow, Carolyn Zahn-Waxler (1984; Zahn-Waxler & Radke-Yarrow, 1982), and their colleagues studied three cohorts of children aged 10, 15, and 20 months over a 9-month period. Mothers, trained as observers and experimenters in this study, reported on their children's responses to naturally occurring events in which their children observed another's negative affect or others' expressions of affection or pleasure. The investigators also made home visits to assess the reliability of behavioral samples and to give children opportunities to respond to a stranger's as well as the mother's distress.

Radke-Yarrow and Zahn-Waxler noted clear developmental changes in how children reacted to other persons' expressions of distress. Ten to 14-month-olds tended to show signs of agitation and general disturbance (e.g., crying, silent tense attending), which continued in later months, but gradually became less common. (However, Hay, Nash, and Pederson [1981] did not find that 6-month-olds responded to peers' distress with distress.) During this early period, children often responded by looking or reaching for their mother. Most likely, children at this age were experiencing either emotional contagion or personal distress.

As agitated responses waned (they decreased significantly by age 2), children began to respond to others' distress in more controlled, positive ways. At first, tentative positive physical contacts such as patting or touching the victim occurred. By the middle or end of the second year, prosocial interventions and imitation of the other's emotion were typical reactions. The children's prosocial responses usually involved physical contact, instrumental acts, and verbal concern (Radke-Yarrow & Zahn-Waxler, 1984). Thus, the 1- to 2-year-olds' prosocial interventions often seemed to reflect some sympathetic responding.

Individual differences in the pattern of responding were evident at an early age (Radke-Yarrow & Zahn-Waxler, 1984). Some children stood out as "affectively prosocial"; their prosocial responses had a large component of emotional arousal and suggested relatively little cognitive analysis of the situation. In contrast, other children, who were equally effective in their prosocial interventions, were more "cognitively prosocial," and approached others' distress by inspecting, exploring, and asking questions. Still other children either manifested an aggressive component in their prosocial interventions (e.g., hitting the person who caused the distress) or shut out signals of others' distress and retreated from them.

These individual differences tended to be consistent over time. For about two thirds of the children, there was continuity in the predominant mode of response exhibited from 1½ years to 6 or 7 years of age. Thus, those who exhibited intense empathic prosocial responses at an early age tended to respond in a similar manner 5 years later, whereas those who responded in a problem-solving, combative, or anxious "guilty" manner as toddlers exhibited similar reaction patterns at age 7. The tendency to respond in an overt, sympathetic manner therefore appeared to emerge early and was relatively stable across individuals, over time.

In the NIMH studies, sympathy or empathy per se was not directly assessed; inferences regarding such responding were derived from observations of the mode of prosocial intervention used by children or the children's reactions to the distress of others. Some children who responded empathically or sympathetically may not have expressed their emotional arousal in their prosocial behavior. Because the investigators were not primarily concerned with measuring empathy, it was not explicitly coded. Nonetheless, their data are consistent with some of the developmental changes hypothesized by Hoffman.

Age differences in response to measures of empathy

A number of people have attempted to measure empathy directly and have examined age differences in individuals' scores. Surprisingly, however, the results of these studies have seldom been reviewed. Feshbach (1978) discussed age differences in several studies in which her measure of empathy was used; we are aware of no other reviews of age differences in empathy.

In reviewing the research concerning age differences in empathy, we encountered many of the same problems we found when reviewing other aspects of the literature on empathy. The most pervasive and unwieldy of these problems is that many researchers' conceptualizations of empathy are ambiguous, especially as reflected in their operationalizations of the concept. In most cases, it is unclear whether the investigator is measuring emotional contagion, sympathy, personal distress, emotional reactivity, or some other aspect of responding. Thus, it is not possible to draw firm conclusions regarding differential age changes in sympathy, empathy, and personal distress.

Our strategy for organizing the relevant data will be the same as that used previously; research findings are grouped according to the method used to assess empathy/sympathy.

Picture/story procedures. Children's scores on picture/story indices appear to increase somewhat in the early years. Marcus et al. (1985) obtained a significant increase in scores for a small sample of subjects ranging from 41 to 81 months of age. Similarly, Bathurst (1933), Lennon et al. (1986), and Marcus, Telleen, and Roke (1979) noted significant age-related increases in empathic responses to stories during the preschool years. Bazar (1977) and Iannotti (1985) did not find a positive relation between preschoolers' empathy and age; however, their samples were relatively homogeneous in age (ranges were 12 and 15 months, respectively).

A positive relation between age and picture/story indices has also been noted in studies involving children ranging in age from preschool to early elementary school age (Cohen, 1974; Powell, 1971, cited in Feshbach, 1978; but not Kuchenbecker, 1977) and from kindergarten or first grade to mid–elementary school age (Fay, 1971; Knudson & Kagen, 1982; Kuchenbecker et al., 1974; Matsuoka, 1983, cited in Asawaka & Shwalb, 1985; Sawin et al., 1981; but not Feshbach & Feshbach, 1969; or Iannotti, 1975b). However, this age-related increase apparently either levels off in the elementary to high school years (Nielson, 1977) or may even decrease in the late elementary school years (Matsuoka, 1983, cited in Asawaka & Shwalb, 1985). Too few data are available to confidently describe age changes after the mid–elementary school years.

The aforementioned findings are consistent with the finding that older elementary school children appear more likely than younger children to attribute emotional responsiveness to the self or others when discussing affect-laden hypothetical situations (Brody & Carter, 1982). The data are more complex, however, when stories are used in which the protagonist's affect, as indicated by his or her facial expression, is not consistent with contextual cues (e.g., a protagonist looks sad at a birthday party). Iannotti (1975a,b) operationalized role-taking empathy as children saying they felt an emotion consistent with the other's facial expression in a situation in which the character's emotion was inconsistent with the situation depicted in the picture. He found that this type of empathy decreased significantly from age 6 to 9. In other words, older children were more likely than younger children to report emotions consistent with contextual rather than facial cues relevant to another's emotional state. Watson (1976) obtained findings consistent with Iannotti's when using a similar measure; however, she found age increases only from preschool to first grade, and primarily for situations involving happy rather than sad emotion.

In summary, it appears that children's empathic (i.e., matching) responses to others in picture/story scenarios increase with age into mid–elementary school and then may level off. With age, children also seem to depend more on contextual cues than others' facial cues in their empathic reactions; this is consistent with Kurdek and Rodgon's (1975) and Watson's (1976) finding that older children are more likely than younger children to identify another's affect on the basis of situational rather than facial cues when the two conflict.

Questionnaire /indices. A number of researchers have used the Mehrabian and Epstein (1972), Bryant (1982), or similar indices to assess empathy in children. As noted earlier, these scales tend to include items tapping sympathy, empathy, personal distress, role taking, emotionality, and other constructs.

In general, researchers have noted age-related increases in questionnaire scores in the early school years (Asakawa & Shwalb, 1985; Bryant, 1982; not Strayer, 1983). However, these findings must be qualified; Asakawa and Shwalb (1985) found that empathy with boys from an outgroup decreased somewhat from fourth to seventh grade. Bryant (1982) also found a decrease in empathy, but only with opposite-sex persons, from first to fourth grade, followed by an increase in empathy with such persons between fourth and seventh grade. Thus, empathy with those different from the self may decrease during the elementary school years.

Findings for somewhat older children are inconsistent. Eysenck et al. (1984) reported an apparent increase in empathy scores for boys but not girls for a sample of 8- to 15-year-olds (no statistics were computed). In contrast, using the same basic questionnaire, Saklofske and Eysenck (1983) found a slight decrease in empathy for 7- to 15-year-old boys, but not girls. Kalliopuska (1980), in a study of Finnish children, found an increase in scores on the Mehrabian and Epstein questionnaire from age 9 to 11, but nonsignificant decreases in scores from age 11 to 12. No age changes in response were reported by Adams, Schvaneveldt, and Jenson (1979) for a group of seventh, eight, and ninth graders and Adams (1983) for a sample of 14-, 15-, 17-, and 18-year-olds (see Bryant, Chapter 11, however). Finally, in a study of 19- to 40-year-old twins, Rushton et al., (1984) obtained a positive correlation between empathy scores and age, whereas for the same measure and similar age groups, Elizur and Rosenheim (1982) and Watson et al. (1984) did not.

In summary, it appears that empathy as measured by questionnaires increases somewhat in the early school years, at least in response to similar persons, whereas no consistent pattern of age-related change is apparent for persons older than approximately age 11.

Self-report of temporary affect in experimental contexts. The questionnaires discussed in the preceding section are designated to measure the trait of empathy. In other studies, researchers have operationalized empathy as the report of emotional arousal consistent with another's state in an experimental situation. The results of this research are inconsistent. Howard and Barnett (1981) asked preschoolers to second graders to think about the feelings of, or just to think about, less fortunate others. After a donation opportunity, children were asked to report their affective responses to the plight of the needy other. Older children reported feeling sadder than did younger children. In contrast, Zahn-Waxler et al. (1983) found no age-related change in the empathy reported by 4-year-olds, kindergarteners, first, second, fifth, and sixth graders in response to hearing the cries of a distressed infant. Nor did Wilson and Cantor (1985) find a significant relation between age and reports of fear in response to viewing a tape of a fearful other; however, there was a nonsignificant tendency ($p<.15$) for older children to report more empathy. In these studies, researchers did not attempt to differentiate between sympathy, empathy, and personal distress; perhaps the differences in findings were due to differences in the nature of the emotional reaction assessed. In Howard and Barnett's study, it is likely that sympathy was assessed, whereas personal distress as well as sympathy probably were assessed by Zahn-Waxler et al. (1983) and Wilson and Cantor (1985).

Facial/gestural indices of empathy. Studies in which researchers have used facial expressions and gestural reactions as indices of empathy are of three kinds: those involving distressed others in lifelike situations, those in which the object of empathy was depicted on tape, and those in which reactions were assessed while children were responding to the picture/story measure of empathy.

In perhaps the only study involving a lifelike distress situation and several age groups of children, Zahn-Waxler and her colleagues (Zahn-Waxler et al., 1983) examined the facial/gestural responses of preschoolers, kindergarteners, and first, second, fifth, and sixth graders when confronted with an adult or infant in distress. They found no significant change in facial/gestural reactions with age.

The findings are mixed for research in which reactions to others depicted on film were assessed. Soloman (1985) and Watson, Solomon, Solomon, and Battistich (1983) found decreases in facial reactions to persons in film clips from kindergarten through sixth grade. Although it is not clear, Solomon apparently used a subset of the children involved in the Watson et al. (1983) study. Similarly, Strayer (1985) found a decrease with age from preschool to adolescence in facial responsiveness to films of others depicting a variety of affects. This decrease was most marked for expressions of fear; expressions of sadness actually increased somewhat with age.

In contrast to the studies just discussed, Lennon et al. (1986) found that age was positively related to the intensity of 4- to 5-year-olds' negative facial reactions in response to viewing films of children in distress. Gestural responses were unrelated to age. In a study involving similar stimuli and a similar age group, Eisenberg et al. (1986) noted no increase with age in worried/anxious, sad/concerned, or happy reactions. In both of these studies, children were told that the events in the film were real. Finally, Kuchenbecker (1977), in a study of 4- to 5-year-olds and 7- to 8-year-olds, and Leiman (1978), in a study of preschoolers, noted no age-related changes in facial expression when the children viewed films of others exhibiting happy and/or sad affect.

In only two studies did investigators examine age-related change in children's facial/gesture reactions while responding to the FASTE. One study involved preschoolers aged 41–81 months (Marcus et al., 1985); the other, first and third graders (Sawin et al., 1981). In neither study was there a relation between age and empathy.

The studies just reviewed suggest that affective responsiveness to others' emotional states may either be stable or may decrease in intensity in the preschool and elementary school years. However, any conclusions regarding age changes in empathy as measured with facial/gestural indices must be tentative given the limited available data.

Physiological measures of empathy. We located only one study in which age was examined in relation to physiological indices of empathy/sympathy. Wilson and Cantor (1985) examined 3- to 5-year-olds' and 9- to 11-year-olds' EMG (muscle) and temperature reactions to a film of a fearful peer. Older children exhibited more evidence of EMG arousal, and less arousal as indexed by temperature. Thus, it is impossible to draw any conclusions from these data.

Teacher ratings of empathy. Only one study was located in which investigators correlated age with teachers' ratings of empathy. Sawin et al. (1981) asked teachers to rate first- and third-grade children with regard to their "sensitivity" to others' emotions, concern with others' unhappiness, awareness of others' feelings, and affect matching in response to three emotions exhibited by others (happiness, anger, fear). Scores on this measure, which appear to tap a combination of sympathy, empathy, and role taking, were positively related to age.

Summary

The findings with regard to age differences in empathy vary with the specific index of empathy. In general, self-report of affect that matches that of hypothetical others in stories and/or pictures seems to increase with age until the mid–elementary school; performance may then level off or decrease. Similarly, self-report of empathy on questionnaire measures has been positively associated with age in the preschool and elementary school years; however, findings are inconsistent for older children and adolescents. Findings pertaining to self-report of empathy in response to others' emotions in lifelike situations are limited and inconsistent, as are the data concerning physiological and teacher report of empathy. Finally, facial/gestural indices appear to be either inversely related or unrelated to age in the early school years, with the possible exception of indices of sadness in reaction to others' distress.

It is difficult to make sense of this conflicting pattern of data. From the data of Zahn-Waxler and Radke-Yarrow (1982; Radke-Yarrow & Zahn-Waxler, 1984), it would appear that the capacity for emotional contagion is present by approximately 1 year of age. Personal distress reactions also seem to be present by this age. Sympathetic responses apparently emerge in the second year of life. Thus, all of the indices reviewed above, because they are all used with persons aged 3 or older, could, at least theoretically, reflect sympathy, empathy, or personal distress.

The fact that facial/gestural responses either are stable or decrease in intensity suggests that children do not increase in empathic responsiveness during the early school years. The findings of Radke-Yarrow and Zahn-Waxler are also consistent with the view that emotional responsiveness to others is stable from the early years. However, it is possible that sympathetic reactions increase with age, whereas personal distress or empathic contagion reactions do not. The decrease in facial responsiveness found in some studies may be due to the process of children learning to mask their emotions during the early school years (Saarni, 1982; Shennum & Bugenthal, 1982).

The findings for self-report measures are inconsistent with the facial/gestural data. However, the age-related increase in the self-report of empathy in the preschool and early school years may not, in fact, reflect increases in empathy, personal distress, or sympathy; this pattern may be due to an increasing awareness of what response is expected in the experimental situation. Consistent with this interpretation are the findings that (1) the sex of the experimenter interacts with the sex of the child in affecting children's responses, and (2) sex differences in empathy favoring women are far greater for those indices for which the intent of the measure is obvious (Eisenberg & Lennon, 1983).

In conclusion, research findings concerning the development of empathy are very difficult to interpret. Much of the research has involved questionable measures of empathy and/or indices that assess a variety of emotional reactions. It is likely that different responses labeled empathy (e.g., personal distress, sympathy) have different developmental courses and are differentially socialized at specific ages (e.g., parents may attempt to socialize empathy and sympathy but not personal distress in the early school years). Whether this is true cannot be determined until better measures of these emotions are developed. Moreover, it is possible that personal distress reactions, because they appear to be related to self-protection and therefore may be crucial to survival early in life, might emerge at an earlier age than do sympathy and empathy. If this were true, the developmental course of personal distress might be more stable and less susceptible to environmental modification with age than is the course for sympathy. Although such ideas are merely speculative at this point in time, differences in the biological bases of empathy, sympathy, and personal distress reactions are not unlikely and would help to explain the way such reactions develop.

Conclusions

It appears that our knowledge of gender differences in empathy/ sympathy and of the developmental course of such vicarious reactions is limited. No doubt this is due, in part, to methodological difficulties in assessing internal psychological states and the lack of differentiation among various emotional responses in much of the research. As methods and theory in the area are refined, our understanding of the role of gender and age in vicarious responding will be enhanced accordingly. Until then, our conclusions regarding these issues must be tentative.

References

Adams, G. R. (1983). Social competence during adolescence: Social sensitivity, locus of control, and peer popularity. *Journal of Youth and Adolescence, 12,* 203–211.

Adams, G. R., Schvaneveldt, J. D., & Jenson, G. O. (1979). Sex, age and perceived competency as correlates of empathic ability in adolescence. *Adolescence, 14,* 811–818.

Archer, R. L., Foushee, H. C., Davis, M. H., & Aderman, D. (1979). Emotional empathy in a courtroom simulation: A person–situation interaction. *Journal of Applied Social Psychology, 3,* 275–291.

Aronfreed, J. (1970). The socialization of altruistic and sympathetic behavior: Some theoretical and experimental analyses. In J. Macauley & L. Berkowitz (Eds.), *Altruism and helping behavior* (pp. 103–126). New York: Academic Press.

Asakawa, K., & Shwalb, D. W. (1985, April). *Empathy and intimacy: An investigation of rural Japanese children.* Paper presented at the biennial meeting of the Society for Research in Child Development, Toronto.

Barnett, M. A. (1984, August). *Empathy as a dependent variable.* Paper presented at the annual meeting of the American Psychological Association, Toronto.

Barnett, M. A., Howard, J. A., Melton, E. M., & Dino, G. A. (1982). Effect of inducing sadness about self or other on helping behavior in high and low empathic children. *Child Development, 53,* 920–923.

Bathurst, J. E. (1933). A study in sympathy and resistance (negativism) among children. *Psychological Bulletin, 30,* 540–541.

Batson, C. D. (1984). *A theory of altruistic motivation.* Unpublished manuscript, University of Kansas.

Batson, C. D., & Coke, J. S. (1983). Empathic motivation of helping behavior. In J. T. Cacioppo & K. E. Petty (Eds.), *Social psychophysiology: A source book* (pp. 417–433). New York: Guilford Press.

Batson, C. D., O'Quin, K., Fultz, J., Vanderplus, M., & Isen, A. M. (1983). Influence of self-reported distress and empathy on egoistic versus altruistic motivation to help. *Journal of Personality and Social Psychology, 45,* 706–718.

Bazar, J. W. (1977). An exploration of the relationship of affect awareness, empathy, and interpersonal strategies to nursery school children's competence in peer interactions (Doctoral dissertation, University of California, Berkeley, 1976). *Dissertation Abstracts International, 37,* 5691A.

Block, J. H. (1976). Assessing sex-differences: Issues, problems, and pitfalls. *Merrill–Palmer Quarterly, 22,* 283–308.

Bohlmeyer, E. M., Burke, J. P., & Helmstadter, G. C. (1985). Differences between education and business students in cooperative and competitive attitudes, emotional empathy, and self-esteem. *Psychological Reports, 56,* 247–253.

Brody, L. R. (1984). Sex and age variations in the quality and intensity of children's emotional attributions to hypothetical situations. *Sex Roles, 11,* 51–59.

Brody, L. R., & Carter, A. S. (1982). Children's emotional attributions to self versus other: An exploration of an assumption underlying projective techniques. *Journal of Consulting and Clinical Psychology, 50,* 665–671.

Bryant, B. (1982). An index of empathy for children and adolescents. *Child Development, 53,* 413–425.

Cohen, E. C. (1974). Empathy, awareness of interpersonal responsibility and consideration for others in young children. *Dissertation Abstracts International, 34,* 6192B. (University Microfilms No. 74–13879)

Craig, K. D., & Lowery, H. J. (1969). Heart-rate components of conditioned vicarious autonomic responses. *Journal of Personality and Social Psychology, 11,* 381–387.

Davis, M. H. (1980). A multidimensional approach to individual differences in empathy. *JSAS Catalog of Selected Documents in Psychology, 10,* 85.

Davis, M. H. (1983). The effects of dispositional empathy on emotional reactions and helping: A multidimensional approach. *Journal of Personality, 51,* 167–184.

Deutsch, H. (1944). *The psychology of women: A psychoanalytic interpretation.* New York: Grune & Stratton.

Dunn, J., Bretherton, I., & Munn, P. (1987). Conversations about feeling states between mothers and their children. *Developmental Psychology, 23,* 132–139.

Eisenberg, N., & Lennon, R. (1983). Sex differences in empathy and related capacities. *Psychological Bulletin, 94,* 100–131.

Eisenberg, N., McCreath, H., & Ahn, R. (1986, August). *Vicarious emotional responsiveness and prosocial behavior: Their interrelations in young children.* Paper presented at the annual meeting of the American Psychological Association, Washington, D.C.

Elizur, A., & Rosenheim, E. (1982). Empathy and attitudes among medical students: The effects of group experience. *Journal of Medical Education, 57,* 675–683.

Erikson, E. (1979). Once more the inner space. In J. H. Williams (Ed.), *Psychology of women* (pp. 71–84). New York: W. W. Norton (original work published 1975).

Eysenck, S. B. G., Easting, G., & Pearson, P. R. (1984). Age norms for impulsiveness, ventureness, and empathy in children. *Personality and Individual Differences, 5,* 315–321.

Fay, B. (1971). The relationship of cognitive moral judgment, generosity, and empathic behavior in six and eight year old children (Doctoral dissertation, University of California, Los Angeles, 1970). *Dissertation Abstracts International, 31,* 3951A.

Feshbach, N. D. (1978). Studies of empathic behavior in children. In B. A. Maher (Ed.), *Progress in experimental personality research* (Vol. 8, pp. 1–47). New York: Academic Press.

Feshbach, N. D., & Feshbach, S. (1969). The relationship between empathy and aggression in two age groups. *Developmental Psychology, 1,* 102–107.

Feshbach, N. D., & Roe, K. (1968). Empathy in six- and seven-year-olds. *Child Development, 39,* 133–145.

Freeman, E. B. (1984). The development of empathy in young children: In search of a definition. *Child Study Journal, 4,* 235–245.

Freud, S. (1950). Some psychological consequences of the anatomical distinction between the sexes.

In J. Strachey (Ed.), *Sigmund Freud: Collected papers* (Vol. 5, pp. 186–197). London: Hogarth Press (original work published 1925).

Frodi, A. M., & Lamb, M. E. (1978). Sex differences in responsiveness to infants: A developmental study of psychophysiological and behavioral responses. *Child Development, 19,* 1182–1188.

Goldstein, D. L. (1985). The effects of sex and sex-role on the empathy process: An explanation of person and contextual factors. *Dissertation Abstracts International, 45,* 3617B–3618B (University Microfilms No. D8500752).

Greif, E. B., Alvarez, M., & Ulman, K. (1981, April). *Recognizing emotions in other people: Sex differences in socialization.* Paper presented at the biennial meeting of the Society for Research in Child Development, Boston.

Hamilton, M. L. (1973). Imitative behavior and expressive-ability in facial expression of emotion. *Developmental Psychology, 8,* 138.

Hay, D. F., Nash, A., & Pederson, J. (1981). Responses of six-month-olds to the distress of their peers. *Child Development, 52,* 1071–1075.

Hoffman, M. L. (1976). Empathy, role-taking, guilt, and development of altruistic motives. In T. Lickona (Ed.), *Moral development and behavior: Theory, research, and social issues* (pp. 124–143). New York: Holt, Rinehart, & Winston.

Hoffman, M. L. (1977). Personality and social development. *Annual Review of Psychology, 28,* 295–321.

Hoffman, M. L. (1981). Is altruism part of human nature? *Journal of Personality and Social Psychology, 40,* 121–137.

Hoffman, M. L. (1982). The measurement of empathy. In C. E. Izard (Ed.), *Measuring emotions in infants and children* (pp. 279–296). Cambridge: Cambridge University Press.

Hoffman, M. L. (1984). Interaction of affect and cognition in empathy. In C. E. Izard, J. Kagan, & R. B. Zajonc (Eds.), *Emotions, cognitive, and behavior* (pp. 103–131). Cambridge: Cambridge University Press.

Howard, J. A. (1983). Preschoolers' empathy for specific affects and their social interaction (Doctoral dissertation, Kansas State University, 1983). *Dissertation Abstracts International, 44,* 3954B.

Howard, J. A., & Barnett, M. A. (1981). Arousal of empathy and subsequent generosity in young children. *Journal of Genetic Psychology, 138,* 307–308.

Iannotti, R. J. (1975a, April). *The effect of role-taking experiences on role-taking, altruism, empathy, and aggression.* Paper presented at the biennial meeting of the Society for Research in Child Development, Denver.

Iannotti, R. J. (1975b, April). *The many faces of empathy: An analysis of the definition and evaluation of empathy in children.* Paper presented at the biennial meeting of the Society for Research in Child Development, Denver.

Iannotti, R. J. (1985). Naturalistic and structured assessments of prosocial behavior in preschool children: The influence of empathy and perspective taking. *Developmental Psychology, 21,* 46–55.

Kalliopuska, M. (1980). Children's helping behaviour: Personality factors and parental influences related to helping behaviour. *Dissertations Humanarum Litterarum, 24.* Helsinki: Academia Scientiarum Fennica.

Knudson, K. H. M., & Kagen, S. (1982). Differential development of empathy and prosocial behavior. *Journal of Genetic Psychology, 140,* 249–251.

Kuchenbecker, S. L. Y. (1971). A developmental investigation of children's behavioral, cognitive, and affective responses to empathically stimulating situations (Doctoral dissertation, University of California, Los Angeles, 1976). *Dissertation Abstracts International, 37,* 5328B–5329B.

Kuchenbecker, S. L. Y., Feshbach, N. D., & Pletcher, G. G. (1974, April). *The effects of age, sex, and modality upon social comprehension and empathy.* Paper presented at the annual meeting of the Western Psychological Association, San Francisco.

Kurdek, L. A., & Rodgon, M. M. (1975). Perceptual, cognitive, and affective perspective taking in kindergarten through sixth-grade children. *Developmental Psychology, 11*, 643–650.

Leftgoff-Sechooler, R. (1979). Helping as a function of pleasure, arousal, and dominance (Doctoral dissertation, University of California, Los Angeles, 1978). *Dissertation Abstracts International, 39*, 3590B.

Leiman, B. (1978, August). *Affective empathy and subsequent altruism in kindergarteners and first graders.* Paper presented at the annual meeting of the American Psychological Association, Toronto.

Lennon, R., Eisenberg, N., & Carroll, J. (1983). The assessment of empathy in early childhood. *Journal of Applied Developmental Psychology, 4*, 295–302.

Lennon, R., Eisenberg, N., & Carroll, J. (1986). The relation between empathy and prosocial behavior in the preschool years. *Journal of Applied Developmental Psychology, 7*, 219–224.

Maccoby, E. E., & Jacklin, C. N. (1974). *The psychology of sex differences.* Stanford: Stanford University Press.

Marcus, R. F., Roke, E. J., & Bruner, C. (1985). Verbal and nonverbal empathy and prediction of social behavior of young children. *Perceptual and Motor Skills, 60*, 229–309.

Marcus, R. F., Telleen, S., & Roke, E. J. (1979). Relation between cooperation and empathy in young children. *Developmental Psychology, 15*, 346–347.

Marsh, D. T., Serafica, F. C., & Barenboim, C. (1981). Interrelationships among perspective taking, interpersonal problem solving, and interpersonal functioning. *Journal of Genetic Psychology, 138*, 37–48.

Martin, G. B., & Clark, R. D. III. (1982). Distress crying in neonates: Species and peer specificity. *Developmental Psychology, 18*, 3–9.

Mehrabian, A., & Epstein, N. A. (1972). A measure of emotional empathy. *Journal of Personality, 40*, 523–543.

Murphy, L. B. (1937). *Social behavior and child personality.* New York: Columbia University Press.

Murray, A. D. (1978). *Infant crying as an activator of altruistic and egoistic motives in adults.* Unpublished doctoral dissertation, Macquarie University, North Ryde, New South Wales, Australia.

Nielson, K. A. (1977). Aggression, empathy, and self esteem in latency aged and adolescent males in a residential treatment center for emotionally disturbed children. *Dissertation Abstracts International*, 6374–6375A. (University Microfilms No. 77–8004)

Parsons, T., & Bales, F. (Eds.) (1955). *Family, socialization, and interaction process.* New York: Free Press.

Radke-Yarrow, M., & Zahn-Waxler, C. (1984). Roots, motives, and patterns in children's prosocial behavior. In E. Staub, D. Bar-Tal, J. Karylowski, & J. Reykowski (Eds.), *Development and maintenance of prosocial behavior: International perspectives* (pp. 81–99). New York: Plenum.

Rein, B. A. (1974). The effects of empathy, similarity, and attraction on level of aggression (Doctoral dissertation, University of California, Riverside, 1974). *Dissertation Abstracts International, 35*, 1395B.

Roe, K. V. (1980). Early empathy development in children and the subsequent internalization of moral values. *Journal of Social Psychology, 110*, 147–148.

Rushton, J. P., Fulker, D. W., Neale, M. C. Blizard, R. A., & Eysenck, H. J. (1984). Altruism and genetics. *Acta Genetical Medicae et Germellologiae, 33*, 265–271.

Rushton, J. P., Russell, R. J. H., & Wells, P. (1984). Genetic similarity theory: Beyond kin selection. *Behavior Genetics, 14*, 179–193.

Saarni, C. (1982). Social and affective functions of nonverbal behavior: Developmental concerns. In R. S. Feldman (Ed.), *Development of nonverbal behavior in children* (pp. 123–147). New York: Springer Verlag.

Sagi, A., & Hoffman, M. L. (1976). Empathic distress in newborns. *Developmental Psychology, 12*, 175–176.

Saklofske, D. H., & Eysenck, S. B. G. (1983). Impulsiveness and venturesomeness in Canadian children. *Psychological Reports, 52*, 147–152.

Sawin, D. B., Underwood, B., Weaver, J., & Mostyn, M. (1981). *Empathy and altruism*. Unpublished manuscript, University of Texas, Austin.

Shennum, W. A., & Bugenthal, D. B. (1982). The development of control over affective expression in nonverbal behavior. In R. S. Feldman (Ed.), *Development of nonverbal behavior in children* (pp. 101–121). New York: Springer Verlag.

Simner, M. L. (1971). Newborn's response to the cry of another infant. *Developmental Psychology, 12*, 175–176.

Soloman, J. (1985, April). *The relationship between affective empathy and prosocial behavior in elementary school children*. Paper presented at the biennial meeting of the Society for Research in Child Development, Toronto.

Staub, E., & Feinberg, H. K. (1980, September). *Regularities in peer interaction, empathy, and sensitivity to others*. Paper presented at the annual meeting of the American Psychological Association, Toronto.

Strayer, J. (1983, April). *Emotional and cognitive components of children's empathy*. Paper presented at the biennial meeting of the Society for Research in Child Development, Detroit.

Strayer, J. (1985, April). *Developmental changes in nonverbal affect expression*. Paper presented at the biennial meeting of the Society for Research in Child Development, Toronto.

Stotland, E. (1969). Exploratory studies in empathy. In L. Berkowitz (Ed.), *Advances in experimental social psychology* (Vol. 4, pp. 271–314). New York: Academic Press.

Vincente, J., Moriera, Y., Moran, G., Comfort, J. C., & Finley, G. E. (1983). Personality in correlations of ordinal family position in Panamanian adolescents. *Journal of Social Psychology, 120*, 7–12.

Watson, M. S. (1976). The development of cognitive and emotional aspects of empathy and their relationship to a verbal measure of altruism (Doctoral dissertation, University of California, Berkeley). *Dissertation Abstracts International, 37*, 446B.

Watson, M. S., Solomon, J., Solomon, D., & Battistich, V. (1983, August). *A measure of social understanding: Relationships with age and behavior*. Paper presented at the annual meeting of the American Psychological Association, Anaheim, CA.

Watson, P. J., Grisham, S. O., Trotter, M. V., & Biderman, M. D. (1984). Narcissism and empathy: Validity evidence for the Narcissistic Personality Inventory. *Journal of Personality Assessment, 48*, 301–305.

Wilson, B. J., & Cantor, J. (1985). Developmental differences in empathy with a television protagonist's fear. *Journal of Experimental Child Psychology, 39*, 284–299.

Wispé, L., Kiecolt, J., & Long, R. E. (1977). Demand characteristics, moods, and helping. *Social Behavior and Personality, 5*, 249–255.

Zahn-Waxler, C., Friedman, S. L., & Cummings, E. M. (1983). Children's emotions and behaviors in response to infants' cries. *Child Development, 54*, 1522–1528.

Zahn-Waxler, C., & Radke-Yarrow, M. (1982). The development of altruism: Alternative research strategies. In N. Eisenberg (Ed.), *The development of prosocial behavior* (pp. 109–137). New York: Academic Press.

Janet Strayer

For both the tough minded and tenderhearted, empathy is a provocative construct, evoking debate over its definition and measurement. A functional answer to the question of what empathy *is* is framed in terms of what empathy does. At a basic level, empathy, as vicariously experienced emotion, enhances our survival value both in terms of the detection of danger and other signal cues and in the communication of positive and negative states among the group members (Darwin, 1872). Functionally, it benefits us and/or others. This acknowledged, we can consider a structural answer, framed in terms of the components of empathy.

Historically, researchers have debated whether empathy is an affective or cognitive construct, or both. Additional complications arise from the confusion of whether empathy is considered in *content* or *process* terms – for example, its content could be defined as affective, whereas its process could be cognitive. Until now, much of our knowledge of empathy has been limited by available technologies, with little integration across methods. Thus, investigations of empathy's function and structure have greatly depended on what we have chosen to measure and on how we have measured it.

In this chapter two main approaches to the study of empathy are examined: the affective and the cognitive perspectives. Each perspective has provoked interesting speculations about empathy and has determined the methods of study and the conclusions that have emerged. As a result of the debate surrounding these perspectives, some researchers are now integrating what is most valuable in each view into a multidimensional consideration of the empathy construct. These new multimethod approaches are also discussed in this chapter.

A cognitive perspective on empathy

From a cognitive perspective, empathy consists of either understanding the psychology of others (i.e., their thoughts, intentions, feelings, etc.) or, more specifically, their feelings. In either case, the processes responsible for such

218

understanding are cognitive. If affect is evoked in us by our understanding of others' feelings, then it is an epiphenomenon of cognition.

Historical roots

Empathy was originally defined *(Einfühlung)* as fairly immediate shared sensory and emotional experience, but this use of the term had only a brief history in psychology until its current renascence. The shift to a cognitive definition of empathic content and process was greatly influenced by Mead, who discussed "the capacity to take the role of the other and to adopt alternative perspectives vis à vis oneself" (1934, p. 27). Instead of the temporary merging of self and other emphasized in earlier affective and motor mimicry definitions of empathy, in applications to empathy of cognitive views such as Mead's, "empathy was no longer viewed as purely a perceptual awareness of an individual's affect or sharing of feeling, but rather as an ability to understand a person's emotional reactions in consort with the context" (Deutsch & Madle, 1975, p. 270).

Thus, regardless of its etymology, empathy, when adopted by English-speaking psychologists, was raised within the school of social cognition. As the cognition involved in understanding others' feelings presumably involved the same processes as did understanding their thoughts, intentions, or perspectives, empathy got lost among its brethren, variously defined as perspective taking, role taking, social sensitivity, and person perception. Measures of empathy ranged from tests of one's stereotypic knowledge of groups, to abilities to predict others' attitudes and opinions, to more specific knowledge of another person's informational, or affective perspective on an event. Although such skills increase with age, they do not necessarily measure the same construct (Shantz, 1983), regardless of what that construct is called.

Given our present understanding, much of the early work on empathy as a cognitive construct seems mislabeled and indistinguisable from general social cognition. Nevertheless, it is useful to scan such research selectively in order to (1) distinguish empathy from constructs with which it is still being confused, and (2) assess viable methods for investigating cognitive factors that may be involved in empathy, conceived of as shared affect. Cognitive measures of empathy fall into three general categories: tests of social prediction accuracy, recognition of affect from situational or pictorial cues, and role-taking tests.

Early empirical attempts to assess empathy as a cognitive skill

Social prediction tests (e.g., Kerr & Speroff, 1954) rest on the mistaken synonymity of empathy and role taking and on the assumption that the ability to predict the behaviors or attitudes of others, typically groups of people or "generalized others," is being assessed. That the results of such studies were not measuring "predictions," but were based upon stereotyping or upon general similarities between self and others, impugned such purported knowledge of other persons (Cronbach, 1955). Whereas such measures may, at best, assess social judgmental accuracy, they do not fit our definition of empathy as shared affect between self and others. They also tap knowledge that could be acquired by processes not involved in empathy.

Such criticisms extend to other cognitive measures of empathy that have remained in more current favor. Such measures do present affective content and assess abilities to detect and label others' affective states (e.g., Borke, 1971; Burns & Cavey, 1957; Gove & Keating, 1979). Study participants identify the emotions of characters portrayed typically in narratives, pictures, audiotapes, or videotapes. Although such measures have been termed "affective role taking" or "empathy," there is, in most cases, little reason to invoke either as the process responsible for accurate judgments of others' emotions. For example, Borke's measure assesses children's report of normative reactions to a birthday party (happiness), and their skill in then detecting and accurately labeling pictorial facial cues to the story character's contrasting emotion (sadness). To infer that attention to facial cues rather than situational cues is a better index of empathy is unwarranted. Yet, it persists in other measures in which empathy is scored only if the child's response accords with the character's facial cues in contrast to the situational cues (Iannotti, 1975). However, giving precedence to facial over situational cues would be particularly misleading when people dissimulate their facial expressions. We would then especially need to recognize the emotional impact of the situational context.

Aside from the question of whether some cues are better than others in assessing empathy, a major problem with many of these measures is that the presence of affective content does not justify the conclusion that empathy is the construct measured. The position taken here is that affective role taking is not empathy, but may be one cognitive skill possibly mediating empathy (Feshbach, 1975; Hoffman 1975). Because detection of affect is necessary for empathy to ensue, I discuss affect discrimination first and then affective role taking.

Recognition of emotions

Recognition of emotions is singled out as one of the two cognitive prerequisites for empathy (the other being role taking) in Feshbach's model (1975). That some analytic skills are involved in recognition of nonverbal cues to emotion is supported by findings of age-related increases in the decoding of nonverbal, especially facial, expressive emotional cues (e.g., Morency & Krauss, 1982).

Recognition of emotions conveyed by situational and verbal content is also important. Children's situational understanding of emotions, studied by Barden, Zelco, Duncan, and Masters (1980) and by Strayer (1986), indicates commonly shared attributions regarding situation–emotion relationships across age, as well as age-related differences in the prevalence of certain situational explanations for emotions.

Nonverbal, situational, and verbal cues of emotion typically are in accord in most naturalistic contexts. Studies involving mixed messages among emotion cues suggest that these would likely promote confusion rather than empathy in young children, who seem less able than older children and adults to compare differing facial, vocal, and bodily emotional cues simultaneously (Mayhew & Strayer, 1985; Rosenthal, Hall, DiMatteo, Rogers & Archer, 1979).

In summary, cognitive factors in the discrimination of emotions include skills in detection, both within and across communication channels, as well as the use of situational information. Further affecting the skills entailed in recognition of emotion is the development of knowledge of both social display rules for emotion (Saarni, 1979), and differences in individual display rules and expressive styles (e.g., the "revealer," "withholder," or "frozen affect" expressors; see Ekman & Friesen, 1975). This addition of person-specific factors to the set of affect recognition skills seems especially necessary for the fine-tuning of empathy as specific to a specific individual in a given situation.

Role taking and empathy

A pervasive confusion in social cognition exists between role taking and empathy. As its legacy is still active, a brief review may help clarify positions. Starting with the studies by Burns and Cavey (1975) and Borke (1971), empathy was defined as understanding others' emotions and was operationalized as the labeling of a story character's facially expressed and situationally incongruent emotions. Empathy was said to depend on the decline in children's cognitive egocentrism (Piaget, 1932) and the corresponding increase in their perspective-taking skills. Unfortunately, the ensuing controversy regarding such measures (Borke, 1972; Chandler & Greenspan, 1972) was not over the misinterpretation of empathy as affective role taking, but over whether the complexity of the task was sufficient to ensure that correct responses were due to role taking. Although such tasks have become more complex in both design and rationale (Gove & Keating, 1979), it is still doubtful whether empathy is involved at all. Such tasks are affective in content only, and not in response or process measures. Correct labeling of others' affect in such tasks requires separate consideration of incongruent cues and situationally given expectations, which together pose a cognitive dilemma for the child to resolve. Whereas this incongruity may be a help to operationalizing role taking, it can be a hindrance to measures of empathy, in which clarity and consistency of cues may be most important.

It seems ironic that the claims made for many early empathy studies, designed to contravene Piaget's views (1932) regarding young children's cognitive egocentrism and inability to consider several viewpoints simultaneously, themselves fell prey to an analogous error when applied to the empathy construct – they failed to differentiate conceptual and affective processes. Piaget asserted that forms of egocentrism were present during all cognitive stages, although perspective-taking skills were considered to be minimal until the emergence of concrete operational thought. Nevertheless, Piaget (1932) also asserted that infants and preoperational children are responsive to others' affect and can even behave altruistically on others' behalf. These early behaviors would thus not be dependent upon cognitive perspective taking.

Given that role taking and empathy are understood as distinct processes, the extent to which role taking may mediate empathy from childhood on justifies its importance to this area. However, there are empirical difficulties in assessing role taking, which is now considered a multi- rather than unidimensional construct, with affective, perceptual, and inferential role-taking measures showing fairly low correlations (Ford, 1979). Affective role taking has the most direct bearing on empathy, and instructions to take the role of the other person have been used successfully to induce empathic emotion in adults (e.g., Toi & Batson, 1982). Nevertheless, the empirical basis for linking role taking and empathy needs further examination, particularly with respect to children.

Affective role taking and children's empathy

Links between affective role taking and empathy, although theoretically justified, are empirically tenuous (Iannotti & Pierrehumbert, 1985; Strayer, 1980). Whereas data show that children's skill in identifying others' emotions correlates significantly with their reported empathy to those characters (Feshbach & Roe, 1986), when role taking and empathy are assessed with independent measures, correlations are modest, at most. For example, preliminary data from our laboratory indicate only modest correlations for children's performance on Selman's (1980) role-taking measure with either their scores on Bryant's (1982) empathy questionnaire or with their mean reported empathy to characters in affectively evocative videodramas.

There are few longitudinal studies relating empathy and role taking. As one example of both the necessity and hazards of such work, Iannotti and Pierrehumbert (1985) conclude that perspective or role taking (i.e., identifying characters' emotions when facial and situational cues are incongruent in a photo-story measure) is a precursor to empathy. However, this is questionable on several grounds. First, only 5-year-olds' situation-based, but not expression-based (the authors' empathy criterion), reports of own and characters' emotion on this measure were found to be related to their earlier perspective-taking skills at age 2. More important, children's empathic responses can be based equally well on expressive or situational cues, and the correlation with perspective taking should, in principle, hold for both. Furthermore, because no measures of empathy were taken when children were 2 years old, the contention that perspective taking is a precursor to empathy (merely because it was tested first) is unfounded. In spite of such problems, there are additional intriguing findings in this study suggesting that children who focused on emotional expressive cues were more socially responsive with peers at both 2 and 5 years of age than were peers who focused on situational cues. These findings thus suggest relations between social functioning and attention to affective cues.

Until we have agreed-upon, valid measures of both affective role taking and empathy, their relationship must remain one that is, at best, theoretically probable. There are, however, a number of empirical lines of evidence that indirectly support this probability.

One reason for linking role taking to empathy is the leap of imagination entailed in feeling as if we were the other person in his or her situation (Stotland, 1969). In one of the few studies to assess spontaneous strategies children use when reacting empathically to videotaped stimuli, Chovil (1985) interviewed a group of children about whether they imagined themselves in the character's role (role taking), imagined what it would be like if the events depicted were happening to them (projection), or were just looking and listening carefully. She found no differences between reports for the two imagination conditions. Both were significantly related to Bryant's (1982) empathy measure and to children's reports of shared affect with videotaped characters. Imaginal processes, whether the direction is allocentric or egocentric, thus seem implicated in empathy.

Empathy may be experienced differently depending upon both the extent of affective involvement and the type of mediators involved (see Hoffman, 1975; 1982). Although I would maintain that empathic affect can occur with only minimal cognitive mediation, the experience of empathy as other-centered probably requires levels of self–other differentiation that continue to develop with age. Role taking may represent a further coordination of such differentiation with self–other imaginal transposition. An information-processing model may be helpful in considering how affect and cognition may interact in the empathic process.

Flavell, Botkin, Fry, Wright, and Jarvis (1968) proposed an information processing model of knowledge of others' perspectives in which information proceeds from:

1. knowledge of the existence of separate realities for people, to
2. recognition of the need to assess the other person's reality or viewpoint,
3. abilities to carry this process through and
4. maintain the results of such analysis in order to
5. apply what has been learned about the other to appropriate behaviors relative to them.

When these five nodes in the information model are examined in relation to empathy, we may find, for example, that all empathy needs at a basic level are skills in existence (e.g., object permanence) and need recognition. Thus, 2-year-olds may evidence empathy at some level. Additional analytic skills, as well as one's own accumulating social-affective experience, may then enhance the accuracy of shared emotion. Deficiencies in the maintenance of self–other distinctions while affect was shared would allow projective errors or self-oriented responses to intrude. Finally, application deficiencies would certainly affect empathy-motivated verbal communication or nonverbal behavioral responses to the other person, as noted in examples of children offering their teddy bears to comfort adults in distress. Clearly, differences in information processing may modulate empathic experience of the other. However, unless one's own affect also is aroused, such processes are insufficient for empathy to occur. Affective development, and not only cognition, may enhance empathy.

The role of social-emotional experience in empathy

Many emotional events we witness offer clear, consistent, and evocative cues. Extensive cognition would not be necessary to arouse our feelings or to understand the other person's. It is most often when cues are puzzling, or when the other person's reactions do not mirror our own experience, that processes such as role taking may be necessary. This points to the importance of social-emotional experience in understanding different emotion cues, experiences, and people. Just as interpersonal interactions are considered to be the arena in which role-taking skills are acquired (Mead, 1934; Piaget, 1932), so too they may help us to distinguish a wider range of emotional reactions in others as well as in ourselves, thus broadening the scope and modulating the intensity of empathic feelings.

Increasing social-emotional experience and reflection upon such experiences should widen the range of stimuli evoking empathy, as well as provide a source of individual differences in empathy. Such factors help to explain both why (1) empathy may increase with age, and (2) children who report little personal distance between themselves and a variety of other persons are more dispositionally empathic than children who distance themselves more from others (Bryant, 1982). Consistent with these notions, a child's own experience of certain emotions enhances his/her empathy with others' experience of those emotions (Barnett, 1984). Moreover, socialization practices that direct a child's attention to a variety of emotions in self and others seem to promote empathy (Hoffman, 1976; Staub, 1979). In conclusion, despite the importance of role taking as a mediator of empathy, individual differences in social-emotional experiences may align role taking to competitive rather than to helpful goals or empathic feelings. An intelligent psychopath may have good role taking skills, but may use them only to manipulate others for personal gain. Again, the affective aspect of empathy is critical. The focus of emotions and empathy is the perspective examined next.

An affective perspective on empathy

Empathy as vicarious affect

In this section I discuss empathy as vicarious or shared affect and consider how it occurs by using both a clinical model of how empathy may be subjectively experienced and developmental models in which different modes of empathic arousal are proposed. I also discuss how content and process variables are distinguished, self versus other differentiation, the directionality of affect, and the search for criterion cues and response measures for affective empathy.

For Lipps (1907), a progenitor of the term *empathy,* its end result is a shared feeling. Lipps's choice of *Einfühlung* or "feeling into," in contrast to *Mitfühlung* or "feeling with" (already in the English lexicon as "sympathy") distinguished the two terms. For Lipps, the mechanism responsible for such shared feeling was rooted not in the cognitive ability to think oneself through to the other person, but in afferent feedback from the body's conscious or unconscious motoric imitations of the other's posture, gesture, and expression.

Lipps's theory of empathy echoes earlier theories of emotion arousal and communication, such as those of Darwin (1872) and William James (1884). Although such views continue to influence present thought, they fail to explain individual differences, or a developmental course for empathy, or why some people and situations evoke more empathy than others do – or, indeed, whether, whenever we attend to stimuli, we always experience some degree of empathic arousal. Lipps viewed the empathizer as a receiver, and specified how affective messages are transmitted; but affect can be amplified, selectively attended to, ignored, or distorted when the empathizer is seen in a more agential role. Perhaps this was in part why subsequent researchers, sufficiently impressed with the empathy concept, nevertheless turned to cognition to elaborate upon it. Lipps's groundbreaking theory of motor mimicry lay dormant in psychological research on empathy until Hoffman (1975) revived it as one of several possible mediators in his model of empathy development, and until methods using nonverbal expressive indices of empathy (discussed later) gained recent prominence.

The affective focus on empathic content and process is clearly conveyed by Hoffman (1976), who stated that "empathy refers to the involuntary, at times forceful, experiencing of another person's emotional state. It is elicited either by expressive cues which directly reflect the other's feelings or by other cues which convey the impact of external events on him" (p. 126). Thus, affective response is the sine qua non of empathy, and this response can be to situational as well as expressive cues. That the affect experienced is "more appropriate to someone else's situation than to one's own situation" (Hoffman, 1982, p. 282) is a major distinction between empathy and direct emotional arousal.

It is probably because of my academic bias that I see developmental psychologists, particularly Norma Feshbach and Martin Hoffman, as the heroes in rescuing empathy from almost complete subjugation by their cognitively oriented contemporaries. In fact, however, there were also clinical psychologists who considered empathy as an affective experience, even if their research did not often generalize to other disciplines.

Clinical perspectives on shared affect and empathy

Carl Rogers (1951) considered empathy to be pivotal in the therapeutic process. Rogers recalled earlier etymological distinctions when noting that empathy, or "feeling into," focuses on and shares others' feelings from an internal frame of reference; whereas sympathy keeps an external frame of reference and "feels about" rather than "into." Although the result of empathy was affect sharing, the process measured was cognitive (Rogers & Truax, 1967). Similar clinical views stress that afferent feedback is essential to empathy as "the human echo to human experience" (Kohut, 1978, p. 700). Many clinicians also stress that empathy is rooted in preconscious process. In particular, Theodore Reik's analysis of empathy had great influence upon clinicians (Goldstein & Michaels, 1985). It seems unfortunate that these views have not received broad empirical testing.

Reik defined empathy as shared affect and proposed four phases of the empathy process. This process was described as moving from:

1. an instinctive imitative activity and relaxation of conscious controls upon becoming absorbed by the object of empathy, through
2. introjection of the other person into ourselves, and the consequent
3. "reverberation" or "resonance" between the internalized feelings of the other and evocations of our own experience and imaginings, to

4. deliberate withdrawal and psychological distancing in order to effect clear differentiation of self and other person in the final phase (Katz, 1963).

What these clinicians and the developmental theorists discussed have in common is their focus upon empathy as shared affect and their inclusion of self–other differentiation as a necessary phase in it. Although empathy can be involuntarily instigated, the requirement of rudimentary self–other differentiation probably limits it during infancy. The question is, can empathy be *experienced* without a rudimentary *self* to experience it? Self-development and further refinements in self–other differentiation occur throughout development. Increasingly deliberative cognitions about what pertains to the other person's versus one's own experience, as in role taking, may be involved, particularly in phase 4. However, such cognitions are kept in abeyance until this phase. The reverberation phase, the core of the empathic experience, is less a function of voluntary deliberative cognition than a "free association" or loosening of self–other boundaries in allowing stimuli impinging on the other to be experienced by the self.

Applying these ideas to children, I would suggest that empathy is initiated when attention is caught by a stimulus. Phase 1 may be driven by the biological signal quality of emotion cues, by motor mimicry, or by arousing person-based and/or contextual cues. Phase 1 may be more easily instigated at young than older ages because the tendency to be captured by stimuli is greater. Phase 2 also may proceed most easily in young children, whose self–other boundaries may be highly permeable. On the other hand, older children, or those with a more distinct, secure sense of self may be better able than younger children to engage in and to maintain such vicarious involvement. Thus, children who are rigid or not "ego resilient" in their personal boundaries (Block & Block, 1980) may abort the process at phase 2 when personal distress is felt.

The affect generated in phases 1 and 2 primes the available mediators in phase 3, which relate the other person's experiences to our own by means of association or imaginal transposition. During phase 3, the reverberation or interplay of our own reactions with those of the introjected person (phase 2) further specifies our affective participation in what the other person may be experiencing. The extent of phase 3 reverberation of external and internal, other person and own cues, may develop with age, particularly given the increasing range of emotional experiences one has available for reverberation. The maintenance of phase 3 reverberation may be more likely with age, given the confusion or self-centered alarm that might result when dysphoric emotions are evoked, particularly when cognitive differentiation and self-controls are limited. As stated previously, phases 1 and 2 may be more or less easily instigated and endured with age; however, phase 3 reverberation is expected to be greater in both range and complexity as a function of age.

The last phase, expected to improve with age, seems particularly necessary to explain empathy as a motivator of prosocial actions and communications. Self–other boundaries, merged in earlier phases, must be reinstated to permit the distance necessary for more objective analysis and decision making regarding the other person. Of course, operations entailed in phase 4 can be exercised without the preceding affective and reverberation phases, in which case I would argue that it is not empathy, but interpersonal cognitions, such as role taking, that are being referenced.

The direction of effects proposed in this conceptualization of empathy is one in which affect primes cognition, and both interact. It may be that during or as a result of phase 4, the affect itself changes from shared or vicarious affect *with* the other (i.e., empathy) to feelings *for* the other (e.g., sympathy). However, a main point is that phase 4 cognitive deliberations are part of the empathic process only when affective involvement with the other has occurred. Although mature empathizers may be most aware of cognitive acts, such as role taking – which they may regard as the initiators of the empathic process – it remains an empirical question whether role taking, itself, is sufficient to prime empathic affect, or, as proposed in this conceptualization, whether it acts in the service of empathy only when affect is aroused to direct the role-taking deliberations. Affect necessarily is involved, and the issue here is the extent to which affect primes cognition or results from it. Although it is hoped that such distinctions help to clarify the empathic process, the challenge for empirical verification is daunting.

The directionality of affect

It may seem paradoxical to assert that empathy requires both self–other merging of affective experience and self–other differentiation. Let me state the obvious. Sharing another's affect is different from experiencing it ourselves, even though our own experiences may be evoked in promoting the shared experience. Experiencing another's feeling of jealousy of a rival is not the same as ourselves being jealous of that rival. A similar distinction holds for a child's shared or vicarious happiness upon viewing televised others at a circus. The child knows he or she is not at the circus, and may be either associating to his or her own experience or "living through" the characters. Even if we use only our personal experience to help inform us about others' affect, this is not egocentric, given the grounding that empathy has in the strata of common human experiences. In this manner, processes of identification and projection, which are anathema to cognitive role taking, are permissible when affective sharing is the criterion. Taken to an extreme, one can agree with Cooley that "it is not essential that there should be any real understanding in order that compassion [or empathy] may be felt'' (1902, p. 137, my bracketed insertion).

The most salient conclusion thus far is that in empathy we are affected by others' affect, with the result that we share it. However, if upon exposure to others' sadness, we only recall our own sadness and limit the focus of our feelings to ourselves, then empathy is not enhanced. The directionality of affect is thus also critical to empathy. One determinant of this self- or other-person direction may be feeling that our own needs are sufficiently satisfied, so that we can afford to empathize with the dysphoria of others. There is some evidence suggestive of such a hypothesis (Barnett, King, & Howard, 1979; Underwood, Froming, & Moore, 1977). Children with histories of emotional disruption or maladjustment are poorer both in judging others' emotions and in empathic responding (Reichenbach & Masters, 1983; Straka & Jacobson, 1981).

Affect as process versus content

As is evident from this discussion, shared affective response is the main criterion of whether empathy has occurred. However, there is still little empirical resolution regarding the processes responsible for this.

Some researchers argue that there is a dispositional factor beyond that measured in any specific situation. In this view, empathic people, whether because of biological or socialization differences, are particularly responsive to affective cues. A number of dispositional questionnaire measures of empathy incorporate items assessing emotionality and affective responsiveness. Consistent with this view, sensitivity to affective cues has been found to differentiate the behaviors of empathic versus nonempathic individuals. For example, only when affective cues are present do lower aggression and higher prosocial behaviors result for empathic but not nonempathic subjects (Feinberg, 1978; Mehrabian & Epstein, 1972). Also, children who are reported to be empathic are more likely than are their less empathic peers to focus on others' affect (Barnett, Howard, Melton, & Dino, 1982). Further discussion of the content–process distinction follows.

Comparison of Hoffman's and Feshbach's empathy models

The two major developmental models of empathy, those of Feshbach and of Hoffman, both agree on its affective definition. However, they differ in process, both temporally (in terms of empathy's ontogeny) and quantitatively (in terms of the number of possible mediators). In contrast to Feshbach, Hoffman proposes many modes of empathic mediation, some of which are not at all or only minimally cognitive. In part, Hoffman's outlook is consistent with that of emotion specificity theorists and those who propose evolutionarily programmed biological feedback systems for emotional recognition and responsiveness (e.g., Ekman, 1973). Given this view, "emotional contagion" noted in newborns' reactive crying to another infant's cries would understandably be included as precursory evidence for empathy in Hoffman's developmental model. Researchers reviewing the other modes of empathic arousal in this model have found evidence for motor mimicry, another precognitive mode of empathic arousal, in both infants (Field, Woodson, Greenberg, & Cohen, 1982) and adults (Bavelas, Black, Lemery, & Mullett, chapter 14). Other involuntary, cognitively rudimentary modes of empathic arousal may include classical conditioning. In contrast, direct association to one's own experience that is triggered by others' affect is somewhat more cognitively advanced than the aforementioned modes. Symbolic recall (e.g., to written material) entails even more voluntary and complex cognitions, the emphasizer being more an agent than a recipient in the process. These modes are still less cognitively demanding than role taking, which for both Hoffman and Feshbach represents the most advanced cognitive mediator of empathy. Nevertheless, empathy, at least for Hoffman, can operate without role taking. The critical point for both models is that role taking, when part of the empathic process, operates in the service of affect.

Although both authors have proposed their models as working ideas rather than finished theories, they have somewhat different implications for empirical research on empathy. Feshbach's model, for example, might foster concentration of effort on identifying age-related developments in emotion discrimination and role taking. These two processes may have different developmental courses as well as different relations to each other and to empathy for different emotions. Hoffman's model, consisting of many modes of empathic arousal, might promote research focused on identifying the cues and developmental differences in attention to cues responsible for eliciting one mode of arousal versus another: For example, salient facial or body cues may foster motor mimicry; narrative events may foster symbolic association, and so on. Given developmental differences in the availability of different modes, certain cues may be more or less likely to elicit empathy at different ages. It also may be that empathy is most likely aroused when several cues are processed and when several modes are elicited in the same empathic process. Furthermore, certain modes of arousal (e.g., direct association) may be more likely to promote personal distress than concern for the other person.

Before I examine empirical findings from the methods of measuring empathic affect, I should underscore several points from the previous discussion. Affect and cognition have been difficult, if not impossible, to dissociate in empirical attempts to measure empathy. Nevertheless, what empathy is (content) and how it occurs (process) are distinguishable issues. They have rarely, however, emerged as distinct issues in empirical research on empathy, which has often ignored or confused this important distinction. To be consistent with the affective definition of empathy, measures of affective arousal to another's affect (e.g., self-report, physiological, or facial expressive indices) are essential to defining empathy. Emotion detection and labeling, social insight, and role-taking tasks do not tell us this. Such factors may, however, operate during reverberation and differentiation phases of the empathic process. Alternatively, noncognitive factors, such as motor mimicry, sometimes may be sufficient to explain empathy. The following review of measures of empathic process is brief and selective.

The search for the criterion cue: expression or context?

The most widely used developmental measure of empathy has been the Affective Situations Test for Empathy (or FASTE, Feshbach & Roe, 1968), in which empathy is scored as a match of the subject's own reported emotion with the emotion considered appropriate to the stimulus character presented in narrative and slides. In derivative measures (e.g., Iannotti, 1978), affect-matching story cues are contrasted with characters' photographed facial expressions. The original assumption, a legacy from role-taking measures, was that children's reliance on expressive cues indicates empathy, whereas reliance on contextual information may indicate projection or egocentrism. As already discussed, this distinction, depending on the information source used, seems logically indefensible as the criterion of empathy.

We use whatever cues seem to us most salient or reliable in inferring others' emotions. At times, contextual cues may outweigh expressive cues, given our appreciation of cultural and personal display rules for emotion. Empirical support for the equipotentiality of different cues was provided by Reichenbach and Masters (1983), who found that preschoolers and third graders were flexible in using either expressive or situational cues, depending on which set provided the clearest or most recognizable affect in a trial. Furthermore, even though preschoolers are able to identify others' emotions when expression and emotion cues are incongruent, their reported empathy on incongruent trials is low (Iannotti & Pierrehumbert, 1985). Use of conflicting affective cues, although perhaps helpful for studying role taking, may hamper empathy. It may be only when redundant or congruent cues are presented that affective evocation, particularly for preschoolers, is sufficient to elicit empathic responses.

Too little attention has been paid to stimulus factors. Particularly when nonverbal or verbal reactions are assessed experimentally, the evocative power of stimuli is critical, and generalizations to life outside the laboratory require that stimuli be evocative and realistic. In one study, for example, children showed greater physiological responses to realistic than cartoon depictions of televised violence (Osborn & Endsley, 1971).

How to assess shared or vicarious affect

On the whole, children do not egocentrically confuse their own and others' emotions. In general, their understanding of others' emotions in stories often is not accompanied by shared feeling, and they attribute emotions to others more often than to themselves in measures using both static picture-story and audiovisual dramas (Brody & Carter, 1982; Feshbach & Roe, 1968; Freeman, 1984; Iannotti, 1975; Mood, Johnson, & Shantz, 1978; Strayer, in press). Thus, children do differentiate cognitive recognition of others' affect from their own affective arousal. Role taking may or may not be implicated in this recognition. Similarly, for adults there need be little correlation between cognitive proclivities to take others' perspectives and either sharing their affect or being responsive to them (Davis, 1983b).

Empathy generally has been scored as a match between children's report of their emotion and the emotion identified by the experimenter as correct for that trial (Feshbach & Roe, 1968; Iannotti, 1975). Yet, regardless of experimental consensus, except in the simplest of instances, an emotional episode is veridically open to several interpretations, which are based both on the occurrence of facial expressive "blends" of emotion (Ekman & Friesen, 1975) and on other cues among which observers select those that are personally most salient for them. Therefore it seems more ecologically valid and meaningful when measuring empathy to use any plausible emotion the subject attributes to the other person as the emotion to be matched in assessing the subject's own reported emotion as empathic (Strayer, 1985).

Depending on the method they have used, a number of experimenters report increases in empathy with age (Eisenberg & Lennon, 1983, and chapter 9; Feshbach & Roe, 1968; Strayer, 1985). Iannotti's (1978) finding that empathy decreases significantly with age can be explained by his restricting empathy to matched emotion based only on characters' expressive cues when these were incongruent with story cues. Such scoring would favor younger rather than older children (Reichenbach & Masters, 1983); this problem has been remedied in Iannotti's subsequent reports.

How is the significant increase with age generally reported for shared affect to be interpreted? Is this an affective or a cognitive phenomenon, or both? Does it reflect simultaneous or separate developments in phases proposed for the empathy process (i.e., in attention to affect cues, affective reverberation, self–other differentiation)? Does it reflect developments not yet considered, such as perhaps greater willingness with age to report dysphoric feelings or greater tolerance for emotional involvement? In the absence of clear answers, I continue to pose the questions I think are relevant and try to narrow down the possibilities while discussing other affective measures of empathy.

Empathy as an emotional dispositional variable

Some affect-based approaches to empathy consider it to be a dispositional or traitlike variable, consistent for individuals across situations. The most widely used measure of the dispositional tendency to respond emotionally and empathically was developed and validated for adults by Mehrabian and Epstein (1972). Children as young as first graders also have been assessed for dispositional empathy using Bryant's adaptation of the Mehrabian and Epstein (1972) scale. Although reading ability and capacity for reflection are required to answer the questions, they all deal with affective responsivity, providing a global index combining items reflecting emotionality, empathy, and sympathy into one scale.

In contrast to these global measures is the multidimensional empathy disposition questionnaire developed by Davis (1983a,b). It consists of two affective subscales that assess empathic concern and personal distress in response to others' emotions; and two cognitive subscales that assess perspective taking and imaginal involvement. Interestingly, the latter correlates more highly with the affectivity subscales than with perspective taking and perhaps suggests that willingness to become imaginally involved in affective events is more related to adult empathic concern, for example, than is perspective-taking skill. Furthermore, although it is important to distinguish empathically experienced emotion that leads to an excess of personal distress rather than concern for the other, "it has been the rule, rather than the exception, that actual feelings of empathic concern and personal distress co-occur to a great degree" (Davis, 1983b, p. 183). Whether this is also true for children, who have poorer self–other differentiation and maintenance skills, remains an interesting question, and adaptation of Davis's measure for use with children seems warranted.

Physiological measures of empathy

Various measures of arousal, such as heart rate and skin conductance, have been used in empathy research, particularly with adults. There is some evidence that direct and vicarious affective arousal produce different patterns of physiological arousal (Craig & Wood, 1969). Nevertheless, the persistent problem with physiological measures in empathy research is to tie them to specific affect. Although some researchers claim that consistent and specific, emotionally differentiated patterns occur within, if not across, individuals (Schwartz & Weinberger, 1980), most maintain that physiological measures assess only general arousal.

Facial expressive measures of empathy

Afferent feedback and internalizer–externalizer models

In contrast to physiological indices, facial expressive measures offer promise of revealing the particular emotion experienced. In the absence of situational information, trained judges can reliably differentiate types of expressions, even among infants (Izard, 1979).

Facial expressions not only portray emotions but also, according to afferent feedback models, influence how the expressor feels: Emotions are intensified when they are facially expressed and are diminished when expression is suppressed (Ekman, Levenson, & Friesen, 1983). Although facial expressions and physiological arousal measures generally show low but significant correlations (Buck, Miller, & Caul, 1974), Buck (1979) has proposed an "internalizer–externalizer" dichotomy in which persons with high physiological arousal are purported to show low expressiveness, and the reverse. However, most of the data reviewed by Buck were based on differences between subjects rather than relative differences within subjects, and seem insufficient at present to challenge the use of facial expressive indices of empathy.

Facial expressions are potent stimuli in evoking similar expressions in the perceiver, as demonstrated by findings that children showed significantly more facial expressions in response to video stimuli that focused on characters' facial expressions than on situational cues to emotion (Wiggers & Willems, 1983). They are also potent response measures, as demonstrated by findings that boys' facial expressions while watching televised violence were more highly related than were their verbal reports to their subsequent aggression (Sawin, 1979).

Does facial expression "show" affective experience?

Granting that facial expressive measures seem promising, several issues need to be considered when using them as affective measure of empathy. Socialization of emotion entails learning both cultural display rules and how to read individually different styles of expressiveness. It is therefore unlikely that the use of such measures taps "pure" emotional responsiveness on the part of the observer, even under conditions of minimal social constraint (Solomon, 1985). Also, as is clearly the case with infants, but also may occur in adults, the face is capable of morphological alignments such as the "contempt" expression of infants that may not reflect the emotion experienced (Izard, 1979). Even when they do, and are used to index empathy, we cannot always be certain that a fearful expression is in response, for example, to a stalking tiger viewed on the screen or to the person who is shown fearfully trying to evade the tiger.

Such expressions may decrease with age given increased thresholds for emotional stimuli and learned expressive control. Or, they may increase given the greater emotional reverberation possible with increasing affective experience. Also, just as there are different developmental timetables for different emotional expressions and experiences, so too may shared affect vary according to the emotion examined. There may be little reason to expect facial measures of empathy to be consistent across stimulus trials: Some stimuli may be more evocative than others for certain ages and individuals. For these reasons, facial expressions, although probably our most promising nonverbal measure of empathy, cannot be used as the definitive criterion. Independent measures of both affect and cognition are needed to survey and analyze the construct of empathy. It also seems increasingly clear that, as empathy is determined by the interaction of affect and cognition, a multidimensional approach offers the most promise.

A multidimensional perspective on empathy

In preceding sections I attempted to differentiate between affective and cognitive factors in the definition and measurement of empathy. Now I consider how their interactions result in a multidimensional conceptualization of empathy. It is admittedly tempting to side with Stewart (1956), who claimed that empathy cannot be studied scientifically. Nonetheless, current progress seems sufficient to warrant further investigation.

Affect and cognition interact in most phases of the empathy process. How they interact has been studied in particular by developmental researchers who have been influenced by Piaget's theory. Piaget, who considered affect and intellect to be "opposite sides of the same coin," nevertheless always flipped the cognitive side up. Current reviews of Piaget's thoughts on affect in development are available (Piaget, 1981), and the only point to be stressed here is that, for Piaget, cognition "acts," whereas affect "energizes" action. Thus, the act of understanding another's feelings may be motivated by our own affective responses to them. Developmentally, however, it is cognition that defines structural development. Affect may demonstrate stagelike properties in the sense of systematic shifts with age (from links to one's actions in the prelanguage period to subsequent social–interactional links); however, its development is tied to cognition. Yet, as Piaget warned that neither affect nor cognition is causal for the other, we remain at a loss to generate from his theory specific cognitive–affective links applicable to empathy development.

Perhaps it is realistic to acknowledge that at present research may artificially compartmentalize cognitive and affective aspects of empathy, which are interacting processes. Accepting that empathy and its measurement are multifaceted, however, does not compel us to accept that there is more than one kind of empathy: for example, role taking as "cognitive empathy" and affective responses to others' affect cues as "affective empathy." My opinion is that empathy has a singular definition: the self's feeling into (*Einfühlung*) the affect of another person. The multidimensional perspective then pertains to *processes* entailed in empathy (consider the phases of the empathic process suggested earlier and the different mediators proposed by Hoffman). Let us consider some present options.

The empirical sway of the data at present suggests that future meta-analyses of affective and cognitive (e.g., affect recognition, role taking) measures used to assess empathy will highlight its multidimensional nature, as has been the case for most other complex phenomena in psychology. Correlations among physiological, somatic, or verbal measures of affect and cognition in empathy may not cohere for several reasons:

1. They do not all measure empathy. (Against what criterion can an empathy measure be assessed as valid?)
2. They are not equally good measures of empathy across different samples (e.g., emotional experience and expressive styles vary within as well as across age groups)
3. They measure separate aspects of empathy, which may not accord unless concurrently assessed
4. They measure separate kinds of empathy.

As stated, I think that all but the last possibility are likely. Although I would maintain that the phenomenon of empathy is shared feeling, there may be several phases of the empathic process calling upon several different kinds of abilities.

Designing measures for a multidimensional study

To review, empathy viewed multidimensionally may be initiated by one's attention to a person in a salient stimulus event (real or symbolic) – salient because of the intensity of the cues, because of their signal quality, because they are different from our immediate experience, and because they are emotionally arousing. Measures at this point would assess stimulus features in laboratory or naturalistic contexts that call attention to an event that is arousing and evocative. I have suggested that stimulus salience is one important feature that may also interact with the familiarity of the person and situation attended to, as well as with the previous emotional state of the observer, all of which can be assessed. Emotional arousal can be measured using verbal reports, and physiological or facial expressive measures with attention to caveats earlier noted.

Subsequent phases of the empathic process may entail motor mimicry, classical conditioning, association, imaginative transposition of self and other, and similar processes as part of the reverberation that links the other person's experience to our own. For example, instructions to adults either to imagine themselves or to imagine the target person's reactions in a painful situation resulted in more physiological arousal than did instructions to observe the target person closely; these results suggest that the latter activity or "close judgmental attention interferes with empathy" (Aderman & Berkowitz, 1970, p. 142, reporting on Stotland's work). Whereas physiological reactions, facial expressions, and motor mimicry can be measured immediately in response to stimuli, other processes, such as imaginative transposition, require either postcondition interview or experimental induction procedures to establish their presence. Similarly, general self–other differentiation can be assessed before or after the empathic episode. However, empathy-specific self–other differentiation, posited as a post–reverberation phase process, would need to be assessed by postcondition interview, which may be problematic, particularly for young children.

There are reasons for singling out component processes and assessing their relationships and perhaps different courses of development. To the extent that empathy mediates such reactions, individual differences in toddlers whose reactions to others' distress are described as either more cognitively or more affectively disposed (Radke-Yarrow, Zahn-Waxler, & Chapman, 1983) may help to suggest the relative weighting of affective or cognitive factors that contribute to individual differences in empathic development. Different measures of the empathic process also may be relevant for different purposes. For example, emotional factors may be important in caring about others' needs; yet behaviors on other's behalf may result only when optimal self–other differentiation balances the personal distress felt. Although cognitive factors may also be implicated (Underwood & Moore, 1982), some recent studies suggest that the emotional and not the cognitive aspect of empathy most strongly predicts behaviors on behalf of others (Rushton, 1980) and that "perspective taking affects helping only as a result of its effect on empathic emotional response" (Coke, Baston, & McDavis, 1978, p. 753). Along these lines, Davis (1983a,b) found that individual differences in the emotional component of his multidimensional dispositional measure of empathy predicted subjects' empathic emotions in response to a distressed victim, whereas their perspective-taking scores did not. Davis's multidimensional measure seems to provide reliable differentiation of cognitive perspective taking (which correlates to measures of social functioning and person perception) and emotional aspects of empathy (which correlate to other measures of emotional responsivity). It is a dispositional measure, however, and does not serve to assess the empathic process. Comparative studies across different methods may help do this.

Relations among measures and recent multimethod studies

In the absence of an agreed-upon definition and theory of empathy, it is not surprising that relations among current measures of empathic process are not impressive. When affective role taking and shared emotion, which need not coincide in general, are assessed in the same situation, they correlate significantly (Feshbach & Roe, 1968; Iannotti, 1975). However, they may often necessarily correlate because such empathy procedures depend upon matching own affect to the affect experimenters ascribe to story characters. In contrast, role taking on the FASTE (considered by its authors to be a prerequisite of empathy) does not correlate with empathy on different measures (Kagan & Knudson, 1982). Preliminary data from a study I am conducting indicate significant correlations between children's empathy with characters and both identification and role taking of characters' emotions, but insignificant correlations between empathy and an independent role-taking (Selman, 1980) measure.

In general, verbal report empathy measures do not intercorrelate well, as noted by a recent review of adult measures (Chlopan, McClain, Carbonell, & Hagen, 1985). The important tasks for future research are to deduce empathy criteria, to integrate criteria across studies, and to establish construct convergence by correlations among different affective measures of empathy, among different cognitive measures implicated in empathy, and between these sets.

Correlations among different methods are important to a multidimensional view of empathy; they are also especially hard to find. Measures of children's facial/gestural responses to watching videotapes of peers in distress did not correlate with their scores on the FASTE (Lennon, Eisenberg, & Carroll, 1983). Similarly, Peraino and Sawin (1981) reported that children's facial/gestural responses to televised peers in distress were not related to their reported emotions in response to these episodes. Yet adults who showed high expressivity while viewing a filmed accident scored higher on emotional empathy disposition than did low expressors (Notarius & Levenson, 1979). Although this is consistent with the report (Mehrabian & Epstein, 1972) that generally low "stimulus screening" thresholds and high emotional responsivity are main features of persons with high empathy on their measure, we do not know whether these expressive adults would have reported empathic responses to this film. Recent studies with children show only modest correlations between facial expressive measures and verbally reported empathy in reaction to stimulus vignettes (Chovil, 1985; Strayer, 1985; Wiggers & Willems, 1983). In the latter study by Wiggers and Willems, children's facial expressions that accorded with emotions shown by videotaped characters (i.e., facial empathy) were observed 47% of the times verbal empathy (self–other affect match) was reported, in contrast to 32% of the times it was not reported. Greater correspondence may occur among nonverbal measures than between verbal and nonverbal measures, as indicated in a cursory report (Sawin, 1979) that correlations between children's physiological arousal and self-reports of shared emotions with videotaped characters were quite low, but that ongoing measures of their physiological and facial expressive responses showed greater correspondence.

Not surprisingly, differences in methods yield somewhat different results. In contrast to the findings (Wiggers & Willems, 1983) that only 26% of young children's responses were empathic, I found (Strayer, 1985) that 5-, 7-, and 13-year-old children reported much more empathy (61%, 74%, 90%, respectively). The stimuli involved children as well as adults, and the vignettes were from film dramas chosen for their emotional evocativeness. The measure of empathy relied upon children's own plausible identifications of characters' emotions in these dramas in which, like life, there was often more than one way of seeing things. Coding of children's facial expressions was also different from that in the first study, since more global, naturalistic, real-time (not microanalytic) judgments were made every 10 seconds, using a scaled euphoric to dysphoric continuum of facial expressions communicated. Significantly more empathy was reported when children's facial expressions were coded as being dysphoric than euphoric, as was generally consistent with stimulus content. Some support also was obtained for the expected greater concordance between facial and verbal reports of own affect with age, owing to developing introspective and labeling skills.

Recently attempts have also been made to include different levels of cognitive mediation and affective arousal in the same measure. For example, an Empathy Continuum System (EC) was developed (Strayer, 1985) for scoring responses to affectively evocative videotapes. The first two EC categories represent no empathy: EC 0 = no recognition of the character's affect; EC 1 = recognition but no shared affect. The remaining 18 categories reflect empathy experienced at three different levels of affective sharing and placed at six different levels of cognitive mediation. The three degrees of affective sharing reflect similar hedonic tone; same emotion, different intensity; or same emotion, same intensity, in response to "How did the character feel? How much – a little or a lot?" and "How did you feel when you watched that? How much – a little or a lot?". These affective values appear at each of six increasingly differentiated and other-focused levels of cognitive mediation (e.g., responses to "Why were you, or what made you feel sad, angry, happy, etc?"). The six levels of cognitive mediation range from the absence of rationale to reliance upon external events only, to increasing transpersonal, other-centered attributions, including those implying role taking. For example, "I felt very sad" is scored at *EC level IV* if the mediation relies on the character's external events (e.g., "because she had to give up her skates"). The obtained *EC category* scores at this level are EC 10 if one's own reported affect is the same in kind and intensity as that reported for a stimulus character, EC 9 if it is the same in kind but not intensity, and EC 8 if it is similar in hedonic tone only. The same three responses for affective sharing would be scored at *EC level VII* (role taking) if the stated mediation were, for example, "because if I were in her place, I'd be so sad having to put up with all she did," and would be scored as EC 19, 18, and 17.

Results confirmed expected increases in EC scores with age among the 5- to 13-year-olds studied, as well as a meaningful age-related distribution of responses at different cognitive levels of the continuum – for example, most responses in the top half of the continuum were made by older subjects, whereas most responses in the lower half of the continuum were made by younger subjects. This system also may be applicable to adults because the highest-placed EC categories were relatively infrequently used by these children.

This multimethod study also included measures of the facial expressions of children viewing affectively evocative videodramas and within-subject correlations of reported empathy and facial expressions. Considerably less facial affect was coded than was verbally reported by these children. This (also found by Wiggers & Willems, 1983) suggests, among other possibilities, different socialization effects for showing versus saying what one feels. Nevertheless, the concordance of both facial and verbal indices may best reflect empathy. In fact, significantly more empathy was reported when there was, versus when there was not, concordance of facial expressions and children's own reported affect. In accord with afferent feedback theorists (e.g., Ekman, Izard) empathy may be enhanced by such concordant trials.

In conclusion, many interesting avenues are open for further investigation. Although the cognitive measures reviewed by Deutsch & Madle (1975) have reportedly low intercorrelations and little construct validity as empathy measures, there are a number of promising affective measures. With regard to these measures, too, researchers will need to tackle the problem of construct validity, which requires a meaningful convergence of both concordant and discriminative evidence. Fundamentally, it also requires some agreement on defining properties of the empathy construct, which, as we have seen, is not always apparent. Empathy research, still in its early stages, has in part suffered the cart-before-the-horse problem of many inductively devised measures tested against one another in the absence of a deductive theory–based rationale. Thus, it is not surprising that many empathy measures do not correlate. Nor, I would argue, should they, given their different foci and the different perspectives outlined in this chapter.

Perhaps developmental dimensions of empathy may at best be represented along a qualitative continuum in which various processes interact at different phases of the empathy process, with somewhat different interactions possible at different points in development. Quantitative changes may occur in certain abilities (e.g., discrimination, associative recall and analogy, conceptual schema for affect, inferences regarding others' emotional attributions), but these are individually unlikely to explain empathy – an essentially interactive process. The past decade has witnessed an increasing tendency to treat empathy as a multidimensional construct entailing both affective and cognitive aspects. This approach has clarified but not simplified the issues involved in defining and measuring empathy. The clarity stems from recognition that cognitive capacities (such as role taking) need not imply emotional reactions, and that emotional aspects of empathy at different phases of the empathy process need not depend upon such cognition. Accepting affect and cognition as separate but interacting variables in empathy does not, however, simplify the task. Both affect and cognition are themselves constructs, each with different measurement indices. Particular measures of empathy may focus more upon affect or cognition, often depending on how many variables one can realistically assess in a study and on the behaviors in response to others' emotions that one is most interested in understanding and predicting – expressive, insightful, communicative, or prosocial. Empathy, as we may all now realize, is not any of these behaviors, but pertains to all of them.

References

Aderman, D., & Berkowitz, L. (1970). Observational set, empathy and helping. *Journal of Personality and Social Psychology, 14,* 141–148.

Barden, R. C., Zelco, F. A., Duncan, S. W., & Masters, J. C. (1980). Children's consensual knowledge about the experiential detriments of emotion. *Journal of Personality and Social Psychology, 39,* 968–976.

Barnett, M. A. (1984). Similarity of experience and empathy in preschoolers. *Journal of Genetic Psychology, 145,* 241–250.

Barnett, M. A., Howard, J. A., Melton, E. M., & Dino, G. A. (1982). Effect of inducing sadness about self or other on helping behavior in high- and low-empathic children. *Child Development, 53,* 920–923.

Barnett, M. A., King, L. M., & Howard, J. A. (1979). Inducing affect about self or other: Effects on generosity in children. *Developmental Psychology, 15,* 164–167.

Block, J. H., & Block, J. (1980). The role of ego-control and ego-resiliency in the organization of behavior. In W. A. Collins (Ed.), *Development of cognition, affect, and social relations.* The Minnesota Symposium on Child Psychology (Vol. 13, pp. 39–101). Hillsdale, N. J.: Erlbaum.

Borke, H. (1971). Interpersonal perception of young children: Egocentrism or empathy. *Developmental Psychology, 5,* 263–269.

Borke, H. (1972). Chandler and Greenspan's "ersatz egocentrism." *Developmental Psychology, 7,* 107–109.

Brody, L. R., & Carter, A. S. (1982). Children's emotional attributions to self versus other: An exploration of an assumption underlying projective techniques. *Journal of Consulting and Clinical Psychology, 50,* 665–671.

Bryant, B. K. (1982). An index of empathy for children and adolescents. *Child Development, 53,* 413–425.

Buck, R. (1979). Individual differences in nonverbal sending accuracy and electrodermal responding: The externalizing–internalizing dimension. In R. Rosenthal (Ed.), *Skill in nonverbal communication: Individual differences.* Cambridge, MA: Oelgeschlager, Gunn & Hain.

Buck, R. W., Miller, R. E., & Caul, W. F. (1974). Sex, personality, and physiological variables in the communication of emotion via facial expression. *Journal of Personality and Social Psychology, 30,* 587–596.

Burns, N., & Cavey, L. (1957). Age differences in empathic ability among children. *Canadian Journal of Psychology, 11,* 227–230.

Chandler, M. J., & Greenspan, S. (1972). Ersatz egocentrism: A reply to H. Borke. *Developmental Psychology, 7,* 104–106.

Chlopan, B. E., McCain, M. L., Carbonell, J. L., & Hagen, R. L. (1985). Empathy: Review of available measures. *Journal of Personality and Social Psychology, 48,* 635–653.

Chovil, N. (1985). *An investigation of sex differences in empathy and imaginal involvement.* Unpublished master's thesis, Simon Fraser University, Burnaby, British Columbia.

Coke, J. S., Baston, C. D., & McDavis, K. (1978) Empathic mediation of helping: A two stage model. *Journal of Personality and Social Psychology, 36,* 752–766.

Cooley, C. H. (1902). *Human nature and social order.* New York: Scribner's.

Craig, K. D., & Wood, K. (1969). Physiological differentiation of direct and vicarious affective arousal. *Canadian Journal of Behavioral Science, 1,* 98–105.

Cronbach, L. J. (1955). Processes affecting scores on "understanding others" and "assumed similarity." *Psychological Bulletin, 52,* 177–193.

Darwin, C. (1872). *The expression of emotions in man and animals.* London: John Murray.

Davis, M. H. (1983a). Measuring individual differences in empathy: Evidence for a multidimensional approach. *Journal of Personality and Social Psychology, 44,* 113–126.

Davis, M. H. (1983b). The effects of dispositional empathy on emotional reactions and helping: A multidimensional approach. *Journal of Personality, 51,* 167–184.

Deutsch, F., & Madle, R. A. (1975). Empathy: Historic and current conceptualizations, measurement, and cognitive theoretical perspective. *Human Development, 18,* 267–287.

Eisenberg, N., & Lennon, R. (1983). Sex differences in empathy and related capacities. *Psychological Bulletin, 94,* 100–131.

Ekman, P. (1973). *Darwin and facial expression: A century of research in review.* New York: Academic Press.

Ekman, P., & Friesen, W. V. (1975). *Unmasking the face: A guide to recognizing emotions from facial cues.* Englewood Cliffs, NJ: Prentice-Hall.

Ekman, P., Levenson, R. W., & Friesen, W. V. (1983). Autonomic nervous system activity distinguishes among emotions. *Science, 221,* 1208–1210.

Feinberg, H. K. (1978). Anatomy of a helping situation: Some personality and situational determinants of helping in a conflict situation involving another's psychological distress (Doctoral dissertation, University of Massachusetts, 1977). *Dissertation Abstracts International, 39,* 357–358B.

Feshbach, N. D. (1975). Empathy in children: Some theoretical and empirical considerations. *The Counseling Psychologist, 4,* 25–30.

Feshbach, N. D., & Roe, K. (1968). Empathy in six- and seven-year olds. *Child Development, 34,* 133–145.

Field, T., Woodson, R., Greenberg, R., & Cohen, D. (1982). Discrimination and imitation of facial expressions by neonates. *Science, 281,* 179–181.

Flavell, J. H., Botkin, P. T., Fry, C. L., Wright, J., & Jarvis, P. (1968). *The development of role-taking and communication skills in children.* New York: Wiley.

Ford, M. E. (1979). The construct validity of egocentrism. *Psychological Bulletin, 86,* 1169–1188.

Freeman, E. B. (1984). The development of empathy in young children: In search of a definition. *Child Study Journal, 13,* 235–244.

Goldstein, A. P., & Michaels, G. Y. (1985). *Empathy: Development, training, and consequences.* Hillsdale, NJ: Erlbaum.

Gove, F. L., & Keating, D. P. (1979). Empathic role-taking precursors. *Developmental Psychology, 15*, 594–600.

Hoffman, M. L. (1975). Developmental synthesis of affect and cognition and its implications for altruistic motivation. *Developmental Psychology, 2*, 607–622.

Hoffman, M. L. (1976). Empathy, role taking, guilt, and the development of altruistic motives. In T. Lickona (Ed.), *Moral development and behavior: Theory, research, and social issues* (pp. 124–143). New York: Holt, Rinehart, & Winston.

Hoffman, M. L. (1982). Development of prosocial motivation: Empathy and guilt. In N. Eisenberg (Ed.), *The development of prosocial behavior* (pp. 281–313). New York: Academic Press.

Iannotti, R. J. (1975). The nature and measurement of empathy in children. *The Counseling Psychologist, 5*, 21–25.

Iannotti, R. J. (1978). The effect of role-taking experiences on role taking, empathy, altruism, and aggression. *Developmental Psychology, 14*, 119–124.

Iannotti, R. J., & Pierrehumbert, B. (1985, April). *The development of empathy in early childhood.* Paper presented at the meeting of the Society for Research in Child Development, Toronto.

Izard, C. E. (1979). *The maximally discriminative facial movement coding system (MAX).* Newark: University of Delaware, Instructional Resources Center.

James, W. (1884). What is an emotion? *Mind, 9*, 188–204.

Kagan, S., & Knudson, K. H. M. (1982). Relationship of empathy and affective role taking in young children. *Journal of Genetic Psychology, 141*, 149–150.

Katz, R. L. (1963). *Empathy: Its nature and uses.* New York: Free Press.

Kerr, W., & Speroff, B. J. (1954). Validation and evaluation of the empathy test. *Journal of General Psychology, 50*, 269–276.

Kohut, H. (1978). *The search for self* (Vol. 2). New York: International Universities Press.

Lennon, R., Eisenberg, N., & Carroll, J. (1983, April). *The relation between nonverbal indices of empathy and preschoolers' prosocial behavior.* Paper presented at the meeting of the Society for Research in Child Development, Detroit.

Lipps, T. (1907). Das Wissen von Fremden Ichen. *Psychologischen Untersuchungen, 1*, 694–722.

Mayhew, J., & Strayer, J. (1985, August) *Developmental changes in the selection of differing emotion cues.* Paper presented at the meeting of the American Psychological Association, Los Angeles.

Mead, G. H. (1934). *Mind, self and society.* Chicago: University of Chicago Press.

Mehrabian, A., & Epstein, W. A. (1972). A measure of emotional empathy. *Journal of Personality, 40*, 523–543.

Mood, D. W., Johnson, J. E., & Shantz, C. (1978). Social comprehension and affect matching in young children. *Merrill–Palmer Quarterly, 24*, 63–66.

Morency, N. L., & Krauss, R. M. (1982). Children's nonverbal encoding and decoding of affect. In R. S. Feldman (Ed.), *Development of nonverbal behavior in children* (pp. 181–199). New York: Springer-Verlag.

Notarius, C. I., & Levenson, R. W. (1979). Expressive tendencies and physiological response to stress. *Journal of Personality and Social Psychology, 37*, 1204–1210.

Osborn, D. K., & Endsley, R. C. (1971). Emotional reactions of young children to TV violence. *Child Development, 42*, 321–331.

Peraino, J. M., & Sawin, D. B. (1981, April). *Empathic distress: Measurement and relation to prosocial behavior.* Paper presented at the meeting of the Society for Research in Child Development, Boston.

Piaget, J. (1932). *The moral judgment of the child* (M. Gabain, Trans.). London: Kegan Paul.

Piaget, J. (1981). *Intelligence and affectivity: Their relationship during child development* (T. A. Brown & C. E. Kaegi, Trans.). Palo Alto, CA: Annual Reviews.

Radke-Yarrow, M., Zahn-Waxler, C., & Chapman, M. (1983). Children's prosocial dispositions and behavior. In P. H. Mussen (Ed.), *Handbook of child psychology*. (Vol. 4, pp. 469-545). New York: Wiley.

Reichenbach, L., & Masters, J. C. (1983). Children's use of expressive and contextual cues in judments of emotion. *Child Development, 121,* 993–1004.

Rogers, C. R. (1951). *Client-centered therapy: Its current practice, implications and theory.* Boston: Houghton-Mifflin.

Rogers, C. R., & Truax, C. B. (1967). The therapeutic conditions antecedent to change: A therapeutic view. In C. R. Rogers (Ed.), *The therapeutic relationship and its impact: A study of psychotherapy with schizophrenics.* Madison: University of Wisconsin Press.

Rosenthal, R., Hall, J. A., DiMatteo, M. R., Rogers, P. L., & Archer, D. (1979). *Sensitivity to nonverbal communication: The PONS test.* Baltimore, MD: Johns Hopkins University Press.

Rushton, J. P. (1980). *Altruism, socialization, and society.* Englewood Cliffs, NJ: Prentice-Hall.

Saarni, C. (1979). Children's understanding of display rules for expressive behavior. *Developmental Psychology, 15,* 424–429.

Sawin, D. B. (1979, April). *Assessing empathy in children: A search for an elusive construct.* Paper presented at the meeting of the Society for Research in Child Development, San Francisco.

Schwartz, G. E., & Weinberger, D. A. (1980). Patterns of emotional responses to affective situations: Relationships among happiness, sadness, anger, fear, depression and anxiety. *Motivation and Emotion, 4,* 175–191.

Selman, R. (1980). *The growth of interpersonal understanding.* New York: Academic Press.

Shantz, C. U. (1983). Social-cognition. In P. H. Mussen (Ed.), *Handbook of Child Psychology* (Vol. 3, pp. 495–555). New York: Wiley.

Solomon, J. (1985, April). *The relationship between affective empathy and prosocial behavior in elementary school children.* Paper presented at the meeting of the Society for Research in Child Development, Toronto.

Staub, E. (1979). *Positive social behavior and morality, Vol. 2,* New York: Academic Press.

Stewart, D. (1956). *Preface to empathy.* New York: Philosophical Library.

Stotland, E. (1969). Exploratory investigations of empathy. In L. Berkowitz (Ed.), *Advances in experimental social psychology.* New York: Academic Press.

Straker, G., & Jacobson, R. S. (1981). Aggression, emotional maladjustment, and empathy in the abused child. *Developmental Psychology, 17,* 762–765.

Strayer, J. (1980). A naturalistic study of empathic behaviors and their relation to affective states and perspective-taking skills in preschool children. *Child Development, 51,* 815–822.

Strayer, J. (1985, August). *Children's affect and empathy in response to TV dramas.* Paper presented at the meeting of the American Psychological Association, Los Angeles.

Strayer, J. (1986). Children's attributions regarding the situational determinants of emotion in self and others. *Developmental Psychology, 17,* 649–654.

Strayer, J. (in press). What children know and feel in response to affective events. In C. Saarni & P. L. Harris (Eds.). *Children's understanding of emotion.* New York: Cambridge University Press.

Toi, M., & Batson, C. D. (1982). More evidence that empathy is a source of altruistic motivation. *Journal of Personality and Social Psychology, 42,* 281–292.

Underwood, B., Froming, W. J., & Moore, B. S. (1977). Mood, attention, and altruism: A search for mediating variables. *Developmental Psychology, 13,* 541–542.

Underwood, B., & Moore, B. S. (1982). Perspective-taking and altruism. *Psychological Bulletin, 91,* 143–173.

Wiggers, M., & Willems, H. (1983). Female preschoolers' verbal and nonverbal empathic responses to emotional situations and facial expression. *International Journal of Behavioral Development, 6,* 427–440.

11 Mental health, temperament, family, and friends: perspectives on children's empathy and social perspective taking

Brenda K. Bryant

My research on empathy has stemmed from an interest in emotional responsiveness and its relation to mental health. I view emotional responsiveness to others as part of a larger issue, the need for relatedness to others. Certainly, issues of relatedness are of central importance to developmental psychologists, beginning with the very survival of the human organism, which requires attachment formation with at least one nurturing other. The need for relatedness remains with us throughout the life cycle, although the nature and extent of this relatedness to others varies with development stages or issues.

Historically, researchers have focused on those aspects of human relatedness that are directly observable and involve instrumental gains for individuals. In contrast to empathy, which is, in large measure, a private experience, social perspective taking has clear external and objective referents for establishing its existence. Being able to take the perspective of another can be viewed as an instrumental activity since it can enable one to make use of this information to negotiate more skillfully with another individual. Empathic experiences, on the other hand, may be viewed more as an expressive competence in that they reflect the quality or ability of one to experience a wide variety of feelings even though no personal, material gain is thereby accured. Consequently, we have a longer and more substantial body of literature on aspects of relatedness such as social perspective taking than on emotional responsiveness to others. Recently, some teachers argued that being both instrumental and expressive is the basis for the richest individual development (see Bem, 1975; Werner & Smith, 1982). The benefit of expressive relatedness characterized by the empathic experiencing of

I am deeply indebted to the steadfast and thorough attention to detail that Pat Worley brought to all aspects of the data analysis. In addition, I thank Curt Acredolo for his statistical consultations and Linda Dougall for her assistance in the final phases of data analysis. I am also very thankful for the extensive and detailed editing provided by Janet Strayer and Larry Harper. Finally, I am graciously aware of the kindly patience Nancy Eisenberg showed me during the writing of this chapter. Funding for this project was provided by the Agriculture Experiment Station, University of California, Davis, the Foundation for Child Development, and the Delta Society.

the perceived emotional experiences of others is less apparent than the benefit of being able to take the objective perspective of another and thus needs to be examined more closely.

Despite the neglect of researchers, clinicians observe daily the despair that ensues when individuals of any age fail to experience an emotional connectedness to others. Although success in many areas of living requires children and adults to understand the thoughts and feelings of others objectively and to behave prosocially, the need to feel an emotional connectedness to others may be equally important, if not paramount, to social perspective taking with respect to one's emotional well-being. Social perspective taking entails cognitive understanding of the feelings and motives of others and, as such, is an instrumental skill. Empathy, on the other hand, entails emotional responsiveness to the feelings experienced by others and, as such, is a personal, subjective experience. Our cultural emphasis on instrumentality has been at the expense of our appreciation of the value of expressivity and its development (see Gilligan, 1982). Researchers, as members of our culture, have not been spared this bias, and so we frequently have equated social perspective taking with empathy, both in their assessment and in our formulation of social-emotional functioning and development.

In this chapter I challenge this bias and attempt to clarify distinctions between social perspective taking and empathy, and provide a foundation for a formulation regarding the development of these two aspects of social-emotional development. More specifically, I use empirical findings to investigate the relevance of both social perspective taking and empathy in predicting mental health. In addition, empirically derived intra- and interpersonal factors associated with the emergence and expression of both social perspective taking and empathy during middle childhood and early adolescence are considered in order to present a formulation of the development and expression of empathy, which I compare with social perspective taking.

An empirical study of empathy and social perspective taking

The data base for this chapter consists of a sample of 168 children who had siblings 2 to 3 years older than themselves and two derivative sets of longitudinal observations. The first derivative set involves 67 (out of an original 72) children first seen at age 7 and followed up 3 years later at age 10. The second derivative set includes 73 (out of an original 96) children first seen at age 10 and followed up four years later at age 14. (See Bryant, 1985, for complete description of sample.)

During the first year of data collection, children were seen during four home visits. On the first visit, the "target" child in the family was taken on a "neighborhood walk" (Bryant, 1985) to assess personal, home, and neighborhood/

community resources. Following this, children responded to Bryant's (1982) index of empathy and Rothenberg's (1970) measure of social perspective taking as well as other indices of social-emotional functioning (not addressed in this chapter). The index of empathy was chosen because of its potential for assessing a wide age range of children over time. The particular measure of social perspective taking was chosen not only because of its applicability to a wide age range of children, but because of the care Rothenberg gave to measuring perspective taking rather than projection. The vignettes in the Rothenberg social perspective–taking tapes involve adult, marital dyads rather than dyads including child participants to help ensure the likelihood that a child appearing to have social perspective–taking ability is actually taking the perspective of another person and not merely attributing feelings and motives to others that are, in fact, merely descriptions of him/herself as experienced in previous, comparable interchanges.

Each of the next three visits involved the target child with one other family member (mother, father, or older sibling) until interactions with all three family members had been assessed. Included in the present analyses are data provided by both the children regarding their perception of treatment they received by each of these three family members as well as data provided by each of these three family members regarding their perception of their treatment of the target child. Aspects of the child's temperament were also assessed by each child's mother, father, and older sibling.

Finally, in the longitudinal follow-ups, mothers provided an assessment of the child's mental health by using the Child Behavior Checklist (Achenbach, 1978; Achenbach & Edelbrock, 1979; Edelbrock & Achenbach, 1980), and children responded to the same measures of empathy and social perspective taking.

Relation of empathy and social perspective taking to mental health

For both groups of children studied longitudinally, six scores were derived from the Child Behavior Checklist. Three focused on social competence: (1) involvement in activities (e.g., participation and skill in sports); (2) social relations (e.g., number of close friends and frequency of contact; getting along with family and friends); and (3) school adjustment (i.e., primarily focused on academic performance). The three other scores focused on behavior problems: (1) internalization problems (e.g., shy; lonely; fearful; obsessive); (2) externalization problems (impulsive or acts without thinking; argues; disobedient; destroys things); and (3) total number of problems. To reflect age and sex differences in the prevalence and patterning of behaviors, separate editions of the Child Behavior Profile were developed and standardized for each sex at ages 6–11 and 12–16; thus normalized T-scores could be used.

In separate analyses, the Bryant (1982) index of empathy and the Rothenberg

(1970) measure of social perspective taking were each tested as a predictor of the mental health/social adjustment scores after partialing sex, family size, sex-of-sibling, and socioeconomic status (using Hollingshead, 1965). Empathy and social perspective–taking scores were obtained at both data gatherings, but the mental health/social adjustment scores were obtained at only the follow-up periods. Empathy or social perspective taking at one age was always partialed when considering the predictive power of empathy or social perspective taking, respectively, at the second age.

Several significant relationships were found between empathy and the indices of mental health, whereas only one significant relationship was found between social perspective taking and these measures. Given the 48 regressions run (24 for social perspective taking and 24 for empathy), social perspective taking was related to mental health no more than one would expect by chance. In other words, children's reported level of empathy was related to their mental health status as judged by mothers, whereas their social perspective taking was not. These findings provided a clear signal that there is a meaningful difference in the mental health implications for the constructs of empathy and social perspective taking.

Concurrent rather than earlier empathy was a better predictor of mental health at both ages 10 and 14, and, with increasing age, empathy predicted more aspects of mental health. Empathy at age 7 was not predictive of any of the Achenbach mental health scores at age 10. At age 10, however, concurrent empathy interacted with the sex of the child to predict both externalization and total number of behavior problems. In both instances, girls' empathy scores were significantly and positively related to the externalization of problems and the total number of behavioral problems, whereas this was not the case for boys. High-empathy girls, however, did not have more problems than high-empathy boys. In other words, 10-year-old, low-empathy girls were unlikely to externalize their feelings behaviorally. In addition, empathy at age 10 tended ($p < .06$) to predict social competence in terms of social relations at age 14 for both sexes. At age 14, concurrent empathy was also significantly and positively related to social relations for both sexes. Partialing procedures reveal that the earlier positive relation between empathy at age 10 and social relations at age 14 is not redundant with the concurrent result, and this makes it very likely that a different group of children contributed to each of these obtained associations.

In other words, we may surmise that empathy is related to mental health differentially according to the age and sex of the child. At the beginning of middle childhood there is no documented relationship between empathy and mental health. By age 10, sex differences in the relation of empathy and mental health indices occur. At this age, girls who report high empathy also tend to be less stereotypically sex typed in the degree to which they externalize their thoughts and feelings since they are not as passive in their expression of feelings as are low-empathy girls. In addition, high empathic arousal among 10-year-old girls is linked to the externalization of feelings to the same degree that is is common for 10-year-old boys, irrespective of empathic arousal. This is not to say that these highly empathic girls look like boys because the externalization factors of the two sexes have some differences in loadings, but externalization problems, in general, are more characteristic of boys than girls (Achenbach & Edelbrock, 1981). One could say that some distress reflected in higher externalization scores is linked to being empathic for 10-year-old girls. By adolescence, however, this early distress related to empathy for girls at age 10 is no longer present and the empathy for these girls, as for boys, even tends to be positively related to enhanced social relations.

Finally, during adolescence itself, empathic experiences among both males and females are clearly positively related to enhanced social relations. In contrast to our traditional view that maturity (i.e., the developmental goal) connotes a separate and detached self-sufficiency, with emotional attachments and interpersonal interdependencies having negative connotations (Gilligan, 1982), the present findings are consistent with the view that adolescents are at risk when they are emotionally detached.

In sum, the present study provides evidence that empathy plays an important role in mental health, particulary as children travel through middle childhood into adolescence. Some emotional distress was observed in one group of children (i.e., 10-year-old girls), although this distress showed no signs of carrying over into adolescence. The lack of relationship between social perspective taking and mental health in this study cautions us that social perspective taking is distinct from empathy. Replication and extension of these findings linking empathy and social perspective taking to indices of mental health are clearly needed.

Child characteristics in relation to empathy and social perspective taking

Researchers are becoming increasingly sensitive to the need for information on both child characteristics and environmental factors as they operate together in the expression of social-emotional functioning and development (Parke, 1985). In this section I examine age, sex, and temperament of children in relation to empathy and social perspective taking.

Age and sex are two child characteristics that have typically received attention. In cross-sectional designs, social perspective taking has been clearly linked with the age but not the sex of the child (Bryant, 1985; Rothenberg, 1970).

Increasing age is associated with increasing social perspective–taking skill. These findings are consistent with those of the present longitudinal study. In the present study, social perspective taking increases significantly from age 7 to age 10, $t(66) = 12.68$, $p < .001$, and from age 10 to 14, $t(72) = 5.92$, $p < .001$. The mean of the younger sample changed from 9.32 (SD = 4.13) to 19.48 (SD = 6.20) over the 3-year testing interval and the mean of the older sample changed from 18.56 (SD = 6.27) to 23.62 (SD = 6.11) over the 4-year testing interval.

On the other hand, sex but not age has been linked to empathic arousal when researchers have used both the child (Bryant, 1982) and the adult version (Mehrabian and Epstein, 1972) of this measure of empathy. With the exception of one sample of 6-year-olds obtained by Strayer (1983) in which there were no sex differences, females of all ages score higher in overall empathy than males on this measure (Barnett, Howard, King, & Dino, 1981; Bryant, 1982; Kalliopuska, 1983; Mehrabian & Epstein, 1972). When cross-sectional designs are used, it is unclear whether age is related to any systematic increase in empathy (Bryant, 1982; Strayer, 1983; Sturtevant, 1985). The present longitudinal analysis of empathy in the same children over time indicates that empathy does not increase from age 7 to 10, but does so from age 10 to 14, $t(72) = 2.59$, $p < .05$. However, this change reflects a miniscule amount of variance given the small mean differences at age 10 (mean = 13.86, SD = 3.16) versus at age 14 (mean = 15.03, SD = 3.15). In view of these longitudinal data plus previously cited cross-sectional data pertaining to the differential responding of different aged children to cross-sex stimuli (Bryant, 1982) and the different factor structures of 7-, 10- and 14-year-olds (Bryant, 1984), the development of empathy appears more characteristically to entail a change in the particular stimuli to which one is emotionally responsive rather than an absolute increase in the number of stimuli that elicit empathy per se.

Temperament is a third child factor that has been considered particularly crucial to aspects of children's initial expression of social-emotional functioning (Campos, Barrett, Lamb, Goldsmith, & Sternberg, 1983), and it appears that the parental assessment of children's temperament is meaningful in predicting their social adjustment (Bates, 1987). The relation of temperament to empathy and social perspective taking had received some attention from Strayer (1983), who found that parents judged empathic children easy to get along with and teachers judged them independent, characteristics that may facilitate competent functioning in family and school settings, respectively. No apparent relationship between temperament and social perspective–taking ability was found by Strayer.

In the present study, temperament and temperament-like variables were assessed in three ways. First, mothers judged the temperament of their 7-year-olds according to the nine categories (e.g., rhythmicity, intensity of response, persistence, and distractibility) specified in the measure developed for parents by Thomas and Chess (1977). Second, mothers judged their children's general style of expressing happy, sad, angry, and worried feelings according to whether they internalized or externalized their expression of these feelings (a sum score was calculated, and a high score indicated high externalization). Third, mothers, fathers, and siblings judged (5-point rating) how easy or difficult it was to tell when the target children were experiencing happiness, sadness, anger, worry, and fear. Again, a sum score was calculated, a high score indicating greater perceived readability of children's emotional experiences. Although it would be conceptually ideal to think that each of these measures taps intrinsic child characteristics, extensive research on the measurement of temperament in infancy cautions us that it is more accurate to say that we are measuring the *caregiver's* experience of child characteristics (Crockenberg & Acredolo, 1983).

To assess the specific predictive value of components of children's temperament, empathy and social perspective taking were separately regressed on each category of temperament identified above in separate hierarchical regressions. Sex of child, family size, and age (when the design allowed for it) were considered possible moderating factors as they have previously been found to function in this way in relation to environmental factors and empathy and/or social perspective taking (Bryant, 1985). The sex of the older sibling was included as a control because it would become a salient factor in later analyses. Socioeconomic status (SES) was included as a control factor so as not to confound family size effects with SES and because it has previously been found to be related to social perspective taking (Bryant, 1985). In each of these regressions, sex of child, family size, sex of older sib, and socioeconomic status were entered simultaneously in a first step. The temperament variable was then entered, followed in subsequent steps by entry of three two-way interactions – sex of the child by temperament, family size by temperament, and sex of child by family size. Finally, one three-way interaction was entered – sex of child by family size by temperament.

This model was broadened for the concurrent regressions using either externalization or one of the three readability-of-emotions ratings as the temperament variable. The age-by-temperament interaction was included among the two-way interactions, and sex by age by temperament, age by family size by temperament, and sex by age by family size were included among the three-way interactions. Finally, one four-way interaction was added – sex of child by age by family size by temperament. Thus, the role of temperament as a main effect or as one of several other child and/or environmental factors in predicting empathy and social perspective taking was considered.

In all, 60 regressions (30 for empathy and 30 for social perspective taking) were run to test the role of temperament in concurrent and longitudinal prediction of empathy and social perspective taking. This included nine temperament variables (see Thomas & Chess, 1977) assessed only for the original 7-year-olds, one temperament variable of internal/externalization of feelings assessed for both samples in the first phase of data collection, and three scores (that of mothers, fathers, and siblings) of readability of the child's feelings, which were also assessed for both samples in the first phase of data collection. Concurrent and longitudinal analyses were made on all these variables. Thus, the role of the Thomas, Chess, and Birch (1968) temperament variables in the expression and development of empathy and social perspective taking was analyzed in 36 regressions (18 consider concurrent relations of these aspects of temperament with empathy and social perspective taking and another 18 consider longitudinal prediction of empathy and social perspective taking.) The roles of general internal/externalization of feelings and the three readability-of-feelings variables in the development of empathy and social perspective taking were analyzed in 24 regressions: 8 (4 for empathy and 4 for social perspective taking) pertained to current relations for the 7- and 10-year-olds combined; 8 (4 for empathy and 4 for social perspective taking) to the longitudinal analyses of 7-year-olds followed up at age 10; and 8 more (4 for empathy and 4 for social perspective taking) to the longitudinal analyses of 10-year-olds followed up at age 14.

Given the number of regressions run, the two significant findings obtained relating temperament to social perspective taking must be considered chance findings. In contrast, there were 11 significant findings relating others' experience of the child's temperament to empathy. Only 7 of these are presented here, as the interactions with family size become too unwieldy to cover in this chapter. Also excluded from the discussion below but listed in the appendix to this chapter are those significant interactions in which the slope between temperament and empathy failed to reach significance for any subgroup involved in the interaction. That is, the differences in slopes were significant despite the fact that no slope was significantly nonzero. These are not discussed here as they take considerable space to explain and do not, in any straightforward way, allow for meaningful discussion in nonstatistical terms.

With respect to the Thomas, Chess, and Birch (1968) dimensions of temperament and concurrent assessment for the 7-years-olds, distractibility was negatively related to empathy, $F(1,61) = 4.02$, $pr^2 = .01$, $p < .05$. Low distractibility has been viewed as not easily soothed when upset (Bates, 1987; Thomas & Chess, 1977) or not easily deterred from one's ongoing affective involvement (Thomas & Chess, 1977). Thus, being able to focus on feeling (e.g., wants, anger, sadness) without being distracted at age 7 appears to be a precursor to the development of empathic experiencing later in middle childhood. Perhaps early low distractibility helps facilitate the development of a tolerance for unpleasant feelings such that, over time, one can tolerate experiencing the unpleasant affect of others as well.

Intensity of response at age 7 interacted with the sex of the child to predict empathy at age 10, $F(1,57) = 4.28$, $pr^2 = .06$, $p < .05$. Strong intensity of response was related to high empathy for girls, $F(1,29) = 5.99$, $p < .05$, whereas for boys there was no relation between intensity and empathy. Young girls who are highly intense emotionally and not easily soothed or distracted are subsequently prone to high empathy. This style of emotional intensity characteristic of empathic 10-year-old girls may also account for the positive relationship between empathy and externalization-type behavioral problems found for this group of children (noted in the previous section).

With respect to the general style of externalizing or internalizing the expression of feelings, externalizing of feelings at age 10 interacted with the sex of the child to predict empathy scores at age 14, $F(1,66) = 9.79$, $pr^2 = .09$, $p < .01$, and this relation was significant and negative for boys, $F(1,31) = 6.92$, $p < .05$, but negligible for girls. This is further evidence that temperament differentially relates to empathy among males and females. This finding is also further evidence that, with age, the relationship between temperament and empathy becomes increasingly linked to the sex of the child. Further research is needed to clarify the processes by which this occurs.

Finally, with respect to clarity by which children express a range of emotions to others, no concurrent relation was found. However, paternal and older sibling ability to read the child's feelings at age 7 each had a straightforward and positive relation to empathy at age 10, $F(1,60) = 9.72$, $pr^2 = .11$, and 8.31, $pr^2 = .10$, respectively, $p < .01$. It appears that early affective expressiveness toward fathers and siblings positively relates to later empathy. The lack of relationship between mother's rating of the child's expressiveness is not due to any apparent measurement artifact as the distribution of mothers' ability to read their children's feelings is comparable to that of fathers and siblings. No ceiling effect for maternal scores was operating. Since this relationship does not hold for mothers' reported ease of knowing what their children are feeling, the relationship between early emotional expressiveness and later empathy does not seem to be a direct one. Rather, these findings suggest that the social relationships between 7-year-old children and their fathers and siblings are influenced by the emotional expressiveness of the child to select individuals or emotional sensitivity of fathers and older siblings, which in turns affects their subsequent development of empathy.

In sum, social perspective taking and empathy are differentially related to the child characteristics studied. Social perspective taking is related to the age but not to the sex or temperament of the child, and this holds from the beginning of middle childhood through early adolescence. The degree of empathy, on the other hand, is related to the sex and the temperament but not to the age of the child. This is further indication not only that empathy is distinct from social perspective taking, but also that early emotional connectedness to fathers and older siblings affects later emotional connectedness to others during middle childhood.

Interpersonal experiences related to empathy and social perspective taking

Specific child characteristics may directly or indirectly affect empathic or social perspective–taking development, and one vehicle for such effects is interpersonal interchanges. Although this study does not focus on this complex of interactions per se, a range of interpersonal experiences is examined in relation to the expression and development of empathy and social perspective taking. Although experiences with family members are the primary focus of the following analyses, some consideration is also given to the effects of familiar persons in the extended family as well as individuals outside the family. Two specific sets of measures were used to examine experiences in the family, one from the child's perspective and the other from the perspective of the caretaker. Children's experiences with mothers, fathers, and siblings 2 to 3 years older than the target child are considered first.

A modified version of the Cornell Parent Behavior Inventory (Devereux, Bronfenbrenner, & Rodgers, 1969) was used to generate data pertaining to caretaker practices from the child's perspective. Variables were determined by factor analyses of children's perceptions of caretaking by mothers, fathers, and older siblings (the details of these factor characteristics are presented in Bryant, in press). The three maternal caretaking dimensions were support, punishment, and concern. The four paternal caretaking dimensions were support, punishment, protectiveness, and indulgence. The four sibling caretaking dimensions were nurturance, challenge, punishment, and concern.

The second set of caretaking practices data took the perspective of each caretaker (i.e., mother, father, and older sibling) separately. Two scores focused on how caretakers tried to respond to children's ordinary stressful experiences, that is, instances of feeling sad, angry, worried, frustrated, disappointed, and afraid. Of the six responses that were rank-ordered for each affective experience, two were analyzed for this presentation: one was clearly expressive (i.e., "Generally talk and reflect that the child is upset") and the other was clearly instrumental (i.e., "Give help or advice for getting rid of the immediate upset feelings"). The number of times the expressive response was ranked as the first response to each of these six stressful experiences determined the expressive score and the number of times the instrumental response was ranked first determined the instrumental score.

Two more scores were determined for each caretaker on the basis of additional structured interview data developed by Rosen (personal communication, 1975). The first assessed their degree of limit-setting behavior, scored according to how frequently the caretaker gave attention to correcting the target child in seven different areas of functioning (i.e., misbehavior in the home or school; having the wrong kind of friends; failing to get along with other kids who are or are not relatives; carelessness about personal appearances; poor school work; and poor use of spare time). The second score assessed the extent of caretakers' participation with the target child in the pleasurable activities of having heart-to-heart talks, sitting down for meals together, having leisure time activities together, and hugging and kissing one another. Guttman consistency coefficients of reliability were calculated for the measures of limit-setting and pleasurable activities. Coefficients for limit setting based on the entire sample ranged from .65 for siblings to .67 for fathers to .70 for mothers. Consistency coefficients for pleasurable activities were .42 for mothers, .50 for fathers, and .57 for siblings. The lower coefficient for maternal consistency is attributable to extremely skewed distribution of two aspects of maternal participation in pleasurable activities (i.e., meals together and hugging and kissing), whereas the problem of skewness existed for only one paternal and sibling item (i.e., meals together).

Finally, four kinds of scores involved both family members and others in the extended family or in the child's community: (1) casual acquaintances with others, recorded according to peer, pet, parent, and grandparent generation; (2) involvement in intimate talks, also recorded according to peer, pet, parent, and grandparent generation; (3) participation with peers in informal meeting places (e.g., going over to other kids' homes to play); and (4) participation with peers in formally sponsored organizations with unstructured activities (e.g., community park; swimming pool). The development and reliability of these measures are presented in detail in Bryant (1985).

Rather than present the results measure by measure, I have organized them according to types of involvement with others: peer generation, parent generation, grandparent generation, and pets. The approach to data analysis was the same as that described for assessing the predictive power of temperament in relation to empathy and social perspective taking. In concurrent analyses where data from 7- and 10-year-olds were combined, age was included as a main effect and in interaction with the other variables. In those measures involving mother, father, and older sibling caretaking, sex of older sibling was also used as a control and as part of the interactions. It was necessary to use sex of sibling in the sibling analyses to know about brothers as compared to sisters, and it provided an opportunity in the analyses of parenting factors to consider family dynamics involving a parent and two of their children (the target child and the older sibling). Bryant (in press) describes the full model in detail.

Peer generation involvement (sibling relationships emphasized)

It has been theorized that peer relations are central to the development of taking the perspective of others (Damon, 1984; Piaget, 1932/1965). The extent to which they are in fact central to the development of social perspective taking and/or empathy is not known.

Neither peer nor sibling involvement in this study predicted empathy. Only two relationships were statistically significant and, given the 36 regression analyses run when considering 4 caretaking variables from the target child's perspective, 4 variables from the older siblings' perspective, and 4 specifically peer variables each analyzed in a current assessment and two longitudinal assessments, the two statistically significant findings obtained could be expected to occur by chance. In contrast, nine significant findings involving peer generation involvement and social perspective taking were found, and these are presented in detail in the following text and in the appendix when no slope in an interaction was significantly nonzero.

It is through conflict, when children disagree with one another, that decentering is thought to occur. If the results of the present research pertaining to children's relations to siblings can be generalized to peers, the role and nature of conflict in peer relations for the development of social perspective taking requires more systematic consideration than has been presumed. Early sibling nurturance (i.e., when the child was 7 years old), not indicators of conflict such as sibling challenge or punishment, predicted the child's later social perspective–taking ability. Specifically, there was a positive relation between receiving sibling nurturance early in middle childhood and social perspective taking later in middle childhood, $F(1,61) = 8.40$, $pr^2 = .11$, $p < .01$. Peer generation conflict did not predict social perspective taking perhaps because sibling relations are not pure peer relations, in that there is greater role asymmetry between siblings than between friends (Brody, Stoneman, & MacKinnon, 1982). In addition, power inequities are less dramatic than in parent–child relations but not as equal as in pure peer relations. Apparently it is not conflict per se that fosters social perspective taking, at least in relations where power asymmetry of any degree exists. Rather, the finding is consistent with the view that social perspective taking develops in relatively low-stress or unthreatening situations characterized by experience with sibling nurturance, at least during middle childhood.

The positive relationship between sibling relations and social perspective taking does not hold if we consider the further development of social perspective taking into adolescence. In fact, if we follow children from middle childhood into adolescence, the role of the peer generation actually appears negative rather than positive. This occurred with respect to older sibling challenge and intimate talks with peers. In particular, experiences at age 10 with older sibling challenge interact with the sex of sibling to predict social perspective–taking ability at age 14, $F(1,64) = 5.52$, $pr^2 = .06$, $p < .05$. The relationship between older sibling challenge and social perspective taking was significant and negative when the older siblings were sisters, $F(1,31) = 5.51$, $p < .05$, and negative but negligible when the older siblings were brothers. Furthermore, contrary to what might be expected as the benefit to perspective taking of sharing peers' perspectives, intimate talks with peers at age 10 also predicted poorer social perspective–taking ability at age 14, $F(1,66) = 5.41$, $pr^2 = .06$, $p < .05$. In other words, in contrast to the expectation from Piaget's theorizing about the role of peer relations in the development of social perspective taking, this documented relationship between experiences in middle childhood and early adolescent development was a negative one, in which more reliance on peers for intimate talks about common childhood stress experiences related to poorer social perspective taking in early adolescence. Therefore, certain aspects of peer generation involvement or unknown related factors during middle childhood probably interfere with the development of social perspective taking during adolescence. Taken together, the findings suggest that, when the peer generation operates during middle childhood in lieu of the adult generation by assuming the role of confidante and/or is a noticeable source of disciplinarian hardship characterized by sibling challenge during middle childhood, the child's social perspective–taking skills are weakly developed by adolescence.

In sum, these peer findings indicate that involvement with one's peer generation is not empirically related to the development of empathy but is significant in relation to the expression and development of social perspective taking during middle childhood. However, involvement with one's peer generation is not unequivocally positive with respect to the development of social perspective–taking ability; that is to say, positive sibling influences occur during the early part of middle childhood and negative influences occur in the transition from middle childhood to adolescence.

Parent generation involvement

The nature of children's involvement with the parent generation was predictive of both their concurrent and longitudinally assessed empathy and social perspective taking. However, the particular aspects of the child's experiences with their parents differed in what exactly predicted empathy in comparison with social perspective taking. Furthermore, the sex of the child interacted with most of the experiences with parents (both fathers and mothers) to predict both empathy and social perspective taking. These findings are discussed in more detail in the next section and in the appendix. Note that only one significant finding pertaining to the parent generation involved adults who were not the child's parents. This factor had to do with the effect of casual relations with adults on perspective taking and is reported in the appendix.

Parental support

It is somewhat of a truism today that principled nurturance will enhance social-emotional development, irrespective of domain. Parental support best describes this prescription for enlightened parenting. In the present study parental support was a factor heavily loaded by items having to do with nurturance (e.g., "she/he comforts me"), principled discipline (e.g., "explains why she/he wants me to do something"), instrumental companionship (e.g., "she/he helps me with homework or lessons if there's something I don't understand"), and consistency of expectation (e.g., "when I do something she/he doesn't like, I know exactly what to expect of him/her"). Contrary to the notion that this enlightened support will promote desirable social-emotional development, extensive relationships between this general style of parental support and both domains of social-emotional functioning of interest here were not found. Children's experience of maternal support was predictive of neither their development of empathy nor social perspective taking; although paternal support was relevant for predicting the development of social perspective taking during middle childhood but not during adolescence, this was not so for empathy. More specifically, concurrent father support was positively correlated with social perspective taking at ages 7 and 10, $F(1,161) = 5.04$, $pr^2 = .02$, $p < .05$. There was also a positive relationship between father support at age 7 and children's social perspective taking at age 10, $F(1,61) = 10.79$, $pr^2 = .14$, $p < .01$. These findings suggest that paternal support is, in one sense, a more salient, treasured, or stress-reducing experience than is maternal support, and as a result children listen and acquire understanding about the perspective of an important other. Furthermore, when this is experienced in middle childhood, it is associated both concurrently and over time (within middle childhood but not into adolescence) with increased understanding of the feelings and motives of others. Given that children typically view fathers as more powerful than mothers (Kagan, 1964), social perspective taking in middle childhood appears enhanced by receiving support from particularly powerful adults. In contrast, general parental support appears to have no bearing on empathic development.

Parental response to children's stressful experiences

Perhaps it is not general parental support during everyday events, but rather parental support during times particularly stressful to children that facilitates social-emotional development. Stress experiences increase self-concern, highlight the need for affective and social skills, and challenge the development of smooth, satisfying patterns of social interaction. Whereas most models of psychopathology take stress to be a critical factor in inducing emotional problems, the effect of the context of stress on healthy development has generally been ignored by both clinical and basic developmental researchers. Most theories of competency development, however, implicate biological and/or psychological processes of stress. Erikson (1950/1963), Piaget (1954), and White (1960) all base their theories of development on notions of the child experiencing stress or crisis that requires some sort of resolution, which in turn evolves into developmental advancement. To investigate the relevance of parental response to children's stressful experiences, expressive (i.e., reflecting with the child about the child's feeling in the stressful situation) and instrumental (i.e., offering help or advice for getting rid of the immediate upset feelings) responses were considered in relation to the development of empathy and social perspective taking.

It was mothers', rather than fathers', reported expressiveness in response to children's stress that appear to facilitate the development of empathy. At both ages 7 and 10, maternal reports of expressive responses to stressful events for children interacted with the sex of the child to predict empathy, $F(1,160) = 5.00$, $pr^2 = .03$, $p < .05$, positively for girls, $F(1,78) = 4.01$, $p < .05$, and negligibly for boys. In addition, mothers' reported expressive responses to children's stressful experiences at age 10 predicted children's subsequent high empathy at age 14, $F(1,67) = 4.22$, $pr^2 = .04$, $p < .05$, and this held for both sexes.

According to these findings. it is not general ongoing parental support but rather mothers' apparent expressive support in situations specifically stressful to children that is conducive to the expression and development of empathy. This picture of mothers focusing on the empathic child's affective state in times of upset is consistent with the obtained relationship between indistractibility and empathy. Both findings highlight the relevance of sustained attention on affective states through either internal or external forces with respect to empathic development. Why paternal report of expressiveness was not predictive of empathy is unexplained. Perhaps fathers' and mothers' reports of their own behavior are not equally valid. Direct observation of fathers and mothers responding to children's stressful experiences is an obvious next step in clarifying these findings.

The relationship between parental expressiveness in stressful situations and social perspective taking differed from that between parental expressiveness and empathy. Mothers' reported intent to respond expressively to the stressful experiences of both 7- and 10-year-olds interacted with the sex of the child to predict social perspective taking, $F(1,160) = 7.47$, $pr^2 = .02$, $p < .01$. The relationship between mothers' reported expressiveness was significantly negative for sons, $F(1,78) = 5.65$, $p < .05$, but negligible for daughters. Fathers' reported expressive responding to the stressful experiences of 7-year-old children interacted with the sex of the child to predict their later social perspective–taking ability at age 10, $F(1,60) = 14.41$, $pr^2 = .18$, $p < .001$. The obtained longitudinal relationship was significant and positive for sons, $F(1,28) = 5.85$, $p < .05$ and significant and negative for daughters, $F(1,29) = 7.70$, $p < .05$. The ability to learn about the feelings and motives of others appears jeopardized if the child's opposite-sex parent focuses discussion on the child's internal feeling states. If it is true that social perspective taking develops in particularly stress-reducing conditions of parental support (i.e., receiving support from the powerful parent), these findings suggest that discussion of the child's feelings is stressful when done with the opposite-sex parent and inhibits the development of social perspective taking. Why this is so is unanswered and may best be understood by looking directly at how men and women, fathers and mothers, actually discuss children's feelings with their children.

Sex-role norms indicate that females are more geared than males to the discussion of feelings and that males, in particular, are uncomfortable with the discussion of intimate feelings (Gilligan, 1982). The findings of the present study suggest that, despite the sex-role norms concerning discussion of feelings, such discussions with the same-sex parent seem useful for both social perspective taking and empathy development during middle childhood. Intimate discussions with the opposite-sex parent appear to be beneficial (assuming a causal relation) over time rather than immediately, at least for boys. This conclusion is based on the finding that discussion of feelings with mothers during middle childhood (i.e., at age 10) does have a positive relation to empathy development for both sexes in adolescence. The reason for this delayed effect among boys, in particular, warrants additional research.

Parental indulgence and protectiveness

Parental intent to support their child's development can often turn into indulgence (e.g., "lets me off lightly when I do something wrong"; "can't bring herself/himself to punish me") and protectiveness (e.g., "won't let me go places because something might happen to me"; "wants to know exactly where I'm going when I go out"). Fathers were uniquely characterized by children (in terms of derived factor structures, see Bryant, in press) according to these dimensions. Paternal indulgence predicted the development of empathy in both longitudinal samples, and paternal protectiveness predicted social perspective taking in the older longitudinal sample.

More specifically, paternal indulgence of 7-year-olds predicted children's poorer empathy at age 10, $F(1,61) = 6.25$, $pr^2 = .08$, $p < .05$. Experiencing paternal indulgence at age 10 interacted with the sex of the child to predict empathy at age 14, $F(1,66) = 10.59$, $pr^2 = .09$, $p < .01$, positively for daughters,

$F(1,32) = 4.28$, $p < .05$, and negatively for sons, $F(1,32) = 4.28$, $p < .05$. The indulgence factor was most heavily loaded by the items, "he lets me off lightly when I do something wrong" and "he cannot bring himself to punish me." In other words, boys who early on experience paternal punishment in connection with wrongdoing are later more empathic; this is true for middle childhood and for early adolescence. Paternal indulgence (or nonindulgence) operates in the same way for girls during middle childhood but in the opposite way if we consider paternal indulgence in response to girls' wrongdoing at age 10 and girls' later empathy scores in early adolescence at age 14. Although paternal disciplinary stress may set the stage for the development of empathy by creating distress in response to a child's wrongdoing – distress that is perhaps designed to have the child think about the distress that the original wrongdoing caused to others – this effect operates only during the first half of middle childhood for girls but on into adolescence for boys in middle childhood. That these paternal effects are present only on the longitudinal data and not the concurrent data informs us of their potential value only over time, and indicates that future research should attempt to clarify how these effects take hold over time differentially for girls and boys.

The relationship between paternal protectiveness and social perspective taking also interacted with the sex of the child, $F(1,66) = 5.95$, $pr^2 = .07$, $p < .05$. Father protectiveness at age 10 predicted boys' poorer social perspective skill at age 14, $F(1,31) = 4.46$, $p < .05$, whereas the effect was nonsignificant for girls. This factor of paternal protectiveness included heavy loadings from items having to do with protectiveness (e.g., "He won't let me go places because something might happen to me"), affective punishment (e.g., "He punishes me by trying to make me feel guilty and ashamed"), and control (e.g., "He wants to know exactly where I am going when I go out"). Thus, paternal protectiveness characterized by attempts to control a boy's personal space and feelings intimately (albeit intrusively) when the child is well into middle childhood is related to lower social perspective taking in early adolescence. The conditions of paternal intimacy and control are unrelated to girls' social-emotional development. Boys in particular and their empathic development appear responsive to nonindulgent fathers, whereas their social perspective–taking development appears at risk when paternal involvement is perceived not simply as nonindulgent in specific times of wrongdoing, but as controlling and protective in general.

Parental punishment

Punitive parenting may or may not be in direct response to a child's wrongdoing. Parental punishment in this study is most heavily loaded by items having to with inflicting physical pain, such as "hitting" and "slapping," and subjecting the child to verbal scolding.

In this regard, maternal punishment at age 7 interacted with the sex of the child to predict social perspective taking at age 10, $F(1,60) = 6.24$, $pr^2 = .90$, $p < .05$. This relationship between maternal punishment and social perspective taking was negative for daughters, $F(1,29) = 5.31$, $p < .05$, but negligible for sons.

Considering the earlier reported results of parental protectiveness with these findings pertaining to punishment, ongoing generally stressful relations with the same-sex parent (i.e., paternal protectiveness for boys and maternal punishment for girls) predicted lower social perspective taking but not empathy at certain times in middle childhood and/or early adolescence. Parental stress associated with indulgence in response to a child's wrongdoing (sometimes only with same-sex parent) predicted empathy and not social perspective taking.

Parental limit setting

At ages 7 and 10, fathers' involvement in limit setting was predictive of high empathy for both sexes, $F(1,160) = 9.56$, $pr^2 = .05$, $p < .01$. Paternal disciplinary stress during middle childhood is associated with greater empathy.

Mothers' limit setting showed effects with their children's empathy and social perspective–taking development only if we also knew how the older sibling behaved in concert with the mother. Longitudinally, the extent to which mothers set limits on their children at age 7 predicted better social perspective taking at age 10, $F(1,58) = 5.36$, $pr^2 = .08$, $p < .05$, for both sexes. In addition, maternal limit setting at age 7 interacted with sex of the older sibling to predict social perspective–taking ability at age 10, $F(1,58) = 6.94$, $pr^2 = .09$, $p < .05$. The relationship between early maternal limit setting and later social perspective taking was especially positive among children with brothers, $F(1,24) = 7.49$, $p < .01$. In this situation, maternal limit setting tended to interact with both sibling punishment and sibling nurturance and sex of sibling to predict social perspective–taking ability, $F(1,56) = 2.46$, $p < .13$ and $F(1,56) = 2.79$, $p < .11$, respectively. In both cases, maternal limit setting tended to be positively correlated with sister involvement, both in terms of punishment, $r(34) = .32$, $p < .06$, and nurturance, $r(34) = 32$, $p < .06$, whereas the relationship between maternal limit setting and older-brother nurturance and punishment of younger sibling was unrelated. In other words, the combination of maternal limit setting and sister intrusiveness interfered with the development of social perspective taking during middle childhood, whereas maternal limit setting, in situations where the behavior of the older sibling remains unrelated to the mother's, enhanced social perspective taking. Furthermore, that social perspective taking develops in relatively low-stress or unthreatening situations is consistent with the finding that maternal limit setting is predictive of greater social perspective taking only when children do not have older sisters joining in with mothers' limit-setting activity by also punishing the target child.

More important, perhaps, these results indicate the value of considering the impact of triadic interaction and varying types of collaborative pressures/ requirements within a family over and above the simple direct effects of parents and/or peer generation individuals on social-emotional development. No clearly interpretable interaction in this regard was found for empathy, although two significant interactions (with ambiguous slopes) between parent and sibling behavior in predicting empathy can be seen in the appendix.

In sum, three parental variables predicted the development of empathy during middle childhood and early adolescence: paternal limit setting, paternal indulgence (or nonindulgence), and maternal expressiveness in response to childhood stresses. Paternal limit setting was concurrently predictive of empathy for both boys and girls at ages 7 and 10. Paternal nonindulgence at age 7 was related to enhanced empathy among both boys and girls at age 10, and the same longitudinal relation held among boys when follow-up work was done from age 10 to 14. In these two respects, empathy appears to be fostered in emotionally ''hot'' situations revolving round aspects of discipline, as suggested by Hoffman (1983). The role of mothers in the development of empathy is more one of stress buffering in the form of acknowledging and, possibly, legitimizing the sustained focus on the child's own feelings of distress. This appears to be the case for girls throughout middle childhood, with lasting effect into adolescence; for boys, this appears to occur only over time in adolescence. Girls' empathy in adolescence also appears to benefit from stress buffering offered by paternal indulgence received at age 10. Children's social perspective taking, on the other hand, did not show such a pattern of relationships to parenting behavior. Principled nurturance provided by fathers was the factor that showed the most pervasive relationship to social perspective taking during middle childhood. Other parental factors of expressiveness, punishment, protectiveness, and limit setting in conjunction with sibling involvement showed unique relations among the two sexes and at different times during middle childhood and early adolescence. Again, there was virtually no overlap in the specific relations found between parenting and empathy as compared to social perspective taking.

Involvement with the ''extended'' family (''pets and grandparents'')

The study of family dynamics need not be limited to the nuclear family. The extended family and its role in social-emotional development also deserves attention. In this study, family and neighborhood pets and grandparents as well as special adults "no longer working" are loosely considered the child's extended family.

Indeed, pets are often viewed as family members so their role in social-emotional development seems relevant. Whereas involvement with pets is predictive of (i.e., correlated with) concurrent expression of empathy at ages 7 and 10 (Bryant, 1985), these experiences did not have any apparent impact on development of empathy over time. Concurrent experiences of intimate talks with pets was associated with more enhanced empathy among 10-year-olds than was true of the 7-year-olds. With respect to social perspective–taking ability, involvement with pets had no predictive power, either concurrently or longitudinally.

Involvement with grandparents at ages 7 and 10 predicted children's concurrent level of empathy and social perspective–taking ability. Involvement at age 7 with grandparent generation predicted later empathy at age 10. However, involvement at age 10 with grandparents or with older adults ("who are no longer working") was not predictive of children's subsequent empathy during adolescence. Social perspective taking in the second half of middle childhood (i.e., age 10) or in adolescence was not related to any of the indices of grandparent involvement when children were 7 or 10 years old, respectively.

Involvement with persons in the grandparents' generation was clearly related to children's expression of empathy at ages 7 and 10. Intimate talks with persons in the grandparents' generation were positively related to expressions of empathy among children of both these ages, $F(1,159) = 5.16$, $pr^2 = .03$, $p < .05$. Clear emotional attachment to persons listed among the 10 most important individuals in the child's life as well as casual knowing and interaction with persons in the grandparent generation both interacted with the sex of the child to predict empathy during middle childhood, $F(1,156) = 8.43$, $pr^2 = .04$, $p < .05$ and $F(1,156) = 5.68$, $pr^2 = .03$, $p < .05$, respectively. Emotional importance of grandparents was positively related, $F(1,76) = 10.94$, $p < .01$, whereas casual knowing and interacting with persons in the grandparent generation was negatively related, $F(1,82) = 4.03$, $p < .05$, to girls' empathy during middle childhood. Neither of these latter grandparent generation factors predicted boys' empathy.

The role of stress-buffering relationships in the expression and development of empathy may well reflect the obtained relationships between experiences with pets and grandparents. This is consistent with the literature that finds grandparents are likely to assume caretaking functions in times of stress or crisis (Albrecht, 1954; Hentig, 1946; Streib, 1958; Tinsley and Parke, 1984) and the research on the stress-buffering role of pets in the lives of the elderly (Lago, Baskey, Green, & Hand, 1982). Both pets and grandparents have been viewed as offering nonjudgmental companionship and delivering unconditional acceptance of persons and their feelings, thereby creating uninterrupted opportunities to explore and acknowledge feelings of selves and others (Bryant, 1985; Lago et al., 1982). This role of stress buffering in fostering empathy needs to be viewed in conjunction with the disciplinarian stress of paternal limit setting and a history of fathers being nonindulgent with respect to the child's obeying the limits. At least, this is the picture for children in middle childhood (i.e., it is based on child experiences at ages 7 and 10, and on child experiences at 7 for empathic development expressed at age 10). Additional research is needed on these matters to inform us about the role of concurrent relations with extended family members in empathy development during adolescence. Meanwhile, it is reasonable to consider the role of pets (i.e., family and neighborhood pets) and grandparents (who in the present samples do not live in the child's household) relevant to children's current functioning in middle childhood but without the socializing power that is suggested by the absence of significant relationships in the longitudinal analyses.

Concurrent versus longitudinal analyses

In reviewing the above findings, I noted that the amount of variance accounted for by individual variables was rather consistently greater in the longitudinal than in the concurrent analyses. This was most notably the case for relationships obtained for the 10-year-olds on the basis of experiences at age 7. More specifically, individual temperament and "family" (including peer involvement) variables accounted for 1–5% of the variance in the concurrent prediction of empathy and social perspective taking, whereas 6–18% of the variance was accounted for by experiences at age 7 in predicting empathy and social perspective taking at age 10, and 4–9% of the variance was accounted for by experiences at age 10 in predicting empathy and social perspective taking at age 14. Since these temperament and family variables are not necessarily independent, however, the variables that reached significance in the earlier analyses were combined into a single hierarchical regression – a reduced or "estimation" model – that cut across the temperament and family variables.

This approach provided six reduced models, three predicting empathy and three predicting social perspective taking. Two were based on concurrent assessments of temperament and family variables in relation to empathy and social perspective taking, two were based on temperament and family variables at age 7 in relation to empathy and social perspective taking at age 10, and two were based on temperament and family variables at age 10 in relation to empathy and social perspective taking at age 14. Entered in the first step of each reduced model were the previously entered control variables of sex of child, age (in concurrent predictions), family size, sex of sibling, and SES, as well as the relevant control variables associated with these selected variables that had attained significance in the individual sets of regressions. Entered in the second step were the specific, select variables that attained significance in the individual, hierarchical regressions.

The total R for the prediction of empathy was .55, $F(13,153) = 5.16$, $p < .001$, in the concurrent analysis; .71, $F(9,53) = 5.93$, $p < .001$, in the analysis of the 7-year-olds followed up at age 10; and .69, $F(9,63) = 6.35$, $p < .001$, in the analysis of the 10-year-olds followed up at age 14. The total R for the prediction of social perspective taking was .74, $F(8,158) = 23.69$, $p < .001$, for the concurrent analysis; .74, $F(12,50) = 4.92$, $p < .001$, for the 7- to 10-year-old follow-up; and .60, $F(9,63) = 3.85$, $p < .001$, for the 10- to 14-year-old follow-up. These findings have three important implications. First, the finding that individual factors were not unduly redundant with one another indicates that the selected network of temperament and family variables in the concurrent at well as the longitudinal samples analyzed added significantly to the predictability of empathy and social perspective taking. Second, the fact that early temperament and family experiences at age 7 are important for later empathic development at age 10 means that empathic responding is not simply a reflection of ongoing life events, but is in part an orientation fostered or hampered by earlier experiences. More longitudinal studies during middle childhood are needed to shed light on the processes by which these early experiences influence later empathic responding. Third, SES is a strong predictor variable of social perspective. SES is a summary variable for many other issues and needs to be explored more carefully in relation to social perspective taking.

Concluding remarks

Empathy should not be equated with social perspective taking either in its function or in its apparent developmental concommitants. In the series of studies presented in this chapter, empathy and social perspective taking were differentially related to individual difference variables such as mental health, age, sex, and temperament. Furthermore, not even one aspect of interpersonal experiences with the peer, parent, grandparent, or pet generation was systematically related to empathy and social perspective taking in the same way. The low-stress context of nurturant sibling relations and principled nurturance in parent–child relations (i.e., parental support) appears particularly central to the development of social perspective taking, and the context of stress appears particularly salient for the development of empathy both in terms of paternal disciplinary stress and in terms of expressive support received from mothers, pets, and/or grandparents directly in response to children's own distress in a stressful situation. The effect of the disciplinary distress is not always immediate and so longitudinal designs are especially important to research in this area. The exact terms of relevant expressive support related to empathy differ according to the age and sex of the child. Direct observation of interpersonal encounters with children in these stressful situations is needed for a more direct validation of the conclusions reported in this chapter. Also needed are research designs that can readily test the cause–effect statements now made on purely correlation data. Finally, additional measures of empathy and social perspective taking need to be applied in comparable studies if we are to delineate further the developmental parameters of empathy and related constructs. In particular, future research needs to examine the effect of adult and peer generation persons on the development of both empathy and social perspective taking.

Appendix A: significant interactions in which no slopes were significantly nonzero

Without significant slopes, the interactions are difficult to interpret accurately. Nonetheless, these interactions can be reliable phenomena and so are reported for reference in future research.

Child temperament

Rhythmicity and persistence at age 7 interacted with the sex of the child to predict empathy at age 10, $F(1,57) = 4.18$ ($pr^2 = .06$) and 4.01 ($pr^2 = .05$), respectively, $p < .05$. Persistence at age 7 was more positively (or less negatively) related to empathy scores at age 10 among girls than among boys. On the other hand, greater regularity (rhythmicity) at age 7 was more positively (or less negatively) related to empathy for boys at age 10 than for girls at the same age.

Peer generation involvement

In the analyses of concurrent effects at ages 7 and 10, sibling concern interacted with sex of older sibling to predict social perspective taking, $F(1,157) = 4.03$, $pr^2 = .01$, $p < .05$. There was a more positive (or less negative) relationship between sibling concern and social perspective taking when the sisters rather than the brothers were showing the concern. In addition, older sibling report of instrumental response to children's stressful experiences interacted with the age of the target child to predict social perspective taking, $F(1,159) = 4.83$, $pr^2 = .02$, $p < .05$. There was a more positive (or less negative) relationship between sibling instrumentality and target child's social perspective–taking ability among the 10-year-olds than among the 7-year-olds. Finally, involvement in organizations with unstructured activities also interacted with age to predict social perspective taking, $F(1,150) = 8.82$, $pr^2 = .03$, $p < .01$. Again, there was a more positive (or less negative) relationship between peer involvement and social perspective taking at age 10 than at age 7.

In contrast, early sibling punishment interacted with sex of sibling to predict later social perspective–taking ability, $F(1,58) = 4.24$, $pr^2 = .06$, $p < .05$, but, in this respect, there was a more negative (or less positive) relationship between early punishment from siblings and social perspective–taking ability when the punishment was delivered by older brothers rather than older sisters. In addition, early experience of older siblings who have the intent of being instrumental in response to common childhood stresses intracted with the sex of the sibling to predict social perspective–taking ability at age 10, $F(1,58) = 4.26$, $pr^2 = .06$, $p < .05$. The relationship between sister instrumentality and social perspective taking was more positive (or less negative) than was true for children with brothers.

Parent generation involvement

The one significant finding concerning the nonparental parent generation was that knowing and interacting with adults at ages 7 and 10 interacted with the sex of the child concurrently to predict the expression of social perspective–taking ability, $F(1,55) = 6.71$, $pr^2 = .02$, $p < .01$. In particular, this relationship was more positive (or less negative) for boys than it was for girls.

Fathers involved in setting limits and engaging in pleasurable activities with their 7-year-old children interacted with the sex of the child to predict empathy at age 10, $F(1,60) = 4.77$, $pr^2 = .06$, $p < .05$ and $F(1,60) = 4.39$, $pr^2 = .06$, $p < .05$, respectively. In each case, the relationship between father involvement and empathy was more positive (or less negative) for daughters than for sons.

Experiences of maternal concern interacted with the sex of the child to predict later empathy, $F(1.66) = 6.14$, $pr^2 = .06$, $p < .05$. The relationship between maternal concern and later empathy was more positive (or less negative) for girls than it was for boys.

Maternal limit setting also interacted with the sex of the child and the sex of the older sibling to predict empathy, $F(1,148) = 4.61$, $pr^2 = .03$, $p < .05$. Children with opposite-sex older siblings had a more negative (or less positive) relationship between maternal limit setting and empathy than did children with same-sex siblings. Follow-up on actual experiences with siblings yielded a tendency for an interaction between maternal limit setting and sibling punishment by sex of child by sex of sibling to predict empathy, $F(1,78) = 2.62$, $p < .11$, among the 10-year-olds. The opposite-sex older siblings of 10-year-olds punished more as mothers set more limits on the younger child [i.e., among boys, the correlation between maternal limit setting and older-sister punishment was $r(22) = .47$, $p < .05$ and, among girls, the correlation between maternal limit setting and older-brother punishment was $r(22) = .41$, $p < .05$. The correlations between maternal limit setting and sibling punishment where the older sibling was the same sex as the younger sibling was .09, n.s.].

Finally, there was an interaction between mothers' reported instrumental response to childhood stresses and sex of the older sibling, $F(1,64) = 7.23$, $pr^2 = .07$, $p < .01$ to predict empathy. The relationship between maternal instrumentality at age 10 and empathy in adolescence was more positive (or less negative) among children with sisters than among those with brothers. Further analysis indicates that maternal instrumentality tended to interact with sibling nurturance and sex of sibling to predict empathy, $F(1,62) = 2.77$, $p < .11$. The relationship between maternal instrumentality and sibling nurturance was more negative where sisters were involved, $r(34) = -.20$, than where brothers were involved, $r(34) = -.09$.

Grandparent generation involvement

With respect to social perspective–taking ability, casual knowing and interacting with, as well as intimate talks with, persons in the grandparent generation both interacted with the sex of the child to predict this ability, $F(1,156) = 5.21$, $pr^2 = .02$, $p < .05$ and $F(1,156) = 9.37$, $pr^2 = .03$, $p < .001$. The relationship between two grandparent-generation factors of involvement and social perspective taking–ability were each more positive (or less negative) for boys than for girls.

References

Achenbach, T. (1978). The child behavior profile: I. Boys aged 6–11. *Journal of Consulting and Clinical Psychology, 46,* 478–488.

Achenbach, T., & Edelbrock, C. (1979). The child behavior profile: II. Boys aged 6–11 and 12–16. *Journal of Consulting and Clinical Psychology, 47,* 223–233.

Achenbach, T., & Edelbrock, C. (1981). Behavioral problems and competencies reported by parents of normal and disturbed children aged 4–16. *Monographs of the Society for Research in Child Development, 46* (1, Serial No. 188).

Albrecht, R. (1954). The parental responsibilities of grandparents. *Marriage and Family Living, 16,* 201–204.

Barnett, M. A., Howard, J. A., King, L. M., & Dino, G. A. (1981). Helping behavior and the transfer of empathy. *The Journal of Social Psychology, 115,* 125–132.

Bates, J. E. (1987). Temperament in infancy. In J. D. Osofsky (Ed.), *Handbook of infant development* (2nd ed). New York: Wiley.

Bem, S. (1975). Sex role adaptability: One consequence of psychological androgyny. *Journal of Personality and Social Psychology, 31,* 634–643.

Brody, G. H., Stoneman, A., & MacKinnon, C. E. (1982). Role asymmetries in interactions among school-aged children, their younger siblings, and their friends. *Child Development, 53,* 1364–1370.

Bryant, B. (1982). An index of empathy for children and adolescents. *Child Development, 53,* 413–425.

Bryant, B. (1984), August). *Self-criticism of the Bryant (1982) empathy index.* In *The construct and assessment of empathy.* Symposium conducted at the annual meeting of the American Psychological Association, Toronto, Canada.

Bryant, B. (1985). The neighborhood walk: Sources of support in middle childhood. *Monographs of the Society for Research in Child Development, 50* (3, Serial No. 210).

Bryant, B. (in press). The child's perspective of sibling caretaking and its relevance to understanding social-emotional functioning and development. In P. Zukow (Ed.), *Sibling interactions across cultures.* New York: Springer-Verlag.

Campos, J. J., Barrett, K. C., Lamb, M. E., Goldsmith, H. H., & Sternberg, G. (1983). Socio-emotional development. In P. H. Mussen (Ed.), *Handbook of child psychology: Vol. 2. Infancy and developmental psychobiology* (pp. 783–915). New York: Wiley.

Crockenberg, S., & Acredolo, C. (1983). Infant temperament ratings: A function of infants, of mothers, or both? *Infant Behavior and Development, 6,* 61–72.

Damon, W. (1984). Peer education: The untapped potential. *Journal of Applied Developmental Psychology, 5,* 331–343.

Devereux, E. C., Bronfenbrenner, U., & Rodgers, R. R. (1969). Child-rearing in England and the United States: A cross-national comparison. *Journal of Marriage and Family, 31,* 257–270.

Edelbrock, C., & Achenbach, T. (1980). A typology of child behavior profile patterns: Distribution and correlates for disturbed children aged 6–16. *Journal of Abnormal Child Psychology, 8* (4), 441–470.

Erikson, E. (1963). *Childhood and society* (2nd ed.). New York: W. W. Norton. (Original work published 1950)

Gilligan, C. (1982). *In a different voice.* Cambridge, MA: Harvard University Press.

Hentig, H. V. (1946). The sociological function of the grandmother. *Social Forces, 24,* 389–392.

Hoffman, M. L. (1983). Affective and cognitive processes in moral internalization. In E. T. Higgins, D. N. Ruble, & W. W. Hartup (Eds.). *Social cognition and social development: A sociocultural perspective* (pp. 236–274). New York: Cambridge University Press.

Hollingshead, A. (1965) *Two factor index of social position.* New Haven, CT: Yale Station.

Kagan, J. (1964). Acquisition and significance of sex typing and sex role identity. In M. L. Hoffman and L. W. Hoffman (Eds.), *Review of child development research* (Vol. 1). New York: Russell Sage.

Kalliopuska, M. (1983). Verbal components of emotional empathy. *Perceptual and Motor Skills, 56,* 487–496.

Lago, D., Baskey, P., Green, C., & Hand, R. (1982). *Do pet companions help when you live alone? Content analysis of a newsletter survey.* Unpublished manuscript from the Companion Animal Project, Pennsylvania State University.

Mehrabian, A., & Epstein, N. (1972). A measure of emotional empathy. *Journal of Personality, 40*(4), 525–543.

Parke, R. D. (1985). Insights from listening to children. Commentary in B. Bryant, The neighborhood walk: Sources of support in middle childhood. *Monographs of the Society for Research in Child Development, 50* (3, Serial No. 210).

Piaget, J. (1954), *The construction of reality by the child.* New York: Basic Books.

Piaget, J. (1965). *The moral judgment of the child.* New York: Free Press (original work published 1932).

Rothenberg, B. (1970). Children's social sensitivity and the relationship to interpersonal competence, intrapersonal comfort and intellectual level. *Developmental Psychology, 2* (3), 335–350.

Strayer, J. (1983, April). *Affective and cognitive components of children's empathy.* Paper presented at the biennial meetings of the Society for Research in Child Development, Detroit, Michigan.

Streib, G. F. (1958). Family patterns in retirement. *Journal of Social Issues, 14,* 46–60.

Sturtevant, A. E. (1985). *The relationship of empathy, mood, prosocial moral reasoning, and altruism in children.* Unpublished doctoral dissertation, New York University.

Tinsley, B. R., & Parke, R. D. (1984). Grandparents as support and socialization agents. In M. Lewis (Ed.), *Beyond the dyad* (pp. 161–194). New York: Plenum.

Thomas, A., & Chess, S. (1977). *Temperament and development.* New York: Brunner/Mazel.

Thomas, A., Chess, S., & Birch, H. (1968). *Temperament and behavior disorders in children.* New York: New York University Press.

Werner, E. E., & Smith, R. S. (1982). *Vulnerable, but invincible: A longitudinal study of resilient children and youth.* New York: McGraw-Hill.

White, R. W. (1960). Competence and the psychosexual stages of development. In M. R. Jones (Ed.), *Nebraskas Symposium on Motivation* (pp. 97–141). Lincoln: University of Nebraska Press.

12 Parental empathy and child adjustment/maladjustment

Norma Deitch Feshbach

The relevance and significance of parental empathy as an important facet of positive parenting is gaining increasing salience in clinical and developmental psychology literature (Goldstein and Michaels, 1985). Parental empathy and related parental attributes such as sympathy, understanding, caring, acceptance, and sensitive parenting are theorized to have positive effects on the child. Conversely, lack of parental empathy, especially in the mother, is conjectured to be responsible for the fragmented self and other forms of psychopathology in the child (Goldberg, 1978; Kohut, 1971). The major aim of this chapter is to explore the theoretical relationship between parental empathy, particularly maternal empathy, and child adjustment and to report preliminary findings from two recent research projects that are pertinent to this association.

Since Freud (1925) first heightened our consciousness of the importance of the early experiences of the child, there have been many efforts to relate parental practices and attitudes to child behaviors and outcomes. Initial theorizing and data gathering regarding these early influences occurred in the context of psychotherapy, especially psychoanalysis. Through free association, interpretation, and reconstruction, many hypotheses were formulated. Maternal behavior, in particular, was conceptualized as having significant and possibly irreversible effects on the psychological development of the child. How and when the mother fed her child, and how she carried out other child-rearing tasks relevant to toilet training, modesty training, and control of aggressive and dependency needs explained the development of the normal personality and the abnormal personality.

An important assumption implicit in these early formulations, and more clearly and fully articulated in the quantified and the more behavioral efforts that followed (Maccoby & Martin, 1983; Sears, Maccoby, & Levin, 1957), was the notion that cold, rejecting parenting was counterproductive to the development of a well-adjusted child and well-adjusted adult. Conversely, a warm, tuned-in, responsive mother, was viewed as being facilitative to the emergence of a psychologically healthy child and subsequently a well-adjusted adult. By and large, the research efforts directed toward establishing empirical validation of hy-

271

potheses linking specific parental antecedents to specific development outcomes have yielded equivocal findings. The efforts relating broader parenting styles to child indices have, in general, been more revealing.

This body of theory and research was not directed specifically to the construct of parental empathy, even though parental variables such as warmth and sensitivity to the child are related to, or are aspects of, empathic responsiveness to the child (Clarke-Stewart, 1973). Even in contemporary literature there are few studies that directly link parental empathy as such to child behavior and development. The breadth of the construct and its diverse theoretical interpretations make it difficult to investigate this process with precision. A related problem is the challenge posed by the need for targeted measures of this attribute/process. Also, since the study of empathy in a socialization framework is relatively recent, I cite empirical literature that deals with parental attributes that are related but not equivalent to empathy. These attributes also tend to be broad in nature.

The construct of empathy

Conceptions of empathy have varied greatly. Empathy is sometimes conceived of as a sympathetic reaction to distress. Also, more broadly, it is said to reflect social understanding and emotional identification. A critical element in cognitive approaches to empathy is the acquisition of social empathy through role taking and imitation (Mead, 1934). Although Mead suggested that empathy involved feeling as well as thinking, it was the latter component that was predominant in his conceptualization of the term. Mead's attention to the activity of role playing anticipated an essential feature of cognitive definitions and explanations of the phenomenon of empathy (Borke, 1971; Chandler, Greenspan, & Barenboim, 1974; Deutsch & Madle, 1975; Hogan, 1969; Shantz, 1975). Although there are a number of different versions of affective approaches to empathy, the requirement of an affective correspondence between the emotional experience of an observer and the observed is, from my perspective, a critical dimension of the empathic response, distinguishing affective approaches to empathy from those employing predominantly cognitive criteria (Berger, 1962; Feshbach, 1975; Feshbach & Roe, 1968; McDougall, 1908; Stotland, 1969; Sullivan, 1953). This requirement of an affective correspondence does not imply that cognitive processes are unimportant in empathy. In fact, the most prevailing current view holds that empathy entails both affective and cognitive elements, the relative role of each varying with the situation and the age and personality of the child or adult (Feshbach, 1973b, 1978b, 1982; Hoffman, 1977, 1982).

The model of empathy that evolved from and guided my research in this area defines empathy as a shared emotional response that is contingent upon cognitive factors. In this integrative–affective model, the affective empathy reaction is postulated to be a function of three factors: (1) the cognitive ability to discriminate affective cues in others, (2) the more mature cognitive skills entailed in assuming the perspective and role of another person, and (3) emotional responsiveness, that is, the affective ability to experience emotions (Feshbach, 1973b, 1975, 1978b; Feshbach and Feshbach, 1969; Feshbach and Kuchenbecker, 1974; Feshbach and Roe, 1968). Implicit in this and other models of empathy is the critical requirement of differentiation of self from object.

Hoffman's (1977) subsequent developmental model of empathy also has three components – cognitive, affective, and motivational – and focuses on empathic responses to distress in others as the motivation for altruistic behaviors. For Hoffman, empathic arousal is already reflected in infant behavior, and although empathic behavior is primarily affective, it subsequently becomes transformed when the cognitive system of the child develops and is afforded a strong role (Hoffman, 1977).

Parental empathy and child adjustment: a theoretical framework

Overview

In both the Feshbach and Hoffman models, empathy is conceived to be the outcome of cognitive and affective processes that operate conjointly. Given the emphasis on elements of emotional sensitivity and discrimination, and on emotional responsiveness as well as role taking, one can anticipate that empathy in a parent will be associated with a range of other parental attributes. Thus, although warmth is not a defining criterion of empathy, parental warmth is likely to be closely associated with parental empathy. The parent who is empathic with his or her child is attending to the child's point of view and feelings, and is able to understand and share these feelings. These behaviors and attributes are not likely to be displayed by parents judged to be cold on the parental warmth–coldness dimension. Similarly, one can anticipate that the parent who lacks empathy would be less emotionally involved in his or her children and less attentive to satisfying their needs. Theoretically, empathy should foster close relationships between parent and child. Shared experiences tend to sustain and contribute to social bonds, and this should be the case for shared emotional experiences. In addition, the empathic response of the parent is probably experienced by the child as a form of validation, a sense of being understood. This kind of reinforcing experience should enhance the child's attachment to the parent. Thus, it appears likely that there is a reciprocal, mutual, sustaining interaction between empathy and the strength of the attachment relationship between parent and child (Feshbach and Feshbach, 1982). Empathy, then, in addition to directly influencing the child's development and adjustment, can influence the child indirectly through its relationship to parent attributes, such as parental warmth and involvement in child rearing, and through the effect of these latter attributes on the child's adjustment.

Theoretical background

The notion of an empathic response functioning as a positive, validating experience for the individual who is the object of empathy is, of course, a basic tenet in Rogerian client-centered therapy (Rogers, 1951; Rogers & Truax, 1967; Truax, 1972). For Rogerian therapists, the process of empathy is central to the therapist–client interaction and relationship. In the Rogerian framework, empathy also plays a critical role in the nature of the parent–child relationship. A parent who can simultaneously express disapproval of an unacceptable action of a child and also convey understanding of the child's perspective and feelings is communicating a fundamental acceptance of the child ("unconditional positive regard"). According to Rogers, the child is then able to acknowledge disapproved impulses while still feeling loved.

A number of psychoanalytically oriented therapists have also called attention to the reinforcing properties of parental empathy and its significance for the child's development. Sullivan (1953) sees mother and infant bound together in a mutually empathic relationship. Sullivan suggests that maternal empathy is manifested in the mother's display of tenderness to her child and in her sensitivity to her child's needs. Object-relation theorists (Winnicott, 1965, 1970) attribute a similar importance to maternal empathy during the early infancy period. There is some debate among the object-relations group regarding the mechanisms mediating maternal empathy. Whereas Winnicott (1965) proposes that the mother is regressively relying on her own early childhood experience as a basis for empathy with her baby, Kaplan (1983) has argued that parental empathy can and should reflect maturity and competence in differentiation from the infant, rather than psychological regression, projection, and dependency.

Perhaps the most extensive treatment of empathy by a psychoanalytic writer is that of Heinz Kohut (1977). The views of Kohut and Rogers are strikingly similar in this regard, although they differ in emphasis and in theoretical context. For Kohut, the maternal empathic response functions as a "mirror" for the child's manifestation of narcissistic grandiosity. This mirroring enables the child to identify with the validating parent, thus facilitating the vicarious acception and assimilation of feelings of grandiosity, and leads to heightened self-esteem in the child. The therapist, when treating patients with fragmented self, the so-called narcissistic personality, responds to the patient's feelings of vulnerability and grandiosity with empathy. This process is referred to as "mirror transference" and is believed to provide a mechanism by which the patient learns to accept formerly rejected narcissistic impulses and to develop internalized controls. Kohut (1978) writes:

> Mirror transference is the reinstatement of the phase in which the gleam in the mother's eye, which mirrors the child's exhibitionistic display and other forms of maternal participation in the child's narcissistic enjoyment, confirms the child's self esteem and by a gradual increasing selectivity of these responses begins to channel it into realistic directions. (p. 489)

For Kohut, as for Sullivan, empathy is a primitive reaction and mode of comprehension of which infants as well as adults are capable. He asserts, ''This primary empathy with the mother prepares us for the recognition that to a large extent the basic inner experience of other people remains similar to our own . . . Nonempathic forms of cognitions are dominant in the adult. Empathy must thus often be achieved specifically before nonempathic modes of observations are interposed'' (Kohut, 1978; pp. 451–452). Whether this concept of a primitive form of empathy that requires minimal cognitive competencies for the apprehension of the affective state of others has some validity is a question that lies outside the scope of the present chapter. I have argued elsewhere that these ''primitive'' forms of ''empathic understanding'' are probably precursors of empathy that are contingent upon affect discrimination and perspective-taking competencies as well as emotional responsiveness. For the present purpose, what is most relevant is the consensus by Kohut and other psychoanalytic writers that parental empathy is of crucial importance to the psychological development of the child. Parental empathy should foster positive psychological development in the child, and the lack of parental empathy should be associated with the development of maladaptive behavior patterns. Thus, parental empathy can influence the child's development and adjustment through validation and reinforcement of the child's experiences, thereby facilitating a secure attachment to the parent. Also, parents who lack empathy are less sensitive to their child's feelings and needs. If a parent is insensitive to a child's feelings or desires, these needs are less likely to be met, even when the parent may wish to meet them. Consequently, one can expect that children will experience a considerable degree of frustration and feelings of not being understood if they are reared in households with nonempathic parents.

Nonempathic parents are likely to have nonempathic offspring. In addition to transmitting empathy to the child through the process of modeling, the empathic parent is likely to be more accepting of the child's feelings and to reinforce specifically empathic responses on the part of the child. Many researchers in this field believe that empathy in the child is correlated with prosocial behavior. There is empirical evidence to support this expectation (Feshbach, 1980, 1982; Feshbach and Feshbach, 1986; Goldstein and Michaels, 1985). The empathic child is likely to be sensitive to the feelings of other children, more able to understand the other child's perspective in conflict situations, and therefore more likely to be generous and cooperative and less aggressive than children low in empathy (Feshbach and Feshbach, 1969). Consequently, another factor linking parental empathy and positive adjustment in the child is stimulation and reinforcement of the child's empathic behavior.

The relationship between parental empathy and child adjustment cannot be adequately examined without considering the phenomenon of physical child abuse. A history of being reared in a physically abusive household is a major predictor of child maladjustment, and there are significant theoretical and empirical reasons to anticipate that parents low in empathy are more likely to engage in physical abuse of the child than parents high in empathy. The empathic parent, by virtue of greater understanding of a child's perspective and feelings, is less likely to misunderstand potential conflict situations. Consequently, there is a lower probability of abuse induced by conflict and misunderstanding in families where the parents are empathic.

Misunderstandings are not the only antecedent of child abuse. A parent burdened with stress or who lacks the skills necessary to modify the child's aversive behavior is disposed to child abuse. However, there is a criticial emotional element in empathy, manifested in the vicarious sharing of another's feelings that should reduce the likelihood of parental abuse. Empathic parents should vicariously experience some degree of the pain and distress of the child who in the object of the physical violence. This empathic response should inhibit abusive behavior in the parent since the abuse, by virtue of empathy, pains the parent as well as the child. The parent low in empathy is less likely to be upset by a maltreated child's distress and is more likely to misunderstand the situation that gave rise to the child's behavior.

A summary model

According to the theoretical analysis that has been presented, parental empathy should have a significant positive role in the socialization process and should facilitate the development of adaptive, positive behavior. However, empathy is not necessarily an "all-embracing good." There are circumstances under which empathy can have negative consequences for a child's development (Feshbach, 1980; Kaplan, 1983). Empathy can be damaging if it is excessive and blocks the parent from engaging in appropriate child-training behaviors that may cause the child some distress or if it fosters intrusiveness into the child's experiences and activities. Empathy can also have deleterious effects if it reflects lack of differentiation between the child and parent. If a parent's emotional reactions are essentially self-centered rather than child-centered, the process may not be empathy but symbiosis.

One might argue that narcissistically based and excessive empathy should be distinguised from "true" empathy. However, the fact remains that there are circumstances under which empathylike responses can reflect pathological rather than constructive emotional processes. In addition, in order to have major child-rearing influence, parental empathy should be coupled with behaviors that reflect sensitivity and understanding. Despite these caveats, one should expect parental empathy to be positively correlated with child adjustment. This hypothesis is based on the several direct and indirect routes that have been described by which parental empathy should enhance the child's psychological development. A schematic illustration of these routes or influences is presented in Figures 12.1 and 12.2.

Several features of these diagrams warrant special comment. The intersecting circles are intended to convey the assumption that parental empathy does not exist in isolation from other parental attributes. Parental empathy is not merely correlated with parental warmth, sensitivity, and involvement with the child. Realistically, it is difficult to conceive of an empathic parent who would not display these other attributes. The converse is less likely to be true. Although an association would be expected between low empathy and low parental sensitivity/low parental involvement, there are undoubtedly many parents who are involved with and sensitive to their child who may not be particularly empathic. Thus, Figure 12.2, although in many ways a mirror of Figure 12.1, is not completely so. One notes also that a stronger empirical association is anticipated between maladjustment in the child and low parental empathy and related correlates than between healthy adjustment and empathy. Similarly, a strong association is anticipated between maladjustment and disturbances in the attachment relationship. Also noteworthy is the proposition implied from the diagrams that the absence or inhibition of child abuse is not predictive of the child's adjustment whereas the presence of child abuse is strongly related to the development of maladaptive behavior patterns.

The variables and interactions depicted in the figures are intended to be schematic rather than exhaustive. Figures 12.1 and 12.2 are not intended to convey a comprehensive description of parental socialization, or of the antecedents of child maladjustment or of the antecedents of physical child abuse.

Research is needed to provide data bearing on the specific hypotheses and interactions conveyed in Figures 12.1 and 12.2, and to supplement the relatively few data available regarding parental behavior correlates of parental empathy. As Goldstein and Michaels (1985) note in their review of the extant literature, "There is little existing research addressing the question of what qualities in the

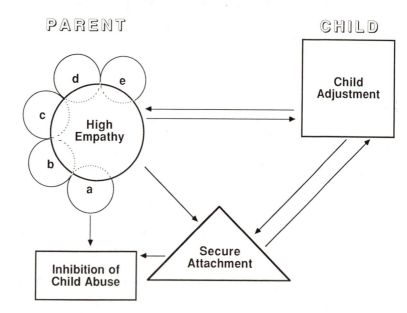

Figure 12.1. A Schematic illustration of the multiconceptual interplay between high parent empathy and child adjustment: (a) parental warmth, (b) parental nurturance and caring, (c) parental responsiveness, (d) involvement with child, (e) sensitive parenting.

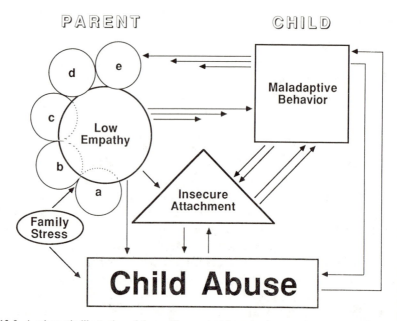

Figure 12.2. A schematic illustration of the multiconceptual interplay between low parent empathy and child maladaptive behaviors: (a) parental hostility and aggressiveness, (b) low nurturance and caring, (c) lack of parental responsiveness, (d) low parental involvement, (e) insensitive parenting.

parent or situation are likely to be associated with either high or low level of parental empathy'' (p. 174). However, there are data linking these hypothesized parental behavior correlates of parent empathy to facets of the child's adjustment. This research is briefly reviewed in the next section. Subsequently, two recent studies bearing directly on parental empathy and child adjustment/maladjustment correlates are presented.

Empathy-related parental behaviors and children's adjustment: empirical summary

One of the principal dimensions that has emerged in factor analyses of parenting behaviors is warmth–hostility. Becker (1964), in a major review evaluating the results yielded by a number of different studies, concluded that hostility in mothers is significantly related to aggressiveness in children. He also reviewed the correlates of parental restrictiveness–permissiveness and arrived at a similar conclusion regarding the effects of restrictiveness. However, subsequent research indicating negative consequences of permissive parenting (Baumrind, 1971; Olweus, 1980; Patterson, 1982) suggests that the significant parent variable moderating the effects of restrictiveness–permissiveness is the warmth versus hostility of the parents.

The degree of parental involvement or noninvolvement, especially in parents of young children, a parental attribute that may be related to empathy, has also been linked to child outcomes. Thus, Egeland and Sroufe (1981a,b), in their longitudinal study of high-risk mothers, found that infants of mothers identified as ''unavailable'' (mothers who were detached, emotionally uninvolved, and uninterested in their children) not only showed disturbances in their attachment relationships but became increasingly dysfunctional with age.

Pulkkinen's (1982) findings from a longitudinal study carried out in Finland also indicate the importance of parental involvement in promoting optimal psychological development in children. At age 14, children of child-centered parents (parents who were interested and involved with their children) were, in general, socially competent, related to their parents, responsible, and achieving. In contrast, the children of parent-centered parents (defined as selfish) were impulsive, had poor emotional control, had more complicated social relationships, and were less achieving. This contrasting pattern became more exaggerated when the sample was evaluated at age 20.

Related to the dimension of parental involvement in the child is parental sensitivity to the child's feelings and needs. Studies of maternal responses to infants indicate that maternal sensitivity is significantly related to the quality of infant attachment. Ainsworth, Bell, and Stayton (1971, 1974) found that mothers of infants considered to be anxiously attached were less sensitive to and were more likely to misidentify infant cues than mothers of securely attached infants. Similarly, Smith and Pederson (1983) observed that mothers of infants who were categorized as anxious-resistant or as anxious-avoidant responded less appropriately to and did less monitoring of the infant than mothers of secure infants.

Moreover, the quality of early attachment has been shown to be predictive of infants' subsequent behavioral adjustment. Infants classified as securely attached at 12 and 18 months were found to be more cooperative, enthusiastic, persistent, and effective at 2 years of age than the insecurely attached children (Matas, Arend, & Sroufe, 1978). These same groups also reflected behavioral differences when observed in a preschool situation 3 years later (Sroufe, Fox, & Pancake, 1983). The children who had been classified earlier as insecurely attached behaved in a more overdependent manner than the securely attached children. Although there is some evidence that the stability of attachment is influenced by situational factors (Thompson, Lamb, & Estes, 1982, 1983), the evidence, on the whole, supports the proposition that an aspect of maternal empathy sensitivity to the child's feelings and needs is positively related to the child's adjustment. Consistent with this proposition is the Zahn-Waxler, Radke-Yarrow, and King (1979) finding that prosocial and empathic caregiving behaviors of 1½–2½-year-old children were associated with such empathy-related maternal behaviors as responding promptly and nurturantly to the child's hurts and anticipating dangers and difficulties.

The final pattern of empathy-related parental behaviors to be reviewed here, in this case inversely related to empathy, is the use of strong physical punishment, particularly as manifested in child abuse. There is considerable evidence that repeated physical punishment by parents is associated with the development of aggressive or delinquent behavior patterns in children (Eron, Walder, & Lefkowitz, 1971; N. Feshbach, 1973a; S. Feshbach, 1970; Patterson, 1982). There is also evidence that children who have been subjected to physical abuse manifest more disturbances and maladjustment than nonabused children. Observations of abused children indicate that they tend to be withdrawn, have low self-esteem, and show hostile and aggressive reaction patterns (Kempe & Kempe, 1978; Martin & Beezely, 1977).

These behavioral difficulties are displayed quite early in the child's development. In a series of observational studies carried out in a child-care setting, George and Main (1979) found that abused toddlers were more aggressive to caretakers and more avoidant of peers than a matched group of nonabused children. In a subsequent paper (Main and George, 1985), they report striking differences between the abused and nonabused preschool children in their responses to distress manifested by a peer, the abused children manifesting either little concern or negative responses. Howes and Espinosa (1984), in a study emerging from a larger project, carried out under the direction of Professor Carollee Howes and myself, similarly report that abused children, in contrast to a nonabused group, responded more aggressively to signs of distress in peers, in both a free-play and a structured situation. The deleterious consequences of physical abuse and other forms of maltreatment of children can be shown, even for a population of children already considered at risk (Egeland & Sroufe, 1981a,b). At age 18 months, a higher proportion of children who were physically abused were anxiously attached to their mothers than children of a nonmaltreated control group. Manifestations of anxious attachment were also displayed by children whose mothers were verbally abusive, psychologically unavailable, or neglectful. Children in the physically abused and other maltreated groups also manifested more anger and noncompliance at 24 months than did the children in the non–high-risk groups. A follow-up study when the children were 42 months and 4½–5 years of age revealed problems in attention and in impulse control in all of the maltreated groups (Egeland, Sroufe, & Erickson, 1983). Abusing children, being hostile to children, and neglecting and being uninvolved with children are clearly parenting styles that foster the development of maladaptive behaviors in the child.

Several studies suggest that physically abusive adults are less empathic than nonabusive adults. Frodi and Lamb (1980) compared the responses of a group of child abusers with those of a matched sample of nonabusers to videotaped scenes of crying and smiling infants. The abuse group had difficulty in discriminating the crying infant scenes from the smiling infant scenes. In addition, the abusive group displayed more anger and less sympathy than the controls when observing the videotapes of crying infants. That is, the abusers displayed less signs of empathy. In a more direct assessment of the relationship between empathy and use of physical abuse, Letourneau (1981) found that the two measures of empathy used in her study were better predictors of physical abuse by mothers than the life-stress measure. More indirect evidence consistent with an inverse relationship between empathy and abuse is provided by Evans (1980), who found that nonabusive mothers, in comparison with abusive mothers, were more likely to produce TAT responses judged as trusting, empathic, and supportive of children.

The empirical findings relating empathy to child abuse and the data on the effects of parental correlates of empathy indicate there is a need for further investigation of parental empathy. Inasmuch as extant scales of adult empathy assess empathy as a widely generalized behavior disposition, my colleagues and I decided to develop a self-report measure that focused specifically on parental empathy. Given the importance of relationships between caretakers for the child's adjustment, the scale also includes items assessing empathy with one's spouse or partner. In addition, we made a systematic effort to construct a parent/partner empathy scale based on the three-component model of empathy described earlier.

Parental empathy and child adjustment: two studies

Two studies recently completed in our laboratory at UCLA provided data bearing on the relationship between parental empathy and child adjustment and are relevant to the theoretical relationships discussed in the preceding section.

Study 1

The first study, part of a broader project carried out by Carollee Howes and myself on sociomoral development in abusive and nonabusive families, was concerned with the influence of maternal empathy, stress, and social support on compliance and self-control in young children (Howes & Feshbach, in preparation). The investigation was carried out with physically abusing families, with families receiving services in mental health clinics, and with a control parent group.

It was anticipated that the two clinical parent samples would manifest less empathy than the control sample and that parental empathy would be positively related to children's compliance and self-control. It was also expected that both cognitive and affective factors involved in parental empathy would contribute to these relationships. Compliance behaviors that emerge in the 9- to 18-month period and self-control behaviors that become evident at about 2 years of age are important parameters in the development of self-regulation in young children (Kopp, 1982). Recent data indicate that compliance and self-control are linked to the presence of sensitive communication and interaction between infants and caregivers (Kopp, 1982; Londerville & Main, 1981; Schaffer, 1984; Stayton, Hogan, & Ainsworth, 1971) and to secure attachment relationships (Sroufe, 1985). Thus, it was expected that compliance and self-control, reasonable indicators of adjustment in young children, would be less well developed in children of low-empathy parents. It was further expected that compliance and self-control would be less well developed in the abused and psychiatric clinical samples of children than in the control children.

Children were observed in a laboratory session that measured child compliance and self-control as well as mothers' investment and involvement in their children's behavior. Mothers also completed a set of instruments measuring empathy, stress, and social support.

The sample included 117 mother-and-child pairs. Twenty-six of the mother–child pairs consisted of physically abused children and their abusing mothers drawn from child guidance clinics, identified by the agency as well as the dependency court as documented cases of physical abuse. Twenty-five of the mother–child pairs were clients of the same child guidance clinics with no history of abuse, nor were they suspected by the therapists of abuse. An additional 66 mother–child pairs were obtained from day-care centers and parent education classes.

The families were predominantly middle class and moderately well educated. About 80% of the families were Anglo, the remaining families were Hispanic, black, and Asian. All of the mothers spoke English. Children in the control sample were younger than children in the abused and clinic samples; there were porportionately more boys in the abused sample and more girls in the clinic sample than in the control sample; there were more single parents in the abused and clinic samples than in the control sample; mothers in the control sample had more years of school than mothers in the abused and clinic sample. These differences were not unexpected, given the known demographic characteristics of abusing families. Further analyses of differences between groups were carried out using age, sex, single parent, and mothers' education as covariates. No other significant demographic differences between the family groups were found.

The data were collected over two sessions, scheduled approximately 1 week apart. During session I the empathy (Feshbach & Caskey, in preparation) and stress (Feshbach, 1985a) questionnaires were administered. During session II the mother–child interaction was observed and the parents completed the social support questionnaire. The empathy variable was assessed by the Parent/Partner Empathy Measure, a new paper-and-pencil inventory developed by N. Feshbach to assess parental empathy toward one's child and toward one's partner (Feshbach & Caskey, in preparation). The measure consists of 40 statements presented in a Likert format in which a respondent indicates whether the statement is always, usually, sometimes, or never true. The measure is based on the three-component conceptual model of empathy described above (Feshbach, 1975, 1978b). Individual items were designed to assess parental and spousal/partner discrimination of affective cues, role-taking skills, emotional expressiveness and general empathy. Cronbach's alpha for the full scale is .87.

A factor analysis of this scale, in which a principal-components solution was employed, yielded four factors that were subject to a varimax rotation. The first factor, labeled *cognitive,* includes 13 parent and partner discrimination and role-taking items. The second factor, labeled *affect expression,* includes 10 items about one's own expressiveness and attitudes about others' expressiveness. Most of the items pertaining to this factor are directed toward children. The third component is a *spouse/partner empathy* factor and includes 9 cognitive, affective, and general empathy items with the object the spouse. The fourth factor, labeled *empathic distress,* consists of 7 items reflecting shared reactions to distress and discomfort in others.

It may be noted that the dimensional structure yielded by the factor analysis is highly consistent with the three-component model of empathy. The two cognitive components appear on one factor and the items reflecting the affective component load on a second factor. Of the two remaining factors, empathic distress is of particular interest in that it corresponds to the function of empathy most emphasized by Hoffman (1982).

Parental stress was assessed by the Feshbach, Jordon, and Hoffman Sources of Stress Inventory, a paper-and-pencil measure designed to tap mothers' and fathers' perceptions of chronic stress (Feshbach, 1985a). Parents rated each of 12 items on a 5-point Likert scale ranging from 1 (little stress) to 5 (severe constant stress). Items include such life areas as money, household chores, time demands, job-related stress, relationships, and health. A total score is obtained by summing the amount of stress indicated for each of the 12 items.

A social support measure included the assessment of network stability, support, contact, integration, and reciprocated help (Howes & Olenick, 1986).

The laboratory sessions were videotaped and included four tasks (Howes & Olenick, 1986). The first task measured the child's ability to comply with the mother's request to complete and remain with a boring task. The second and fourth tasks measured the child's ability for self-control in the presence of the mother, and the third task measured the child's ability to comply with the mother's request to complete a familiar cleanup task.

Factors measured among children included *compliance,* the extent to which the child completed tasks 1 and 3, and *self-control,* the data yielded by the child's behavior in tasks 2 and 4. *Child expressions of positive and negative affect* were derived from frequencies of these responses observed during the four tasks.

Several parental measures were derived from the observations. *Parent involvement in child compliance* was the extent to which the mother helped the child in the boring and cleanup tasks combined with the rating of parental physical restraint in the forbidden toy task (task 2). *Parental investment in child's compliance* was derived from the mother's insistence on the child doing the various tasks, and the measures of *parental expressions of positive and negative affect* were summed from frequencies of these behaviors across the four tasks.

Of principal interest are the findings bearing on the differences between the clinical and control groups on the empathy measure and, especially, on the relationship between parental empathy and the indices of the child's social functioning. A comparison of the means of the three parent groups on the Parent/ Partner Empathy Measure and its factorial components is presented in Table 12.1. With the exception of the empathic distress factor, the control parents manifested significantly greater empathy on each of the empathy factors than did the abuse or psychiatric parent groups, the mean scores of the latter two groups being quite similar. With regard to empathic distress, the control mean was almost identical to the psychiatric group mean, both groups manifesting greater empathic distress than the abuse group.

Table 12.1. *A comparison of mean scores of control, psychiatric, and child abuse groups on Parent/Partner Empathy Measure and its factorial components*

	Mean scores				
	Total empathy	Cognitive (F-1)	Affect expression (F-2)	Partner empathy (F-3)	Empathic distress (F-4)
Control	131.7	42.3	35.2	30.3	21.8
High risk	124.8	38.8	34.2	28.8	21.6
Abuse	122.8	39.2	34.1	27.2	20.2
$p<$	.001	.001	.05	.05	.05

Source: Feshbach & Caskey (in preparation).

Table 12.2. *Relationships between empathy and mother and child behaviors when controlling for social support and stress*[a]

	Empathy scales				
	Cognitive	Express	Spousal	Distress	Total
Child					
compliance	.09	−.17	.05	.06	.16
self-control	.12	−.53**	−.05	.56**	.49**
positive affect	.31*	.01	.29*	.11	.20
negative affect	−.19	.31*	−.14	−.31*	−.27
Parent					
investment	.23*	.15	.03	.65***	.67**
involvement	.39**	.11	−.17	.32*	.51*
positive affect	.14	−.04	.12	.34**	.39**
negative affect	−.10	.09	−.18	.35**	−.39**

[a]Partial correlation $df = 109$; $*p<.05$, $**p<.01$, $***p<.001$.
Source: Howes and Feshbach (in preparation).

The correlations of the empathy scale factors with the child behaviors in the laboratory situation are presented in Table 12.2. These are partial correlations, in which social support and stress are held constant. The partial correlations of the empathy factors with measures of maternal behavior in the laboratory situation are reported here because these correlations bear on the validity of the empathy measure. On the whole, the correlations are consistent with theoretical expectation. Although the measure of child compliance is unrelated to the total empathy score, there is a significant positive correlation of .49 between total empathy score of the mother and the amount of self-control manifested by the child in the laboratory situation. It also would appear that the children of mothers who encourage affect expression tend to display greater affect expression in the form of less self-control and more negative affect display. It is of theoretical interest that the correlations obtained with the empathic distress factor are most consonant with those found for the total empathy score. Both the total score and emotional distress factor scores correlate positively with child self-control, negatively with child negative affect, and positively with maternal investment, maternal involvement, and maternal positive affect. Only in the case of maternal negative affect was there a difference in the direction of the correlation. The findings of this first study indicate that parent/partner empathy is related to a significant feature of the child's adjustment – degree of self-regulation. The children of more empathic parents tend to display greater self-control. In addition, the findings indicate that the new Parent/Partner Empathy Measure has theoretical and empirical utility.

Study 2

Study 2 was concerned with the interrelationships between family environment, parental characteristics, and adjustment in school-age children (Repetti, Feshbach, & Nelms, in preparation). It was part of a larger project, codirected by Norma Feshbach and Seymour Feshbach (1986), which included a series of interrelated field studies on affective processes and academic achievement in nonpathological samples of elementary school–age children.

Although a variety of family and individual difference variables were included in the study, only the variables under consideration in this chapter are discussed.

A correlation design was used to relate parent variables to symptoms of maladjustment in children. Fifty-six mothers and 41 fathers (29 parent pairs) of 62 children aged 8½ to 11½ attending a university elementary school completed a series of questionnaires. These included the Parent/Partner Empathy Measure, the Block (1969), and the widely used Child Behavior Checklist (CBCL) (Achenbach and Edelbrock, 1981). The Externalizing Scale, which measures symptoms such as aggressiveness and conduct problems, and the Internalizing Scale, which assesses symptoms such as social isolation and depression, were our chief targets of interest. It was predicted that higher levels of parental empathy would be associated with fewer adjustment problems in children. As the data in Table 12.3 reflect, the hypothesis was supported by the findings. For mothers there is a significant inverse correlation between empathy and symptomatology across both adjustment scales, whereas for the fathers the inverse association holds only between empathy and externalizing symptoms.

The 29 mother-and-father pairs provided another opportunity to assess the

Table 12.3. *Intercorrelations between Parent/Partner Empathy Measure and child adjustment scales*

	Child Behavior Checklist	
Empathy	Internalizing Scale	Externalizing Scale
Fathers ($N = 21$)	−.16	−.41*
Mothers ($N = 38$)	−.37**	−.42**

Note: Probability levels are based on one-tailed tests; $*p \leq .05$, $**p \leq .01$.

utility of the empathy measure. Discrepancy scores between parents were determined for each of the discipline items on the Block Scale, and then summed across all items. This discipline discrepancy score was then correlated with mothers' and fathers' total empathy scores, respectively. It was anticipated that greater empathy on the part of parents would be associated with greater sharing of discipline attitudes and practices. The obtained correlations were consistent with this expectation. The correlation between maternal empathy and discipline discrepancy was − .55 ($p < .01$) and that for paternal empathy was − .54 ($p < .01$).

Although the data analysis for this study is still in progress, the results yielded thus far support the positive role that parental empathy is hypothesized to play in the child's adjustment. Low parental empathy is associated with greater behavioral symptomatology in the child and is also indicative of inconsistencies between the parents in their discipline attitudes and practices. At the same time, the findings again point to the utility of the Parent/Partner Empathy Measure.

Conclusion

Parental empathy has been proposed as a significant parameter of socialization. In this chapter, it has been theoretically linked to major dimensions of parental attributes and practices such as parental warmth, parental involvement in the child, and parental sensitivity to the child. It is believed to be a major element in the attachment relationship between parent and child. In general, it is suggested that parental empathy fosters positive social response patterns and facilitates the development of adaptive behavior in children. At the same time, it has been hypothesized that the negative influence of low empathy on children's adjustment is likely to be stronger than the positive influence of high empathy. Thus, low empathy on children's adjustment is likely to be stronger than the positive influence of high empathy. Thus, low parental empathy has been suggested as a very important element in the matrix of factors involved in physical child abuse. This proposed negative effect of low empathy leads to a number of other hypotheses that warrant empirical evaluation. For example, low empathy may have particularly deleterious effects in interaction with development problems presented by the child or stressful conditions presented by the environment. On an empirical level, the role that empathy plays in the socialization process is yet to be investigated. Extant data are limited, and the two studies reviewed here constitute only a beginning effort. The measurement of parental empathy has always been a challenge and a stumbling block. Although the data indicate that the Parent/Partner Empathy Measure is useful, the instrument has only recently been developed and requires further analysis and testing. Further work with the measure should help clarify the component structure of empathy, especially the different properties of the empathic distress and affect expression factors.

The findings of the two studies are consistent with the theoretical properties ascribed to parental empathy. Parents who physically abuse their children are low in empathy; parents who are low in empathy tend to have children who have problems in self-regulatory behavior and other symptoms indicative of maladjustment. These relationships need to be explored in other contests, especially among populations that include fathers as well as mothers. From theoretical, empirical, and clinical standpoints, the further investigation of parental empathy appears to be an important and fruitful endeavor to pursue.

References

Achenbach, T. M., & Edelbrock, C. S. (1981). Behavioral and competencies reported by parents of normal and disturbed children aged four through sixteen. *Monographs of the Society for Research in Child Development, 66* (Serial No. 188).

Ainsworth, M. D. S., Bell, S. M., & Stayton, D. J. (1971). Individual differences in strange situation behavior of one-year-olds. In H. R. Schatter (Ed.), *The origins of human social relations.* London: Academic Press.

Ainsworth, M. D. S., Bell, S. M., & Stayton, D. J. (1974). Infant–mother attachment and social development. In M. P. M. Richards (Ed.), *The integration of the child into a social world.* Cambridge: Cambridge University Press.

Baumrind, D. (1971). Current patterns of parental authority. *Developmental Psychology Monograph, 4*(1, Pt. 2).

Becker, W. C. (1964). Consequences of different kinds of parental discipline. In M. L. Hoffman and L. W. Hoffman (Eds.), *Review of child development research* (Vol. 1). New York: Russell Sage.

Berger, S. M. (1962). Conditioning through vicarious instigation. *Psychological Review, 69*(5), 450–466.

Block, J. (1969). *Q Sort: Child rearing attitudes.* University of California, Berkeley.

Borke, H. (1971). Interpersonal perception of young children: Egocentrism or empathy. *Developmental Psychology, 5*(2), 263–269.

Chandler, M. J., Greenspan, S., & Barenboim, C. (1974). Assessment and training of role-taking and referential communication skills in institutionalized emotionally disturbed children. *Developmental Psychology, 10*(4), 546–553.

Clarke-Stewart, K. A. (1973). Interactions between mothers and their young children: Characteristics and consequences. *Monographs of the Society for Research in Child Development, 38* (5–6, Serial No. 153).

Deutsch, F., & Madle, R. A. (1975). Empathy: Historic and current conceptualizations, measurement, and a cognitive theoretical perspective. *Human Development, 18,* 267–287.

Egeland, B., & Sroufe, L. A. (1981a). Attachment and early maltreatment. *Child Development, 52,* 44–52.

Egeland, B., & Sroufe, L. A. (1981b). Developmental sequelae of maltreatment in infancy. In R. Rizley & D. Cicchetti (Eds.), *Developmental perspectives in child maltreatment* (pp. 77–82). San Francisco: Jossey Bass.

Egeland, B., Sroufe, L. A., & Erickson, M. (1983). The developmental consequence of different patterns of maltreatment. *Child Abuse and Neglect, 7*(4), 459–470.

Eron, L. O., Walder, L. O., & Lefkowitz, M. M. (1971). *Learning of aggression in children.* Boston: Little, Brown.

Evans, A. L. (1980). Personality characteristics and disciplinary attitudes of child-abusing mothers. *Child Abuse and Neglect, 4,* 179–187.

Feshbach, N. D. (1973a). The effects of violence in childhood. *Journal of Clinical Child Psychology, 11*(3), 28–31.

Feshbach, N. (1973b). Empathy: An interpersonal process. In W. Hartup (Chair), *Social understanding in children and adults: Perspectives on social cognition.* Symposium presented at the meeting of the American Psychological Association, Montreal.

Feshbach, N. D. (1975). Empathy in children: Some theoretical and empirical considerations. *Counseling Psychologist, 5*(2), 25–30.

Feshbach, N. D. (1978a). *Empathy training: A field study in affective education.* An invited address presented at the American Educational Research Association meetings, Toronto.

Feshbach, N.D. (1978b). Studies of empathic behavior in children. *Progress in Experimental Personality Research, 8,* 1–47.

Feshbach, N. D. (1980). *The psychology of empathy and the empathy of psychology.* Presidential address, 60th Annual Meeting of the Western Psychological Association, Honolulu, Hawaii.

Feshbach, N. D. (1982). Sex differences in empathy and social behavior in children. In N. Eisenberg (Ed.), *The development of prosocial behavior* (pp. 315–338). New York: Academic Press.

Feshbach, N. D. (1985a). Chronic maternal stress and its assessment. In J. N. Butcher & C. D. Spielberger (Eds.), *Advances in personality assessment* (Vol. 5). Hillsdale, NJ: Erlbaum.

Feshbach, N. D. (1985b). The construct of empathy and the phenomenon of physical maltreatment of children. University of California, Los Angeles. (Unpublished manuscript.)

Feshbach, N. D., & Caskey, N. (in preparation). A new scale for measuring parent empathy and partner empathy: Factorial structure, correlates and clinical discrimination.

Feshbach, N. D., & Feshbach, S. (1969). The relationship between empathy and aggression in two age groups. *Developmental Psychology, 1,* 102–107.

Feshbach, N. D., & Feshbach, S. (1982). Empathy training and the regulation of aggression: Potentialities and limitations. *Academic Psychology Bulletin, 4,* 399–413.

Feshbach, N. D., & Feshbach, S. (1986). *Affective processes and academic achievement.* (Unpublished manuscript.)

Feshbach, N. D., & Kuchenbecker, S. (1974). *A three-component model of empathy.* Symposium presented at the meeting of the American Psychological Association, New Orleans, Louisiana.

Feshbach, N. D., and Roe, K. (1968). Empathy in six and seven year olds. *Child Development, 39*(1), 133–145.

Feshbach, S. (1970). Aggression. In P. H. Mussen (Ed.), *Carmichael's manual of child psychology.* New York: John Wiley & Sons.

Feshbach, S., & Feshbach, N. (1986). Aggression and altruism: A personality perspective. In C.

Zahn-Waxler, M. Chapman, & M. Radke-Yarrow (Eds.), *Aggression and altruism: Biological and social origins*. Cambridge: Cambridge University Press.

Freud, S. (1925). *Collected papers*. London: Hogarth.

Frodi, A. M., & Lamb, M. E. (1980). Child abuser's responses to infant smiles and cries. *Child Development, 51*, 238–241.

George, C., & Main, M. (1979). Social interactions of young abused children: Approach, avoidance and aggression. *Child Development, 50*, 306–318.

Goldberg, A. (1978). *The psychology of the self*. New York: International Universities Press.

Goldstein, A. P., & Michaels, G. Y. (1985). Empathy training: A components approach. *Empathy: Development, training and consequences*. Hillsdale, NJ: Erlbaum Associates.

Hoffman, M. L. (1977). Empathy, its development and prosocial implications. In H. E. Howe (Ed.), *1977 Nebraska Symposium on Motivation, 25*, 169–217.

Hoffman, M. L. (1982). Development of prosocial motivation: Empathy and guilt. In N. Eisenberg (Ed.), *The development of prosocial behavior* (pp. 281–311). New York: Academic Press.

Hogan, R. (1969). Development of an empathy scale. *Journal of Consulting and Clinical Psychology, 33*, 307–316.

Howes, C., & Espinosa, M. P. (1985). The consequences of child abuse for peer interaction. *International Journal of Child Abuse and Neglect, 9*, 397–404.

Howes, C., & Feshbach, N. D. (in preparation). Compliance and self control in young children from varying family contexts: Relationships with parent empathy, stress and social support.

Howes, C., & Olenick, M. (1986). Family and child care influences on toddlers' compliance. *Child Development, 57*, 202–216.

Kaplan, A. G. (1983). Empathic communication in the psychotherapy relationship. *Work in progress, Stone Center*. Wellesley, MA: Wellesley College.

Kempe, R., & Kempe, C. H. (1978). *Child Abuse*. London: Fontana/Open Books.

Kohut, H. (1971). *The analysis of the self: Psychoanalysis of the child*. Monograph No. 4. New York: International Universities Press.

Kohut, H. (1977). *The restoration of the self*. New York: International Universities Press.

Kohut, H. (1978). *The search for the self. Selected writings of Heinz Kohut: 1950–1978* (Vol. 1). New York: International Universities Press.

Kopp, C. B. (1982). Antecedents of self-regulation: A development perspective. *Developmental Psychology, 18*, 199–214.

Letourneau, C. (1981). Empathy and stress: How they affect parental aggression. *Journal of Social Work, 26*, 383–389.

Londerville, S., & Main, M. (1981). Security of attachment, compliance, and maternal training methods in the second year of life. *Development Psychology, 17*, 289–299.

Maccoby, E. E., & Martin, J. A. (1983). Socialization in the context of the family: Parent–child interaction. In P. H. Mussen (Ed.), *Handbook of child psychology* (Vol. 4). New York: John Wiley & Sons.

McDougall, W. (1908). *Introduction to social psychology*. Longon: Methuen.

Main, M., & George, C. (1985). Responses of abused and disadvantaged toddlers to distress in agemates: A study in the day care setting. *Developmental Psychology, 21*, 407–412.

Martin, H. P., & Beezley, P. (1977). Behavioral observations of abused children. *Developmental Medicine and Child Neurology, 19*, 373–387.

Matas, L., Arend, R., & Sroufe, L. (1978). Continuity of adaptation in the second year: The relationship between quality of attachment and later competence. *Child Development, 49*, 547–556.

Mead, G. H. (1934). *Mind, self, and society*. Chicago: University of Chicago Press.

Olweus, D. (1980). Familial and temperamental determinants of aggression behavior in adolescents – A causal analysis. *Developmental Psychology, 16*, 644–660.

Patterson, G. R. (1982). *Coercive family process*. Eugene, OR: Custalia Press.

Pulkkinen, L. (1982). Self-control and continuity from childhood to adolescence. In P. B. Baltes & O. G. Brim (Eds.), *Life-span development and behavior* (Vol. 4). New York: Academic Press.

Repetti, R., Feshbach, N. D., & Nelms, B. (in preparation). Family environment, parental characteristics, and school-aged children's adjustment.

Rogers, C. R. (1951). *Client-centered therapy: Its current practice, implications, and theory.* Boston: Houghton Mifflin.

Rogers, C. R., & Truax, C. B. (1967). The therapeutic conditions antecedent to change: A theoretical view. In C. R. Rogers (Ed.), *The therapeutic relationship and its impact: A study of psychotherapy with schizophrenics.* Madison: University of Wisconsin Press.

Schaffer, H. R. (1984). *The child's entry into a social world.* New York: Academic Press.

Sears, R. R., Maccoby, E. E., & Levin, H. (1957). *Patterns of child rearing.* New York: Harper and Row.

Shantz, C. U. (1975). The development of social cognition. In E. M. Hetherington (Ed.), *Review of child development research* (Vol. 5). Chicago: University of Chicago Press.

Smith, P. B., & Pederson, D. R. (1983). *Maternal sensitivity and patterns of infant–mother attachment.* Paper presented at the biennial meeting of the Society for Research in Child Development, Detroit, Michigan.

Sroufe, L. A. (1985). Attachment classifications from the perspective of infant–caregiver relationships and infant temperament. *Child Development, 56,* 1–14.

Sroufe, L. A., Fox, N., & Pancake, V. (1983). Attachment and dependency in developmental perspective. *Child Development, 54,* 1615–1627.

Stayton, D., Hogan, R., and Ainsworth, M. (1971). Infant obedience and maternal behaviors: The origins of socialization reconsidered. *Child Development, 42,* 1057–1069.

Stotland, E. (1969). Exploratory investigations of empathy. In L. Berkowitz (Ed.), *Advances in experimental social psychology.* New York: Academic Press.

Sullivan, H. S. (1953). *The interpersonal theory of psychiatry.* New York: W. W. Norton.

Thompson, R., Lamb, M., & Estes, D. (1982). Stability of infant–mother attachment and its relationship to changing circumstances in an unselected middle-class sample. *Child Development, 53,* 144–148.

Thompson, R., Lamb, M., & Estes, D. (1983). Harmonizing discordant notes: A reply to Waters. *Child Development, 54,* 521–524.

Truax, C. B. (1972). The meaning and reliability of accurate empathy ratings: A rejoinder. *Psychological Bulletin, 77,* 397–399.

Winnicott, D. W. (1965). *The maturational processes and the facilitating environment.* New York: International Universities Press.

Winnicott, D. W. (1970). The mother–infant experience of mutuality. In E. J. Anthony and T. Bewedek (Eds.), *Parenthood: Its psychology and psychopathology.* Boston: Little, Brown.

Zahn-Waxler, C., Radke-Yarrow, M., & King, R. (1979). Child rearing and children's prosocial initiations toward victims of distress. *Child Development, 50,* 319–330.

13   Empathy, sympathy, and altruism: empirical and conceptual links

Nancy Eisenberg and Paul A. Miller

One of the primary reasons psychologists have been interested in the concepts of empathy and sympathy is that they play an important role in theories concerning altruism. Specifically, many psychologists and philosophers have suggested that empathy or sympathy mediates much moral, including altruistic, behavior (e.g., Blum, 1981; Hoffman, 1981; Hume, 1777/1966; Staub, 1978). However, the validity of this assumption is a topic of current debate (cf. Batson & Coke, 1981; Underwood & Moore, 1982).

In this chapter, we briefly consider current theory concerning the relation of empathy and sympathy to altruism and present a review of the relevant empirical research. We define sympathy as an emotional response stemming from another's emotional state or condition that is not identical to the other's emotion, but consists of feelings of sorrow or concern for another, and we define empathy as an affective state that stems from the apprehension of another's emotional state or condition and that is congruent with it (see chapter 1). Altruism is defined as intentional, voluntary behavior that benefits another and is not performed with the expectation of receiving external rewards or avoiding external punishments or aversive stimuli.

Often, in both theoretical and empirical discussions, it is impossible to determine whether writers are referring to empathy, sympathy, or both. For ease of reading, we generally use the term *empathy* rather than *sympathy and empathy* when discussing the literature in which the two concepts have not been clearly differentiated.

Theory

Theoretical discussions of the association between altruism and sympathy or empathy appear in several other chapters in this volume (chapters 3 and 8). Thus, we examine these theories only briefly prior to reviewing the relevant empirical research.

Justin Aronfreed and Martin Hoffman are among the few psychologists who

292

have proposed developmental accounts of the relation between empathy and pro-social behavior (defined as intentional, voluntary behavior that benefits another; but, unlike the definition of altruism, the motive is unspecified). According to Aronfreed (1970), empathy is acquired by the repeated pairing of the child's own feelings of pleasure or pain (elicited by external stimuli) with corresponding emotions in others. As a result of this conditioning process, cues indicating others' emotional states acquire the capacity to elicit corresponding emotions in the child. Moreover, the child learns that behaviors that make others happy or relieve their distress are pleasurable for the self as well. Thus, prosocial behaviors are, in essence, self-reinforcing and frequently are performed because of the child's experiencing of others' affective states.

Hoffman (1982a, chap. 3) has proposed the most detailed developmental account of the association between empathy and altruism. Very briefly, he has suggested that very young children are able to experience others' emotional states, and that once children differentiate between self and other, they frequently react to this vicarious emotion by attempting to assist others in need. However, because the 1–2-year old has difficulty differentiating between another's and one's own distress, Hoffman (1976) has suggested that early helping behaviors may be "quasi-hedonistic" in motive, in that young children may provide assistance in part to alleviate their own distress. Moreover, Hoffman noted, young children's helping may be inappropriate because they cannot differentiate between methods that are useful for alleviating another's distress and those that reduce their own distress.

According to Hoffman (1984, chap. 3), with developmental advances in role-taking skills, children are increasingly able to differentiate between their own and others' emotional states. As a consequence, they become capable of experiencing compassion or "sympathetic distress," in addition to empathic distress (the latter being a more or less exact replica of the victim's presumed feeling of distress). Thus, at this stage (starting around age 1–2), children's assistance may be motivated by concern for another as well as by the desire to relieve their own empathic distress.

With developments in role taking, children also become more skilled at assisting others in appropriate ways. Moreover, in late childhood, advances in children's understanding of persons as beings with continuing identities appear to make it possible for them to understand and sympathize with another's general life condition. This development is likely to facilitate prosocial behavior directed at persons in chronic distress, even if their distress is not readily visible.

Hoffman's theory is unique because he has delineated developmental change in the contributions of both affect (empathy/sympathy) and cognition to prosocial behavior. Most psychologists who have examined the relation of empathy to prosocial behavior have focused on adults and older children. Perhaps the most elaborate of such theories are those of Piliavin, Dovidio, Gaertner, and Clark (1981) and Batson (Batson & Coke, 1981, chap. 8).

Piliavin et al. (1981) proposed a model to explain bystander interventions in emergencies and crises. In this model, emotional arousal and the cognitive calculation of potential costs and rewards in a particular situation are central. Arousal from observing an emergency is viewed as aversive, so much so that the bystander is motivated to reduce his or her empathic arousal. To do so, bystanders will select the response to the emergency that will reduce their arousal the most quickly and effectively while incurring as few costs (e.g., psychological or material) as possible. Thus, in some situations, empathic arousal will lead to helping, whereas in others, a cost–benefit analysis leads the bystander to escape the situation rather than assist. Piliavin et al. also noted that for some people with specific personality characteristics and in some situations (e.g., when arousal is very high), emergency helping may be impulsive and irrational.

In their model, Piliavin et al. attempted to differentiate between feelings of concern for oneself or personal distress and sympathy. However, although Piliavin et al. clearly believe that people experiencing personal distress will help primarily to reduce their own arousal, it is unclear whether they think sympathetic reactions lead to helping for the same reason.

Batson and his colleagues (e.g., Batson & Coke, 1981, chap. 8) have proposed a model of prosocial responding similar in some respects to that of Piliavin. In their view, taking the perspective of another in need often leads to sympathizing (concern for another), which in turn increases the potential helper's motivation to see the other's need reduced. Thus, sympathizing is viewed as producing altruistically motivated acts of assistance. However, Batson has pointed out that another type of emotional arousal may occur in helping situations: Observers may experience personal distress (self-oriented emotions such as anxiety or worry), which tends to engender egoistic helping (i.e., helping motivated by the desire to reduce one's own aversive state of arousal).

Batson has proposed a means of distinguishing between altruistically (sympathetically) motivated helping and egoistically motivated helping. In his view, because the altruist's goal is to reduce the other's distress, there is a cost for not helping and little gain for the potential helper in escaping without helping. In contrast, if the motive for assisting is primarily egoistic (the reduction of personal distress), this goal can be achieved more easily by escaping than helping, if escape is possible and easy. Thus, the cost–benefit analyses for egoistic and altruistic helping should vary, and the patterns of helping behavior should differ.

The theoretical models of Hoffman, Piliavin et al., and Batson are all complex and lead one to conclude that the relation between empathy and prosocial behavior is not simple or constant across situations and persons. We next considered a few of the conceptual complexities raised by these theories.

Conceptual issues

Although theorists frequently have posited a relation between empathy or sympathy and prosocial behavior, few if any would expect them to relate consistently to prosocial behavior. There are several reasons for this, some of which are now considered briefly (see Eisenberg, 1986, for more discussion of these issues).

Implicitly or explicitly, most theorists who have proposed that sympathy or empathy mediates prosocial behavior have confined their assertions to those prosocial behaviors that are altruistic in motivation. In other words, most have assumed that empathy mediates prosocial behaviors that are voluntary and intentional, benefit others, and are not motivated by self-concern or externally produced rewards or pressures. In contrast, nonaltruistic prosocial behaviors are viewed as being motivated by factors such as the desire for social approval, concrete rewards, or the need to relieve one's own personal distress.

There is considerable evidence to support the notion that apparently altruistic behaviors are often mediated by nonsympathetic, pragmatic, or self-oriented considerations (e.g., Bar-Tal, 1982; Batson & Coke, 1981; Eisenberg, 1982). Moreover, some research indicates that truly altruistic behaviors can be motivated by factors other than sympathy, for example, internalized moral values (e.g., Eisenberg-Berg, 1979; Fellner & Marshall, 1981). Thus, in many instances there is no theoretical reason to expect an association between sympathy or empathy and a given prosocial behavior.

Many researchers have not adequately considered this issue when choosing indices of prosocial behavior. In many cases, the mode of prosocial behavior expected to correlate with empathy has been one that is likely to be motivated by factors other than empathy. For example, donating to an organized charity at the office on a yearly basis or in front of one's superiors is less likely to be motivated by empathy than is assisting an individual whose need or distress is clearly visible at a time when no one else is near.

Another factor that might influence the degree of empirical association between sympathy/empathy and indices of altruistic behavior is the index of emotional response selected. Although many theorists apparently believe that altruism is related to both state empathy (empathy in the given situation) and trait empathy (the general disposition to be empathic), it is likely that the association between altruism and state empathy (or sympathy) is the stronger of the two (Peraino & Sawin, 1981). The reason is that, in any given situation in which an individual could assist another, those empathy-eliciting cues that are present may or may not evoke empathy in any specific person who is, in general, ranked high on the trait of empathy. In other words, owing to factors either within the individual or specific to the circumstances (e.g., the nature of the cues), an individual's typical level of empathic responding may be irrelevant to whether the individual will assist in that particular circumstance.

As is evident in the forthcoming review of the research, sympathy or empathy has been operationalized as a trait in most of the work with children (that is, empathy has been measured in reaction to several stimuli and then related to prosocial behavior in an unrelated situation). In contrast, many investigators have used both trait and state indices in studies with adults. This difference in method may be responsible in part for age differences in the results of research concerning the link between sympathy/empathy and prosocial behavior.

A third conceptual issue concerns the need to differentiate among the various emotional responses that have been called empathy. If, as discussed in chapter 1, empathy is conceptualized as an affective response that can lead to personal distress or sympathy for another, one would expect empathy to relate positively to prosocial behavior in only specific circumstances. If empathy turns into personal distress because of a weak self–other differentiation or excessive association between self and other, one should expect an association between empathy (and the resultant personal distress) and prosocial behavior only if the prosocial act can be expected to reduce one's own distress. If one's own distress could be relieved with some other, perhaps less costly behavior, empathy that is transformed into personal distress would not be expected to be associated with prosocial behavior (see Batson & Coke, 1981). In contrast, if an empathic response engenders sympathy for the other, one would expect an association between empathy (or sympathy) and prosocial behavior across a wide variety of situations. Thus, distinctions among empathy, sympathy, and personal distress are crucial for predicting the pattern and strength of the association between vicariously produced affective responding and prosocial behavior. Some of the inconsistencies evident in the empirical research are no doubt the result of the failure to consider these critical distinctions.

The empirical data

In most of the research concerning the association between sympathy/empathy and altruism, empathy or sympathy has been assessed with one of the following types of measures:

1. picture-story indices,
2. questionnaires,
3. self-report of reactions in experimental situations,
4. other-report of sympathy,
5. facial/gestural indices,
6. physiological indices, or
7. experimental inductions of empathy.

Because the method of assessing sympathy/empathy seems to be related to the empirical findings, we have organized our review of the data on the sympathy–altruism link around the methods used to measure sympathy.

Picture-story measures of empathy

One of the most popular methods for assessing children's empathy is the picture-story technique (e.g., the FASTE, Feshbach & Roe, 1968). Typically, a child listens to a narrative while viewing a peer of the same age and the same sex who is depicted in slides or pictures as experiencing a variety of emotion-evoking events (at times pictures without narratives are used). After each scenario, children are asked how they feel; they are considered empathic if they report feelings that match or generally correspond with those that the story's protoganist is likely to have experienced.

Consistent with earlier reviews (e.g., Underwood & Moore, 1982), we found that the results of studies based on picture-story indicies point to an inconsistent, if not somewhat negative, pattern of relations between empathy and prosocial behavior. For example, significant positive relations have been found between children's or adolescents' empathy and donating to peers (Cohen, 1974; Miller, 1979), helping (Liebhart, 1972), sharing (Panofsky, 1976), caring responses toward peers (Roe, 1980), and self-report of caring reactions (Watson, 1976). However, nonsignificant, inconsistent, or negative relations also have been found between children's empathy and helping (Bazar, 1977; Feshbach, 1980, 1982; Howard, 1983; Kameya, 1976; Lennon, Eisenberg, & Carroll, 1986), sharing or donating (Fay, 1970; Iannotti, 1975, 1977, 1985; Kameya, 1976; Kuchenbecker, 1977; Miller, 1979; Sawin, Underwood, Weaver, & Mostyn, 1981; Staub & Feinberg, 1980; unpublished data), composite scores of spontaneous prosocial behaviors (Eisenberg-Berg & Lennon, 1980; Iannotti, 1985), and other measures of prosocial responding (Cohen, 1974; Feshbach, 1982; Knudson & Kagen, 1982).

These results run counter to the prevailing notion among researchers that empathy mediates altruistic behavior. However, a number of conceptual and methodological problems have been raised with regard to picture-story techniques that may be responsible, at least in part, for the inconsistent results in the research.

Measurement of empathy. In virtually all the studies involving picture-story techniques, children's vicarious affective responses have been operationalized as empathy (the degree to which the child's response matches that of the protagonist) rather than sympathy (other-oriented concern). On a conceptual basis, however, one would expect sympathetic reactions to be more highly related to altruism than empathic reactions because of the other-orientation inherent in sympathetic reactions. Consistent with this notion, in one of the few studies in which sympathetic responses to stories were assessed, Liebhart (1972) found that adolescents high in sympathy (as well as in the tendency to take instrumental action) helped a person in distress more quickly than those low in sympathy. Similarly, Staub and Feinberg (Staub, personal communication, 1985; unreported data from their 1980 study) found that girls' reports of sympathetic reactions to pictures of others were positively related to cooperative behavior and spontaneous sharing (but not to helping or sharing in response to requests). Scores reflecting the degree to which girls merely reported feeling the same emotion as the other were negatively related to spontaneous sharing and unrelated to cooperation, helping, or requested sharing. Similar scores for boys were negatively related to cooperation and requested sharing and unrelated to helping or spontaneous sharing. (Interestingly, the boys in this study did not verbalize any sympathetic responses.) These results are consistent with the view that the lack of differentiation between children's sympathetic responses and other emotional responses such as emotional contagion may be one reason for the inconsistent findings in research involving picture/story indices.

Unidimensionality of the empathy construct. When using picture-story assessments of empathy, researchers usually have assumed that empathic individuals are equally responsive to the range of human emotions, including both euphoric and dysphoric notions. Thus, a child's responses are summed across stories reflecting different affects to compute a total empathy score. However, Sawin (1979) and Hoffman (1982b), among others, have suggested that empathy may not in fact be a unitary construct.

Children's sympathy/empathy for others probably is influenced by previous learning experiences, the degree of similarity between the situations they have experienced and those depicted in the story stimuli, and the differential costs and rewards for empathizing with positive versus negative emotions (Eisenberg, 1986). If this is true, children's empathic responses to positive versus negative affects may relate in different ways to their prosocial behavior. Indeed, there is some reason to believe that empathy with dysphoric states is more highly related to prosocial behavior than is empathy with positive states (Feshbach, 1980, 1982; Sawin, 1979; Sawin et al., 1981). However, the data are not entirely consistent (see Kuchenbecker, 1977); thus, more research is needed to determine whether this is so and whether such a pattern is dependent upon the particular index of empathy (see section on facial/gestural indices).

Social desirability. Demand characteristics are quite salient in picture-story assessments of children's empathy because children repeatedly are asked to report how they are feeling. Such repeated questioning may induce the child to report experiencing the emotion displayed in the stories either to meet implicit experimenter expectations or because the child adopts the response set consistent with the affective stimuli. Notably, females score higher than males on verbal self-report procedures but not on nonverbal, somatic, or physiological indices of empathy (Eisenberg & Lennon, 1983). These results are compatible with the notion that demand characteristics affect people's self-report of empathy because empathic responsiveness and sympathy are more consistent with the social stereotypes and sex-role expectations for females than males (Block, 1973).

Similarly, if children's verbal self-report of empathy in reaction to picture-story stimuli is affected primarily by experimental demands, one would expect these self-reports to be unrelated or negatively related to their naturally occurring, unsolicited prosocial behavior. Generally, this is what has been found (Eisenberg-Berg & Lennon, 1980; Howard, 1983; Iannotti, 1985). Conversely, if self-report of empathy in picture-story assessments reflects the child's concern for social approval, positive correlations would be expected between children's scores and measures of their compliant (solicited), prosocial behavior. This is because the motivation for approval would be expected to be relatively high when one is directly requested to assist and may elicit disapproval if they do not. In fact, females' self-reported empathy has been positively correlated with their donating in a "visible" situation (Miller, 1979), as has preschool children's empathy with requested prosocial behaviors (Eisenberg-Berg & Lennon, 1980).

Other methodological issues. Another major concern with regard to picture-story indices is that the scores of children's reported empathy may confound verbal ability with the expression of empathic feelings. Indeed, children's empathy scores have been found to relate positively to measures of verbal ability (Sawin, 1979) and reading comprehension (Feshbach, 1978). Moreover, picture-story measures generally consist of short, hypothetical events that may not sufficiently evoke the child's emotions, especially over repeated trials. In fact, the repeated trials themselves may inure the child to the emotional depictions in the stories.

These apparent problems lead one to question the validity of children's empathy scores on picture-story measures. Thus, although picture-story techniques inaugurated a decade of research on children's empathy, researchers must address these conceptual and methodological issues if this procedure is to be useful in future research on the relation between children's empathy and altruism.

Questionnaire indices of sympathy, empathy, and personal distress

Questionnaire measures of sympathy, like picture-story indices, have been used in many studies of the relation between sympathy and prosocial behavior, perhaps because of their ease of administration. Most of these studies have been conducted with adults, although a few have involved elementary school children.

Four questionnaires have been used in most of the research. The most widely used is the Mehrabian and Epstein (1972) questionnaire measure of emotional tendency (ET). According to Mehrabian and Epstein, this 33-item scale contains items that tap susceptibility to emotional contagion, appreciation of the feelings of unfamiliar and distant others, extreme emotional responsiveness, the tendency to be moved by others' positive emotional experiences, sympathetic tendency, and willingness to have contact with others who have problems. In a recent factor analysis involving the responses of 9–12-year-old Finnish children, the scale factored into five components: emotional receptivity, hardened feelings, lability of emotional control, complete rejection of feelings of others combined with extreme agitation in some situations, and readiness to identify oneself with others (Kalliopuska, 1983). In brief, the questionnaire would seem to tap sympathy, personal distress, susceptibility to emotional arousal, perspective taking, and a variety of other factors.

Bryant (1982) adapted the ET scale for children. Her scale contains items similar to the ET and thus also seems to assess a variety of factors, including sympathy, personal distress, emotional arousability, and perspective taking. In unpublished studies, both Bryant (1985, personal communication) and Eisenberg have obtained factors related to sympathy (or possibly sympathy and personal distress) and ease of crying in an emotional situation.

In an attempt to differentiate among components of empathy, Stotland, Mathews, Sherman, Hansson, and Richardson (1978) constructed the following five questionnaire scales: Denial-Avoidance (i.e., refusal to empathize), Involvement-Concern (including primarily items concerning role taking), Hostility-Empathy, Friend-Empathy, and Fantasy-Empathy (concerning involvement with characters in stories, plays, or movies). From initial validation studies, Stotland et al. concluded that the Fantasy-Empathy Scale was the most valid and used this scale in nearly all subsequent work.

Only Davis (1980, 1983a,b) has attempted to differentiate between personal distress and empathic concern (i.e., sympathy). His questionnaire, the Interpersonal Reactivity Index (IRI), contains four subscales: empathic concern, personal distress, fantasy, and perspective taking. The personal distress and empathic concern subscales obviously are most relevant to the issue at hand.

The results across questionnaire indices suggest that there is a positive relation between empathy and prosocial behavior, especially among adults. For adult samples, empathy scores have been positively related to volunteering to assist others (e.g., Archer, Diaz-Loving, Gollwitzer, Davis, & Foushee, 1981; Barnett, Feighy, & Esper, 1983; Earle, Diaz-Loving, & Archer, 1982; Fultz, Batson, Fortenbach, McCarthy, & Varney, 1985; Leftgoff-Sechooler, 1979; Mehrabian & Epstein, 1972; Seaman, 1979), self-report of altruistic or cooperative behaviors, attitudes, and values (Bohlmeyer & Helmstadter, 1985; Crandall & Harris, 1976; Davis, 1983b; Rushton, Chrisjohn, & Fekken, 1981; Hansson, reported in Stotland et al., 1978), self-report of the inclination to pick up a crying infant (Wiesenfeld, Whitman, & Malatesta, 1984), time on a crisis hotline phone dealing with crisis calls (Mathews study, reported in Stotland et al., 1978), and the reported use of effective comforting verbalizations (Burleson, 1983). Researchers who did not find a consistent positive relation between prosocial behavior and empathy, sometimes found a positive relation for some persons but not others (e.g., first but not second borns, Hammersala's study, reported in Stotland et al., 1978) or under some conditions (e.g., Davis, 1983a, when the subject was not provided with an empathy/inducing set; see also Earle et al., 1982). In only a few studies involving adults has empathy been unrelated (Batson, Bolen, Cross, & Neuringer-Benefiel, 1986; Harnett, 1981; Van Ornum, Foley, Burns, DeWolfe, & Kennedy, 1981) or negatively related (Harnett, 1981, for one of four correlations; Davis, Hansson, & Jones study, reported in Stotland et al., 1978; Mathews & Stotland study, in Stotland et al., 1978) to prosocial indices. In contrast, many have found personal distress scales to be unrelated to prosocial responding (Batson et al., 1986; Davis, 1983b), although Batson et al. (1986) obtained a positive relation with helping when it was difficult for subjects to escape from dealing with the needy other.

Results for adolescents and children are somewhat less consistent, although there seems to be a weak-to-moderate positive association between questionnaire indices of empathy and prosocial behavior. Significant or marginally significant positive relations have been obtained in several studies with adolescents (Barnett, Howard, King, & Dino, 1981; Eisenberg-Berg & Mussen, 1978, for males but not females) and children (Reichman, 1982; Strayer, 1983). Inconsistent findings across prosocial measures and/or age groups have been noted in other studies (Eisenberg, Pasternack, & Lennon, 1984; Kalliopuska, 1980), empathy being both positively related and unrelated to indices of prosocial responding. To our knowledge, only one study obtained no positive associations (Peraino, 1977), and we are aware of no research in which a negative relation was reported.

In summary, questionnaire measures of empathy are, in general, diverse in content. Nonetheless, there tends to be a positive association between these indices and measures of prosocial responding. In the few studies based on a measure of sympathy (the Davis measure) (Batson et al., 1986; Davis, 1983a,b), the results are not any more consistent than in studies involving other indices of empathy. Thus, it is not clear which component or components of the empathy questionnaire are responsible for the positive association with prosocial behavior. Indeed, the positive relation between questionnaire indices and prosocial behavior may be due in part to the fact that these questionnaires tap more domains of vicarious affective response than do picture-story indices.

Self-report of reactions in experimental settings

In a number of studies participants have been exposed to lifelike empathy-inducing stimuli (eg., videotapes) and then asked to rate or otherwise report their affective reactions (prior to being provided the opportunity to assist the needy other). Many of these studies were conducted by Batson and his colleagues and therefore involve self-report of both sympathy and personal distress. Very little of this research has involved child participants.

In a number of these studies, especially those involving adults, self-report of sympathy (Archer, Diaz-Loving, Gollwitzer, Davis, & Foushee, 1981; Batson, Cowles, & Coke, 1979; Coke, Batson, & McDavis, 1978; Rultz et al., 1985), general upset or anxiety (Gaertner & Dovidio, 1977; Marks, Penner, & Stone, 1982), or both (Shelton & Rogers, 1981), have been positively associated with prosocial behavior. The association between sympathy and helping seems to be especially strong in situations in which it is easy to escape the distressing stimulus (Batson, O'Quin, Fultz, Vanderplus, & Isen, 1983, study 1; Toi & Batson, 1982). Personal distress as assessed by Batson and his colleagues generally has not been associated with assisting (Archer et al., 1981; Batson, 1986; Batson et al., 1983, studies 1, 2, & 3; Coke et al., 1978; Fultz, 1982; Fultz et al., 1985; Toi & Batson, 1982), although a positive relation was found by Coke (1980). Not surprisingly however, the data are not entirely consistent; in some studies, no significant relation between sympathy and helping has been obtained (Batson et al., 1983, studies 2 & 3; Coke, 1980; Fultz, 1982). Moreover, in studies with children, self-report of emotional reactions to another's distress tends to be unrelated (Brehm, Powell, & Coke, 1984; Zahn-Waxler, Friedman, & Cummings, 1982) or inconsistently, positively related (Eisenberg, McCreath, & Ahn, in press; Kuchenbecker, 1977; Peraino & Sawin, 1981) to prosocial action. The weak association between self-report of empathy and children's prosocial behavior may be due either to children's difficulty in veridically asserting and/or reporting their emotional states or to a weaker link between affect and behavior among the young.

In summary, there appears to be a moderate positive association between adults' reports of experiencing negative affect, especially sympathy, and their subsequent assisting of the distressed other. The data pertaining to children are considerably weaker, although there is some evidence of an association in the predicted direction. Whether the discrepancy in findings between adults and children is due to differences in the nature of children's and adults' self-reports of sympathy/empathy or to the strength of the relation between sympathy and prosocial behavior is unclear.

Other-report of children's sympathy

Ratings of children's sympathy/empathy by significant others (e.g., teachers, parents, and/or peers) has not been employed by researchers until recently. Typically, children are rated on various aspects of their emotional responsiveness to others, including indicators of concern and emotional matching, across a wide variety of situations. Consequently, this approach may allow researchers to obtain a larger sampling of children's empathic responsiveness than can be obtained during experimental sessions or one-time assessments of empathy.

The results of the few studies using other-reports of children's empathy are mixed. Teacher and/or peer ratings of children's empathy have been positively related to other-reports, of helping and sharing (Sawin et al., 1981; Strayer, 1983) and actual helping behaviors (Barnett, Howard, Melton, & Dino, 1982). However, in Sawin et al.'s study (1981), teachers' ratings of empathy did not relate to donating in a laboratory setting, although they were positively associated with teachers' reports of helpfulness. Similarly, Strayer (1983) found parental reports of empathy to be positively related to parental but not to teachers' reports of prosocial behavior. Thus, the relation between other-reports of empathy and prosocial behavior appears to be strong primarily when the reports of both modes of functioning are obtained from the same informant; in such instances, however, the interrelation may be due to a halo effect.

Nonverbal facial/gestural indices

Three procedures have been used to study the relation between facial/gestural indices of empathy (henceforth called somatic indices) and prosocial behavior:

1. Participants' reactions have been observed while they were responding to a picture-story index of empathy.
2. Participants' reactions have been observed while they viewed tapes of persons who were not the potential recipients of assistance.
3. Participants have been observed while viewing those persons who were subsequently the potential recipients of aid.

Each procedure is discussed in turn, although in some instances a given study may have used more than one procedure.

In only three studies have investigators assessed somatic reactions while participants were responding to picture/story measures of empathy. Sawin et al. (1981) correlated the somatic reactions of first and third graders while responding to the FASTE with scores on an anonymous donation task. There were no significant relations when scores for the total sample were combined. Nor were there significant relations when the sample was broken into groups by age and sex. However, when Sawin et al. examined the facial data in response to each of the four emotions (sad, happy, anger, fear) depicted in FASTE stories, they found a positive relation between happy empathic facial affect and donations for first-grade girls, and a positive, marginally significant relation between empathic fear and donations for first-grade boys. There were no significant associations for third-grade girls or boys; furthermore, empathic sadness and anger were unrelated to donating.

Howard (1983) conducted a similar study in which he examined the relation between preschoolers' facial empathy in reaction to stories concerning happy, sad, angry, and hurt peers and the helping of peers. He found that helpfulness in boys was positively related to facial empathy with others' happiness, but negatively related to empathy with sad others. Girls who were more helpful exhibited more empathy with sad peers than did less helpful girls.

In the third study involving preschoolers and second graders, Cohen (1974) found that facial/gestural reactions to a picture-story presentation were marginally, negatively related to preschool boys' donating, whereas empathy with happy feelings was positively related to teachers' ratings of consideration for others, especially for second graders. Similarly, Marcus, Roke, and Bruner (1985) found that preschoolers' facial empathy was negatively related to teachers' ratings of cooperation; however, the measure of cooperation was more an index of sociability than prosocial behavior. In brief, the results in studies involving somatic reactions to picture-story indices are inconsistent and vary considerably with sex of child and type of empathic affect.

We located one study in which investigators examined the relation between children's reactions to empathy-inducing films of peers and the assisting of persons not in the films. Solomon (1985) showed kindergarten, second, fourth, and sixth graders tapes that depicted sad, angry, and pleasurable events involving other children and assessed prosocial behaviors (as well as aggressive and socially responsible behaviors) via teacher ratings. For girls, facial empathic sadness was positively related to ratings of prosocial and socially responsible behavior, and negatively related to aggression. For boys, empathic anger was negatively related to ratings of prosocial and socially responsible behavior. Given that children generally could respond with either sadness or anger to the same film clips and that anger may have represented the more hostile response, the fact that boys' empathic anger was negatively related to prosocial ratings is not inconsistent with the finding that girls' empathic sadness was positively related to prosocial ratings.

We located six studies in which facial empathy with a particular individual was examined in relation to subsequent helping of that person. Kuchenbecker (1977) found that 4–5- and 7–8-year-olds' sharing with a peer was negatively related to hostile behavior (facial and verbal) directed toward the peer when the children viewed a tape of the peer. Sad and positive facial/verbal empathic responses were unrelated to generosity. However, in several other studies, negative facial reactions to a videotaped needy peer were positively related to young children's anonymous sharing and/or helping behaviors (Leiman, 1978; Lennon, Eisenberg, & Carroll, 1983; Peraino & Sawin, 1981). For example, Peraino and Sawin (1981) assessed first-grade girls' facial and gestural reactions to three tapes of three different needy peers and provided the children with opportunities to assist each of the three needy peers. Facial responsiveness (negative affect) in reaction to viewing a specific film was positively related to assisting the peer in each of the three instances. Moreover, speed of reaction was positively related for two of the three recipients. Gestural indices were inconsistently related to assisting. The associations were considerably stronger between empathizing with a given person and assisting that same person than between empathizing with one peer and prosocial behavior directed toward a different peer. In other words, empathy and assisting were more highly related if both were assessed in the same situation and involved the same person.

Unlike Leiman, Lennon et al., and Peraino and Sawin, Zahn-Waxler et al. (1983) noted a negative relation between preschoolers' and school-age children's facial/gestural displays of negative emotion when hearing an infant cry and subsequently helping to look for a bottle for the infant. Moreover, Chapman, Iannotti, Cooperman, and Zahn-Waxler (1984), using the same sample and some of the same data, found that the positive affect displayed when the infant cried was positively related to helping the infant but not to helping a woman who hurt her back or to helping to find a can opener to feed a kitten. Perhaps positive emotion expressed when hearing a baby cry was more an index of how much the children liked or were interested in babies than empathy or sympathy.

In none of the studies reviewed above were different negative facial reactions differentiated from one another. Thus, scores on negative affect in reaction to another's distress could indicate purely vicarious reactions, sympathy, personal distress, or merely negative mood. This is a problem because recent theory and research suggest that personal distress is positively associated with prosocial behavior primarily when escape from the distressing stimulus (e.g., the needy other) is difficult (Batson & Coke, 1981). In a recent study, Eisenberg et al. (in press) attempted to differentiate between sympathy and personal distress and examine the relation of each to various instances of prosocial behavior. Children's facial/gestural reactions when viewing two tapes (on two separate days) of peers experiencing distress were taped and coded for concerned/sad and anxious/worried reactions (or both). The former reactions were thought to reflect a primarily sympathetic reaction whereas the latter were thought to reflect personal distress. Intensity of these reactions was correlated with spontaneous (self-initiated) and peer-requested prosocial behavior assessed when dyads of peers were playing with a single attractive toy. We reasoned that spontaneous prosocial behaviors could be viewed as assisting in an easy escape situation because the benefactor need not have spontaneously offered help. In contrast, the peer-requested actions were viewed as analogous to assisting in a difficult escape situation because one has to continue to deal with the requester and his or her request if one refuses to assist.

The data, for the most part, supported Batson's predictions. Children's sad/concerned reactions were positively related to spontaneous prosocial behaviors, whereas worried/concerned reactions were positively associated with requested behaviors. For girls only, sad/concerned reactions also were positively correlated with requested prosocial actions. Happy reactions were marginally, negatively related to helping when the children were given the opportunity to assist the injured children in the film. On the basis of these data, it seems reasonable to suggest that some of the inconsistent findings in prior research concerning the relation between empathy with another's distress and prosocial responding were due to the failure to differentiate between sympathy and personal distress or among various modes of prosocial behavior.

In summary, the data concerning the relation between somatic indices of empathy and prosocial behavior are somewhat inconsistent. However, considerable data support the view that dysphoric reactions (sad or worried, not angry or hostile) when viewing another's distress are positively associated with prosocial responding. The findings are clearest in studies in which videotapes rather than stories were used to evoke empathy and are likely to be stronger if composite measures of prosocial behavior are used (e.g., Lennon et al., 1983) or discriminations are made among modes of both negative somatic reactions (e.g., personal distress versus sympathy) and prosocial behaviors.

Physiological indices

We could locate only four studies in which physiological indices of empathy were examined in relation to prosocial behavior. In two of those studies, a positive correlation between helping and physiological responsiveness was obtained. Both Gaertner and Dovidio (1977) and Sterling and Gaertner (1984) obtained a positive association between heart rate acceleration and speed of helping in unambiguous emergency situations. However, in an ambiguous emergency situation, the association tended (nonsignificantly, for the most part) to reverse itself (Sterling & Gaertner, 1984). In the third study, palmar sweating in reaction to viewing an empathy-inducing tape was not related to the time spent by nurses interacting with patients (Mathews & Stotland, reported by Stotland et al., 1978). Finally, Epstein (1975) found no relation between skin conductance and emotional reactivity when individuals viewed another exhibit pleasant and unpleasant emotions.

It is unknown at this time if heart rate (HR) responsiveness in reaction to another's distress is an index of sympathy, empathy, personal distress, or some other emotional reaction. It has been shown, however, that anxiety and self-concern are positively associated with heart rate acceleration (e.g., Darley & Katz, 1973; Lazarus, Speisman, Mordkoff, & Davison, 1962). Moreover, researchers have hypothesized that heart rate acceleration is positively related to self-focus whereas an outward or other-orientation is associated with heart rate deceleration (Lacey, Kagan, Lacey, & Moss, 1963). Thus, it is reasonable to hypothesize that a self-oriented, personal distress reaction should be associated with HR acceleration whereas an other-oriented, sympathetic response may be associated with relative HR deceleration (Campos, Butterfield, & Klinnert, 1985). In the unambiguous emergency situations studied by Gaertner and his colleagues, HR acceleration may have indicated personal distress, and therefore was positively correlated with helping because it was difficult to escape from the distressing stimulus (the injured person was in the next room); recall that personal distress is expected to enhance helping if there is no other way to reduce one's own distress. Consistent with this view is Sterling and Gaertner's (1984) finding that HR acceleration was nonsignificantly negatively related to helping when the emergency was ambiguous and when escape via cognitive mechanisms (such as denial) was easier. Indeed, HR acceleration in the ambiguous emergency situation was negatively associated with participants' report of how serious they judged the other individual's injuries to be.

Unfortunately, both studies involving heart rate assessed helping in an emergency situation. It is quite likely that the patterns of association between assisting and sympathy or personal distress differ in emergency versus nonemergency situations (owing to the average level of arousal and the immediacy of the situation). Consequently, further research is needed in which HR as well as other physiological indices of sympathy and personal distress are examined in relation to subsequent prosocial responding.

Empathic inductions

A common procedure in studies of the relation between empathy and prosocial behavior has been to attempt to induce or inhibit empathy/sympathy via experimental procedures (in lieu of or in addition to exposing subjects to a distressed or needy other). In general, a given induction procedure is used with some study participants, and their subsequent prosocial responding is compared with that of participants in control groups or those receiving an alternative induction procedure.

Most of the induction procedures fall into the following categories:

1. observational set manipulations,
2. procedures that alter persons' attributions regarding their own physiological arousal,
3. manipulations of actual physiological arousal,
4. empathic mood inductions, and
5. similarity manipulations whereby perceived similarity with a needy other is manipulated.

Training studies in which individuals are provided with experiences designed to enhance empathic responding can also be viewed as a type of empathic induction, although it is the trait rather than a temporary empathic reaction that the experimenter hopes to alter. Research related to each of these modes of induction is examined in turn.

Observational set. The most commonly used method of inducing empathy in research involving adults has been to manipulate the participants' observational set. Typically, some participants are instructed to "imagine" themselves in the needy other's position or imagine how the other feels, and their subsequent helping or sharing is contrasted with that of participants instructed to merely observe, watch, listen to, or evaluate the needy other.

The results of the research involving observational set inductions are complex. In some studies, researchers have found that the empathic inductions were associated with self-reported empathic reactions (e.g., Davis, 1983a; Fultz et al., 1985; Howard & Barnett, 1981; Toi & Batson, 1982); in other studies, the set manipulation apparently did not induce empathy (Coke, 1980). Moreover, in some studies, persons who received the empathy-inducing instructions (sometimes in combination with other induction procedures, e.g., Coke et al., 1978) prior to exposure to a needy other were more likely to assist the other (Coke et al., 1978; Fultz et al., 1985; Howard & Barnett, 1981; Shelton & Rogers, 1981; Toi & Batson, 1982); in other studies the empathic set increased helping for only one sex (Brehm et al., 1984, for boys; Curry, 1978, for girls on one of three measures; Davis, 1983a, for girls) or did not produce the expected pattern of helping (Coke, 1980; Wispé, Kiecolt, & Long, 1977).

Despite some inconsistencies, the overall pattern of the findings seems to support the assertion that sympathy/empathy is positively associated with performance of prosocial behavior. Especially when the induction manipulation worked, inducing an empathic set frequently resulted in more helping than did inducing an uninvolved set.

Attributions regarding arousal. For the most part, the findings from studies concerning manipulations of attributions related to physiological responding indicate that sympathizing mediates prosocial responding, but can be inhibited if individuals are led to misinterpret empathic arousal. In studies in which adults were induced to attribute their arousal in an emergency or an otherwise arousing situation to another source (e.g., a drug believed to induce arousal or exercise), bystanders helped less or after a longer interval than did other persons who had not been induced to misattribute their arousal (Coke et al., 1978; Gaertner & Dovidio, 1977; Harris & Huang, 1973). Indeed, Batson, Duncan, Ackerman, Buckley, and Birch (1981) found that misattribution procedures could be used to induce feelings of either sympathy or personal distress, and that they could produce the expected pattern of assisting with their misattribution procedures.

An exception to this general pattern was reported by Sterling and Gaertner (1984), who found that males who were aroused by high levels of exercise helped more than other persons in an unambiguous emergency, but less in an ambiguous emergency. Apparently, when the emergency is clear, some residual arousal from performance of the exercise may be mistakenly attributed to reacting to the emergency, given that people would expect an unambiguous emergency to elicit high levels of arousal.

Arousal induction. In other studies researchers have attempted to induce arousal in adults that would be misinterpreted as empathy or sympathy. Typically, either real arousal has been created by manipulations, or perceived arousal has been induced by false physiological feedback. Persons who are administered the experimental manipulations are expected to attribute their arousal to sympathetic processes and, consequently, to assist faster or to a greater degree.

The limited findings in this area of research are generally positive. Leftgoff-Sechooler (1979) found that helping was greatest if induced arousal was moderate rather than very low or very high. Moreover, Peraino (1977) found that arousal produced by exposure to unpleasant pictures increased adolescent boys' generous behavior. However, Archer et al. (1981) found that false skin conductance feedback to adults increased helping only for persons who ranked high on a dispositional (questionnaire) measure of empathy and were in a situation in which the experimenter was purportedly monitoring the subjects' physiological responses (i.e., a situation in which evaluation was more likely).

Similarity manipulations. For decades, researchers have assumed that inducing an individual to identify with another increases empathic responding. One technique used to enhance identification is to encourage persons to believe they are similar to another in attitudes, values, or preferences (e.g., Stotland, 1969).

We located only a few studies in which empathy, as induced by a similarity manipulation, was examined in relation to subsequent prosocial responding. In these investigations, adults (Batson et al., 1981; Krebs, 1975) and children (Panofsky, 1976) who believed themselves similar to a needy other subsequently assisted the other more than did persons who believed themselves dissimilar. In the Krebs study, physiological indices supported the assumption that the similarity manipulation was successful. In brief, the results of both studies are consistent with the view that empathy/sympathy mediates adults' altruistic responding.

Summary

A distinct pattern is evident in the results from empirical studies of the relation between prosocial behavior and sympathy and empathy. For adults, a variety of measures of empathy have been found that, in general, relate positively to indices of prosocial behavior. For children the results are mixed. Self-report indices such as responses to picture-story indices and empathy questionnaires have not been consistently associated with measures of prosocial behavior; however, the data for facial/gestural indices are somewhat more consistent with the notion of a positive relation between sympathy or empathy and prosocial behavior.

One possible explanation for the discrepancy between the data on children and adults is that different methods were used to assess sympathy at different ages. In most studies with children, the measure of empathy traditionally has been a picture-story procedure. As mentioned earlier, such techniques are of questionable validity (see Eisenberg & Lennon, 1983; Hoffman, 1982b). Moreover, although one must always interpret the results of self-report questionnaires with caution, such caution is especially merited when questionnaires are used with children who may have difficulty reporting their typical emotional reactions.

The research conducted with children and adults differs in another respect. Most of the research involving self-report of sympathy or empathy in a specific situation or empathy inductions in an experimental setting has been based on adult samples. In these studies, empathy with a specific person in a particular situation is assessed, and usually is examined in association with prosocial behavior in that same situation. As already mentioned, this method of assessing the empathy–prosocial link is likely to be more powerful than simply correlating a measure of the trait of empathy with an unrelated measure of prosocial behavior.

Interestingly, where such state measures of sympathy or empathy have been used with children (some of the work with facial/gestural measures), the overall results point to an empathy–prosocial behavior link. Thus, one interpretation of the existing pattern of data is that the relation between empathy and prosocial behavior is weaker for children because few researchers have measured the relation between children's empathy in a specific situation and their subsequent assistance in that same situation. In addition, some measures used with adults, such as self-report in experimental situations and empathy inductions, seem more likely to measure sympathy, as opposed to mere emotional contagion or diffuse emotional arousal, than the picture-story indices typically used with children. Given that a stronger relation can be expected between sympathy and altruism than between empathy and altruism, the use of different instruments with children and adults could account for the stronger pattern of results for adults.

Of course, it is also quite possible that there are real age differences in the strength of the positive association between empathy and altruism. Certainly, in the first two or three years of life, because children may have considerable difficulty both in interpreting their own emotional reactions and in understanding when and how to assist others, one would expect a relatively weak association between the two aspects of functioning. Moreover, even somewhat older children may be more inhibited in their prosocial behavior than are adults owing to their lesser competence (e.g., Peterson, 1983). In addition, it is likely that children, because of their lesser role-taking abilities, are more likely than adults to experience vicarious arousal as personal distress rather than sympathy, and are therefore less likely to assist a needy other. In brief, differences in the association between empathy (or sympathy) and altruism for children and adults probably reflects differences that are both developmentally based and related to the methodologies used.

What is clear from our review of the empirical literature is that the research concerning sympathy and empathy lacks much in the way of both conceptual and methodological sophistication. Distinctions among sympathy, personal distress reactions, and emotional contagion are needed; moreover, the question of when these emotional responses can be expected to relate to altruistic and other modes of prosocial behavior must be taken more seriously. In addition, better methods must be devised to assess sympathy, empathy, and personal distress, methods that are less likely than self-report indices to be contaminated by demand characteristics or self-presentational concerns. Perhaps just as important, sorely needed is a multimethod approach for assessing vicariously produced emotional reactions and their correlates. A multimethod study might include qualitative methods such as ethnographic reports that may help to explain unique person–situation interactions. Thus, there is much to challenge researchers in the future, and much to be done before we can truly understand the nature of the relation between sympathy/empathy and prosocial behavior.

References

Archer, R. L., Diaz-Loving, R., Gollwitzer, P. M., Davis, M. H., & Foushee, H. C. (1981). The role of dispositional empathy and social evaluation in the empathic mediation of helping. *Journal of Personality and Social Psychology, 40,* 786–796.

Aronfreed, J. (1970). The socialization of altruistic and sympathetic behavior: Some theoretical and experimental analyses. In J. Macauley & L. Berkowitz (Eds.), *Altruism and helping behavior* (pp. 103–126). New York: Academic Press.

Barnett, M. A., Feighy, K. M., & Esper, J. A. (1983). Effects of anticipated victim responsiveness and empathy upon volunteering. *Journal of Social Psychology, 119,* 211–218.

Barnett, M. A., Howard, J. A., King, L. M., & Dino, G. A. (1981). Helping behavior and the transfer of empathy. *Journal of Social Psychology, 115,* 125–132.

Barnett, M. A., Howard, J. A., Melton, E. M., & Dino, G. A. (1982). Effect of inducing sadness about self or other on helping behavior in high and low empathic children. *Child Development, 53,* 920–923.

Bar-Tal, D. (1982). Sequential development of helping behavior: A cognitive-learning approach. *Developmental Review, 2,* 101–124.

Batson, C. D., Bolen, M. H., Cross, J. A., & Neuringer-Benefield, H. E. (1986). Where is the altruism in the altruistic personality? *Journal of Personality and Social Psychology, 50,* 212–220.

Batson, C. D., & Coke, J. S. (1981). Empathy: A source of altruistic motivation for helping? In J. P. Rushton & R. M. Sorrentino (Eds.), *Altruism and helping behavior: Social, personality, and developmental perspectives* (pp. 167–211). Hillsdale, NJ: Erlbaum.

Batson, C. D., Cowles, C., & Coke, J. S. (1979). *Empathic motivation for helping: Could it be altruistic?* Unpublished paper, University of Kansas.

Batson, C. D., Duncan, B. D., Ackerman, P., Buckey, T., & Birch, K. (1981). Is empathic emotion a source of altruistic motivation? *Journal of Personality and Social Psychology, 40,* 290–302.

Batson, C. D., O'Quin, K., Fultz, J., Vanderplus, M., & Isen, A. M. (1983). Influence of self-reported distress and empathy on egoistic versus altruistic motivation to help. *Journal of Personality and Social Psychology, 45,* 706–718.

Bazar, J. W. (1977). An exploration of the relationship of affect awareness, empathy, and interpersonal strategies to nursery school children's competence in peer interactions. *Dissertation Abstracts International, 37,* 5691A. (University Microfilms No. 77-4373)

Block, J. H. (1973). Conceptions of sex role: Some cross-cultural and longitudinal perspectives. *American Psychologist, 28,* 512–526.

Blum, L. A. (1980). *Friendship, altruism and morality.* London: Routledge–Kegan Paul.

Bohlmeyer, E. M., & Helmstadter, G. C. (1985, March). *Cooperative and competitive attitudes as predictors of emotional empathy.* Paper presented at the annual meeting of the National Association of School Psychology, Las Vegas.

Brehm, S. S., Powell, L. K., & Coke, J. S. (1984). The effects of empathic instructions upon donating behavior: Sex differences in young children. *Sex Roles, 10,* 405–416.

Bryant, B. (1982). An index of empathy for children and adolescents. *Child Development, 53,* 413–425.

Burleson, B. R. (1983). Social cognition, empathic motivation, and adults' comforting strategies. *Human Communication Research, 10,* 295–304.

Campos, J. J., Butterfield, P., & Klinnert, M. (1985, April). *Cardiac and behavioral differentiation of negative emotional signals: An individual differences perspective.* Paper presented at the biennial meeting of the Society for Research on Child Development, Toronto.

Chapman, M., Iannotti, R., Cooperman, G., & Zahn-Waxler, C. (1984). *Cognition, affect, and attributions as predictors of children's helping.* Unpublished manuscript, Max Planck Institute for Human Development and Education, Berlin.

Cohen, E. C. (1974). Empathy, awareness of interpersonal responsibility and consideration for others in young children (Doctoral dissertation, Michigan State University, 1973). *Dissertation Abstracts International, 34,* 6192B.

Coke, J. S. (1980). Empathic mediation of helping: Egoistic or altruistic? (Doctoral dissertation, University of Kansas, 1979). *Dissertation Abstracts International, 41,* 405B.

Coke, J. S., Batson, C. D., & McDavis, K. (1978). Empathic mediation of helping: A two-stage model. *Journal of Personality and Social Psychology, 36,* 752–766.

Crandall, J. E., & Harris, M. D. (1976). Social interest, cooperation, and altruism. *Journal of Individual Psychology, 32,* 50–54.

Curry, J. F. (1978). Effects of locus of control and empathy on attributions and altruism. *Dissertation Abstracts International, 39,* 1947B. (University Microfilms No. 78-17587)

Darley, S. A., & Katz, I. (1973). Heart rate changes in children as a function of test versus game instructions and test anxiety. *Child Development, 44,* 783–789.

Davis, M. (1980). A multidimensional approach to individual differences in empathy. *JSAS Catalog of Selected Documents In Psychology, 10,* 85.

Davis, M. H. (1983a). Empathic concern and the muscular dystrophy telethon: Empathy as a multidimensional construct. *Personality and Social Psychology Bulletin, 9,* 223–229.

Davis, M. H. (1983b). The effects of dispositional empathy on emotional reactions and helping: A multidimensional approach. *Journal of Personality, 51,* 167–184.

Earle, W. B., Diaz-Loving, R., & Archer, R. L. (1982, August). *Antecedents of helping: Assessing the role of empathy and values.* Paper presented at the annual meeting of the American Psychological Association, Washington, D.C.

Eisenberg, N. (1982). The development of reasoning regarding prosocial behavior. In N. Eisenberg (Ed.), *The development of prosocial behavior* (pp. 219–249). New York: Academic Press.

Eisenberg, N. (1986). *Altruistic cognition, emotion, and behavior.* Hillsdale, NJ: Erlbaum.

Eisenberg, N., & Lennon, R. (1983). Sex differences in empathy and related capacities. *Psychological Bulletin, 94,* 100–131.

Eisenberg, N., McCreath, H., & Ahn, R. (in press). Sympathy, personal distress, and prosocial behavior in children. *Personality and Social Psychology Bulletin.*

Eisenberg, N., Pasternack, J. F., & Lennon, R. (1984, March). *Prosocial development in middle childhood.* Paper presented at the biennial meeting of the Southwestern Society for Research in Human Development, Denver.

Eisenberg-Berg, N. (1979). Development of children's prosocial moral judgment. *Developmental Psychology, 15,* 128–137.

Eisenberg-Berg, N., & Lennon, R. (1980). Altruism and the assessment of empathy in the preschool years. *Child Development, 51,* 552–557.

Eisenberg-Berg, N., & Mussen, P. (1978). Empathy and moral development in adolescence. *Developmental Psychology, 14,* 185–186.

Fay, B. (1971). The relationships of cognitive moral judgment, generosity, and empathic behavior in six and eight year old children. *Dissertation Abstracts International, 31,* 3951A. (University Microfilms No. 71-4868)

Fellner, C. H., & Marshall, J. R. (1981). Kidney donors revisited. In J. P. Rushton & R. M. Sorrentino (Eds.), *Altruism and helping behavior: Social, personality and developmental perspectives* (pp. 351-365). Hillsdale, NJ: Erlbaum.

Feshbach, N. D. (1978). Studies of empathic behavior in children. In B. A. Maher (Ed.), *Progress in experimental personality research* (Vol. 8, pp. 1–47). New York: Academic Press.

Feshbach, N. D. (1980, May). *The psychology of empathy and the empathy of psychology*. Presidential address presented at the annual meeting of the Western Psychological Association, Honolulu.

Feshbach, N. D. (1982). Sex differences in empathy and social behavior in children. In N. Eisenberg (Ed.), *The development of prosocial behavior* (pp. 315–338). New York: Academic Press.

Feshbach, N. D., & Roe, K. (1968). Empathy in six- and seven-year-olds. *Child Development, 39*, 133–145.

Fultz, J. N. (1982). *Influence of potential for self-reward on egoistically and altruistically motivated helping*. Unpublished master's thesis, University of Kansas, Lawrence, Kansas.

Fultz, J. N., Batson, C. D., Fortenbach, V. A., McCarthy, P. M., & Varney, L. L. (1985). *Social evaluation and the empathy–altruism hypothesis*. Unpublished manuscript, University of Kansas.

Gaertner, S. L., & Dovidio, J. F. (1977). The subtlety of white racism, arousal, and helping behavior. *Journal of Personality and Social Psychology, 35*, 691–707.

Harnett, C. B. (1981) Personality traits, values, and empathic capabilities as predictors of prosocial behavior. *Dissertation Abstracts International, 42*, 1587B. (University Microfilms No. 81-21271)

Harris, M. B., & Huang, L. C. (1973). Competence and helping. *Journal of Social Psychology, 89*, 203–210.

Hoffman, M. L. (1976). Empathy, role-taking, guilt, and development of altruistic motives. In T. Lickona (Ed.), *Moral development and behavior: Theory, research and social issues* (pp. 124–143). New York: Holt, Rinehart, and Winston.

Hoffman, M. L. (1981). Is altruism part of human nature? *Journal of Personality and Social Psychology, 40*, 121–137.

Hoffman, M. L. (1982a). Development of prosocial motivation: Empathy and guilt. In N. Eisenberg (Ed.), *The development of prosocial behavior* (pp. 218–231). New York: Academic Press.

Hoffman, M. L. (1982b). The measurement of empathy. In C. E. Izard (Ed.), *Measuring emotions in infants and children* (pp. 279–296). Cambridge: Cambridge University Press.

Hoffman, M. L. (1984). Interaction of affect and cognition in empathy. In C. E. Izard, J. Kagan, & R. B. Zajonc (Eds.), *Emotions, cognitions, and behavior* (pp. 103–131). Cambridge: Cambridge University Press.

Howard, J. A. (1983). Preschoolers' empathy for specific affects and their social interaction. *Dissertation Abstracts International, 44*, 3954B. (University Microfilms No. DA 8407675)

Howard, J. A., & Barnett, M. A. (1981). Arousal of empathy and subsequent generosity in young children. *Journal of Genetic Psychology, 138*, 307–308.

Hume, D. (1966). *Enquiries concerning the human understanding and concerning the principles of morals* (2nd ed.); Oxford: Claredon Press (original work published 1777).

Iannotti, R. J. (1975, April). *The effect of role-taking experiences on role-taking, altruism, empathy, and aggression*. Paper presented at the biennial meeting of the Society for Research in Child Development, Denver.

Iannotti, R. J. (1977). *Empathy and the relationship to role taking and altruism: A longitudinal investigation*. Unpublished manuscript, Marietta College.

Iannotti, R. J. (1985). Naturalistic and structured assessments of prosocial behavior in preschool children: The influence of empathy and perspective taking. *Developmental Psychology, 21*, 46–55.

Kalliopuska, M. (1980). Children's helping behaviour: Personality factors and parental influences related to helping behaviour. *Dissertationes Humanarum Litteraum, 24*, Helsinki.

Kalliopuska, M. (1983). Verbal components of emotional empathy. *Perceptual and Motor Skills, 56*, 487–496.

Kameya, L. I. (1976). The effect of empathy level and role-taking training upon prosocial level. *Dissertation Abstracts International, 37*, 3151B. (University Microfilms No. 76-29, 321)

Knudson, K. H. M., & Kagan, S. (1982). Differential development of empathy and prosocial behavior. *Journal of Genetic Psychology, 140.* 249–251.

Krebs, D. (1975). Empathy and altruism. *Journal of Personality and Social Psychology, 32,* 1134–1146.

Kuchenbecker, S. L. Y. (1977). A developmental investigation of children's behavioral, cognitive, and affective responses to empathically stimulating situations. (Doctoral dissertation, University of California, Los Angeles, 1976). *Dissertation Abstracts International, 37,* 5328B–5329B.

Lacey, J. I., Kagan, J., Lacey, B. C., & Moss, H. A. (1963). The visceral level: Situational determinants and behavioral correlates of autonomic response patterns. In P. H. Knapp (Ed.), *Expression of the emotions in man.* New York: International Universities Press.

Lazarus, R. S., Speisman, J. C., Mordkoff, A. M., & Davison, L. A. (1962). A laboratory study of psychological stress produced by a motion picture story. *Psychological Monographs, 76,* 1–35.

Leftgoff-Sechooler, R. (1979). Helping as a function of pleasure, arousal, and dominance. *Dissertation Abstracts International, 39,* 3590B. (University Microfilms No. 79-01374)

Leiman, B. (1978, August). *Affective empathy and subsequent altruism in kindergarteners and first graders.* Paper presented at the annual meeting of the American Psychological Association, Toronto.

Lennon, R., Eisenberg, N., & Carroll, J. (1986). The relation between nonverbal indices of empathy and preschoolers' prosocial behavior. *Journal of Applied Developmental Psychology 3,* 219–224.

Liebhart, E. H. (1972). Empathy and emergency helping: The effects of personality, self-concern and acquaintance. *Journal of Experimental Social Psychology, 8,* 404–411.

Marcus, R. F., Roke, E. J., & Bruner, C. (1985). Verbal and nonverbal empathy and prediction of social behavior of young children. *Perceptual and Motor Skills, 60,* 299–309.

Marks, E. L., Penner, L. A., & Stone, A. V. W. (1982). Helping as a function of empathic responses and sociopathy. *Journal of Research in Personality, 16,* 1–20.

Mehrabian, A., & Epstein, N. A. (1972). A measure of emotional empathy. *Journal of Personality, 40,* 523–543.

Miller, S. M. (1979). Interrelationships among dependency, empathy and sharing: A preliminary study. *Motivation and Emotion, 3,* 183–199.

Panofsky, A. D. (1976). The effect of similarity/dissimilarity of race and personal interests on empathy and altruism in second graders. *Dissertation Abstracts International, 37,* 200A. (University Microfilms No. 76-16659)

Peraino, J. M. (1977). *Role-taking training, affect arousal, empathy, and generosity.* Unpublished manuscript, University of California, Berkeley.

Peraino, J. M., & Sawin, D. B. (1981, April). *Empathic distress: Measurement and relation to prosocial behavior.* Paper presented at the biennial meeting of the Society for Research in Child Development, Boston.

Peterson, L. (1983). Influence of age, task competence, and responsibility focus on children's altruism. *Developmental Psychology, 19,* 141–148.

Piliavin, J. A., Dovidio, J. F., Gaertner, S. L., & Clark, R. D. III. (1981). *Emergency intervention.* New York: Academic Press.

Reichman, F. L. (1982). Empathy and trait anxiety in relation to altruism in children. *Dissertation Abstracts International, 43,* 1626B. (University Microfilms No. 82-23889)

Roe, K. V. (1980). Early empathy development in children and the subsequent internalization of moral values. *Journal of Social Psychology, 110,* 147–148.

Rushton, J. P., Chrisjohn, R. D., & Fekken, G. C. (1984). The altruistic personality and the self-report altruism scale. *Personality and Individual Differences, 2,* 1–11.

Sawin, D. (1979, March). *Assessing empathy in children: A search for an elusive concept.* Paper presented at the biennial meeting of the Society for Research in Child Development, San Francisco.

Sawin, D. B., Underwood, B., Weaver, J., & Mostyn, M. (1981). *Empathy and altruism.* Unpublished manuscript, University of Texas, Austin.

Seaman, R. P. (1979). Variables affecting bystander intervention in a simulated minor emergency: Empathy, locus of control, and social responsibility. *Dissertation Abstracts International, 39,* 5152B. (University Microfilms, No. 7907828)

Shelton, M. L., & Rogers, R. W. (1981). Fear-arousing and empathy-arousing appeals to help: The paths of persuasion. *Journal of Applied Social Psychology, 11,* 366–378.

Solomon, J. (1985, April). *The relation between affective empathy and prosocial behavior in elementary school children.* Paper presented at the biennial meeting of the Society for Research in Child Development, Toronto.

Staub, E. (1978). *Positive social behavior and morality: Social and personal influences* (Vol. 1). New York: Academic Press.

Staub, E., & Feinberg, H. K. (1980, September). *Regularities in peer interaction, empathy, and sensitivity to others.* Paper presented at the annual meeting of the American Psychological Association, Montreal.

Sterling, B., & Gaertner, S. L. (1984). The attribution of arousal and emergency helping: A bidirectional process. *Journal of Experimental Social Psychology, 20,* 286–296.

Stotland, E. (1969). Exploratory studies in empathy. In L. Berkowitz (Ed.), *Advances in Experimental social psychology* (Vol. 4, pp. 271–314). New York: Academic Press.

Stotland, E., Mathews, K. E., Sherman, S. E., Hansson, R. O., & Richardson, B. E. (1978). *Empathy, fantasy, and helping.* Beverly Hills: Sage.

Strayer, J. (1983, April). *Emotional and cognitive components of children's empathy.* Paper presented at the biennial meeting of the Society for Research in Child Development, Detroit.

Toi, M., & Batson, C. D. (1982). More evidence that empathy is a source of altruistic motivation. *Journal of Personality and Social Psychology, 43,* 281–292.

Underwood, B., & Moore, B. (1982). Perspective-taking and altruism. *Psychological Bulletin, 91,* 143–173.

Van Ornum, W., Foley, J. M., Burns, R. R., DeWolfe, A. S., & Kennedy, E. C. (1981). Empathy, altruism, and self-interest in college students. *Adolescence, 16,* 799–808.

Watson, M. S. (1976). The development of cognitive and emotional aspects of empathy and their relationship to a verbal measure of altruism (Doctoral dissertation, University of California, Berkeley, 1976). *Dissertation Abstracts International, 37,* 446B.

Wiesenfeld, A. R., Whitman, P. B., & Malatesta, C. Z. (1984). Individual differences among adult women in sensitivity to infants: Evidence in support of an empathy concept. *Journal of Personality and Social Psychology, 46,* 118–124.

Wispé, L., Kiecolt, J., & Long, R. E. (1977). Demand characteristics, moods, and helping. *Social Behavior and Personality, 5,* 249–255.

Zahn-Waxler, C., Friedman, S. L., & Cummings, E. M. (1983). Children's emotions and behaviors in response to infants' cries. *Child Development, 54,* 1522–1528.

14   Motor mimicry as primitive empathy

Janet Beavin Bavelas, Alex Black, Charles R. Lemery, and Jennifer Mullett

History of the topic

The "most primitive form" of sympathy

In 1759, Adam Smith described a familiar phenomenon:

> When we see a stroke aimed, and just ready to fall upon the leg or arm of another person, we naturally shrink and draw back on our leg or our own arm. (1759/1966, p. 4)

This is elementary motor mimicry, overt action by an observer that is appropriate to or mimetic of the situation of the other person, rather than one's own. The observer acts as if in the other's place to the point of wincing at his pain, smiling at her delight, or (as Smith described) trying to avoid that person's danger.

In his review of sympathy and imitation, Allport (1968, pp. 24–32) documented the long – and yet humble – history of motor mimicry. From Smith on, many social theorists described it as a form of "sympathy," but always as the most primitive form. Smith felt it was "almost a reflex." Spencer (1870) called it "presentative" sympathy because it is immediate and apparently reflexive, in contrast to "representative" sympathy, which is conscious and reflective, and to the even higher (i.e., more intellectualized) "re-representative" sympathy. Ribot (1897) also proposed three kinds of sympathy. The first included, for example, "imitating the movements of a rope-walker while watching him" (1897, p. 232) and was described by Ribot as "its primitive form . . . reflex, automatic, or very slightly conscious" (p. 231). Scheler (1912/1970) reached the limit of subtle distinctions by identifying eight forms of sympathy, three of which were

The Social Sciences and Humanities Research Council of Canada and the University of Victoria have provided financial support since the earliest phases of this project. The order of authors on project publications is alphabetical.

We are indebted to Dr. George Mackie and the Biology Department staff for photographing the figures.

seen as "low grade, really pseudosympathy" (Allport, 1968, p. 27). Elementary motor mimicry (*Einfühlung*) was at the bottom of the hierarchy.

> *Einfühlung* [as treated by Scheler] is the primitive, reflex process mentioned by Smith, Spencer, Ribot, and others. The term "empathy" is a fair translation, provided it is understood to mean only elementary motor mimicry and is not employed in the broad sense of "an ability to understand people," as is sometimes the case today. (Allport, 1968, p. 27)

Indeed, it was from *Einfühlung* that the word *empathy* entered our language in 1912 (see *Shorter Oxford English Dictionary*).

Notice that in early usage, the standard general term was *sympathy,* and *empathy* was specific to motor mimicry. In the latter half of the twentieth century, *empathy* has come to be used as the general term, replacing old-fashioned *sympathy*. Recent usage has also turned away from fine distinctions (cf. Allport, 1961; Strunk, 1957), so that *empathy* has become a global term encompassing vicarious emotion, role taking, and the ability to understand others (and/or to project this nonverbally). Allport had a strong, even harsh, opinion of this:

> It is regrettable that with passing years the original meaning of empathy as "objective motor mimicry" became hopelessly confused and lost to view. . . . The theoretical coin has depreciated, probably beyond redemption (Allport, 1961, pp. 536–537)

In point of fact, this potential confusion has been present from the start. Both Allport (1961, pp. 533–534) and Strunk (1957, p. 47) credit the German psychologist Lipps with introducing the concept of *Einfühlung* in 1907, and both make clear that he was referring to motor mimicry, although the term itself means "feeling oneself into." Lipps assumed that the overt act led to projective understanding, not only of works of art but also of other people. In our view, the terminological problem of empathy arises from this failure to distinguish between an overt behavior and a psychological process that is inferred from it. We do not require, as Allport seemed to, a historical purity in which empathy continues to mean only motor mimicry. However, we do agree with Smith, Spencer, Ribot, and Scheler in their distinctions among various *kinds* of empathy. More is to be gained by identifying clearly what is an observed behavior (motor mimicry) and what is a hypothesized process or construct inferred from that behavior (e.g., projective understanding or vicarious feeling) than by prematurely equating the behavior with these inferences. Our hypothesis is that "primitive empathy" (that is, motor mimicry) functions independently of other empathic processes, that it is instead part of a parallel, communicative process.

Early theory and research

Allport (1968) described early theorists as both attracted to and baffled by motor mimicry. For example, Baldwin (1895, 1897) seemed to rely on "the little understood tendency to elementary motor mimicry" as an explanation of "nondeliberate imitation," noting that

> the child tends to assume the movements, strains, and attitudes of the model. He is "a veritable copying machine" and cannot help doing so. (Allport, 1968, p. 29)

Blanton and Blanton (1927) also emphasized the importance of the infant's assuming the postural tensions of the mother. McDougall (1908) had postulated "primitive passive sympathy," as well as a "nonspecific innate tendency to imitate"; but these could not explain precise overt mimesis, and Allport proposed that McDougall

> was much troubled by the process of precision which enables a child (or a parrot) to [imitate], as well as by the manifest tendency of spectators to assume the postural strains of the dancers or athletes they are watching. (p. 30)

Allport himself felt that motor mimicry "would seem to be genetically and conceptually basic to social learning and to lie at the heart of any theory of imitation" (p. 30). Nonetheless, he did not agree with those who thought that it could be explained as conditioning. He concluded that "this process of *empathy* remains a riddle in social psychology" (p. 30).

We can add other observers to those Allport reviewed. Darwin (1872/1965) described several instances of the nonverbal expression of "sympathy," especially tears for the grief or joy of another (pp. 215–217). He also noticed that his own 4-month-old son would match his (Darwin's) smile and that, by 6 months, the infant "instantly assumed a melancholy expression" when his nurse pretended to cry (p. 358). Indeed, he anticipated our view of the communicative function and social importance of such nonverbal expressions (see the section "Motor mimicry as solely communicative"):

> We readily perceive sympathy in others by their expression; our sufferings are thus mitigated and our pleasures increased; and mutual good feeling is thus strengthened. (p. 364)

Anthropologists have reported ritual "couvade" in which, classically, the father appears to undergo labor pains along with the mother (e.g., Kupferer, 1965). Margaret Mead (1968) described "empathy or imitation" in Manus culture:

> For example, a number of people are standing on opposite sides of a house, supporting themselves by holding onto rafters above their heads; as those on one side initially raise their hands to the rafters, the group facing them will also shift and grasp the rafters – empathetically – and if someone shifts from right hand to left hand, this act will be mirrored by the group on the opposite side. (p. 56)

Relatively early in this century, there were two developments that forecast the possibility of modern experimental work. Köhler (1927) and Allport (1937, 1961)

Figure 14.1. Köhler's (1927, Plate IV) photograph of Sultan watching Grande reach for bananas. Köhler added, parenthetically, "Note Sultan's sympathetic left hand."

were able to go beyond anecdotes and offer photographs of the phenomenon (see Figures 14.1–14.3). It was Clark Hull (1933, pp. 41–44) who brought motor mimicry into the experimental laboratory by arranging for an incident to occur and be recorded. He noted, "Every one has at one time or another caught himself unintentionally performing the actions which he is observing in some other person." Hull, "wishing to secure a graphic record of this fairly well known but little studied tendency," created the first laboratory demonstration. He arranged for an observer to see another person straining and reaching. By surreptitiously pinning a string to the observer's clothing and attaching this string to a rotary event recorder, Hull obtained a trace of the mimetic movements.

O'Toole and Dubin (1968) went on to conduct two full-scale investigations, one based on Hull's, of observers swaying forward while an actor strained to reach forward, and a second one of mothers opening their own mouths while

Figure 14.2. Allport's (1937, p. 531) illustration of "empathy."

spoon-feeding their infants. They saw these as instances as George Herbert Mead's (1934) "taking the role of the other." Both their empirical expression of Mead's theory and the logic of their measurements were major advances. In the first study, O'Toole and Dubin looked for and found evidence that the mother most often opened her own mouth *after* her baby had; hence she was truly mimicking and not merely trying to induce the infant to imitate. In the second study, they had an actor reach forward, with effort, from several different positions relative to the observing subject. The observer consistently swayed forward as well (more than in other directions), thus mimicking the actor's effort.

However, there are some problems with O'Toole and Dubin's data. In their body/sway study, they did not show that they had eliminated the alternative explanation of static ataxia (Edwards, 1942, 1943), which will produce forward movement (more than in other directions) even when the individual is trying to stand still. Another problem, which applies to both studies, is that these researchers were greatly handicapped by not being able to film their subjects; their live

Figure 14.3. Allport's (1961, p. 535) illustration of "empathy."

observations without reported interobserver reliabilities must be treated with some caution. Even though there is a question whether these findings meet today's standards for the study of nonverbal behavior, O'Toole and Dubin's data stand until empirically rebutted. They brought motor mimicry into the beginning of an experimental era and reestablished it as a contemporary topic.

Finally, MacInnis (1979) introduced standard, videotaped stimuli; his observers viewed up to five different incidents evocative of motor mimicry. Even under poor observational conditions, he found that an average of 40% of the subjects displayed mimetic reactions. He also obtained interjudge reliability for the observers' self-reported feelings of empathy ("as if it were happening to me") in his main study and for overt mimetic reactions to pain in a small, live pilot study. He found (as we have in all subsequent studies) that there was a strong effect of stimulus, no evidence for individual differences in the tendency to react, and no relation between the overt facial reaction and self-reported feelings of empathy.

As the above review suggests, motor mimicry is something of a persistent historical puzzle: It has been recorded as a social phenomenon for at least two centuries. Over that period, it has also been observed repeatedly, although, naturally, these observations must be judged by the standards of their time (from anecdotes to photographs to demonstrations to early experiments). It has been explained as reflex, imitation, conditioning, and taking the role of the other; it has been viewed as an indicator of sympathy or, more recently, as an indicator of empathy in the broad sense of this term. Throughout this history, it has been minimized and dismissed, labeled as "primitive," and always considered too simple to be meaningful in itself. But it has also eluded all of our theories, and it does not go away.

Current research on motor mimicry

Motor mimicry intrigued our research group both because of this history and because these simple, natural, and often fleeting acts are, on further reflection, quite subtle. The observer after all is *not* being injured, nor eating baby food, nor straining to reach something. It is, in a sense, inappropriate to "do" the other person's behavior. Such acts give – even advertise – a false and inappropriate impression, namely, that the observer is momentarily the other person in that person's situation rather than his or her own. Why should people do this? Indeed, do they really do it?

Methods for studying motor mimicry

The prerequisite for answering these questions was to improve the methodological and technical state of research on the topic. In order to understand motor mimicry, we first had to capture it for analysis and measure it objectively. Moreover, it was highly desirable to seek a wide variety of instances, in order to show that motor mimicry is a class of behaviors rather than just a few isolated cases. The details of the methods developed are described in Bavelas, Black, Lemery, MacInnis, and Mullett (1986).

Because of the importance of having a permanent record, both for reliability and for frame-by-frame analysis, all experiments are videotaped. Typically, the observer is presented with an incident likely to evoke motor mimicry while being videotaped in split-screen so that both the stimulus and the response are on the final tape.

The stimuli have been presented "live," on videotape, or in narrative. That is, we have enacted incidents that were real, or apparently real, in front of the observer; we have used videotaped excerpts from documentary films or from television and have also produced our own incidents on videotape; and we have simply described incidents or told stories. The typical episode is quite short. Indeed, as it has become clear how precise and synchronous the responses are, we have shortened our stimuli from a minute or so to only a few seconds long.

A broad class of incidents has been found to evoke motor mimicry. These include pain (caused in different episodes by an apparent cut, burn, shock, hammer blow, or crushed finger), laughter, smiling, affection, embarrassment, discomfort, disgust, facing a thrown projectile, ducking away from being hit, stuttering, word-finding, reaching with effort, and succeeding and failing at a timed task.

Having evoked a mimetic reaction and captured it on videotape, the final pre-requisite is to score it. In our working definition, motor mimicry is identified as a reaction by the observer that is

1. similar to one made by the other person (e.g., leaning or smiling when the other does); or
2. one that the other person might make in his or her situation (e.g., Adam Smith's description of shrinking from a blow to another – whether or not the other does); but
3. not what the observer would do as observer (e.g., verbal expressions of concern); and
4. not irrelevant or involuntary behaviors (e.g., startle or ataxia).

These are the principles by which motor mimicry can be distinguished from other behaviors in any given situation. The behaviors thus identified have been reliably scored simply for presence or absence and also for clarity, pattern, quantitative parameters, and microanalysis of synchrony (see Bavelas, Black, Lemery, MacInnis, & Mullett, 1986; Bavelas, Black, Lemery, & Mullett, 1986).

The microsynchrony of the reaction is worth emphasizing here. Motor mim-icry is by no means a single diffuse or global reaction to the evoking incident. When an observer is filmed in split-screen with a sequential stimulus, it becomes obvious that he or she makes several different responses, which are minutely synchronized to the stimulus as it unfolds. For example, in one study (Bavelas, Black, Chant, Lemery, & Mullett, 1987a), we found that virtually all reactions to a 2-minute video clip showing a series of medical procedures were closely related to the immediate stimulus. When *all* voluntary behaviors were counted in 5-second segments, they were shown to be nonrandomly distributed over time and significantly related to the degree of intensity of the stimulus at that partic-ular moment in the stimulus.

A communicative theory

The usual way of approaching motor mimicry has been as a manifesta-tion of an intrapersonal state. For Smith, Spencer, Ribot, Scheler, and Darwin, motor mimicry was hardly separate from primitive feelings of sympathy, for they saw it as an expression of such feelings. Lipps associated motor mimicry with projective understanding. O'Toole and Dubin (following G. H. Mead) inter-preted it as a manifestation of the cognitive process of taking the role of the other. In all of these theories, the overt behavior itself is seen as a kind of over-flow from the primary event, which is an intrapersonal one.

Contemporary psychological approaches to nonverbal behavior would see mo-tor mimicry as an expression of vicarious emotion or empathic feelings. So, although the earlier theories (with the exception of Mead's) probably appear very old-fashioned to modern readers, in fact the paradigm is the same. This traditional psychological model of expressive behavior proposes that the stimulus initiates an intrapersonal process (whether it be called sympathy or vicarious emotion) and that this process leads to nonverbal behaviors that indicate or express the internal state.

In contrast, we propose that motor mimicry is not necessarily expressive *of* any internal state; however, it is expressive *to* the other person in the situation. Our theoretical framework (e.g., Watzlawick, Beavin, & Jackson, 1967) views any behavior that occurs in a social context as potentially communicative. So we would point out that there is always an *other person* in the situation when motor mimicry occurs. Therefore, the focus of study should be expanded to include this other person as well as the potential effect of the behavior on him or her.

Watzlawick et al. (1967) went on to propose (pp. 62–67) that nonverbal behaviors in particular convey analogic information to others about our relationships to them. Applying this principle to motor mimicry, we can see that the observer momentarily portrays him/herself as feeling like the other by leaning, wincing, or smiling as if in the other's situation. Rather than simply saying, "I know how you feel," the observer actually *shows* how you feel, in the analogically coded equivalent of the verbal statement. This suggests that motor mimicry is more than a nonverbal behavior; it is a nonverbal communication intended to convey "fellow feeling" to the other person. (At this point, there is an immediate, obvious question; namely, Why do people show motor mimicry when they are alone, as they apparently do? This issue is addressed at the end of this section.)

Thus we propose that, although the eliciting stimulus may also evoke intrapersonal reactions, it is not these that lead to motor mimicry, the visible display. Motor mimicry is a function of the interpersonal, communicative situation, not the by-product of private experience. We propose that these are parallel processes: The same stimulus may set off both internal reactions and overt display, but these function independently, just as they do for the case of verbal language. Language is not the simple product of emotion or cognition, not the involuntary consequence of any intrapersonal state; rather it has a domain of its own, in human interaction. Yet the usual model of nonverbal behavior is that, unlike language, it is merely a behavioral "indicator" that reveals, often inadvertently, the individual's internal experience. We sought data that would test this model against a communicative one.

Experimental evidence

There is a fairly direct experimental test of our theory, based on a straightforward deduction: If motor mimicry is a communicative act, then it should be affected by communicative variables in the interpersonal situation in which it is evoked. If, on the other hand, it is solely the manifestation of an intrapersonal process, then such variables should have no effect.

Therefore we (Bavelas, Black, Lemery, & Mullett, 1986) enacted the same painful injury, in which a male experimenter dropped a heavy TV monitor on an apparently already injured finger, in two different versions. In one condition, because of his initial orientation, eye contact with the victim appeared probable and did indeed occur shortly after the injury. In the other condition, eye contact appeared unlikely at the time of the injury and did not occur. If motor mimicry (in this case, any expression of pain such as wincing) expresses the observer's own or vicarious emotional reaction to the injury, then only the constant injury should matter; hence there should be no difference between experimental conditions. If instead motor mimicry is meant to be seen, then the availability of the victim as a receiver should affect its display.

The experiment, which is described in detail in Bavelas et al. (1986), proceeded as follows: Forty-two female undergraduate volunteers were instructed simply to act as observers. Because the injury itself would take only a few seconds and was to appear as an accident, the experiment began with another, irrelevant task. After that, the main experimenter ($E1$) and a helper ($E2$) began setting up equipment so that the observer (O) could watch TV. While they were carrying in the TV monitor together, $E1$ (who had a conspicuous splint on his left middle finger) slowed down at a point about 4 feet in front of O and suggested to $E2$ that they set the TV down on the table there. As they tried to do so, the end of the monitor that was closest to O landed directly on $E1$'s splinted finger. There were two versions of what followed, both carefully rehearsed for precise enactment:

Eye Contact	*No Eye Contact*
Injury and sharp intake of breath; $E1$'s face begins to show pain.	Injury and sharp intake of breath; $E1$'s face begins to show pain.
$E1$ brings head up and glances at O (with defocused eyes) as head rolls back.	$E1$ hunches down over TV, with face (still showing pain) visible to O in profile.
Two seconds after start of injury, $E2$ lifts TV off $E1$'s hand.	Two seconds after start of injury, $E2$ lifts TV off $E1$'s hand.
$E1$ pivots fully toward O, in semicrouch, holding his hand. Looks at hand, then directly at O for 1 second, with "blank" face.	$E1$ pivots fully toward $E2$, in semicrouch, holding his hand. Looks at hand, then directly at $E2$ for 1 second, with back to O.

Four seconds after the start of the injury in both conditions, $E2$ asked, "Are you okay?" $E1$ looked at $E2$, then said, "Yeah, I think so," examined his hand again, and concluded, "It just hurt for a minute." (They went on to hook up the equipment without looking at *O*; then *E*1 told *O* about the video episodes she would be watching. After watching these, *O* was interviewed and asked to describe everything she saw during the experiment.)

Because of our previous data on the microsynchrony of an observer's mimetic behavior to a stimulus, it was vital that the injury sequence, which was only 4 seconds long, be precisely planned, rehearsed, and executed. Manipulation checks showed that this was in fact done. Although data from five observers could not be used because they interrupted the sequence and threw it off, and there were two videotaping problems, in only three cases did the experimenters themselves fail to execute the sequence exactly. For the 32 usable cases (15 Eye Contact and 17 No Eye Contact), all common points of the two scripts were enacted identically to within tenths of seconds; there were no significant differences in timing between the Eye Contact and No Eye Contact conditions.

As predicted, there were significant variations in the pattern and display of motor mimicry as a function of the probability of eye contact (see Bavelas, Black, Lemery, & Mullett, 1986, for full details). When this probability increased, the observer's mimetic expression typically occurred quickly and either continued or actually increased in intensity. When, in the other condition, the probability of eye contact decreased, motor mimicry usually either began but then faded or did not occur at all. Direct evidence for the "delivery" of motor mimicry can be found in the expressions at the precise point of eye contact, where 10 of 15 observers were displaying clear motor mimicry.

A plausible alternative explanation would be that, because of fuller facial visibility, the injury seemed more painful in the Eye Contact than the No Eye Contact condition. For this reason, a great deal of planning and pilot work had gone into making the latter injury appear just as painful. There is also the evidence of the observers' other behaviors: Observers in the Eye Contact condition *smiled* (usually in addition to wincing) significantly more often than did their counterparts – an unlikely response if the injury indeed appeared more painful. (We interpret these smiles not as "sadism" or amusement, which would presumably have been more likely to be displayed when not seen, but rather as "sympathetic smiles," which were reassuring or face-saving, that is, as communicative acts as well.)

It is possible that a modification of the intrapersonal model could incorporate these effects of visual availability as follows: In the minimally communicative condition, the injury itself led to the hypothesized internal process (e.g., taking the role of the other or vicarious emotion), which led to some motor mimicry. The amount occurring here is thus seen as a "base rate" of the primary reaction. When the other person was more visually available, a secondary social process enhanced the reaction, thereby increasing the probability of its being manifested.

This model is consistent with the usual view in which intrapersonal processes are "primary" and social behavior is "secondary." A simple derivation from this model leads to an empirical test: The hypothesized secondary, social process would take some time, however short – time that would be added onto the primary, internal reaction that must occur before it. Therefore, the reactions produced in this condition would have to occur somewhat later. However, there was no significant difference in the time at which the first mimetic expression appeared. On the contrary, the reactions in the Eye Contact condition were, on average, *faster* than those in the No Eye Contact condition (1.04 vs. 1.32 seconds). These data cannot support a sequential, two-stage model.

In the second part of this experiment, we went on to test a corollary deduction, that if motor mimicry is a nonverbal message sent to the other, then it should be systematically decoded by receivers. A second set of 10 subjects rated the videotapes of the 32 observers' faces for their meaning. These "naive decoders" were first told about the injury the observers were witnessing, although of course not about the two experimental conditions. They were then asked to rate the extent to which the nonverbal behavior of each observer indicated that she *knew* how the victim felt, *cared* about what had happened to the victim, and had reacted *appropriately* to what happened.

There was a good consensus on the meaning of the expressions (intraclass r's = .87 to .89), and the averages for the "knows" and "cares" scales differed significantly, as predicted, for the two experimental conditions. The behaviors of observers in the Eye Contact condition were rated as significantly more knowing and caring than were those of observers in the No Eye Contact condition. The "message" the former sent was apparently understood; the latter group, on the other hand, were sending no message or one that faded quickly.

In our most recent study (Bavelas, Black, Chovil, Lemery, & Mullett, 1987b), we examined the *form* of mimetic reactions in order to establish their communicative function. By a somewhat more complicated process of deduction than described above, it is possible in some instances to distinguish between communicative and intrapersonal causes of the behavior. Most intrapersonal theories propose that motor mimicry occurs because the observer psychologically supplants the other. The most explicit example is Mead's (1934) "taking the role of the other" from the standpoint of the other, as applied by O'Toole and Dubin (1968) to motor mimicry. These authors proposed that the individual momentarily puts him/herself into the place of the other person, seeing the situation from that point of view and even acting, on that basis, like the other. Similarly, most theorists who cast empathy as projection, identification, or vicarious emotion implicitly make the assumption that the empathizer has "put himself in the place of the other" and is having the other's reaction.

The difference between this family of theories and ours is a subtle one. They propose that the observer takes the other's place momentarily, feels the other's feelings, and *has* the other's reaction. (Indeed, these elements are usually seen as the criteria of true empathy.) We propose that the observer is not having the other's reaction but is portraying it. He or she is sending the message, "It is *as if* I feel as you do." In other words, the motor mimicry is an encoded representation quite different from, say, actual pain. It is, in Ekman and Friesen's (1969) terms, a nonverbal illustrator or, in McNeill's (1985), a referential gesture, functioning like verbal language but (in our view) with a certain advantage of eloquence owing to its analogic coding. In most instances, motor mimicry would look the same regardless of which process lies behind it. For example, if the observer took the role of another person who was in pain, he or she would wince in much the same way as if representing that person's pain. This is an inherent characteristic of analogic coding – it is highly similar to the reaction it represents.

However, there is one instance in which reactions governed by the two processes would differ, and that is left–right leaning. Imagine that the observer and the other are facing each other. Suppose the other ducks to her right to avoid something; the observer might also lean quickly, in motor mimicry. Freeze this scene for a moment and consider the two different possibilities, based on the observer's possible psychological processes: If the observer has taken the role of the other, he will have (psychologically) rotated into her position and will therefore also duck to his right. This would mean moving in the *opposite* direction from the other's movement (i.e., to her left). Other intrapersonal theories might dispute that such an elaborate cognitive process could be happening so quickly and accurately. Such theories would have to predict no differences – left and right leaning should be equally probable.

Yet, for some reason, any movement in the opposite direction strikes us as looking odd. We propose that it looks odd because it breaks the principle of analogic coding. If, as in our theory, the observer is sending a message by leaning, specifically, conveying that he feels *like* the other – then he would move *like* her, in a way that is clear to her. He would therefore move in the same direction she did, to her right with her, which is to his left. Note that, in this case, the observer remains (psychologically) in his place and *in relation to the other*, rather than supplanting her in any way. (The term *mirroring* has been used in the nonverbal synchrony literature for such movement in the same direction, but there is no consistent term for the opposite movement. We prefer the topological terms, *reflection symmetry* and *rotation symmetry*, respectively.)

Thus, there is one instance in which form may reveal function, where the topography of the mimetic response would be different depending on the causal process behind it. If a communicative process is determining the behavior, then mimetic reactions should take the reflected form. If instead the process is one of taking the role of the other, then motor mimicry in this situation should follow rotation symmetry. If some other, less cognitive vicarious process is involved, then the direction would not matter, so both forms should occur, with equal probability.

The experiment was, therefore, a simple one. A female experimenter told 23 male or female volunteer subjects two stories about "near misses." After the first, warm-up story she told one about nearly being hit (accidentally) by the wild arm-swings of a much taller person at a party. There were two points at which she enacted a sharp duck to her right. The videotapes were analyzed for left–right movements occurring within 1 second after each of these two incidents. Twelve of 23 observers leaned at least once. Eleven of these leaned left, reflecting the experimenter; one leaned right.

In this experiment, the form that motor mimicry took was the one predicted by a communicative theory. Role-taking and equiprobable responding are obviously eliminated by these data. In a series of subsequent decoding studies, subjects were asked which form conveyed "involvement" or "being together." Reflection symmetry was consistently chosen over rotation symmetry. An unexpected finding was that the eye contact variable reappeared in these decoding studies: Even in photographs shown to third parties, there was an effect of whether or not there was eye contact between the two people in the photo; where there was no eye contact, the choices were random.

We do not believe that any intrapersonal theory can find in its particulars any way to predict the bias toward reflection symmetry. Such mirroring makes sense only when the other person is in the picture as well. Thus, these results cannot support the theory that intrapersonal processes lead to motor mimicry, which then has a secondary or incidental social function. The form of the behavior suggests that communication is its primary or original function.

Motor mimicry as solely communicative

In summary, we have data indicating that

1. motor mimicry is differentially affected by the visual availability of a receiver;
2. its display is synchronized to this visual availability;
3. decoders agree on its meaning;
4. it occurs very rapidly, with a reaction time that seems to rule out prior internal processes; and
5. its form (reflection symmetry) is consistent with analogic coding rather than role taking or vicarious experiencing.

These data make sense if we go back to historical distinctions among various forms of sympathy (or empathy) rather than grouping them so that a single global process must include all instances. Motor mimicry is no more and no less than the overt behavior visible to others. We propose that this behavior is parallel to, and independent of, any intrapersonal reaction that the same stimulus may elicit. Incidents such as the experimenter's injury or the "near miss" story may well evoke some of the intrapersonal processes proposed by such theories. But these processes neither lead to nor shape the form of motor mimicry, which occurs for a different reason.

It is important not to confuse our theory with a "behaviorism" that denies the existence of processes that cannot be observed. We simply propose that the overt reaction occurs in parallel to any intrapersonal reaction rather than serially, which is the usual model. Motor mimicry itself is best (and, in our opinion, only) accounted for by its interpersonal function, which operates separately and by its own process, a communicative one.

There are two interesting speculations that could be put to our theory. First, if motor mimicry is a purely communicative act, why would it ever occur when the individual is alone? Second, if it is indeed independent of internal feelings, what would be the function of such a behavior?

The first question can be rephrased more formally: We have shown that *some* motor mimicry is communicative; is it the case that *all* motor mimicry is communicative, that is, that there are no noncommunicative instances? This possibility would seem to be eliminated by the occurrence of motor mimicry in non-social settings, for example, when one is watching TV or a movie. We have three alternative, communicative explanations for such displays. First, in our experiments using video stimuli (Bavelas, Block, Lemery, MacInnis, & Mullett, 1986), the observers were still in the presence of an experimenter and a camera, both of which are potential receivers. Similarly, as is well known to those who cry in movies, one can be seen by others even in a darkened theater. Second, when this is not the case (e.g., when the individual is home alone watching TV), the personification on the screen may well become, momentarily, a person real enough to be a receiver. Consider that we easily accept the notion that the *plot* can become psychologically real and thereby cause considerable emotion. It is no more far-fetched to propose that motor mimicry can be caused by a fictitious receiver than to propose that emotions can be caused by fictitious plots. Or, third, the "totally alone" case can be explained by analogy with language. When alone, we often think in words, and these words are sometimes mouthed or actually said (e.g., "Oh NO!" when a big mistake is made). Similarly, we represent some reactions nonverbally, and these too may be expressed even when alone.

If a plausible case can be made for motor mimicry's being solely communicative, then why would this occur? Why should people display to others something that may or may not reflect their current internal state? Even more, why should this display be so rapid and so precisely tuned to the receiver's availability and decoding? We propose that this happens because motor mimicry conveys a message that is of vital importance to our relationships with others: I can feel as you do; I am like you.

Humphrey (1983) has reasoned that human consciousness evolved principally to anticipate other humans' reactions and, in aid of this, to empathize with their experiences. Yet if this had not led to behavior, it would have had no selective advantage. Empathy has been of interest to social theorists because of its importance for society (e.g., Clark, 1980). Yet empathy that is merely felt and never acted on has no social implications. Agony or joy for another is a private experience unless it appears as words or actions. Conversely, appropriately expressed words or actions can have their salutary effect whether or not accompanied by the private experience of empathy.

In our view, the search for the elusive link between empathic experience and overt behavior has overlooked the humble instance of motor mimicry, which gets on with the job of expressing empathy to the other. Recall Darwin: "We readily perceive sympathy in others by their expression; our sufferings are thus mitigated" (1872/1965, p. 364). It is in this sense that motor mimicry can still be called primitive empathy; it may be the prototype rather than a trivial instance. Motor mimicry does not wait for full comprehension of the situation of the other. Nor does it require that the observer first experience the other person's feelings him/herself. The first priority is to display similarity to the other, and this it does rapidly and precisely. We propose that humans are "primed" for such primitive empathy. That is, they are acutely tuned to the situations of their fellows; they process this information quickly and then immediately register, nonverbally, that they have done so. They may go on to understand or feel the other's situation in a more deliberative sense, and this may well lead to words or further action. But the social priority is so high that immediate communication comes first.

Mimetic synchrony as a class of nonverbal behaviors

Motor mimicry is similar in many respects to certain other nonverbal behaviors such as posture sharing and movement mirroring, which are usually found in the quite separate literature on nonverbal synchrony. We propose that part of this literature is in fact a separate class of its own, which we will call *mimetic synchrony*, of which motor mimicry is a special case.

Nonverbal synchrony was "discovered" by the microanalyses of Scheflen (1963) and Condon (1963), both of whom noticed the striking synchronicity of nonverbal behaviors in the flow of interaction. A substantial and diverse literature has ensued (e.g., Davis, 1982). It is our interpretation of this literature that two different kinds of synchrony, rhythmic and mimetic, have been found. By far the dominant interest has been in rhythm. For example, Condon and Ogston (1966) identified two kinds of rhythmic synchrony: self-synchrony, which is the timing of the speaker's nonverbal behaviors to his or her own speech, and interactional synchrony, the timing of the listener's nonverbal behaviors to the speaker's speech. Interaction rhythms seem to function to achieve and maintain the coordinated flow that characterizes, and makes possible, spontaneous dialogue. A remarkable variety of behaviors and channels may be interwoven in such synchronies, but the focus of interest is the entrainment or coinciding of these words and actions. Investigators of this kind of synchrony usually find it by extremely fine microanalysis, because their "events" are the onsets and offsets of behavior; these changes of state are the essence of rhythm.

A second class of behaviors, although similar in many respects, is nevertheless distinguished by *the simultaneous display of similar behaviors*. These mimetic synchronies – for example, similar postures or mirrored movements – are not cross-modal, and they are observable in real time. We found that most of the researchers who have included this kind of synchrony have also implied that it reveals or is caused by the relationship between the interactants (rather than serving to coordinate the interaction).

Scheflen (1964) suggested that congruence of posture indicates similarity in views or roles. In 1969, Dabbs reported two experiments in which he varied whether a confederate interviewee either mimicked or took positions opposite to those of the subject; he found that this led to strong differences in the evaluation of the confederate. Kendon (1970) observed synchronous movement among interactants in a public drinking house. He noted that "movement mirroring" appeared only between speaker and addressee. Kendon speculated that this heightens the bond between these two and at the same time differentiates them from the others present.

Goodwin (1981) noted a relation between nonverbal "congruence" and topic. Congruent (similar) postures reflected mutuality of topic and interest, whereas moving out of congruent postures was associated with a change of topic. (He also noted that such fine movements as eyebrow flashes were mimicked by the other person within less than 0.1 second.) Matching behaviors and their relation to speech content and rapport have also been studied in therapeutic interactions by Scheflen (1963), Charney (1966), Trout and Rosenfeld (1980), and Daubenmire and Searles (1982)

La France (e.g., 1982) explicitly connected posture mirroring with motor mimicry and with the relationship between the interactants. Elaborating on Scheflen's (1964) hypotheses, she proposed that postural coordination could lead to a feeling of rapport and reflect a common definition of the situation or a common orientation; lack of such mirroring could signal discord or even cause it. Two correlational studies (La France, 1979; La France & Broadbent, 1976) showed that rapport in seminar classes correlated significantly with posture sharing. An experiment (La France, 1985) confirmed that arm mirroring varied as a function of cooperative versus competitive orientation in pairs of dyads listening to a tape.

Davies (1984) independently found the same effect in our laboratory. He asked four strangers to have a debate, one pair against the other. Individuals were randomly assigned to these two "teams," and the initial level of movement synchrony was a significant function of this pairing (higher for cooperating pairs than for competing pairs). Moreover, as the teams were reassigned by the experimenter in all possible combinations, the synchrony tracked the relationship – the new cooperating pairs synchronized with each other more than with their previous partners.

Finally, mimetic synchrony has been observed in infants. Lieberman (1967) studied mimetic changes in intonation and found that the child tracked the adult frequencies. That is, the fundamental frequencies that measure pitch were highest when playing by himself, lower with his mother, and lowest with his father. Rosenthal (1982) showed that mothers and their 3-day-old infants co-vocalized significantly above chance; that is, when one vocalized, the other "chimed in." Meltzoff and Moore (1977) have reported facial mimesis in very young infants, although this finding is a disputed one (Koepke, Hamm, Legerstee, & Russell, 1983).

In brief, there seems to be a sizable and widespread group of mimetic synchronies, in which A's behavior is followed closely by a matching behavior by B. These bear an interesting similarity to motor mimicry; both involve the virtually simultaneous display of similar behaviors, and both seem to convey, analogically, the relationship between the interactants ("I am like you"). Indeed, some of the classic motor mimicries such as leaning and body sway appear indistinguishable from the larger set.

In most cases, however, motor mimicry forms a special subset having three identifying features: Motor mimicry has a unilateral pattern; that is, the observer mimicks the other but not the reverse, whereas other mimetic synchronies are reciprocal actions that either person may "lead," or that may be shared. Second, motor mimicry is typically fleeting rather than slow-moving or even static (as, for example, sitting in the same posture). Finally, most mimetic synchrony remains in the background; indeed, the interactants are often self-conscious if they become aware of it. In contrast, motor mimicry (especially a facial expression such as a wince in our experiment) is often the "figure" for that moment in the interaction. Thus the broader class contains nonverbal signals that may be "left on" for minutes at a time, so that the relationship message is being quietly broadcast almost constantly, while the verbal content changes more rapidly. Motor mimicries, on the other hand, follow this shorter-term flow of the interaction, often acting in conjunction with verbal phrases (e.g., a wince followed by "Are you okay?").

A communicative view of nonverbal behavior

As Trevarthen (1977) has implied, movement itself has been treated as "mere movement," almost as trivial, principally because its precision cannot be seen in real time. Our work with motor mimicry has led us to respect the "merely motoric" and to see nonverbal behavior in general in a new light. In our reading of the literature, nonverbal behavior is usually treated as the weak servant of the mind. For example, nonverbal behavior has often been of interest because it is thought to be under less control than verbal language, so that it will "leak" the truth despite the individual's control of what he or she says verbally. Even when nonverbal behavior is seen as expressing attitudes or feelings directly, it is considered to be imprecise and ineloquent. The information to be gathered from nonverbal behavior is seen as global and diffuse (e.g., simply a positive/negative attitude or a dominant/submissive orientation), with none of the subtlety of verbal language. Even terms like *nonverbal communication* or *body language* are usually misnomers, because nonverbal behavior is not treated as true language or communication. In the rare instances where nonverbal behavior qualifies to be called nonverbal communication, it still seems to be cast as the redundant inferior to true language.

Furthermore, human nonverbal behavior is rarely treated as interactional. Kraut and Johnston (1979) have made this point particularly well by comparing the approach of most psychologists to that of ethologists. The former tradition sees nonverbal behavior almost exclusively as emotional expression:

> As a result, it has often embedded the study of nonverbal behavior in individualistic psychology by treating individuals as socially encapsulated. (p. 1552)

Ethologists, on the other hand, have not been concerned with any emotions behind the nonverbal behavior of the animals they study. Rather, they have

> stayed concerned with the functions of nonverbal displays and their social consequences. (Kraut & Johnston, 1979, p. 1552)

Indeed, the ethological term *display* emphasizes this interactional focus.

There is an important methodological implication in this difference. Kraut and Johnston point out that Ekman, Friesen, and Ellsworth (1972) reviewed over 100 studies since Darwin on human facial expression of emotion and found *no* studies examining the effects of nonverbal expression on social interaction. Therefore, we would add, no such effects could be discovered. The study of nonverbal behavior as expressive of intrapersonal events is self-confirming in its methodology; if social factors are not studied, their effects will not be uncovered. As Spitz and Wolf (1946, p. 59) pointed out, this is like trying to understand the law of gravitation by studying one body.

We propose that, rather than being an extension or indicator of an emotional state, nonverbal expressions *represent* such states to other people. It is a classic error to confuse a word with what it represents. Similarly, we should not confuse an analogic or iconic behavior with what it represents. Nonverbal expressions can occur before, during, or after an emotional state; they are independent of such feeling, to the same degree words are. (And, just as words, they can express a much wider variety of ideas than only feelings.)

When the necessary methodology has been used to look at nonverbal behavior in this way, the results are encouraging. Spitz and Wolf (1946) found that infants smile at human eyes, virtually independently of emotional state. Trevarthen (1977) has proposed that the earliest mother–infant interaction is content-free; it seems solely to establish the process of communicating with each other. Kraut and Johnston (1979) showed that smiling (by adults) is a function of the availability of a receiver, not the emotional state of the sender. Our data, reported here, confirm this principle with a new set of nonverbal behaviors. McNeill (1985) has argued that many gestures should not be considered "nonverbal" but rather part of the same processing that produces verbal speech.

If we could see nonverbal behavior without preconceptions, then we would be led by parsimony to propose first that it may be communicative. Why would such a behavior appear if it were not meant to be seen? Why should it merely "spill over" from internal events? Nature is neither slipshod nor wasteful; other human behaviors are precise and functional. Therefore, if a behavior is made visible to others, it is reasonable to start with the assumption that it is communicative. There is a good deal of evidence to suggest that nonverbal behavior expresses precise information to others and that it is part of the communicative process through which we are connected to others. Rather than using it as a route into the mind, we can follow it outward, into the social interaction.

References

Allport, G. W. (1937). *Personality. A psychological interpretation.* New York: Holt.

Allport, G. W. (1961). *Pattern and growth in personality.* New York: Holt, Rinehart, and Winston.

Allport, G. W. (1968). The historical background of modern social psychology. In G. Lindzey & E. Aronson (Eds.) *Handbook of social psychology* (2nd ed., Vol. 1, pp. 1–80). Reading, MA: Addison-Wesley.

Baldwin, J. M. (1895). *Mental development in the child and in the race.* New York: Macmillan.

Baldwin, J. M. (1897). *Social and ethical interpretations in mental development.* New York: Macmillan.

Bavelas, J. B., Black, A., Lemery, C. R., MacInnis, S., & Mullett, J. (1986). Experimental methods for studying "elementary motor mimicry." *Journal of Nonverbal Behavior, 10,* 102–119.

Bevelas, J. B., Black, A., Lemery, C. R., & Mullett, J. (1986). "I *show* how you feel": Motor mimicry as a communicative act. *Journal of Personality and Social Psychology, 50*, 322–329.

Bavelas, J. B., Black, A., Chovil, N., Lemery, C. R., & Mullett, J. (1987a). Evidence for microsynchrony of nonverbal behaviour to a video stimulus. Unpublished manuscript, University of Victoria.

Bavelas, J. B., Black, A., Chovil, N., Lemery, C. R., & Mullett, J. (1987b). *Form and function in motor mimicry.* Manuscript under revision for *Human Communication Research.*

Blanton, S., & Blanton, M. (1927). *Child guidance.* New York: Century.

Charney, E. J. (1966). Psychosomatic manifestations of rapport in psychotherapy. *Psychosomatic Medicine, 28*, 305–315.

Clark, K. B. (1980). Empathy. A neglected topic in psychological research. *American Psychologist, 35*, 187–190.

Condon, W. S. (1963). *Synchrony units and the communicational hierarchy.* Paper presented at the Western Psychiatric Institute, Pittsburgh.

Condon, W. S., & Ogston, W. D. (1966). Sound film analysis of normal and pathological behaviour patterns. *Journal of Nervous and Mental Disease, 143*, 338–347.

Dabbs, J. M. (1969). Similarity of gestures and interpersonal influence. *Proceedings of the 77th Annual Convention of the American Psychological Association, 4*, 337–338.

Darwin, C. (1965). *The expression of the emotions in man and animals.* Chicago: University of Chicago Press. (Original work published 1872)

Daubenmire, M. J., & Searles, S. (1982). A dyadic model for the study of convergence in nurse–patient interactions. In M. Davis (Ed.), *Interactional rhythms.* New York: Human Sciences Press.

Davies, J. P. A. (1984). *Situational determinants of interaction synchrony.* Unpublished honours thesis, Department of Psychology, University of Victoria.

Davis, M. (Ed.) (1982). *Interaction rhythms.* New York: Human Sciences Press.

Edwards, A. S. (1942). The measurement of static ataxia. *American Journal of Psychology, 55*, 171–188.

Edwards, A. S. (1943). Factors tending to decrease the steadiness of the body at rest. *American Journal of Psychology, 56*, 599–602.

Ekman, P., & Friesen, W. V. (1969). The repertoire of nonverbal behavior: Categories, origins, usage, and coding. *Semiotica, 1*, 49–98.

Ekman, P., Friesen, W. V., & Ellsworth, P. (1972). *Emotion in the human face.* New York: Pergamon.

Goodwin, C. (1981). *Conversational organization: Interaction between speakers and hearers.* New York: Academic Press.

Hull, C. L. (1933). *Hypnosis and suggestibility.* New York: Appleton-Century.

Humphrey, N. (1983). *Consciousness regained. Chapters in the development of mind.* Oxford: Oxford University Press.

Kendon, A. (1970). Movement coordination in social interaction: Some examples described. *Acta Psychologica, 32*, 100–125.

Koepke, J. E., Hamm, M., Legerstee, M., & Russell, M. (1983). Neonatal imitation: Two failures to replicate. *Infant Behavior and Development, 6*, 97–102.

Köhler, W. (1927). *The mentality of apes* (2nd ed.). (E. Winter, Trans.). New York: Harcourt.

Kupferer, H. J. K. (1965). Couvade: Ritual or real illness. *American Anthropologist, 67*, 99–102.

Kraut, R. E., & Johnston, R. E. (1979). Social and emotional messages of smiling: An ethological approach. *Journal of Personality and Social Psychology, 37*, 1539–1553.

La France, M. (1979). Nonverbal synchrony and rapport: Analysis by the cross-lag panel technique. *Social Psychology Quarterly, 42*, 66–70.

La France, M. (1982). Posture mirroring and rapport. In M. Davis (Ed.), *Interaction rhythms.* New York: Human Sciences Press.

La France, M. (1985). Postural mirroring and intergroup relations. *Personality and Social Psychology Bulletin, 11,* 207–217.

La France, M., & Broadbent, M. (1976). Group rapport: Posture sharing as a nonverbal indicator. *Group and Organizational Studies, 1,* 328–333.

Lieberman, P. (1967). *Intonation, perception and language.* Cambridge, MA: MIT Press.

McDougall, W. (1908). *Introduction to social psychology.* London: Methuen, 1908.

MacInnis, S. (1979). *The nature of the empathy process.* Unpublished honours thesis, Department of Psychology, University of Victoria.

McNeill, D. (1985). So you think gestures are nonverbal? *Psychological Review, 92,* 350–371.

Mead, G. H. (1934). *Mind, self, and society* (C. M. Morris, Ed.). Chicago: University of Chicago Press.

Mead, M. (1968). *Continuities in cultural evolution.* New Haven: Yale University Press.

Meltzoff, A. N., & Moore, M. K. (1977). Imitation of facial and manual gestures by human neonates. *Science, 198,* 75–78.

O'Toole, R., and Dubin, R. (1968). Baby feeding and body sway: An experiment in George Herbert Mead's "taking the role of the other." *Journal of Personality and Social Psychology, 10,* 59–65.

Ribot, T. (1897). *The psychology of the emotions.* London: Walter Scott.

Rosenthal, M. K. (1982). Vocal dialogues in the neonatal period. *Developmental Psychology, 18,* 17–21.

Scheflen, A. E. (1963). Communication and regulation in psychotherapy. *Psychiatry, 26,* 126–136.

Scheflen, A. E. (1964). The significance of posture in communication systems. *Psychiatry, 27,* 316–331.

Scheler, M. (1970). *The nature of sympathy* (P. Heath, Trans). Hamden, Conn.: Archon Books. (Original work published 1912).

Smith, A. (1966). *The theory of moral sentiments.* New York: Augustus M. Kelley. (Original work published 1759).

Spencer, H. (1870). *The principles of psychology* (2nd ed., Vol. 1). London: Williams and Norgate.

Spitz, R. A., & Wolf, K. M. (1946). The smiling response: A contribution to the ontogenesis of social relations. *Genetic Psychology Monographs, 34,* 57–125.

Strunk, O., Jr. (1957). Empathy: A review of theory and research. *Psychological Newsletter, 9,* 47–57.

Trevarthen, C. (1977). Descriptive analysis of infant communicative behavior. In H. R. Schaffer (Ed.), *Studies in mother–infant interaction.* London: Academic Press.

Trout, P. L. & Rosenfeld, H. (1980). The effect of postural lean and body congruence on the judgement of psychotherapeutic rapport. *Journal of Nonverbal Behavior, 4,* 176–190.

Watzlawick, P., Beavin, J., & Jackson, D. D. (1967). *Pragmatics of human communication: A study of interactional patterns, pathologies, and paradoxes.* New York: Norton.

Commentary on Part III

Bert S. Moore

The role of commentator is in many respects an enviable one in that you bask, to some extent, in the reflected glory of the insightful observations made by the authors of the chapters on which you comment. You also have the advantage of drawing upon each of the contributions in coming to conclusions on the difficult issues posed in an examination of empathy. At the same time, there is an incumbency to impose order on the various chapters that have already imposed order on certain domains – to provide the glue among contributions that are disparate in their purpose. Luckily, in the present case, the authors have all made substantial and interesting contributions to our understanding of empathy.

Each of the chapters, while addressing a particular issue related to empathy, went to some length to address the fundamental problem that has plagued research in this domain – the problem of definition. Although the authors do not always agree on how the problem might be resolved, they do agree that research has been hindered by the absence of clear, restrictive definitions. In the present volume, Batson has distinguished among the various emotional reactions that we may have to the emotions of others. Personal distress may be one outcome, where the distress of another evokes self-focused affect. Emotional contagion is experienced when the emotion of one evokes an analogous affective experience in the other. This second reaction most closely approximates what is meant by *empathy* here. Finally, a third type of vicarious emotional reaction to the emotions of another is concern for the other. The chapters by Strayer, Eisenberg and Miller, and Bryant specifically address the overlapping definitions of empathy, sympathy, and social perspective taking.

Clearly, the definitional distinctions that are drawn are important ones and help bring order to a field where, up until now, the terms employed in research have been applied as loosely as they are in everyday conversation. What also becomes apparent in the chapters here is that these distinctions *do* have implications for both the range of characteristics associated with the phenomena and the predictive differences hypothesized from studies of behavior such as altruism or social competence.

339

In general, the authors in this section have argued the importance of restricting empathy to affective reactions engendered by the apprehension of another's emotional state that are congruent with that state. Sympathy, on the other hand, refers to a nonidentical emotional state that results from sorrow or concern. Often in previous writing, it has been impossible to determine which construct an author was discussing, and the terms were frequently used interchangeably.

For me, the distinction is most finely drawn when I consider the variety of affects associated with various people whose affect I encounter. When I listen to the plight of an acquaintance who is undergoing a painful divorce, even though I experience concern and sympathy, it does not have the affective kick of a true empathic response. What is missing is the affect; the true experiencing of the affect of the other. When I compare this to the wrenching affect I experience as I watch my son bumble his way through his lines in a school play, the important difference in experience becomes salient. It is not just the difference in the closeness of the relationship, although that may be part of it. I can imagine the responses being reversed. It is those phenomena of direct emotional contagion that are of central interest here. The relation of those affective responses to cognitive processes and sympathetic concern inevitably come to the fore also. Empathy then is closely associated with sympathy in what I shall term the empathy/ sympathy complex, but the movement to sympathy is not automatic, and may involve cognitive mediation.

One of the central questions posed by these contributions concerns the relation between cognitive processes (role taking, emotion discrimination, self–other differentiation) and affect (empathy). The notion of an empathy/sympathy complex articulated by a number of the contributors to this volume implies an interrelation but partial autonomy of empathy and sympathy. If we restrict empathy to mean the feeling of what another feels, then one consequence of those feelings may be sympathy when the affect perceived in the other is distress, but it is only a possible consequence.

Although no one seriously questions the interactive effects of cognitive and affective processes in the empathy/sympathy complex, there is a serious question as to whether the term *empathy* ought to be restricted to emotion directly engendered by the affect of another. Essentially, the question being posed is whether affect can occur without prior cognitive mediation. Although this question is as old as theorizing about the nature of emotion, it takes on new meaning in the context of empathy, for some definitions and empirical approaches have treated empathy as if it necessarily involved the observer taking the role of the other before an affective experience could occur. Several of the chapters in Part III highlight the importance of this distinction between affective and cognitive processes. Another central concern in these chapters is the developmental course in the empathy/sympathy complex. Finally, given restrictive definitions of empathy, what is the relation between empathy and important behaviors such as altruism and social adjustment?

In Chapter 10 Strayer makes a number of useful distinctions regarding the construct of empathy. She points out that although empathy, by definition, has to do with affective responding, much of the research has focused on cognitive indices of role taking. Strayer argues that investigations of empathy need to concentrate on understanding affective responding. Strayer maintains that empathic affect can occur as a result of being exposed to another's affect with minimal cognitive mediation. Once cognitive mediation enters the process, the empathic response may be transformed. According to Strayer, cognitive developmental factors act to influence the range and subtlety of emotional responsiveness. These cognitive skills become important in the transition from reciprocal affective responding to sympathetic concern.

Strayer, borrowing from clinical theorizing, proposes a four-stage model describing the empathy–sympathy relation. This model also suggests ways in which cognitive developmental factors may shape affective experiencing. According to the model, the empathic response is initiated when our attention is caught by emotional cues in others. Strayer suggests that the tendency to be caught may be greater at young rather than older ages in that younger children have fewer cognitive controls. In the second stage, the other person is introjected into ourselves. It is possible that, as self–other boundaries become more distinct, the affect experienced at this stage becomes less intense. During these first stages of emotional responding, motor mimicry – as described by Bavelas et al. – may be initiated and contribute to the subsequent two stages.

The third phase involves a "reverberation" of the affect of the other and the affective homologues of the individual. An important aspect of the transition to sympathetic concern is the recognition and discrimination of these self-generated affects from the affect of the other person.

The final phase involves a withdrawal and differentiation of self and other. The central contention in Strayer's analysis is that affect has primacy in these processes. Cognition is initiated and organized by the operation of affective reactions. In turn, the direction and sophistication of the cognitive processes shape the change from feeling *with* (empathy) to feeling *for* (sympathy).

With these distinctions in mind, we may ask how, in general, empathy has been assessed in empirical investigations. One point that soon becomes apparent is that our ability to differentiate conceptually among the various affective reactions that one may have to the affect of others has, up until now, far outstripped our ability to assess those different reactions. Eisenberg and Miller's chapter, as well as Strayer's, briefly reviews the various techniques that have been employed to assess empathy. They point out that although empathy has been defined in two ways – as the cognitive awareness of another person's internal states (thoughts, feelings, point of view, goals or intentions) and the emotional experiencing of some version of another person's affective experience – the measurement techniques purporting to assess empathy often show low-order or zero intercorrelations and low-order relations to theoretically close behaviors.

Strayer follows her theoretical analysis with an overview of the various methods of assessment that have been used to investigate empathy. She argues that the most frequently employed indices show low intercorrelations for several reasons. First, some of the measures, particularly the frequently used FASTE, may be only tangentially related to affective expression, and instead may tap social-cognition abilities. Other indices of empathy such as paper-and-pencil instruments may tap dispositional self-described emotional reactivity, but may not take into account moderating situational factors. Facial/gestural measures may be influenced by display rules. Given that the measures tap such different components of the empathy/sympathy complex, it is not surprising that correlations among them are low.

Strayer concludes her chapter by outlining an approach to empathy research that is based on the distinctions she has drawn. The multidimensional focus that she articulates parallels the arguments put forth by Eisenberg and Miller. As noted in some of the chapters of this book (e.g., chapter 9) this multidimensional view of empathic responding is beginning to be implemented and holds great promise for clarifying what has been a contradictory and murky domain of research. The other chapters in Part III provide empirical reviews of important areas of empathy research.

Bryant's chapter helps clarify the distinction between empathy and social perspective taking through a description of a large, complex longitudinal study of affective development and mental health. The point made in her chapter is that confusion has existed between the ability to take the role of others and our emotional responsiveness to others. Bryant persuasively argues that empathy entails emotional responsiveness to the feelings experienced by others and is not primarily an instrumental ability, as is social perspective taking. Bryant argues that when the meaning of empathy is restricted to emotional expressiveness, its developmental course and its role in the social-emotional development of children is different from that of social perspective taking.

Bryant's research is particularly valuable in that it represents one of the few attempts to trace the developmental course of empathy and place it in the larger context of emotional development. She has followed two samples of children, one from age 7 to age 10, the other from age 10 to age 14, and obtained a number of parental, peer, school, and self ratings. Using the measure of empathy that she has developed from the Mehrabian and Epstein instrument, Bryant also obtained measures of social perspective taking and other indices of social development. Bryant has used these rich data sources to examine both the antecedents and sequelae of empathy and social perspective taking.

Bryant's findings are complex, but clearly indicate that emotional responsiveness to others (at least as measured by the Bryant instrument) bears a different relation to social adjustment than does social perspective taking. Furthermore, there are significant interactions with age and gender. For example, Bryant finds that empathy at age 10 is associated with concurrent behavior problems for girls, but not for boys, but that empathy at age 10 also predicts social competence for both sexes at age 14. These findings suggest that emotional expressiveness may have different adaptive consequences at different ages and for males and females.

Bryant's findings on parent-rated temperament variables and empathy suggest similar conclusions. Thus, being able to focus on feelings without distractions at age 7 appears to be a precursor to the development of empathy in later childhood. Intensity of response at age 7 was related to high empathy at age 10 for females. It appears that, for girls, being able to focus on feelings and having intense feelings lead to high empathy scores at age 10, which in turn is associated with behavior problems at age 10, but social competence at age 14. Very different patterns exist for boys. This complex picture then, should not lead us to expect simple relations between empathy and social behaviors. When it is recalled that paper-and-pencil measures of empathy such as those employed by Bryant show different gender and age relations than do other measures of empathy, the picture becomes even more complex. Thus, one task for future research is to make explicit how the conceptual definition of emotional expressiveness relates to the measure used to assess that responsiveness.

Bryant also provides some interesting, suggestive findings on the family contextual factors associated with empathy development. In a number of the relations she documents, parental discipline and parental handling of children's stressful experiences emerge as particularly important factors.

The data presented by Bryant, taken as a whole, provide strong support for the differential developmental pattern of behaviors associated with social perspective taking and empathy.

Feshbach, like Bryant, provides some illuminating data both on parental factors associated with empathy and on the relations between empathy and children's adjustment. She drew her data from comparisons of families in which children had been abused, families that had come to a clinic for other reasons, and nonclinical controls. Using a model that examines parental empathy, abuse, and adjustment in children, she finds important links between maternal empathy and parental affect and abuse. Maternal empathy also is associated with measures of children's affect and self-control. Feshbach argues that maternal empathy is part of a complex of behaviors that are conducive to children's social adjustment and a secure attachment.

The studies by Bryant and by Feshbach, although concerned with different issues, provide evidence that parental factors play an important role in the evolution of emotional development, including empathy. Their data also emphasize the complexity of those socialization relations. Although empathy may beget empathy, it does not do so in a simple way. The ways in which caretakers respond to children's stress, the ways in which they label and respond to children's affect, and the way in which discipline is handled may all be important antecedents of empathy development. These inferences regarding socialization are based on the belief that emotional states and experiences are, in part, a consequence of how the child's social environment responds to the child's behavior. Socialization, then, is, in part, communication through selective responsivity. What emerges throughout these chapters is the notion that the components of affective responsiveness that have been investigated under the empathy/sympathy rubric may show relatively modest interrelations and may be influenced by different factors. Future work must be more explicit regarding the components that are being investigated and should expect to find different predictors for different components. This point becomes more obvious when we examine age and gender differences in empathy.

In chapter 9, Lennon and Eisenberg review findings related to gender and age. They update the findings of a very helpful review of gender differences in a 1983 *Psychological Bulletin* article in which meta-analyses were used to calculate the magnitude of effects for different measures of empathy. As already mentioned, some widely used methods of assessing empathy such as the FASTE and paper-and-pencil measures show gender differences in accord with gender stereotypes, females being found to be more empathic than males. However, these measures appear to have heavy demand characteristics, and the gender differences may reflect different societal expectancies regarding reports of feelings rather than true differences in experienced affect. This possibility is supported by the researcher's findings that gender differences are small or nonexistent when more direct behavioral assessments of empathy are used, such as facial/gestural measures and physiological indices. Although they do not rule out gender differences in affective experiencing, the authors conclude that the prevailing societal stereotypes regarding empathic responding are not strongly supported. Again, the heterogeneity of measures and the corresponding different findings point to the need for greater conceptual and methodological precision.

A similar conclusion emerges from Lennon and Eisenberg's review of research on changes with age. Most theoretical formulations of empathy development suggest a positive relation between age and empathy. This relation has been said to provide the basis for the generally positive correlation between age and altruism and age, empathy, and altruism (see chapter 9). However, Lennon and Eisenberg's results on this question differ with the different measures of empathy. In general, self-report measures show increases in empathy up until the middle–elementary school years, whereas facial/gestural measures do not show such increases and may, in fact, be inversely related to age. These findings, like those related to gender, suggest that the various measures of empathy may tap a variety of emotional responses subject to different moderating factors or perhaps different developmental courses.

An alternative view is that we should not expect a positive relation between affective responding and age above early elementary school and that the changes in the empathy/sympathy complex that do occur are governed by cognitive factors through which children and adolescents become gradually more aware of the inner experiences of others. What emerges over time is an increasingly subtle and elaborated network of affective and cognitive responding to the emotions of others. Age may not lead to an increase in empathy if what we mean by empathy is "an affective state that stems from the apprehension of another's emotional state or condition and that is congruent with it." Although the ability to apprehend others' emotional states may increase with age in terms of decoding confounded emotions, interpreting situational regulators of affect and understanding "unexpressed" affect, the emotional *reactions* to others' affect, may asymptote at a relatively young age and have a significant biological contribution. Part of the developmental process may consist of acquiring more elaborated empathy/sympathy complex behaviors – more occasions that evoke affect *and* buffers against such evocation – as well as better distancing, distracting, display, and avoidance patterns. Empathic emotional response in the young child may be stronger whereas sympathy may increase with age.

In chapter 14, Bavelas, Black, Lemery, and Mullett trace the historical roots of research on empathy and examine that particular set of empathic phenomena called motor mimicry. Motor mimicry has received renewed interest as it is thought to represent important components of more elaborated forms of empathic responding.

Motor mimicry refers to the specific forms of frequently noted postural and motoric imitation that occur between individuals in social exchanges. Bavelas et al. suggest that motor mimicry's place in understanding the empathy/sympathy complex has been prematurely relegated to the state of being a fascinating curiosity that bears little relation to more affective responding to another's affect. The authors describe an intriguing program of research in which they and their colleagues have performed microanalyses of the imitative acts of individuals as they observe a variety of episodes. The question guiding the research is this:

What function(s) is served by the frequently observed tendency of subjects to enact the posture, facial expressions, and partial motor responses appropriate to the individual being observed rather than to themselves, the observers?

Contrary to the prevailing assumption among many psychologists that motor mimicry is an expression of vicarious emotion or empathic feelings, Bavelas, Black, Lemery, and Mullett argue that motor mimicry represents a communicative expression to the other party. The distinction is a subtle one, but the authors argue that although motor mimicry may co-occur with empathic affective responses, it is not the product of those private responses. They argue that motor mimicry functions to communicate to the other person that ''I know what you feel,'' by showing the display appropriate to those feelings. This is not the same as *feeling* what the other feels. Motor mimicry is explained by its interpersonal communicative function rather than our capacities for experiencing others' affect.

The interesting research presented by these authors, although it does not entirely rule out alternative explanations for these phenomena, makes a convincing case for the independence of these components of reciprocal responding. Further, it raises the question of the functional value of the empathy/sympathy complex. The cognitive, affective, and motoric reactions to the analogous reactions of others appear to function as part of a number of systems designed to assure social cohesion. Although motor mimicry is seen as being independent of intrapersonal responses, it also has the function of communicating awareness of such responses to others. Therefore, motor mimicry establishes an initial communicative link with others that may allow the subsequent elaborated empathic/sympathetic response to occur. Motor mimicry may also serve as part of a reverberating circuit that promotes empathic responding, since we not only appear as we feel, but also feel as we appear.

Chapter 13 by Eisenberg and Miller provides a helpful review of empathy/sympathy measures and prosocial behavior. This relation is one of the most theoretically obvious predictions regarding empathy. Experiencing the distress of another is widely discussed as a primary mediating mechanism for altruistic intervention. Eisenberg and Miller note that recent formulations regarding empathy and altruism make differing claims, depending on the affective sequelae of the empathic response. As we have noted, empathic response may be a relatively early component of the empathy/sympathy complex, which may follow several courses. Because our response to another's affect may lead to self-focused personal distress or to other-focused sympathetic responding, the relation between reciprocal affect and altruism is a complicated one; which outcome eventually occurs will be determined, in part, by a variety of factors, including a self–other differentiation, excessive association between self and other, availability of an intervening response, and costliness of the response. For individuals who experience personal distress, we would expect subjects to engage in prosocial acts only when avoidance of the situation is not easily achieved. For individuals whose affective response to another's distress leads to sympathetic concern, prosocial behavior is more likely. Unfortunately, most of the measures of empathy that have been employed to investigate the empirical relation between empathy and altruism are not sensitive to these distinctions.

Eisenberg and Miller review the research that has been conducted on empathy and prosocial behavior using the most commonly employed measures of empathy. As might be expected, given the very different assessment devices that have been used to investigate the empathy–altruism link, different patterns of association emerge. Furthermore, although the data are not definitive on this count, it appears that the association between empathic response and altruism may become stronger with age. Direct behavioral assessments such as facial/gestural indices appear to show stronger associations, although situational factors surrounding the performance of the prosocial act may interact with the relation between assessment of empathy and altruism. For instance, empathy may be strongly associated with altruism in situations where demand characteristics regarding the performance of the prosocial act are low, but the association may be wiped out by strong demand characteristics.

Eisenberg and Miller provide a valuable contribution to investigations in this domain by clearly delineating when the association and empathy should be expected and the types of measurement indices that are most likely to be useful in revealing those relations. Future work needs to clearly define distinctions among sympathy, personal distress reactions, and emotional contagion. The developmental course of the relation between empathy and prosocial behavior still warrants extensive investigation.

Summary

The chapters in Part III have made several significant contributions to the study of empathy. Each has addressed the definitional problem that has plagued previous research and pointed out that future studies need to employ a restrictive affect-based definition. The chapters by Strayer, Bryant, Eisenberg and Miller, and Lennon and Eisenberg provide powerful demonstrations of the complexity of relations that exist when measures of empathy are employed that tap cognitive, self-descriptive, and behavioral components of the empathy/sympathy complex. Although each of these components represents an important part of affective concern, we should not expect each to be equally predictive of all behaviors. Researchers must carefully define their target behaviors in terms of the predicted theoretical links to components of the empathy/sympathy complex. If we are to understand the relation between an affect-based empathy and important behavioral outcomes, we must refine our measures of empathy to tap affective responding in a more restrictive fashion.

The developmental course of empathy and empathy-based behaviors is clearly a complex one. However, the contributors here provide us with a much firmer foundation from which to explore the development processes. The picture that seems to emerge is one of early, perhaps biologically determined, tempermental differences in terms of emotional reactivity. These early differences are subject to both cognitive, developmentally based shifts in expression and the influence of socialization forces. Even in the case of behaviors such as altruism, where the conceptual links with empathy appear to be straightforward, the relations appear to be complex across age. As for behaviors such as self-control or social adjustment, the associations appear to be important but difficult to interpret. A great deal more developmental research is needed to elucidate these complex relations. Bryant's and Feschbach's chapters are excellent examples of the work that is beginning to appear on the important role of socialization and contextual determinants of empathic expression. These influences show many interactions with age and gender and call for the multimethod strategies described by Strayer and Eisenberg and Miller.

These chapters have helped to clarify what has been a confused and contradictory area of research. They place us in a much stronger position to proceed, but the tasks before us are daunting because the relations are complex and the methods necessary to address the questions posed by these chapters are taxing. In sum, these contributors have given us a much clearer path to follow than existed previously.

Part IV

Methodological issues

Janet Strayer

Our intent in the following discussion is not to review the many interview based, picture-story indices that have been used to measure empathy, but rather to point out, in general, the positive and negative features of the use of such methods. Because many relevant points are discussed elsewhere in this volume, our discussion will be brief.

Picture-story indices of empathy present participants, typically children, with a series of story narratives in which the characters are described and portrayed (by drawings, photos, slides, or, most recently, by videotapes) in contexts likely to evoke sadness, fear, or other emotions (see Feshbach & Roe, 1968, for the prototype measure). For each story, participants are asked to label the character's emotion and to report if they, themselves, feel any emotion. Credit for empathy on each trial is given when the participants report that they feel the same (highest score) or similar emotion (fewer points scored) as the story protagonist.

Pros

There are at least four distinct advantages to interview based, picture-story methods for assessing empathy in the laboratory. Most important, the response measures in such procedures typically are consistent with the primary definition of empathy as shared affect, and do not equate empathy with any of the sociocognitive skills with which it previously has been confused. Second, the criterion response of shared affect must be the participant's report of *subjective* experience of a specific affect that is shared with a story character. Given that this rendition may be facially, as well as verbally, expressed by participants, it may be best to include both nonverbal and verbal expressive measures concurrently. The advantage or necessity of the verbal response is that the criterion of empathy as subjectively experienced shared affect requires that we assess what participants, themselves, experience. Indeed, it is true that such reports are affected by the subject's introspective and verbal skills, as well as by social communication and perhaps demand features of the interview. Nevertheless, if we used only facial expressive responses or other nonverbal measures, we (the experimenters) and not the participants would decide if affect were being shared. It seems most appropriate that empathy remain, in large part, the property of the experiencer. The researcher's task, then, is to find methods that assess the validity of these verbal reports of their experience.

The last two points in favor of such methods pertain to pragmatic considerations and experimental feasibility. First, methods using picture-story stimuli and verbal responses are less time-consuming to administer and require less training in scoring procedures than do other nonverbal methods such as coding of facial expressions of emotion. Furthermore, it seems that picture-story measures, and recent updatings of such procedures using videotaped dramatic episodes, remain among the most feasible of interview-based methods for assessing empathetic affective responsiveness. Such methods ensure consistency across settings in stimulus materials, and seem particularly useful when validated for affective content. These methods, particularly when procedures are made standard across different laboratories, also ensure consistency in mode-of-response assessment and thus allow some progress to be made on age- and gender-related, normative, or comparative investigations of empathy.

Cons

In spite of the importance and clear viability of interview-based picture-story methods, they have some evident drawbacks on both the stimulus and response dimensions of these measures. Some of these difficulties can be remedied, whereas others may remain intractable.

For the five intractable problems I discuss, the only remedy appears to be attention to, or covariation of, their effects in data analyses. For example, social desirability pressures may induce participants in studies either to underestimate empathy (e.g., given response sets not to report emotion, particularly dysphoric emotion) or to overestimate it (e.g., if participants accept a favorable interpretation of empathy and are attuned to what most experimenters probably want to hear). Experimental instructions emphasizing the equal value of neutral or inconsistent feelings, or feelings different from those of stimulus characters, as well as independent assessments of social desirability (with established indices available for children and adults, as proposed by Crandall, Crandall, & Katkowsky, 1965; Crowne & Marlow, 1960) might be helpful to reduce, assess, and control for such effects in studies of empathy.

Another problem is particularly evident among young children, who frequently report themselves to be ''happy'' regardless of antecedent conditions (Mood, Johnson, & Shantz, 1978). Keeping fatigue to a minimum, as well as providing carefully chosen experimental probes or judiciously repeating the choice of alternatives, may help redress this problem. However, for participants of all ages, there is also the general constraint of reporting one's feelings to a stranger in a laboratory. Such a constraint, typical of any experiment, may be particularly likely to hamper investigations of empathy. On the other hand, given the hypothesis-testing advantages of laboratory work, there may be little recourse other than ensuring that participants are familiarized and relaxed, and using informal, even if structured, interviews.

The two remaining "intractable" problems are related and are less easily addressed by procedural remedies. They concern limitations, for adults as well as children, in introspective access to what one really feels, as well as in the verbal ability to label emotions, both of which are entailed in responses to picture-story methods. However, the participant's difficulty in knowing what to label the emotion experienced may or may not be a confounding variable in such self-report measures. Controlling for this verbal skill may not be the answer because persons with ready access to emotional experiences may be precisely those persons who become skilled at labeling emotion states. It therefore seems likely that researchers who wish to deal with the possible confounding of verbal skill with self-reported measures of empathy might better rely on the strategy of covarying some general measure of verbal skill, rather than controlling for more specific emotion-labeling abilities.

Now we turn to the more tractable and remediable problems, in the sense that they can be eliminated by changes in stimuli and procedures. Three points can be highlighted regarding stimulus materials. Many of the early picture-story methods used narratives and pictures (photos, etc.) that seem less ecologically valid and evocative than current videotaped stimuli portraying people reacting to others or to events that are likely to be witnessed or reported in life. Lifelike stimuli may make it more difficult to identify and experimentally to control the contextual narrative or pictorial cues for empathy. Yet, they extend both the ecological validity and the applicability of picture-story methods to adults as well as children and thus permit life span studies of empathic responses to the same stimulus set. There also seems little reason, when using lifelike stimuli, for pictorial cues to conflict with contextual cues (as has occurred in some picture-story indices, e.g., Iannotti, 1975, 1978). Empathy may be no less valid when it is in reaction to situational than to facial expressive or other pictorial cues of emotion. Furthermore, concordant affective arousal and empathy may be promoted by the salience of concurrent cues, rather than by conflicting or confusing cues. The third point regarding stimuli concerns an empirical question yet to be tested: that is, whether the presentation of a series of stimuli vignettes may overload the "empathic system" to the extent that observers may be unable to arouse or switch their emotional reactions as quickly as most stimulus series require. Comparisons of the effects on empathic responses of primacy versus recency of stimuli, presented in a series, for example, may be useful.

Another empirical issue pertains to the possibly biasing effects due to the sex of the experimenter. Any gender-related findings concerning reported emotions may be attributable to the fact that most studies of empathy with children have been conducted by female experimenters. Comparative studies employing both male and female experimenters would address this issue (see Eisenberg & Lennon, 1983; Lennon, Eisenberg, & Carroll, 1983).

There are yet other changes concerning response indices that researchers should consider. One concerns the degree of emotional match required for shared affect to be scored. Most researchers in this area now agree that the emotions reported for self and for story characters need only be similar and not identical. However, there remains the question of how and by whom this match is decided. Whereas many researchers (e.g., Feshbach & Roe, 1968; Iannotti, 1975, 1978) have required that children first identify the character's emotion in accordance with labels assigned by experimenters or a panel of judges, I would advocate the use of any plausible emotion identified by the child for the story character as the "standard" to be matched in assessing empathy. Given both that affective experience is subjective and that affective stimuli often evoke several plausible labels and interpretations, particularly when complex videotaped interactions are depicted, it seems less advisable to assess empathy in terms of affective consensus, rather than in terms of what is plausible and is reported to be affectively salient and evocative for the individual.

Last, with most picture-story measures, participants are asked only what they and the story character feel. Somewhat more extensive interviewing regarding the participant's reason for his or her feelings (see chapter 10) may allow one to assess whether the score for empathy better reflects personal distress or concern for the other.

In conclusion, there are many problems with interview-based, picture-story methods. Yet, many of these problems can be remedied or mitigated. Such efforts seem particularly worthwhile because these methods attempt to go to the heart of the matter by asking people what they feel when other people's feelings are at issue.

References

Crandall, V. C., Crandall, V. J., & Katkowsky, W. (1965). A children's social desirability questionnaire. *Journal of Consulting and Clinical Psychology, 29,* 27–36.

Crowne, D. P., & Marlowe, D. (1960). A *new* scale of social desirability independent of psychopathology. *Journal of Consulting Psychology, 24,* 349–354.

Eisenberg, N., & Lennon, R. (1983). Sex differences in empathy and related capacities. *Psychological Bulletin, 94,* 100–131.

Feshbach, N. D., & Roe, K. (1968). Empathy in six- and seven-year-olds. *Child Development, 34,* 133–145.

Iannotti, R. J. (1975). The nature and measurement of empathy in children. *The Counseling Psychologist, 5,* 21–25.

Iannotti, R. J. (1978). The affect of role-taking experiences on role taking, empathy, altruism, and aggression. *Developmental Psychology, 14,* 119–124.

Lennon, R., Eisenberg, N., & Carroll, J. (1983, April). *The relation between nonverbal indices of empathy and preschoolers' prosocial behavior.* Paper presented at the meeting of the Society for Research in Child Development, Detroit.

Mood, D. W., Johnson, J. E., & Shantz, C. U. (1978). Social comprehension and affect matching in young children. *Merrill–Palmer Quarterly, 24,* 63–66.

16   Self-report ratings of empathic emotion

C. Daniel Batson

If you want to know how someone is feeling, why don't you just ask them? Most researchers studying emotional reactions to the distress of others have been tempted to follow this simple suggestion. And many have yielded to temptation, myself included. But as is true for every other known approach to measuring emotional reactions, there are both pros and cons to using self-reports.

Pros

The advantages of measuring emotional reactions to the distress of others using self-reports are probably obvious. First, it is easy to do. One need only place subjects in the role of observers, present them with a person in distress, and then ask them to report their emotional response to observing the person. Typically, these self-reports are obtained by giving adult subjects a rating questionnaire containing a series of 10–30 adjectives describing possible emotional reactions to the situation – sympathetic, compassionate, alarmed, grieved, upset, softhearted, tender, and the like. Subjects are asked to rate the degree to which they are experiencing each emotion listed on the questionnaire by marking unidirectional 1–7 or 1–9 scales, with the endpoints labeled "not at all" and "extremely." With such a questionnaire, the entire measurement process can be completed within a minute or two, and it requires no equipment other than a pencil and a copy of the rating questionnaire.

The second major advantage to using self-report ratings is that they can provide a relatively differentiated measure of emotion. With many other measures, all one can hope to obtain is a gross index of general emotional arousal. But with self-reports, subjects can be asked to rate a variety of different emotion adjectives. One can then look at the interrelationships among these ratings to determine which ratings are closely associated and which are not – and thereby deter-

Preparation of this paper was supported in part by NSF Grant BNS-8507110, C. Daniel Batson, principal investigator.

mine whether there is a single underlying dimension of emotional response or multiple dimensions, respectively.

In recent years important progress has been made in the effort to develop physiological or facial-expression measures that can detect qualitative differences in emotional response. I look forward to the time when these more objective measures can reliably detect subtle qualitative differences. But that time is not yet. Even though encouraging initial attempts are under way (Eisenberg, personal communication, April 1985), most researchers using physiological measures would be hard pressed to know how to differentiate between, for example, empathic feelings when witnessing another person suffer (feeling sympathetic, compassionate, softhearted, tender, etc.) and feelings of personal distress (alarmed, grieved, upset, distressed, disturbed, perturbed, etc.). Yet, as discussed in some detail in chapter 8, factor analyses of adult subjects' self-reports clearly and consistently pick up this difference (Table 8.1 summarized the results of factor analyses from six different studies). Moreover, as also pointed out in chapter 8, research assessing the motivational consequences of these two qualitatively distinct emotional reactions to another's distress suggests that subjects' self-reports reflect a real qualitative difference in emotional reaction, not simply a semantic difference. The validity of self-report ratings is further supported by those studies in which both physiological and self-report measures have been taken and the two types of measures found to be positively associated (see Krebs, 1975; Stotland, 1969)

Cons

If these two advantages of using self-report ratings are obvious, then so are its several disadvantages. The value of self-report ratings rests on two assumptions: (1) Our research participants know what they are feeling, and (2) they will tell us – accurately. But, at least under certain circumstances, there is reason to doubt each of these assumptions.

First, concerning knowledge of their feelings, it seems likely that some subjects, even if they are experiencing some distinct emotion such as empathy rather than distress, do not have the language skills to interpret this experience accurately – at least not in the terms provided on our rating scales. This problem is likely to be especially severe when experimenters try to use self-report ratings with young children, which may account for the infrequent use of self-reports with young children, but it can also exist with adults. To illustrate the difficulties one can encounter, Coke, Batson, and McDavis (1978) originally used the term *empathic concern* to describe their index for measuring empathic or sympathetic reactions to witnessing another person's suffering. But it proved necessary to drop the adjective *empathic* from the empathic concern index because too many college student subjects were not certain what the word meant. (This, of course, only puts them in the same company with us psychologists, as Lauren Wispé has pointed out in chapter 2.)

In addition to the problem of respondents not knowing the meaning of the adjectives on a self-report rating scale in some absolute sense, there is the problem of contextual meaning. Some adjectives describing emotional reactions to another's distress have multiple meanings depending on context, and respondents may interpret the words differently as result. Consider, for example, the adjective *concerned*. In experiment 2 reported by Coke et al. (1978), subjects were asked to report their emotional reactions after learning that a master's student in education needed volunteers to participate in her thesis research. In response to this relatively bland need situation, subjects clearly interpreted *concerned* as an other-directed emotion. Ratings of this adjective were highly correlated with ratings of empathic, compassionate, softhearted, and warm. But in subsequent studies in which subjects have been confronted with more upsetting need situations – for example, watching someone who is apparently suffering as a result of receiving electric shocks (Batson, O'Quin, Fultz, Vanderplas, & Isen, 1983) – most subjects have interpreted *concerned* in the more self-directed sense of worried, troubled, or upset. Ratings of it have correlated highly with ratings of these distress adjectives, and not with ratings of the other-directed empathy adjectives. This contextual shift led to the exclusion of *concerned* from what was initially called the empathic concern index. So now neither *empathic* nor *concerned* appears on the index, and we are left with severe doubts about the wisdom of our initial name for this index. We still call it an empathy index, but others now prefer to call it a sympathy index.

The second major problem with using self-report measures is self-presentation. Even if (1) subjects know what they are feeling and (2) they are thinking about their feelings in the same way we are – the two necessary conditions for them to be able to communicate their true feelings to us – they may not want to communicate their true feelings. Instead, at least some subjects may want to present themselves as more sympathetic, compassionate, and so on, than they really are, believing either that this is the way they should react to another's distress or that it is the way that will most impress other people. Other subjects may want to underreport their emotional reactions in order to appear strong and unruffled by adversity and crisis.

Fortunately, there is some evidence that it may be possible to control psychometrically for these self-presentational biases. The control technique uses dispositional empathy measures – but in a very different way from the way they were designed to be used. The intent of researchers developing measures of empathy as a dispositional personality variable was to detect individuals who are more likely to respond with sympathy, compassion, and so on to another's distress. But some recent evidence (Archer, Diaz-Loving, Gollwitzer, Davis, & Foushee, 1981; Batson, Bolen, Cross, & Neuringer-Benefiel, 1986) suggests that these dispositional measures are more effective in detecting individuals who want to see themselves, and to be seen by others, as this kind of person. This recent research suggests that if one considers that part of situational self-reports of empathy (sympathy) that is *not* related to scores on dispositional empathy measures, then one may have a self-report less contaminated by self-presentation concerns.

Self-presentation concerns may also underlie at least some of the sex differences in the self-report of emotional reactions, especially in reports of empathy (sympathy) and personal distress. Although not always, males often report less of each of these types of emotion. That this sex difference is due at least in part to self-presentation concerns and not to sex differences in emotional experience is suggested by the fact that these sex differences tend to disappear when one takes less obtrusive physiological and facial-expression measures of emotion (see Eisenberg & Lennon, 1983).

Depending on the particular research question being addressed, one may be able to deal with this sex-role based self-presentation bias either by restricting subject samples to only one sex or by looking at relationships separately for the two sexes. Alternatively, one may use a within-subject difference between self-reported empathy (sympathy) and self-reported distress, so as to create an index of the relative predominance of the two emotional responses. This last technique takes advantage of the fact that the sex-related self-presentation concerns seem to affect self-reports of both empathy and personal distress in the same direction.

In sum, I know of no researchers studying emotional reactions who do not wish for better measures than we now have. We need measures that are more accurate, more sensitive, and more objective. The most likely area for a measurement breakthrough is, I think, the physiological domain. The future almost certainly lies there. But the distance to that future is unclear. It may be less than a decade; it may be more than a century. In the interim, there is much to be said for using self-reports. As long as we do not take their answers at face value, we may be able to learn a lot about what people are feeling simply by asking them.

References

Archer, R. L., Diaz-Loving, R., Gollwitzer, P. M., Davis, M. H., & Foushee, H. C. (1981). The role of dispositional empathy and social evaluation in the empathic mediation of helping. *Journal of Personality and Social Psychology, 40,* 786–796.

Batson, C. D., Boleen, M. H., Cross, J. A., & Neuringer-Benefiel, H. E. (1986). Where is the altruism in the altruistic personality? *Journal of Personality and Social Psychology, 50,* 212–220.

Batson, C. D, O'Quin, K., Fultz, J., Vanderplas, M., & Isen, A. (1983). Self-reported distress and empathy and egoistic versus altruistic motivation for helping. *Journal of Personality and Social Psychology, 45,* 706–718.

Coke, J. S., Batson, C. D., & McDavis, K. (1978). Empathic mediation of helping: A two-stage model. *Journal of Personality and Social Psychology, 36,* 752–766.

Eisenberg, N., & Lennon, R. (1983). Sex differences in empathy and related capacities. *Psychological Bulletin, 94,* 100–131.

Krebs, D. L. (1975). Empathy and altruism. *Journal of Personality and Social Psychology, 32,* 1134–1146.

Stotland, E. (1969). Exploratory studies of empathy. In L. Berkowitz (Ed.), *Advances in experimental social psychology* (Vol. 4). New York: Academic Press.

Brenda K. Bryant

Paper-and-pencil measures used to study the development of empathy (i.e., Bryant, 1982; Mehrabian & Epstein, N., 1972) over a wide age range have focused on empathy as a vicarious emotional response to the perceived emotional experiences of others, in particular, the experience of perceived sharing of feelings, at least at the gross affect (pleasant–unpleasant) level. The approach taken by researchers using paper-and-pencil measures contrasts with approaches that focus on cognitive insight per se or on nonverbal, physiological indices of emotional arousal in that the individual's conscious experience of emotions is held paramount. Such a perspective is in keeping with Kagan's (1984) position that how an individual experiences life is more relevant to his/her behavior than how someone else thinks that person experiences it. In sum, the paper-and-pencil measures of empathy highlight the metaexperience and reporting of vicarious emotional response to the perceived emotional experiences of others and emphasize emotional responsiveness rather than accuracy of cognitive insight.

Description of measures

Two paper-and-pencil measures are evaluated here: The Mehrabian and Epstein measure of empathy in adults and the Bryant adaptation of this measure for use with children and adolescents. The Mehrabian and Epstein (1972) measure consists of 33 items requiring a response to each item on a +4 (very strong agreement) to −4 (very strong disagreement) scale. Sixteen items require agreement and the remaining 17 items require disagreement to be scored as an empathic response. Items vary in content: some indicate external behavioral cues (e.g., another's laughter or cries), some identify or refer to an internal emotional state of another (e.g., feelings of characters in a novel; seeing someone who is depressed), some describe situational cues (e.g., seeing someone be ill-treated), some describe general emotional atmosphere (e.g., excitement around me), and some describe salient psychosocial states of persons (e.g., foreigners who inherently must deal with psychosocial issues of belonging and not belonging). These

361

particular distinctions in the variety of items have not been documented in factor analyses of the items, although selection of items for this scale was based in part on content validity inferred from factor analyses of a larger set of items. Unfortunately, these factor analyses are not clearly detailed in any available reports. Although the measure represents a variety of situations and possible dimensions of empathy, each item has been found to correlate at $p < .01$ with the total score on the scale (Mehrabian & Epstein, 1972). This measure was designed, then, to be global in its consideration of empathy as a general disposition of perceived emotional responsiveness to others' emotional experiences.

Bryant (1982) adapted 18 of the original 33 items from the Mehrabian and Epstein (1972) measure as a way of accommodating a wide age range of children and adolescents and, at the same time, yielding a measure comparable to one already available for use with adults. From these 18 items, 22 items were generated for use with children. First, each of the 18 items was reworded in order to be appropriate for use with children. For example, ''I often find public displays of affection annoying'' became ''People who kiss and hug in public are silly.'' Second, four of the original Mehrabian and Epstein items were used to generate two items, each varying in sex of the stimulus person. For example, the adult Mehrabian and Epstein form reads, ''It makes me sad to see a lonely stranger in a group,'' whereas the form for younger persons reads, ''It makes me sad to see a girl (boy) who can't find anyone to play with.'' These items provide a basis for assessing same- versus cross-sex empathy and the development of such phenomena. Three formats have been used in administering the resulting children's version of empathy assessment. First graders do not actually use a paper-and-pencil measure as they place cards (one empathy item per card) in a ME or NOT ME box; older children circle YES or NO in response to each item; and seventh graders have responded to the children's wording using either the yes/no or the Mehrabian and Epstein 9-point format. Both the Mehrabian and Epstein measure for adults and Bryant's measure for use with children and adolescents have been administered to groups and to individuals and in all cases a higher score has been used to reflect greater empathy. What follows now is a review of currently available research that informs us about the reliability and construct validity of these two measures of empathy.

Measure characteristics

Table 17.1 presents a summary of currently available studies that have used either the Mehrabian and Epstein (1972) or the Bryant (1982) measure of empathy and highlights for the reader the nature of the sample, the specific empathy measure used, the mode of administration, and the empathy issues addressed. For a full discussion of age and sex differences in empathic responding

Table 17.1. *Summary of studies using Mehrabian & Epstein (1972) and Bryant (1982) measures of empathy*

Reference	Version	Age/grade	n	Sex	Mode	Format	Issues
Archer, Diaz-Loving, Gollwitzer, Davis, & Foushee (1981)	Adult	College students	120	All f	Group	9-point	Altruism, social influence
Barnett, Feighny, & Esper (1983)	Adult	College students	96	Approximately 48m 48f	Group	9-point	Altruism
Barnett, Howard, King, & Dino (1981)	Adult	High school (10–12th graders)	103	33m 70f	Group	9-point	Altruism
Barnett & Thompson (1985)	Child	4th & 5th graders	117	64m 53f	Group	YES/NO	Altruism, machiavellianism
Bryant (1982)	Child	1st grade	56	27m 29f	Individual	ME/NOT ME	Other measures of empathy, social desirability, aggression, achievement, acceptance of individual differences, reading level[a]
	Child	4th grade	115	56m 59f	Group	YES/NO	
	(& Adult)	7th grade	87	43m 44f		9-point	
	Child	1st grade	72	36m 36f	Individual	ME/NOT ME	
	(& Adult)	7th grade	94	42m 52f	Group	YES/NO	
Bryant (1984)	Child	7–10-yr-olds	67	33m 34f	Individual	YES/NO	Mental health

Table 17.1. (*cont.*)

Reference	Version	Age/grade	n	Sex	Mode	Format	Issues
		10–14-yr-olds	73	36m 37f	Individual		Factor analysis
		7-yr-olds	128	63m 65f			
		10-yr-olds	163	81m 82f			
		14-yr-olds	73	36m 37f			
		10-yr-olds	115	56m 59f	Group		
Bryant (1985); also (1980)	Child	7-yr-olds	72	36m 36f			Relation to other components of social-emotional functioning
		10-yr-olds	96	48m 48f			
Eisenberg, Pasternack, & Lennon (1984)	Child	9-10-yr-olds	32	16m 16f	Individual	YES/NO	Altruism, moral reasoning
		4th graders	39	17m 22f			
Foushee, Davis & Archer (1979)	Adult[b]	College students	591	246m 345f	Group	9-point	Expressiveness; emotional vulnerability
Hoppe & Singer (1976, 1977)	Adult	Criminal offenders	115	All m	Group	9-point	Violence
Kalle & Suls (1978)	Adult	College students	90	All m	Group (45/group)	9-point	Moral judgment

Study	Type	Population	N	Sex	Administration	Response	Factor analysis
Kalliopuska (1983)	Adult	Parents of 9–12-yr-olds	338			9-point	
Mehrabian & Epstein (1972)	Adult	College students	91[c]	37m 51f	Group (10/group)	9-point	Aggression, social desirability
		College students	104[d]	47m 47f			
		College students	81	All f	Individual	9-point	Altruism, emotion
Strayer (1983)	Child	6-yr-olds	33	18m 15f	Individual	ME/NOT ME	Prosocial development;
		8-yr-olds	38	20m 18f		YES/NO	Verbal ability; creative emotions
Sturtevant (1985)	Child	4–6th grade	161	78m 83f	Group	YES/NO	Altruism; intelligence

[a] See text for details on which age groups received which particular measures.
[b] Items 3, 6, 14, 17, and 22 were deleted.
[c] 3 discarded.
[d] 10 discarded.

on these measures, see chapter 9. Note that preliminary factor analyses of responses to the Bryant measure indicate that there is virtually no concordance between the factor structures of responses provided by 10-year-olds in group versus individual administration (Bryant, 1984). Thus, the Bryant measure appears to be vulnerable to the mode of administration, and, until suitable data suggest otherwise for either measure, the mode of administration should be taken into account in comparisons of findings.

Reliability

The internal consistency of the Mehrabian and Epstein adult measure has been documented to be .79 among adults (Kalliopuska, 1983) and .48 among seventh graders (Bryant, 1982). The internal consistency of the children's version varies according to the age of the respondent, ranging from .54 for first-grade children, .68 for fourth-grade children, and .79 for seventh-grade children (Bryant, 1982). Consistent with the relatively high internal consistency obtained for adults, split-half reliability for the adult measure has been reported to be .84 (Mehrabian & Epstein, 1972). Short-term stability of scores has been based on 2-week test–retest reliability coefficients and, consistent with the notion that these measures of empathy reflect relatively stable dispositions, it has been reported to be $r(53) = .74$ for first graders and $r(108) = .81$ for fourth graders; for seventh graders, it was $r(80) = .83$ using the children's version and .85 using the adult scale (Bryant, 1982). Although reliability is adequate for the younger children, internal consistency and short-term stability of scores do increase with the age of the respondent. Although the structure of responses distinguish seventh graders from adults (these young adolescents show more internal consistency on the children's version of empathy), other aspects of reliability of seventh graders appear equivalent to that of adults.

Construct validity

The relations of empathy to aggression/violence, altruism, and moral reasoning have been central to establishing the construct validity of the Mehrabian and Epstein and the Bryant child measure of empathy. In addition, some work has been done on the relation of these two measures of empathy to other aspects of emotional life and well-being. Finally, divergent validity has been examined by considering the relation of these two measures of empathy to cognitive functioning and social desirability.

Aggression/violence

Empathy has been found to be linked to reduced aggression among first- and fourth-grade males but not females (Bryant, 1982) and adults (Mehrabian & Epstein, 1972). Hoppe and Singer (1976) failed to find a relationship between empathy and criminal violence but, what seems odd to this reviewer, they categorized child molestation as nonviolent. Since child molesters constituted 71% of the "nonviolent" offenders in their sample, the lack of difference in empathy between the groups, in this reviewer's opinion, does not challenge the validity of paper-and-pencil measures of empathy.

Altruism/prosocial behavior

The preponderance of the evidence supports a positive relationship between empathy and altruism. Adolescents and adults have demonstrated a positive relationship between empathy and helping (Archer, Diaz-Loving, Gollwitzer, Davis, & Foushee, 1981; Barnett, Howard, King, & Dino, 1981; Mehrabian & Epstein, 1972). Mehrabian and Epstein (1972) have documented that this positive relationship was not confounded by liking of or perceived similarity to the person being helped. One qualification of this positive association between empathy and altruism, however, is needed. That is, highly empathic adults volunteered more time to supervise the recreational activities of physically handicapped children described as responsive than did low-empathy adults, but this was not the case when the handicapped children were described as unresponsive (Barnett, Feighny, & Esper, 1983). Thus, the anticipated responsiveness of the potential recipient of help may be a moderating factor in the positive association between empathy and helping among adults.

Whereas the link between empathy and prosocial behavior is clear among adults, the relationship for persons earlier in the life span is less well established. Among elementary school children in particular, Barnett and Thompson (1985) found that highly empathic children were rated by their teachers as being more helpful than low-empathy children when another individual's need is obvious and salient. With respect to donating behavior, Eisenberg, Pasternack, and Lennon (1984) found no relationship, whereas Sturtevant (1985) found a positive relationship. A UNICEF poster in conjunction with describing the children as poor (i.e., the procedure used by Eisenberg et al.) did not pull an association, but a call for donating to poor *and* hungry children (i.e., the procedure used by Sturtevant) did. Empathy has also been positively linked to expressing acceptance of individual differences in others (Bryant, 1982). In contrast, Sturtevant (1985) found no relationship between empathy and helping, and Eisenberg et al. (1984)

found a negative relationship between empathy and helping to pick up a box of spilled paper clips and no relationship to helping to pick up toys. In addition, Strayer (1983) did not find empathy significantly linked to teacher ratings of considerateness at school (i.e., "is agreeable and easy to get along with"; "tries not to do or say anything that would hurt another").

It is unclear whether the lack of association found at times reflects difficulties in measuring empathy or prosocial development or actual developmental inconsistencies. Considering the actual associations found, at best empathy is linked to altruism and prosocial behavior when the need of another is salient, the other is emotionally responsive, and the need is relatively important in that the prosocial behavior can be viewed by the donor as relieving some clear emotional distress. Even this picture must be tempered for children by the number of studies (with the various operational definitions of prosocial behavior) that did not reflect this description.

Moral reasoning

Both adults and children have demonstrated some relationship between their empathy scores and moral reasoning. Eisenberg et al. (1984) found empathy was negatively related to hedonistic reasoning, and positively related to sympathetic reasoning, a prosocial composite score, and the number of stories in which the children said the protagonist would assist. Consistent with this, Barnett and Thompson (1985) found that highly empathic children had significantly lower machiavellianism scores and cited other-oriented reasons for their own helping behavior more frequently than less empathic children. More equivocal, Kalle and Suls (1978), studying adults, found a significant relationship of empathy to conventional morality (stage 4) but no relationship to stages 2, 3, 5, or 6 of Kohlberg's moral judgment stages. Finally, Eisenberg et al. (1984) did not find a relationship between empathy and Kohlberg's moral maturity scores of 9- and 10-year-olds. These findings are consistent with Gilligan's (1982) evaluation that Kohlberg's stages of moral development are not sensitive to developmental components of moral reasoning based on emotional connectedness and responsibility for others. Overall, empathy as assessed by these paper-and-pencil measures is not clearly related to moral maturity as assessed by Kohlberg's scoring system but is related to measures of moral reasoning that focus on the individual's perceived motives for behaving that take into account the needs and wishes of others.

Emotions and well-being

Empathic tendency among adults has been found to be positively associated with higher characteristic arousal by others' emotional experiences (Mehrabian & Epstein, 1972), a willingness to express emotional vulnerability, and a ready awareness of the feelings and needs of others (Foushee, Davis, & Archer, 1979). Among children, it has been associated with imaginal processes, ego resiliency, and creativity (Strayer, 1983), with acceptance of help (Bryant, 1985), and with general adaptability, in that parents judge empathic children to be easy to get along with and teachers judge the same children to be independent (Strayer, 1983). The picture of the emotional status of persons (children and/or adults) scoring high on these measures of empathy is one of being characteristically aroused by the feelings and needs of others, able to express their own vulnerability, emotionally independent, and creative.

Bryant (1984) also assessed the relation between empathy and children's mental health status using parental reports of behavioral problems and social competencies assessed by the Child Behavioral Checklist (Achenbach, 1978; Achenbach & Edelbrock, 1979). Her study reveals that girls' but not boys' empathy at age 10 is related to the externalization of problems and total number of behavioral problems. The implication here is that "empathic" girls at this age have more behavioral problems than do "nonempathic" girls. Johnson–Neyman contrasts reveal that although low-empathy girls have fewer behavioral problems than low-empathy boys, high-empathy girls do not differ from high-empathy boys in these relevant categories of mental health. It is important to replicate this finding because the implication is that highly empathic 10-year-old girls do not fit the sex-role stereotype of "good little girls" but rather are awkward or troublesome in response to their emotional arousal. Empathy at age 10 did not predict later mental health status in early adolescence (age 14) for either boys or girls. Concurrent evaluation of empathy and mental health at age 14, however, predicted several components of mental health at the same age. Specifically, higher empathy among children from large (3 or more children) families was related to lower internalization, externalization and total number of behavioral problems as well as to better social relations. In contrast, among children from small 2-child families, empathy was related to lower school adjustment. These findings suggest that the meaning of relatedness to others in the form of self-reported empathy on the Bryant (1982) index is different for children at age 10 and at age 14, for males and for females, and for children from small versus large families. Indeed, factor analyses provide preliminary support for this contention (Bryant, 1984).

Divergent aspects of construct validity

To understand the meaning of self-reported empathy, it has been critical to know the relation between obtained empathy scores and scores on other measures that theoretically should be independent of empathy, such as cognitive ability and social desirability per se, or that should be related only marginally with constructs such as affective role taking. In fact, the discriminant validity of the two paper-and-pencil measures of empathy appears rather good.

No relationship has been found between such empathy measures and level of cognitive functioning. Neither reading ability (Bryant, 1982) nor verbal ability (Strayer, 1983), nor intelligence (Sturtevant, 1985) has been found to be significantly related to children's empathy scores.

With respect to social desirability, neither Mehrabian and Epstein (1972) using the Crowne and Marlowe (1960) measure of social desirability nor Bryant (1982) using the Crandall, Crandall, and Katkovsky (1965) measure of social desirability found any significant relationship between empathy scores and social desirability scores. Using a large sample of more than 300 adults, Kalliopuska found a slight negative correlation ($-.08$) between the Crowne and Marlowe measure of social desirability and adult empathy scores, but the correlation accounts for so little variance that it is of no practical significance. Although Eisenberg et al. (1984) did not report a correlation between children's empathy and social desirability, the pattern of correlates of these two measures to aspects of moral judgment were dissimilar. To date no direct and substantial link has been found between social desirability scores and empathy scores, but there does appear to be a positive link between empathy scores and responsiveness to social influence (Archer et al., 1981).

Future research needed

Future research must address several questions. First, is it appropriate to consider empathy as a generalized phenomenon in contrast to the measurement guidelines requiring analysis of subscales? Tradition leads us to determine neat, reliable, and well-specified components of a construct that hold across ages and both sexes. Unfortunately, there is also a tendency not to see this predetermined similarity of structure across individuals that we force upon our conceptualization of development. We need to be studying in detail the role that individual differences may play in empathy development, including the development of the structure of empathic arousal.

An alternative or additional approach to factor analyses of how empathy questionnaire items covary with one another is to determine the differential and overlapping meaning of particular items by what "outcomes" of interest individual items predict. Bryant (1984), for example, assessed which particular items of the children's index of empathy predicted the mental health variables already documented as relevant by analyses using "total" empathy scores. When hierarchical regressions were used for each item in conjunction with the relevant controls for sex of child, sex of sibling, family size, and socioeconomic status, all but item 12 predicted at least one of the previously described aspects of mental health. A more conservative stepwise regression was attempted next. The variance accounted for by the item most predictive of the mental health factors was selected before assessing whether another item could significantly add to the predictability of the mental health factor. This was done until no further item added to the predictability of the mental health factor. Ten items were relevant here: items 1, 2, 3, 4, 7, 9, 10, 14, 16, and 20. These results suggest that items that most consistently load on a factor (items 1, 6, 12, and 14) are not the only meaningful items on this empathy measure and that individual items each appear to have predictive value, roughly half of the items having predictive value that does not overlap with one another. These findings lead me to argue for further consideration of even more content areas of empathic arousal and to avoid premature narrowing of our empirical understanding of empathy and its relation to human development.

In addition, before these indices of empathy can be truly life span in nature, older adults need to be included in our research samples. Relevant or uniquely sensitive content issues may become increasingly salient as we consider a wider age range in our examination of human development.

The second important question is do these paper-and-pencil measures of empathy confuse empathy with projection, and if so, how can we get around such a problem? We need to tap an individual's ability to feel the comfort of another individual in a situation that would arouse discomfort if the perceiver was in the same situation or an individual's ability to feel the discomfort of another individual in a setting that would not be uncomfortable to the perceiver if he or she were in the same setting. Although projection may facilitate empathic arousal in many situations, projection as a basis for empathy in these two types of situations would interfere with empathic arousal.

The third point is that, although the existing paper-and-pencil measures assess the extent of empathy in terms of the variety of situations in which the individual reports an empathic response, it would be conceptually useful to incorporate an assessment of intensity of empathic arousal that is distinct from the range of empathic arousal. In particular, empathic arousal that is debilitating in intensity rather than facilitating of constructive response is at issue. Davis (1983) approaches this issue indirectly when he attempts to differentiate between adults' empathic concern and personal distress as a general orientation. More direct attention needs to be given to the transition from facilitating to debilitating emotional arousal and individual differences in tolerance for discomfort that may buffer against debilitating empathic arousal.

References

Achenbach, T. (1978). The child behavior profile: I. Boys aged 6–11. *Journal of Consulting and Clinical Psychology, 46,* 478–488.

Achenbach, T., & Edelbrock, C. (1979). The child behavior profile: II. Boys aged 12–16. *Journal of Consulting and Clinical Psychology, 47,* 223–233.

Archer, R. L., Diaz-Loving, R., Gollwitzer, P. M., Davis, M. H., & Foushee, H. C. (1981). The role of dispositional empathy and social evaluation in the empathic mediation of helping. *Journal of Personality and Social Psychology, 40* (4), 786–796.

Barnett, M. A., Feighny, K. M., & Esper, J. A. (1983). Effects of anticipated victim responsiveness and empathy upon volunteering. *The Journal of Social Psychology, 119,* 211–218.

Barnett, M. A., Howard, J. A., King, L. M., & Dino, G. A. (1981). Helping behavior and the transfer of empathy. *The Journal of Social Psychology, 115,* 125–132.

Barnett, M. A., & Thompson, S. (1985). The role of affective perspective-taking ability and empathic disposition in the child's machiavellianism, prosocial behavior, and motive for helping. *Journal of Genetic Psycholgoy, 146* (3), 295–305.

Bryant, B. K. (1980). *Developmental perspective on sources of support and psychological well-being.* Final report submitted to the Foundation for Child Development.

Bryant, B. K. (1982). An index of empathy for children and adolescents. *Child Development, 53,* 413–425.

Bryant, B. K. (1984, August). Self-criticism of the Bryant (1982) empathy index. In *The Construct and Assessment of Empathy.* Symposium conducted at the annual meeting of the American Psychological Association, Toronto, Canada.

Bryant, B. K. (1985). The neighborhood walk: Sources of support in middle childhood. *Society for Research in Child Development Monograph, 50* (3, Serial No. 210).

Crandall, V. C, Crandall, V. J., & Katkovsky, W. (1965). A children's social desirability questionnaire. *Journal of Consulting Psychology, 29*(1), 27–36.

Crowne, D. P., & Marlowe, D. (1960). A new scale of social desirability independent of psychopathology. *Journal of Consulting Psychology, 24,* 349–354.

Davis, M. H. (1983). Measuring individual differences in empathy: Evidence for a multidimensional approach. *Journal of Personality and Social Psychology, 44,* (1), 13–126.

Eisenberg, N., Pasternack, J., & Lennon, R. (1984, March). *Prosocial development in middle childhood.* Paper presented at the Southwestern Society of Research in Human Development, Denver, Colorado.

Foushee, H. C., Davis, M. H., & Archer, R. L. (1979). Empathy, masculinity, and femininity. *Catalog of Selected Documents in Psychology, 9,*(4), 85.

Gilligan, C. (1982). *In a different voice.* Cambridge, MA: Harvard University Press.

Hoppe, C. M., & Singer, R. D. (1976). Overcontrolled hostility, empathy, and egocentric balance in violent and nonviolent psychiatric offenders. *Psychological Reports, 39,* 1303–1308.

Hoppe, C. M., & Singer, R. D. (1977). Interpersonal violence and its relationship to some personality measures. *Aggressive Behavior, 3,* 261–270.

Kagan, J. (1984). *The nature of the child.* New York: Basic Books.

Kalle, R. J., & Suls, J. (1978). The relationship between Kohlberg's moral judgment stages and emotional empathy. *Bulletin of the Psychonomic Society, 11*(3), 191–192.

Kalliopuska, M. (1983). Verbal components of emotional empathy. *Perceptual and Motor Skills, 56,* 487–496.

Mehrabian, A., & Epstein, N. (1972). A measure of emotional empathy. *Journal of Personality. 40*(4), 525–543.

Strayer, J. (1983, April). *Affective and cognitive components of children's empathy*. Paper presented at the biennial meetings of the Society for Research in Child Development, Detroit, Michigan.

Sturtevant, A. E. (1985). The relationship of empathy, mood, prosocial moral reasoning, and altruism in children. Unpublished doctoral dissertation, New York University.

Robert F. Marcus

A good measure of empathy should function in ways that accord with the meaning of the construct and that reliably and consistently convey this meaning across appropriate measurement contexts. It should demonstrate discriminant validity to convince us that empathy, rather than other possibly related constructs, is being assessed. A measure of empathy should predict theoretically related behavior, relate to other measures of empathy and have an acceptable level of reliability (i.e., internal consistency and replicability). Unfortunately, criterion measures of empathy, against which somatic indices may be compared, are themselves not well developed. It therefore appears paradoxical that somatic indices such as facial ratings, which some believe may turn out to be the most valid and reliable measures of empathy (Hoffman, 1982), cannot themselves be securely assessed with respect to other established and confirmed validity checks at this point.

The variety of somatic indices to be reviewed here makes it difficult to compare studies. Researchers typically evaluate empathic responses to one to four affective stimuli with little rationale for inclusion of particular affective stimuli. The samples studied generally have included preschool and school-age children. Because few published studies can be found, this review is based largely on professional papers and dissertations. The methods used in these studies have involved exposure of children to slide-story or videotaped, affectively charged stories with videotapes made of children's responses. Ratings have then been made of children's facial, gestural, or vocal empathic responses.

Pros

Children's facial, gestural, or vocal responses to others' affect are highly accessible targets for ratings of both a global and more specific nature. Considerable research has been done detailing the range of universal facial emotional responses, and this groundwork can easily serve as a training format for raters (Ekman & Friesen, 1975). Interrater agreement has been consistently high on measures of facial empathy across various affective stimuli (Barnett, 1984; Cohen, 1973; Howard, 1983; Leiman, 1978; Marcus, Roke, & Bruner, 1985). Vocal empathic responses also have been reliably assessed in one study of empathy (Marcus, Roke, & Bruner, 1985) and in another study of children's responses to distress (Cummings, Iannotti, & Zahn-Waxler, 1985).

Nonverbal indices are obviously not dependent upon the sophistication level of expressive language used by the individual and, thus, facial measures have not been found to correlate with age (Cohen, 1973; Howard, 1983; Marcus et al., 1985) or sex (Cohen, 1973; Eisenberg & Lennon, 1983; Lennon, Eisenberg, & Carroll, 1986; Marcus et al., 1985). Strayer (1985a) however, found that facial expressions of particular emotions did correlate with sex, as might be consistent with Saarni's (1979) work on socialization of display rules. Boys showed less fearful facial expressions than girls. It should be added that very different patterns of correlations emerge when facial empathy measures are related to behavioral measures for one sex versus the other (Howard, 1983; Sawin, 1979). Gestural and vocal empathy measures have not been studied sufficiently to delineate patterns of age and sex differences.

It is important that researchers have a good measure of empathy that varies in conceptually meaningful ways with the presence of emotional stimuli and other situational factors. Children's nonverbal emotional responses to adults' arguing and in friendly and neutral interaction were examined in a recent study (Cummings et al. 1985). This was not designed as a study of empathy but as a study of children's emotional responses. However, the emotional responses could be interpreted as either self- or other-directed (i.e., empathic), or both. Nonverbal signs of distress were greatest under the background anger condition; distress was most evident in body posture or movement (60% of the sample by second exposure, a procedure employed to heighten emotional impact), in facial responses (33.6% of the sample), and in their voices or crying (23.1% of the sample) (Cummings et al., 1985). Similarly, Strayer (1985b) recently found that children's facial expressions appropriately reflected the dysphoric valence of TV vignettes they viewed. Moreover, Barnett (1984) found that facial empathic responses were greater when children had had previous sad experiences similar to those of an actor in a videotaped presentation that they watched, thus again showing enhanced empathy in certain situations. Similarity of experiences to the plight of another has often been thought to enhance one's empathic feelings for the other, and this enhanced empathy should be reflected in facial empathy ratings. In brief, there is evidence that somatic indices of emotion, including empathic responsiveness, vary in a manner consistent with conceptual expectations (Barnett's results show empathic variation with similarity of previous experience, and Strayer and Cummings et al.'s show variation with kind and intensity of exposure to emotional stimuli).

Somatic indices have been found to be consistently unrelated to verbal matching measures of empathy, as collected during slide-story presentations (Cohen,
1973; Howard, 1983; Kuchenbecker, 1976; Marcus et al., 1985). However, this
may be more a reflection of the inadequacy of verbal matching measures than
the criterion validity of somatic measures (see critique by Hoffman, 1982). It is
more important that somatic indices show some consistency among one another,
and this generally has been supported by modest correlations among measures
(Cummings, personal communication; Lennon, Eisenberg, & Carroll, 1986; Marcus
et al., 1985).

Facial measures of empathy may have an edge over verbal reports of empathic
responses because they can be collected in such a way as to make them less
subject to self-presentation bias. Those who have used slide-story measures of
empathy with 3- and 4-year-old children are familiar with a common response to
the question "How do you feel?" after watching and listening to an affectively
charged story. The responses "fine" or "good" show an awareness of socially
desired verbal responses in polite conversation. Sex differences that occasionally
appear on verbal but not nonverbal measures of empathy have, in part, been
attributed to self-presentational biases (Eisenberg & Lennon, 1983). Facial
expressions of emotion in response to slide presentations have been found to
vary with the sex of the experimenter and the presence or absence of others
(Yarczower & Daruns, 1982). The presence of a male experimenter has been
found to inhibit spontaneous expressions of tenderness in male but not female
subjects (Blumberg, Solomon, & Perloe, 1981). Although this might appear to
make both verbal and facial measures vulnerable to situational influences, it is
possible to devise a method whereby children are left alone to watch videotaped
presentations, so that less obtrusive videotaping of the children's responses can
be obtained. Situational pressures can thus be minimized.

Finally, somatic indices have shown consistent relations with theoretically
predicted behaviors, although the direction of correlation has at times been the
reverse of what was predicted. Howard (1983) found that facial ratings of empathy with four emotions predicted helping behavior in another situation for both
boys and girls. However, a negative relation was found for boys and a positive
relation for girls. Marcus et al. (1985) found a negative association between
facial empathy in reaction to a slide-story presentation and cooperation in the
preschool classroom. In addition, Cohen (1973) found negative correlations between facial empathy and candy donations. A suggestion as to how these contrary findings might be understood is dealt with in the next section (Cons). However, when researchers have limited the stimulus conditions to single dysphoric
affects, and have used videotaped stimuli rather than slide-story measures to
elicit empathy, ratings of facial empathy have been found to be positively related
to generosity (Leiman, 1978), sharing (Peraino & Sawin, 1981), and to a com-

posite measure of anonymous prosocial behavior (Lennon et al., 1986). Such stimuli may be more effective in eliciting empathy for a number of reasons, including children's familiarity with the television medium and the personal and engaging quality of the videotapes. Slide-story presentations may, in some instances, evoke empathic responses that are then muted or suppressed as a result of the child being less involved. Or, as discussed in the next section, the character of the empathic response itself may be different under slide-story conditions. Thus, there is evidence that empathy with another's negative affective state, especially if elicited with realistic stimuli, is related to prosocial behavior directed toward the object of empathy.

Cons

The findings with regard to cross-situational and cross-time stability of somatic indices are somewhat mixed. Howard (1983) found that stability of facial ratings of children retested using a slide-story measure after two weeks was poor, and, in some cases negative correlations were discovered. Moreover, correlations between teachers' ratings (of how well empathic vs. nonempathic statements fit each child) and facial ratings were low ($r = .26$). However, Lennon et al. (1986) found facial empathy ratings in response to peer affect to be stable over a week's time; however, gestural responses were not. Within-situation correlations between somatic indices have been found to be more highly correlated than cross-situational correlations (Peraino & Sawin, 1981).

The general theoretical expectation is that empathy will be positively related to prosocial and negatively related to antisocial behavior. There are, however, research findings to the contrary. Researchers who have looked at the relation between physiological measures and overt responses (i.e., body, face) have sometimes found a negative correlation between the two (Field, 1982; Field & Walden, 1982; Jones, 1950, 1960; Notarius & Levinson, 1979). Thus it may be possible for the intensity of facial responsiveness to actually be negatively related to inner emotional experiences. Both theoretical and methodological advances are needed to disentangle these complexities.

Recent research concerning individual differences on somatic measures of empathy suggest some limitations on their use. Notarius and Levinson (1979) divided subjects into natural expressors and natural inhibitors on the basis of their facial/gestural responses to an emotion-packed videotape. Expressors and inhibitors were then exposed to a threat of a shock, and natural inhibitors showed less facial expressivity and more physiological reactivity than did the natural expressors. Thus, facial measures may not be adequate measures of empathy for those who usually inhibit somatic expression. Although conclusions concerning sex and age differences in facial expressivity cannot be made at this time, Buck

(1975, 1977) has found evidence that as boys (but not girls) become older, they show less spontaneous facial/gestural expressiveness. Thus, there is some suggestion in the literature that style of emotional expression, and age and sex of the child are variables that may limit the usefulness of somatic indices. More research is needed in this area.

Measurement of emotion or empathy in one's voice may present certain complexities not found with other somatic indices. Frick (1985) has recently reviewed research concerning the prosodic features of voice and concluded that emotion could be accurately detected in vocal pitch, loudness, and so on. However, accurate judgments required an adequate sample in order to capture the contour pattern and other complex features, and the signs of various affects were not always consistent across individuals. Thus, judging empathy from vocal responses may require methodological refinement that is different from dimensions necessary for judging facial responses.

Summary

Research utilizing somatic measures of empathy has shown considerable promise in a number of important ways. Somatic measures are easy to collect. Experimental procedures designed to yield or enhance facial and gestural expressions of empathy have been successful. Somatic measures have been found to be internally consistent within the context of an emotionally stimulating situation. Somatic measures have reliably predicted theoretically linked behaviors. Whereas some reasonable theoretical explanations for reversals in the direction of such hypotheses are beginning to appear, none are well accepted at this point.

Suggestions have been made with regard to possible limitations of somatic measures. As a result of such preliminary findings, researchers would be well advised to use multiple somatic and nonsomatic (i.e., physiological, self-report, and questionnaire) measures until such time as styles of empathic responsivity are better understood.

References

Barnett, M. A. (1984). Similarity of experiences and empathy in preschoolers. *Journal of Genetic Psychology, 145*(2), 241–250.

Blumberg, S. H., Solomon, G. E., & Perloe, S. I. (1981). *Display rules and the facial communication of emotions.* Unpublished manuscript, Haverford College.

Buck, R. W. (1975). Nonverbal communication of affect in children. *Journal of Personality and Social Psychology, 31,* 644–653.

Buck, R. W. (1977). Nonverbal communication accuracy in preschool children: Relationships with personality and skin conductance. *Journal of Personality and Social Psychology, 33,* 225–236.

Cohen, E. C. (1973). Empathy, awareness of interpersonal responsibility and consideration for others in young children. *Dissertation Abstracts International, 34,* 619B (University Microfilms No. 7413879).

Cummings, E. M., Iannotti, R., & Zahn-Waxler. (1985). The influence of conflict between adults on the emotions and aggression of young children. *Developmental Psychology, 21*, 495–507.

Eisenberg, N., & Lennon, R. (1983). Sex differences in empathy and related capacities. *Psychological Bulletin, 94*, 100–131.

Ekman, P., & Friesen, W. V. (1975). *Unmasking the face.* Englewood Cliffs, NJ: Prentice Hall.

Field, T. (1982). Individual differences in the expressivity of neonates and young infants. In R. W. Feldman (Ed.), *Development of nonverbal behavior in children.* New York: Springer Verlag.

Field, T., & Walden, T. A. (1982). Perception and production of facial expressions in infancy and early childhood. In H. Reese & L. Syssett (Eds.), *Advances in child development and behavior* (Vol. 16). New York: Academic.

Frick, R. W. (1985). Communicating emotion: The role of prosodic features. *Psychological Bulletin, 97*, 412–429.

Hoffman, M. F. (1982). The measurement of empathy. In C. E. Izard (Ed.), *Measuring emotions in infants and children* (pp. 279–296). New York: Cambridge University Press.

Howard, J. A. (1983). Preschoolers' empathy for specific affects and their social interaction. *Dissertation Abstracts International, 44*, 3954B (University Microfilms No. 8407675).

Jones, H. E. (1950). The study of patterns of emotional expression. In M. Reymert (Ed.), *Feelings and emotions.* New York: McGraw-Hill.

Jones, H. E. (1960). The longitudinal method in the study of personality. In I. Iscoe & H. W. Stevenson (Eds.), *Personality development in children.* Chicago: University of Chicago Press.

Kuchenbecker, S. L. Y. (1976). A developmental investigation of children's behavioral, cognitive, and affective responses to empathically stimulating situations. *Dissertation Abstracts International, 37*, 5328B (University Microfilms No. 7708523).

Leiman, B. (1978). *Affective empathy and subsequent altruism in kindergartners and first graders.* Paper presented at the annual meeting of the American Psychological Association, Toronto.

Lennon, R., Eisenberg, N., & Carroll, J. (1986). The relations between nonverbal indices of empathy and preschooler's prosocial behavior. *Journal of Applied Developmental Psychology, 3*, 219–224.

Marcus, R. F., Roke, E. J., & Bruner, C. (1985). Verbal and nonverbal empathy and prediction of social behavior of young children. *Perceptual and Motor Skills, 60*, 299–309.

Notarius, C. I., & Levenson, R. W. (1979). Expressive tendencies and physiological response to stress. *Journal of Personality and Social Psychology, 37*, 1204–1210.

Peraino, J., & Sawain, D. (1981). *Empathic distress and prosocial behavior.* Paper presented at the meeting of the Society for Research in Child Development.

Saarni, C. (1979). Children's understanding of display rules for expressive behavior. *Developmental Psychology, 15*, 424–429.

Sawin, D. (1979). *Assessing empathy in children: A search for an elusive construct.* Paper presented at the meeting of the Society for Research in Child Development, San Francisco.

Strayer, J. (1985a). *Developmental changes in nonverbal affect expression.* Paper presented at the biennial meeting of the Society for Research in Child Development, Toronto.

Strayer, J. (1985b). *Children's affect and empathy in response to TV dramas.* Paper presented at the annual meeting of the American Psychological Association, Los Angeles.

Yarczower, M., & Daruns, L. (1982). Social inhibition of spontaneous facial expressions in children. *Journal of Personality and Social Psychology, 43*, 831–837.

19 Physiological indices of empathy

Nancy Eisenberg, Richard A. Fabes,
Denise Bustamante, and Robin M. Mathy

There are clear disadvantages to all the methods of assessing empathy/sympathy described by Fesbach, Bryant, Batson, and Marcus in previous sections of this book. Most marked of these disadvantages is the role that self-presentational factors may play in all types of verbal report indices, as well as in nonverbal facial/gestural indices. This disadvantage may increase in importance during the preschool years as males become increasingly reluctant to express negative affect verbally (e.g., Brody, 1984) and nonverbally (e.g., Shennum & Bugenthal, 1982; Strayer, 1985). Moreover, for self-report indices, there is the additional major disadvantage that people, especially young children, may be unable to decipher or accurately communicate their emotional states.

The great advantage of using physiological indices to measure empathy and related reactions is that such indices should suffer minimally from the aforementioned disadvantages of self-report measures and, to some degree, facial/gestural indices. This chapter is about the positive features as well as the disadvantages of physiological indices.

Advantages

Physiological measures have been used for several decades to assess empathic and related reactions (e.g., Berger, 1962; Craig & Lower, 1969; Craig & Wood, 1969; Lazarus, Speisman, Mordoff, & Davison, 1962; Stotland, 1969). In general, both in this research and in the larger body of psychophysiological research, investigators have found that emotional arousal tends to be associated with changes in physiological responses as assessed by skin conductance, heart rate, palmar sweating, skin temperature, vasoconstriction, and electromyographic (EMG) procedures (see Buck, 1984; Cacioppo & Petty, 1983; Schwartz, Brown, & Ahern, 1980; Stotland, Mathews, Sherman, Hansson, & Richardson, 1978).

Thus, there is good reason to assume that physiological measures can be used

380

to tap the autonomic changes in the nervous system associated with emotional reactions. Given that most people do not consciously control physiological responses in their normal functioning – although certain aspects of responding such as heart rate can be consciously controlled to some degree – it is also reasonable to assume that such responding usually is relatively uncontaminated by an individual's desire to present a socially desirable image to the world or to the self.

Until recently, physiological indices were thought to measure generally undifferentiated states of arousal. However, in recent research there is some evidence that certain physiological indices may be useful for differentiating between discrete emotions. For example, Ekman, Levenson, and Friesen (1983) found different patterns of heart rate, temperature, and skin conductance for adults experiencing a variety of emotions. More relevant to the study of sympathy and empathy is the evidence suggesting that one can differentiate between personal distress reactions (anxiety related to one's own well-being) and vicarious sympathetic or empathic reactions. Whereas adults, children, and infants have been found to exhibit heart rate acceleration in situations that create anxiety (e.g., Craig, 1968; Darley & Katz, 1973; Lazarus et al., 1962), heart rate decelerations have been found in circumstances in which adults were exposed to negative stimuli involving others in a context in which the observer was unlikely to experience self-concern. Specifically, heart rate decelerations have been noted when adults view others receiving, or about to receive, noxious stimulation (Craig, 1968; Craig & Lowery, 1969). For example, Craig (1968) found that adults who watched another person submerge his or her hand in cold water exhibited heart rate deceleration, whereas those who submerged their own hands or imagined submerging their own hands exhibited heart rate acceleration. Moreover, Krebs (1975) found that observers who believed themselves similar to the distressed other were especially likely to exhibit heart rate decelerations and were also the most likely to assist the other at a cost to the self. Similarly, Campos, Butterfield, and Klinnert (1985) found that 14-month-old children exhibited cardiac deceleration when they viewed an adult who was sad, and moderate nonsignificant acceleration when the adult was fearful. Moreover heart rate changes were associated with behavioral correlates of fear and sadness.

In brief, it is likely that heart rate, and perhaps some other physiological indices (e.g., temperature; see Ekman et al., 1983), can be useful for differentiating among various emotions that have been labeled empathy. If so, physiological data may be extremely valuable in studying the development and elicitation of sympathy and personal distress.

There are other procedural advantages to using physiological measures. First, most indices can be recorded in a manner such that the raw data can be fed directly into the computer. Such procedures minimize human error in scoring and coding the data. Second, once study participants are comfortable with the equipment, reactions can be unobtrusively and continuously monitored, unless uncomfortable equipment is used. Thus, one need not continually interrupt the experimental procedure to obtain indices of the dependent variable, as is the case when subjects must be asked to report on their emotional reactions. Moreover, if data for the entire experimental sessions are stored on tape or some other form of hard copy, they are available for further analyses at a later time if new hypotheses are formulated. With self-report indices, it is often impossible to test alternative hypotheses because the self-report measure was given at only one specific point in time. Last, when physiological indices are used, the probability that experimenter bias will contaminate the data is reduced, although not entirely eliminated.

Disadvantages

The major disadvantages of physiological measures are, for the most part, ones of practicality. There are, however, some disadvantages of conceptual and methodological significance. We start with a discussion of these.

One drawback is that it is as yet unclear to what degree physiological indices can be used to differentiate between various emotional states. Moreover, given that people can experience more than one emotion at a time (e.g., personal distress and sympathy; see Chapter 8), there may be problems in interpreting data reflecting multiple simultaneous emotional reactions. It is quite possible that the predominant emotion will be evident in the analyses of physiological data, but it is also possible that the physiological correlates of different emotions, when combined, will sometimes mask one another. For example, it is not clear whether the experiencing of two emotional reactions, one associated with cardiac deceleration and one with acceleration, will result in alternating patterns of acceleration and deceleration, one predominant reaction, or a canceling of significant change in either direction. Although this problem is not unique to physiological indices, it is a concern for the researcher.

Another methodological problem is that study participants may react to the physiological equipment being used. Some physiological equipment not only constrains the participants' movement, but is uncomfortable and even frightening. For example, when electrodes are placed on the face to measure EMG, the participant is quite likely to experience an emotional reaction that may affect his or her reactions in the experimental setting.

This problem of reactivity is especially significant when the participants are young children. The equipment, even if it feels comfortable, may frighten them and thus affect their physiological reactions. Indeed, Wilson and Cantor (1985), in a study involving preschoolers and elementary school children, found that electromyogram (EMG) decreased substantially across the experimental session, probably in tandem with a decline in the fear or excitement that had been induced by the equipment.

There are ways to deal with the problem of reactivity and constraints, at least to some degree. For example, familiarizing people, especially children, with the equipment prior to use appears to be very effective in reducing anxiety during the study. Moreover, one can make the equipment more attractive to children by simple measures such as putting colored stars on the electrodes or by pointing out that astronauts and athletes use such equipment. A particularly ingenious method devised by Gottman (personal communication) is to place the monitors in a space suit the children don, and then constrain them by strapping them in a space capsule.

A problem related to subject reactivity is teacher or parent reactivity. Many adults feel uneasy about using physiological equipment with children, especially if the equipment must be attached under the clothes. In such cases, the equipment may have to be placed somewhere else (e.g., on the shoulder or arm rather than the chest).

A number of other problems are associated with the use of physiological equipment during experimental sessions. First, it is often necessary to control the subject's activities throughout data collection because movement, as well as speech (Campos & Johnson, 1966), can dramatically affect some indices. Second, some physiological measures are so sensitive that extraneous external stimuli uncontrolled by the investigator may influence the data. For example, an unexpected sound in the room may elicit a change in heart rate deceleration. Third, difficult decisions must be made regarding the data to be used in analyses – for example, one may have to decide whether to use continuous data recorded throughout the presentation of a stimulus or only the data recorded intermittently at precise critical points during stimulus presentation. Moreover, decisions regarding the proper baseline and how to handle individual differences in normal physiological responding are tricky ones. Fourth, we know relatively little about changes in psychophysiological responses with age and how these may affect physiological measures (Shields, 1983). Fifth, the data base created by the use of physiological indices generally is quite large, so that special procedures and software may be needed for the analyses. Sixth, physiological research generally requires a considerable amount of equipment, much of which is highly specialized and expensive. Needless to say, what can go wrong usually does. Moreover, the complexity of the equipment makes training of experimenters more time-consuming, and provides a host of opportunities for human error.

Summary

Among the distinct advantages of using physiological equipment to assess empathy and related reactions, the most important is that it provides an alternative to reliance on self-report indices. However, there are also numerous disadvantages, including reactivity, difficulties in handling and analyzing the data, and equipment dependency. Nonetheless, given the necessity of dealing with self-presentational problems when studying sympathy, we believe that physiological indices are among the most promising methods for future research, especially with children. Furthermore, if physiological data are combined with facial/gestural and/or self-report indices, the possibilities of differentiating between personal distress and sympathy and of assessing these emotions accurately should increase.

References

Berger, S. M. (1962). Conditioning through vicarious instigation. *Psychological Review, 69,* 450–466.

Brody, L. R. (1984). Sex and age variations in the quality and intensity of children's emotional attributions to hypothetical situations. *Sex Roles, 11,* 51–59.

Buck, R. (1984). *The communication of emotion.* New York: Guilford Press.

Cacioppo, J. T., & Petty, R. E. (Eds.). (1983). *Social psychophysiology.* New York: Guilford Press.

Campos, J. J., Butterfield, P., & Klinnert, M. (1985, April). *Cardiac and behavioral differentiation of negative emotional signals: An individual differences perspective.* Paper presented at the biennial meeting of the Society for Research in Child Development, Toronto.

Campos, J. J., & Johnson, H. J. (1966). The effects of verbalization instructions and visual attention on heart rate and skin conductance. *Psychophysiology, 2,* 305–310.

Craig, K. D. (1968). Physiological arousal as a function of imagined, vicarious, and direct stress experiences. *Journal of Abnormal Psychology, 73,* 513–520.

Craig, K. D., & Lowery, H. J. (1969). Heart-rate components of conditioned vicarious autonomic responses. *Journal of Personality and Social Psychology, 11,* 381–387.

Craig, K. D., & Wood, K. (1969). Physiological differentiation of direct and vicarious affective arousal. *Canadian Journal of the Behavioral Sciences, 1,* 98–105.

Darley, S. A., & Katz, I. (1973). Heart rate changes in children as a function of test versus game instructions and test anxiety. *Child Development, 44,* 783–789.

Ekman, P., Levenson, R. W., & Friesen, W. V. (1983). Autonomic nervous system activity distinguishes among emotions. *Science, 221,* 1208–1210.

Krebs, D. (1975). Empathy and altruism. *Journal of Personality and Social Psychology, 32,* 1134–1146.

Lazarus, R. S., Speisman, J. S., Mordkoff, A. M., & Davison, L. A. (1962). A laboratory study of psychological stress produced by a motion picture story. *Psychological Monographs, 76,* 1–35.

Schwartz, G. E., Brown, S., & Ahern, G. L. (1980). Facial muscle patterning and subjective experiences during affective imagery: Sex differences. *Psychophysiology, 17,* 75–82.

Shennum, W. A., & Bugenthal, D. B. (1982). The development of control over affective expression in nonverbal behavior. In R. S. Feldman (Ed.), *Development of nonverbal behavior in children* (pp. 101–121). New York: Springer Verlag.

Shields, S. A. (1983). Development of autonomic nervous system responsitivity in children: A review of the literature. *International Journal of Behavioral Development, 6,* 291–319.

Stotland, E. (1969). Exploratory studies in empathy. In L. Berkowitz (Ed.), *Advances in experimental social psychology* (Vol. 4, pp. 271–314). New York: Academic Press.

Stotland, E., Mathews, K. E., Sherman, S. E., Hansson, R. O., & Richardson, B. E. (1978). *Empathy, fantasy, and helping.* Beverly Hills, CA: Sage.

Strayer, J. (1985, April). *Developmental changes in nonverbal affect expression.* Paper presented at the biennial meeting of the Society for Research in Child Development, Toronto.

Wilson, B. J., & Cantor, J. (1985). Developmental differences in empathy with a television protagonist's fear. *Journal of Experimental Child Psychology, 39,* 284–299.

Conclusions

20   Empathy viewed in context

Janet Strayer and Nancy Eisenberg

The time of reckoning has come. It is incumbent upon us in this concluding chapter to draw attention to the scope of topics examined regarding empathy and its development and to assess, from this panoramic perspective, the critical questions that have been raised. In addition, we should indicate which of these have been answered; which remain unanswered, puzzling, or problematic; and what important new questions have been generated that can provide directions for future research.

It is a well-known maxim of science that the secret to resolving many issues lies as much in posing the right questions as in finding the right answers. Here, in summary, are the questions the contributors initially posed, followed by a synthesis of some of the pertinent points made in connection with each question. The conclusions that emerge represent to us the best integration of what we know about empathy thus far and what we can propose as guidelines for further research. The gamut of questions we started out with include the following:

> What is empathy?
> Why does it occur?
> Why is it important?
> How does it occur?
> How does it develop?
> What consequences does empathy have for self and for others?
> How can it be measured?

The questions present challenges in a field of inquiry that has a long general history but a short specific memory. The history of the construct of empathy, its synonyms, cognates, and associated terms as expressed in diverse scholars' writings long precedes the minting of the word empathy. Its specific meaning as an affective ''feeling into'' another's affect only fairly recently captured the attention of empirical researchers. Given the relatively young state of empathy research, particularly in a developmental context, it would be especially foolhardy to assume that, even after surveying the chapters in this volume, we can assure

389

ourselves of having provided the right answers, But, on an optimistic note, we think that some of the right questions have been posed and addressed by the talented professionals represented in this volume.

This volume was designed to address several broad and related topics. The first two objectives were (1) to provide a conceptual and theoretical framework for the definition and further consideration of "empathy" (Part I), and (2) to review selectively research pertaining to empathy across the life span (Part II). The third objective (Part III) was to present empirical findings concerning more specific topics such as

a. the role of motor mimicry as a basic empathic phenomenon (Bavelas, Black, Lemery, & Mullett, chapter 14);

b. the role of affect and cognition in empathy considered as a process variable (Strayer, chapter 10);

c. age and gender differences in empathy considered as an outcome variable (Lennon & Eisenberg, chapter 9);

d. the motivational role for empathy considered in relation to altruism (Eisenberg & Miller, chapter 13);

e. the socialization concomitants of empathy and individual differences in its development (Bryant, chapter 11); and

f. the relations of empathy to parental abuse and child adjustment (Feshbach, chapter 12).

The last objective, covered by the authors contributing to Part IV, was to review methods used in research on empathy and to evaluate their advantages and shortcomings with an eye to benefiting future research on empathy.

What is empathy?

The definitional question was the first one posed. What do we mean by *empathy?* The etymological fact that empathy is a relative newcomer to the English lexicon[1] is illustrated by the following example. A year ago students in a Canadian psychology seminar where asked to interview people in their community, their parents, and others at the corner store or recreation center, asking them if they had ever heard of the word *empathy* and what it meant. Many persons outside the university had not heard of it, and most responded that it meant sympathy.

A brief time afterward, one of us was seated next to a famous English actor during a plane trip and took this opportunity to ask him the same question. In contrast to the people surveyed informally, he reacted as if a key concept had been broached; he knew precisely that empathy entailed feeling in oneself the feelings of others, and discussed at some length the importance of the concept to his work. Empathy was a crucial process, he said, not only in his rendering of character, but also in his reading of plays. He went on to distinguish works he liked especially well; these were ones in which he regarded the authors as having mastered and conveyed an empathic position with respect to their characters.

The definitional issues addressed in Part I are particularly relevant to establishing the framework for the study of empathy, an idea whose time has come. In particular, what *empathy* means derives from its history (Wispé, chapter 2), its function (Plutchik, chapter 3), its structure and motivational features (Hoffman, chapter 4), and its psychotherapeutic application (Marcia, chapter 5). Points raised in these chapters are echoed in many of the others in this volume. This is encouraging because it seems particularly useful in consolidating the findings from contemporary psychological investigations to both attend and attempt to resolve definitional issues. This permits us, in Wispé's words, to "investigate the parameters of empathy," even if one takes the position that we "cannot explain empathy, any more than one can explain memory or imagination."

Wispé's focus on different ways in which the term *empathy* has been transposed by scholars in different traditions, often for different purposes, provides a historically illustrative caveat for those doing empirical work on empathy. Researchers' operational definitions in studies of empathy proceed from their selective focus on certain phenomena or processes (affective, cognitive, motivational, dispositional) to the exclusion of others. The operationalizations in any one study rarely can be fitted easily to operationalization in another study of empathy, thus limiting construct convergence. This problem increases the need for a consensus (or plan) regarding the general meaning of the construct of empathy. It is necessary for researchers to differentiate and to specify carefully what is being measured in investigations of empathy in the light of the historical context in which this term has both proliferated and been burdened by surplus meaning. In chapter 10 Strayer further emphasizes that careful consideration of affective and cognitive components of empathy may help us to clarify this construct, which in the past has been used to signify phenomena, intervening variables, and hypothetical constructs (e.g., motor mimicry, cognitive role taking, empathy). One optimistic conclusion we draw from a review of the chapters is that there now appears to be more cross-disciplinary agreement that affect is a central component of empathy and, thus, that empathy is the act of "feeling into" another's affective experience. Why empathy occurs, how it occurs, and what consequences may ensue once it occurs are questions introduced in the remaining chapters of Part I and further discussed throughout the volume.

Why does empathy occur?

Why empathy occurs is addressed by Plutchik (chapter 3), who discusses its biological-evolutionary bases. He highlights the survival and communication functions of empathy and notes the evolution of specialized signals that typically trigger similar affect and appropriate contingent action in observers. In Plutchik's view, regardless of whether such action removes the observer from danger or comes to the aid of the signaler, it is of survival value. Plutchik's ideas suggest that even if empathic arousal in response to another's plight leads to acts on their behalf that are motivated by reduction of personal distress rather than by more "noble sentiments," such arousal is a biological mechanism by which the future is secured for the development of noble sentiments. Plutchik's two major themes, the biologically based adaptive functions of affect and the communicative context for empathy, are elaborated in other chapters, particularly in Thompson's chapter on infants' emotional development and its relations to empathy, (chapter 6) and in Bavelas et al.'s chapter on motor mimicry (chapter 14) as a basis for empathic communication.

Why is empathy important?

Questions that ask why are notorious for their teleological hazards. To avoid these, we can rephrase the question "Why does empathy occur?" and instead ask "Why is empathy important?" In addition to having adaptive and communicative functions, as already discussed, empathy plays a central role in the model of morality Hoffman has presented as an alternative to cognitive theories based on the principle of justice. Empathy also is considered important to personality development, as well as to the conduct of psychotherapy.

Given the contribution of clinical psychologists in the formulation and application of the concept of empathy (see Wispé, chapter 2), the discussion of empathy by Marcia provides both a historically connective and a contemporary perspective. He considers how empathy contributes to adult personality development, and how it functions in the process of psychotherapy according to different psychotherapeutic formulations. The more important the "relationship" aspect is to a given psychotherapeutic formulation, the more important is empathy's function as a psychotherapeutic ingredient. The personal insights based on Marcia's work recall Kohut's suggestion that empathy need not always be perceived as "good," either in terms of the empathizer (also, see Batson et al., chapter 8) or in terms of the recipient. Nevertheless, the importance of empathy as a motivator for prosocial behavior is a well-recognized topic in psychology, as discussed by various contributors to this volume (see Batson et al., chapter 8, Eisenberg & Miller, chapter 13, and Hoffman, chapter 4).

How does empathy occur?

The contributors have suggested a number of ways to explain how empathy occurs. Some of these suggestions center around the expressive signals that may trigger empathy (see Plutchik, chapter 3, and Thompson, chapter 6) and others around the processes involved, such as motor mimicry (Bavelas, chapter 14) and vicarious or reciprocal affective arousal, with or without explicit cognitive inference (e.g., role taking; see Strayer, chapter 10). Our answers to the question of how empathy occurs depend in part upon our answers to the question of how it develops. Processes such as motor mimicry have been described as occurring in both infants and adults, and generally may undergo little developmental change with age (although this possibility has not been investigated empirically). Similarly, as Strayer proposes, individually different thresholds for affective arousal may remain relatively constant within persons across the life span.

Nevertheless, the range of stimuli capable of evoking affective arousal should change as a function of both social experience and cognitive development. Furthermore, some of the different mediators proposed for empathy such as role taking would be expected to increase with development. Empathy, then, is viewed as a process that can occur both with and without complex inference – just as cognitive inference can occur without empathy.

How does empathy develop?

The question of how empathy develops, first addressed in Hoffman's chapter, is examined in more detail in Part II. As Mussen points out in his commentary, even though the contributors to Part II by and large agree with the definition of empathy put forth in our introduction, each one focuses on a different aspect of empathy. Thus, for example, empathy can be regarded as an affective *response* entailing sensory transmission or translation of another's affect (Strayer, chapter 10); or it can be regarded as a *capacity* (e.g., referring to how much or how extensively a child can empathize). Moreover, empathy may be viewed not so much as itself not developing with age but as being affected by other skills or intervening variables (cognitive role taking, social experience, etc.). Alternatively, empathy may be seen as changing with age, as when developments in semiotics are thought to change the quality of responses. Empathy also can be regarded as a *process,* with attention given to affective experiences and cognitive intervening variables that may help to explain how empathy is experienced.

With these distinctions in mind, we see that Thompson's discussion of empathy in infancy focuses first on empathy as a sensory-perceptual response, the signs of which are noted in early infant nonverbal social signals and contingent responsiveness to such signals in others. These early developments appear to rely on some biologically given modes of response, similar to those in Plutchik's consideration of empathy in nonhuman primates. Thompson also considers early attachment and caregiver–child interactions to be relevant to the refinement of the empathic response. In Thompson's view, particularly during and after the second year of life, empathy includes responses that "translate" (i.e., involve inference), as well as "transport by sensory means," the other's affective experience. That Thompson takes into account the research on early social-emotional interactions as the context for the development of empathy seems particularly important in explaining subsequent individual differences in empathic responsiveness. His viewpoint blends well both with Marcia's discussion of the development of empathic responsiveness according to psychotherapeutic outlooks and with Bryant's (chapter 11) and Feshbach's (chapter 12) focus on socialization and adjustment as related to empathy in childhood. Although Thompson is concerned with infants' empathic responsiveness in general, the factors he discusses also can be considered early precursors to individual differences in empathic responding, which is a major focus of Barnett's discussion of empathy in childhood (chapter 7).

The research reviewed in Barnett's chapter makes clear that there is unlikely to be one necessary and sufficient antecedent for the development of empathy. Barnett suggests that empathy is enhanced by environments in which socializers pay explicit attention to and satisfy the child's emotional needs; in such an environment the child's self-concern may be lessened and he/she may be encouraged to focus on a range of emotions in others. As a consequence, the emotional and experiential bases for empathy responsiveness may be enhanced. Moreover, the modeling and cognitive bases for the development of understanding one's own and others' affect may be strengthened.

Barnett's view that variations in child rearing and patterns of family interaction are important to the development of empathy is mirrored in Bryant's report of caregiver and sibling socioemotional variables associated with empathy and Feshbach's discussion of parental empathy. From these chapters, we gain an appreciation of the fact that the development of empathy and its associations with individual adjustment as well as with family variables is not uniform across age. Empathy, which we generally value as a personal characteristic, can be associated with emotional stresses as well as with competencies at certain points in development and with respect to different aspects of behavior or personality.

Questions of development all too characteristically stop at adolescence. Changes in empathy in adulthood versus childhood more often are thought to rest on accretions or decrements in attention, skill, and the like (i.e., an additive model) rather than on new developments in adulthood that construct or reformulate reality in qualitatively different ways (i.e., a stage-constructivist model).

This observation is supported by an examination of the content of Batson and colleagues' chapter (8) on empathy in adulthood. There is little said in their chapter about the *development* of empathy in individuals, perhaps because many psychologists believe that the internal changes during adulthood are less dramatic, and that more of the variation among adults is due to situational factors than is true for children (Flavell, 1963). Perhaps because of these factors, the emphasis on empathy in adulthood is on the environmental variables that affect empathic responsiveness (e.g., similarity to others or emotional intensity of the stimuli) and on the consequences of empathizing for prosocial action. Although some research has been done on dispositional empathy in adulthood, the approach in such research is not developmental.

One conclusion to be drawn from the discussion of Batson and his colleagues is that qualitative distinction needs to be made with respect to the direction of one's emotional responsiveness to others. Such emotional involvement may lead to personal distress and avoidance rather than an empathic focus on the other person's needs. That there indeed may be individual differences in empathic disposition is considered by Batson et al., who conclude that one cannot assume concordance between dispositional empathy assessed by means of self-report measures and empathy assessed by behavioral responses to situational variables. Certainly, as is true for all psychological discussions, what we can conclude is based very much on the limits and properties of our measures. This implies, as do the methodological chapters in Part IV, that multimodal measures and methods may be the best route to examining empathy.

Indeed, a major problem in trying to determine how empathy develops is that comparable measures are not available across the life span. Instead, we must, as in other areas of psychology, ask whether measures that are available for different ages provide analogous information about empathy. The conclusion reached by Lennon and Eisenberg (chapter 9) is that this is "more or less" the case. For example, the naturalistic behavioral data reviewed in this chapter are consistent with the conclusion that empathy is a dispositional variable, that is, that there is intra-individual consistency from toddlerhood to early school age in patterns of reaction to others' distress. In contrast, results from picture-story measures of empathy suggest that scores increase from preschool to middle childhood years, at which time scores seem to level off, perhaps more because of a ceiling effect for the measurement instrument than the fact that empathy reaches asymptote. Similarly, empathy scores increase with age on questionnaire indices until about early adolescence, after which there is no consistent relation with age. There are too few age-related studies of nonverbal indices of empathy to warrant any generalizations. Overall, then, the findings concerning age-related change in empathy are inconclusive, owing, in part to discrepancies in findings across different methodological approaches.

In summary, the question of how empathy develops has been addressed by most theorists and researchers surveyed in this volume in terms of

1. biological–genetic factors, which may provide the basis for empathy, but, nevertheless, may still vary across individuals;
2. early conditioning, affective training, and observational learning;
3. socioemotional experiences enhanced or attenuated by child-rearing factors;
4. social-cognitive development, particularly of imaginative skills and affective role taking; and
5. situational factors interacting with dispositional characteristics.

An important consideration for those who are particularly interested in examining age-related developments in empathy is that there are serious gaps in our knowledge, notably in the design of suitable instruments and measures for use across the life span, and in our understanding of the relations among different kinds of measurement methods.

What consequences does empathy have for self and for others?

Hoffman (chapter 4) is one contributor to this volume who asks what consequences follow from, or are motivated by, empathy. He believes that empathic affect kindles "hot cognitions," which contribute to moral judgments and action. His notion that different developmental levels of empathy result from the interaction of different modes of affective arousal with different levels of social cognition sets the conceptual framework for the subsequent developmental consideration of many issues related to empathy. For example, Strayer, who regards affect as the central defining feature in her discussion of the development of empathy, also discusses a model in which concordant affective arousal is a necessary precondition for the process that may result in empathy and understanding. Her argument – that only when shared affect is engaged is the understanding of others' feelings likely to lead to actions on their behalf – shares some common conceptual ground with Hoffman's proposal that moral principles are shaped and informed by affect as well as intellect. Related themes are developed and discussed by Batson et al. (chapter 8) and by Eisenberg and Miller (chapter 13), who relate empathy to prosocial behavior.

Specifically, the long-standing issue in the psychological literature concerning the link between empathy and prosocial behavior is critically examined in the chapters by Batson et al. and by Eisenberg and Miller. In general, a variety of measures have been found to relate positively to adults' prosocial behavior, whereas the relation for children is less consistently positive (although not negative). This difference in data for adults versus children may reflect the greater variability or inconsistency in children's versus adults' behavior across situations, or the fact that, in studies with children, a wider and somewhat different range of methods has been used than in research with adults.

Issues pertaining to the consequences of empathy for self and others are also touched on by Strayer, who maintains that there is only a probable, rather than a necessary or sufficient link, between empathy and prosocial intervention. Similarly, Marcia, speaking from a psychotherapist's vantage, cautions us about both the emotional weight absorbed by empathic individuals (e.g., psychotherapists) and the possible intrusiveness of empathy when communicated to others who wish to remain more distant from us. Again, we are reminded of Kohut's (1984) rejoinder that being empathic is not synonymous with being nice, kind, or loving, but, when engaged in psychotherapy is, among other things, an attitude and means of "prehending" and gathering information about the other.

How can empathy be measured?

In Part IV of the volume, the contributors directly address the question underlying all the other questions raised: How can empathy be measured? They review methods by which empathy has been measured and conclude that a multimodal approach seems to be the best approach for future investigations. Questionnaires and picture-story methods are limited by age constraints as well as by possible demand characteristics; the former problem can be remedied in part by downward or upward extensions of the items or stimuli used. Nevertheless, such indices are not appropriate for infants and very young children, for whom we must rely on behavioral or somatic indicators as a basis from which to infer empathy. Nonverbal methods (e.g., facial expression and physiological measures) are promising and can be applied across the life span; however, their use as indices of empathy involves an inference on the part of the researcher.

Obviously, all that we can use to measure empathy are stimulus features and responses. However, empathy is a process as well as a response. Part of the process entails a subjective experience, the phenomenology of which depends upon what the subject can tell us. Appreciating that confounding variables may enter into the report of subjective experience, we can try to include appropriate control measures in studies of empathy. In addition, more than one measure of empathy may be needed in any one study. We do not think that putting several poor measures together in one study is better than using one poor measure alone. However, at present many refinements are being made including both the recalibrating of old instruments (chapter 14 is a case in point), as well as attempts to devise new and better ones (see chapters 15–17). We favor the use of a variety of these improved measures to assess the elusive phenomenon of empathy.

Most of us know very well that research generates even more questions than originally were posed. This is both a frustrating and sustaining experience. Originally, we, the editors, cordoned off an area for examination and posed a number of questions concerning what, for increasing numbers of us, is a topic of great interest, but one also in need of clarification, integration, and careful evaluation. In our view, there was a need to assess where we have come, and, even more important, to suggest the directions for the future. It is our hope that the contents of this volume will be useful in addressing this need and will serve as a compass by which theorists and researchers can guide future investigations of empathy.

Note

1. "Empathy" does not appear in the regular text of the *Oxford English Dictionary,* but only in its *Supplement* covering the years since 1928, in which this example of empathy's usage provides an interesting initiator–respondent distinction (from Rebecca West, *Strange Necessity, 1928*): "The active power of empathy which makes the creative artist, or the passive power of empathy which makes the appreciator of art."

References

Flavell, J. H. (1963). *The developmental psychology of Jean Piaget*. Princeton, NJ: Van Nostrand.
Kohut, H. (1984). Introspection, empathy, and the semicircle of mental health. In J. Lichtenberg, M. Bornstein, and D. Silver (Eds.). *Empathy I*. Hillsdale, NJ: Erlbaum.

Index